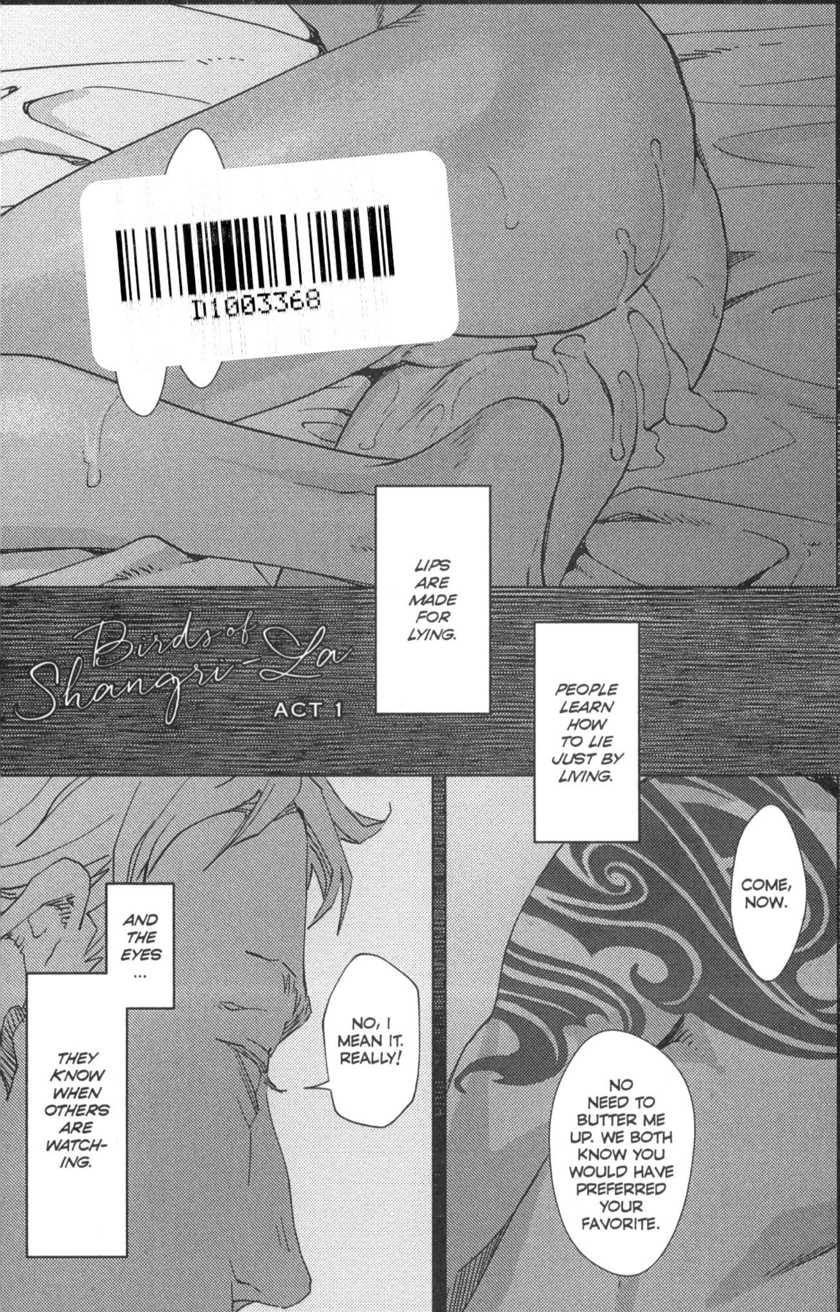
LIPS ARE MADE FOR LYING.
Birds of Shangri-La
ACT 1
PEOPLE LEARN HOW TO LIE JUST BY LIVING.
COME, NOW.
NO NEED TO BUTTER ME UP. WE BOTH KNOW YOU WOULD HAVE PREFERRED YOUR FAVORITE.
NO, I MEAN IT. REALLY!
AND THE EYES...
THEY KNOW WHEN OTHERS ARE WATCHING.

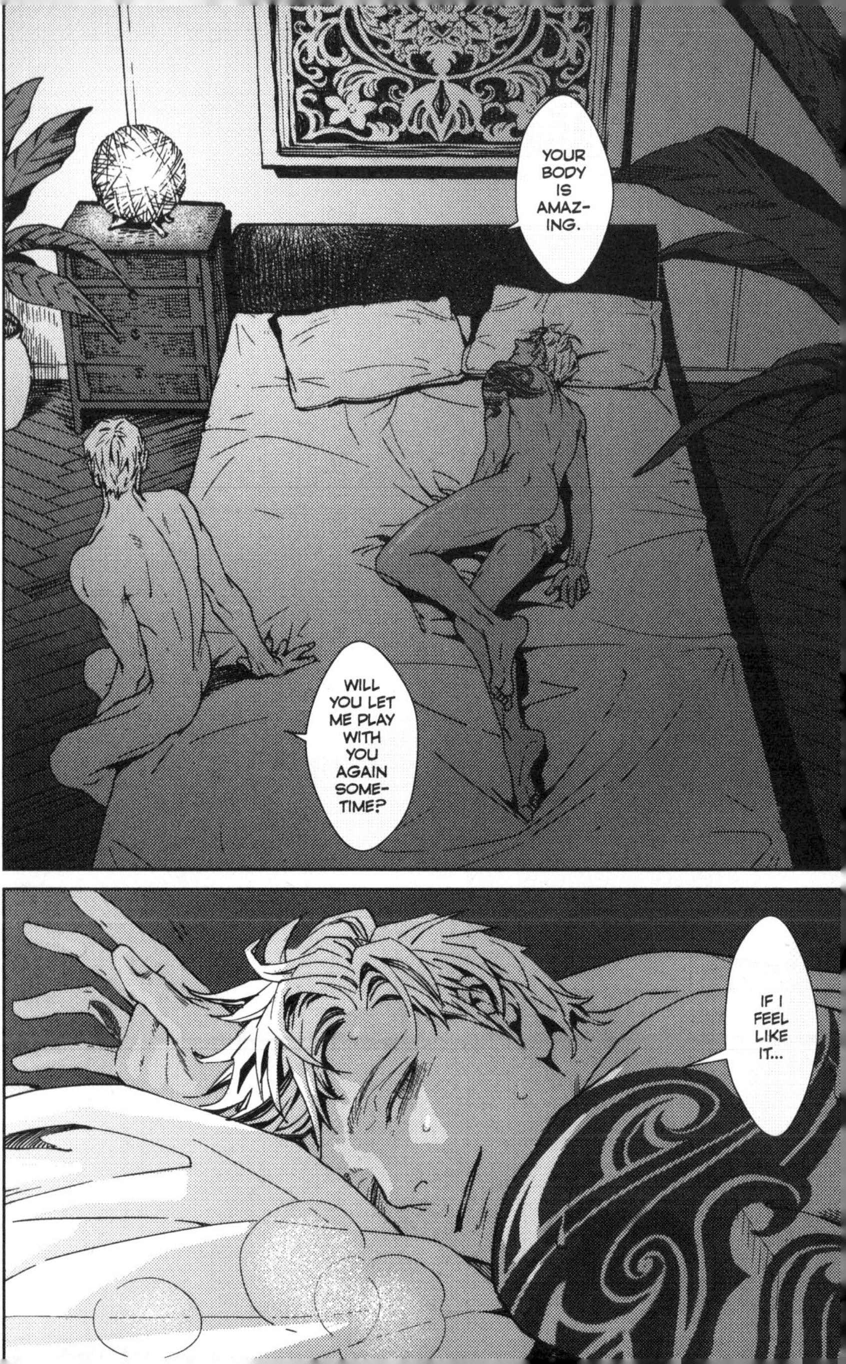
YOUR BODY IS AMAZ-ING.
WILL YOU LET ME PLAY WITH YOU AGAIN SOME-TIME?
IF I FEEL LIKE IT...

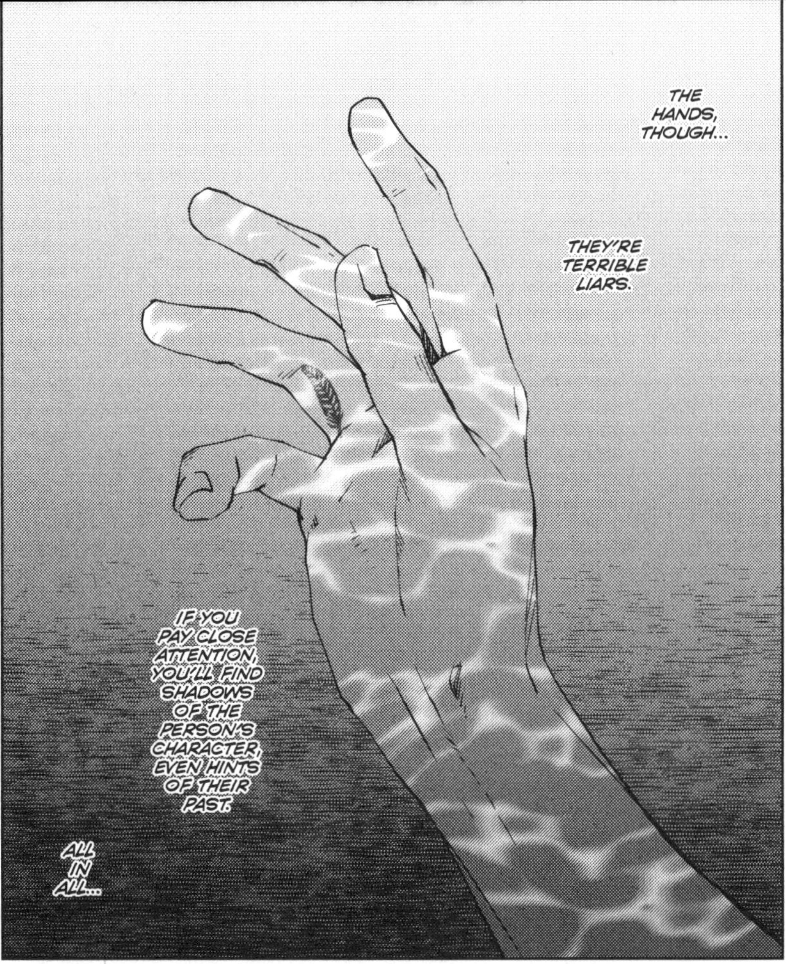
THE HANDS, THOUGH...
THEY'RE TERRIBLE LIARS.
IF YOU PAY CLOSE ATTENTION, YOU'LL FIND SHADOWS OF THE PERSON'S CHARACTER, EVEN HINTS OF THEIR PAST.
ALL IN ALL...
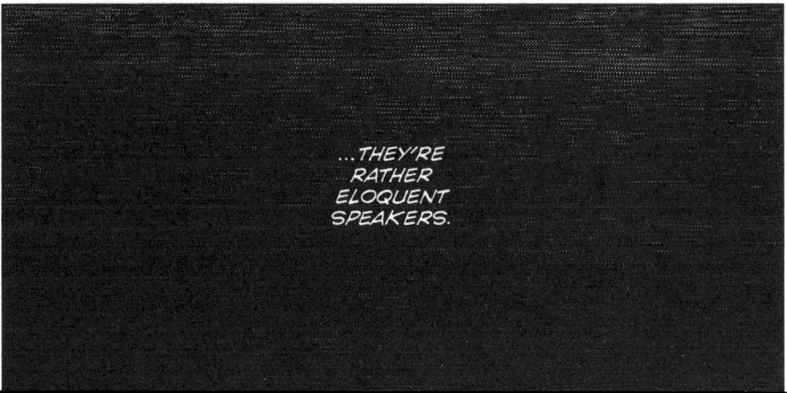
...THEY'RE RATHER ELOQUENT SPEAKERS.

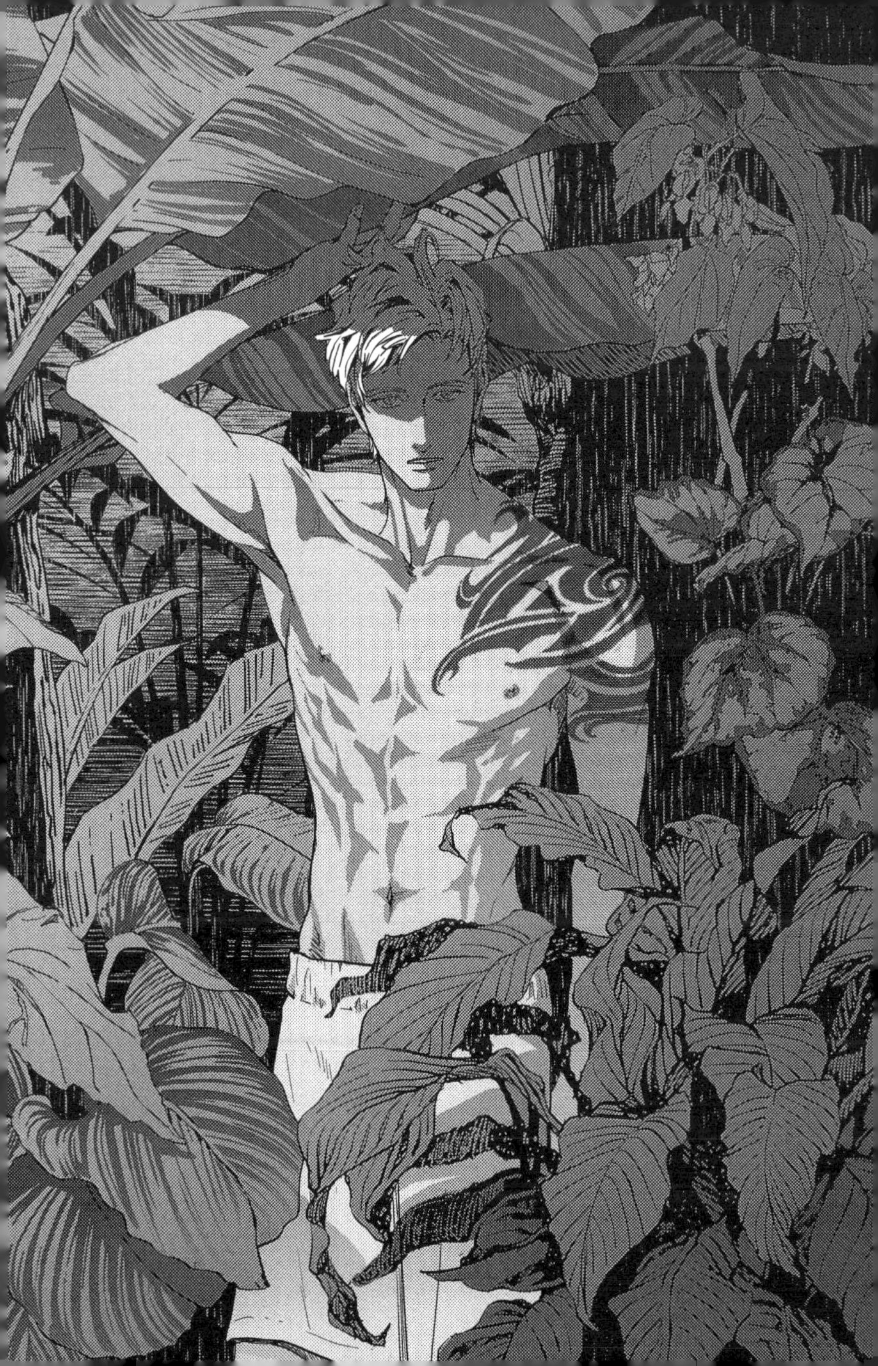

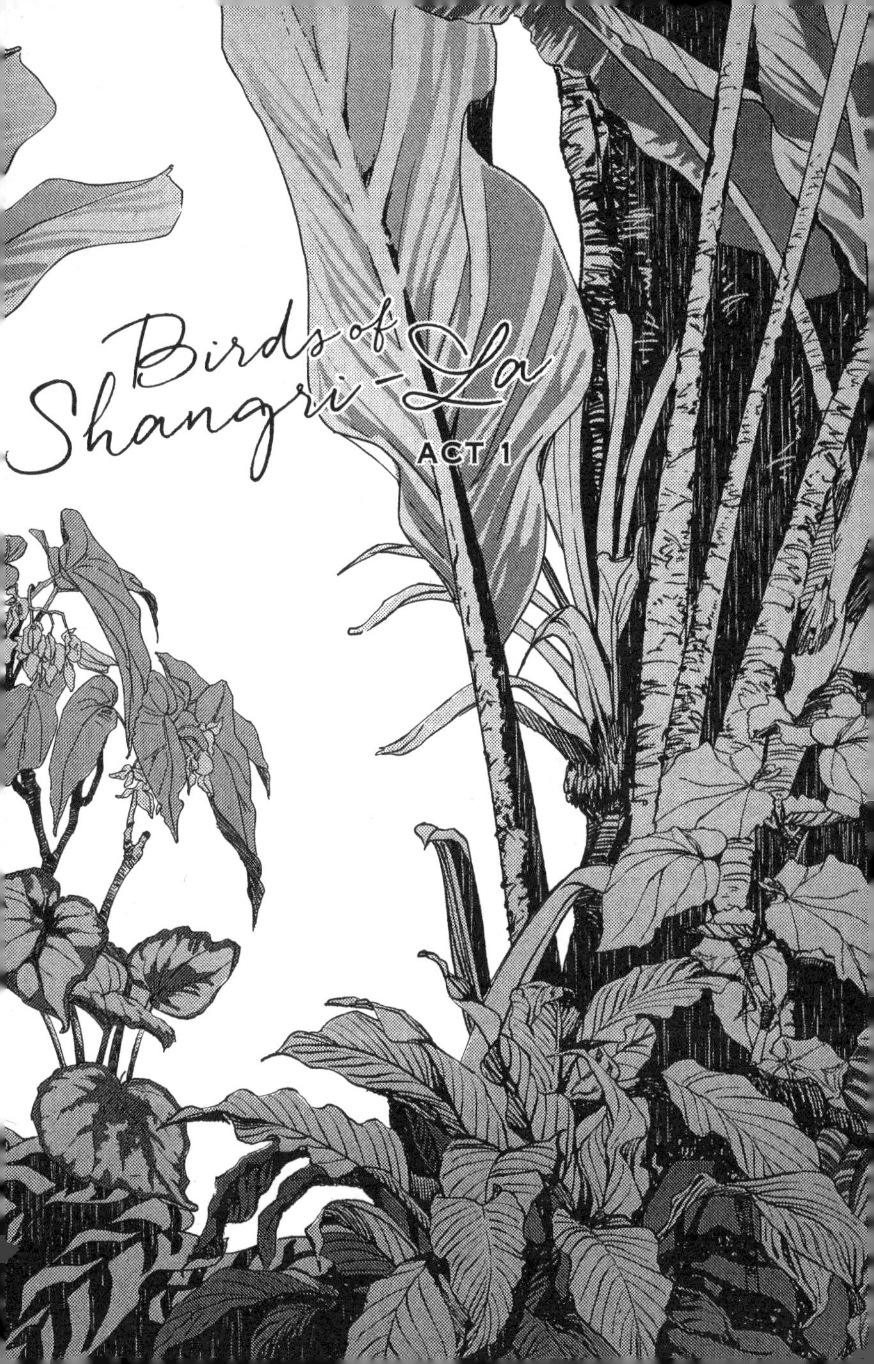
Birds of Shangri-La
ACT 1

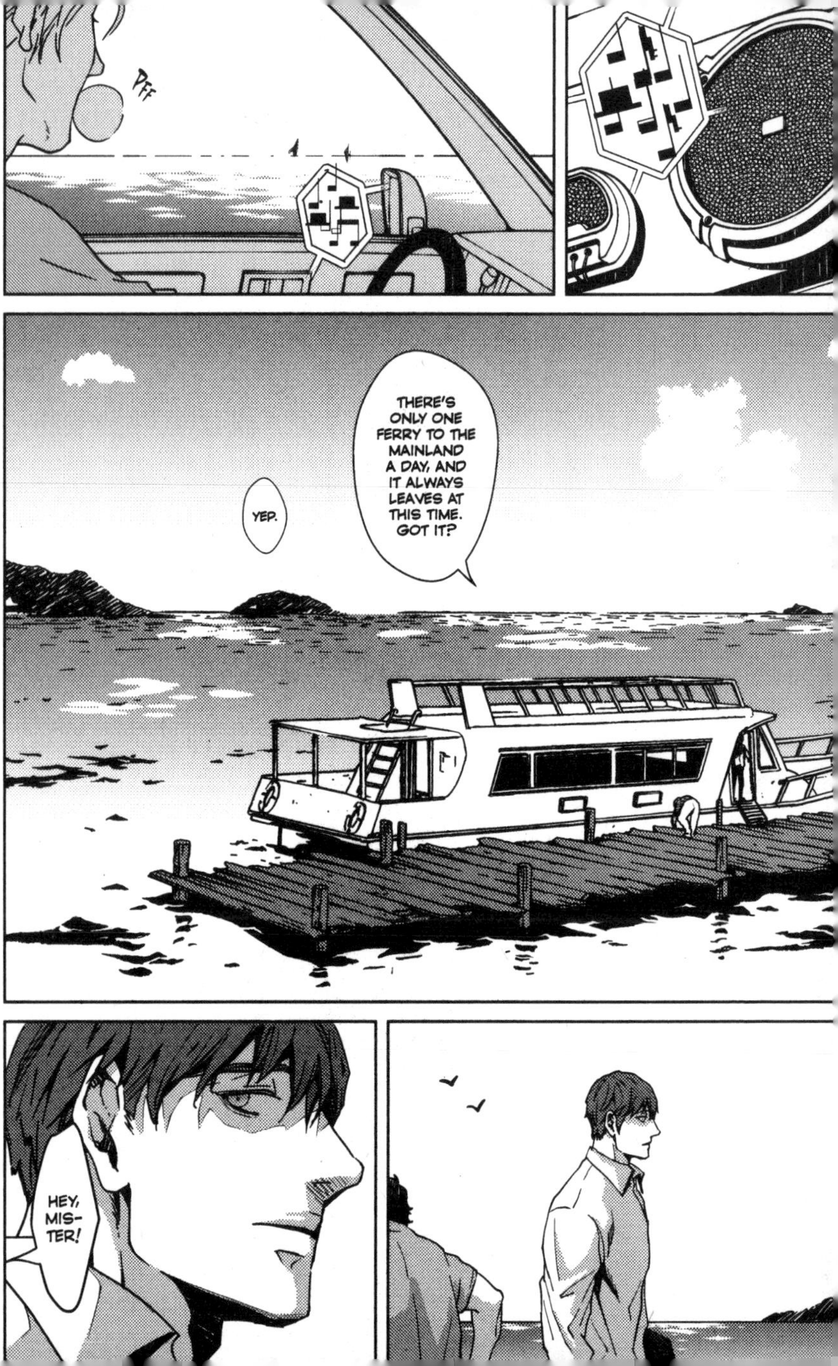
Pff
THERE'S ONLY ONE FERRY TO THE MAINLAND A DAY, AND IT ALWAYS LEAVES AT THIS TIME. GOT IT?
YEP.
HEY, MIS-TER!

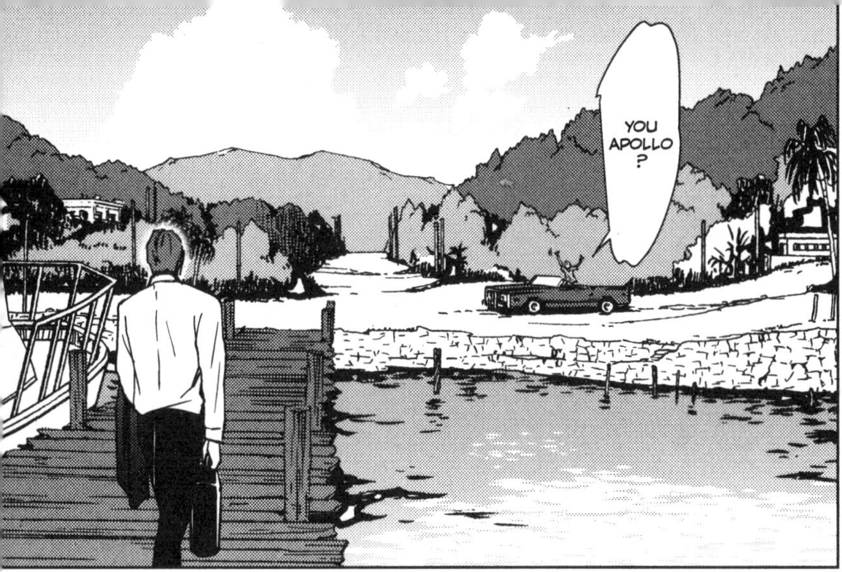
YOU APOLLO?
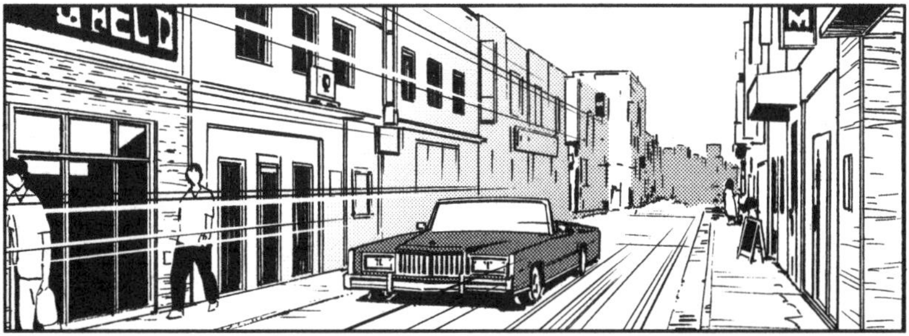
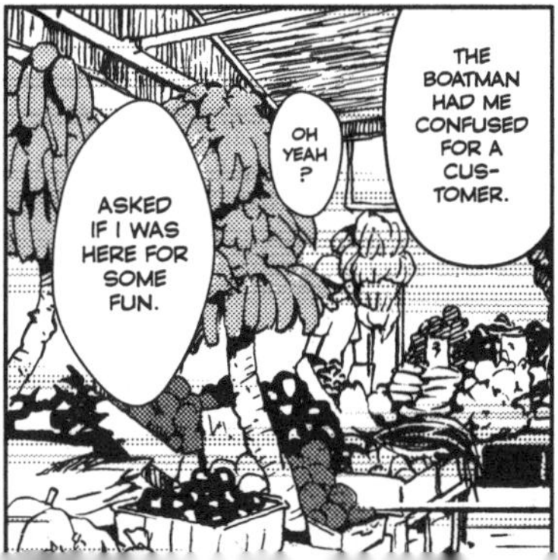
THE BOATMAN HAD ME CONFUSED FOR A CUS-TOMER.
OH YEAH?
ASKED IF I WAS HERE FOR SOME FUN.
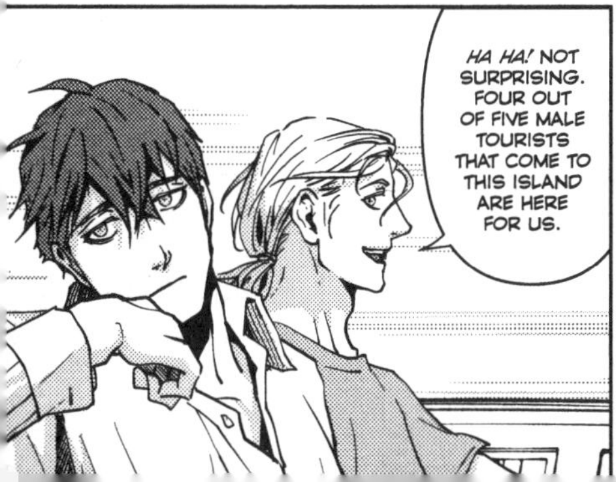
HA HA! NOT SURPRISING. FOUR OUT OF FIVE MALE TOURISTS THAT COME TO THIS ISLAND ARE HERE FOR US.

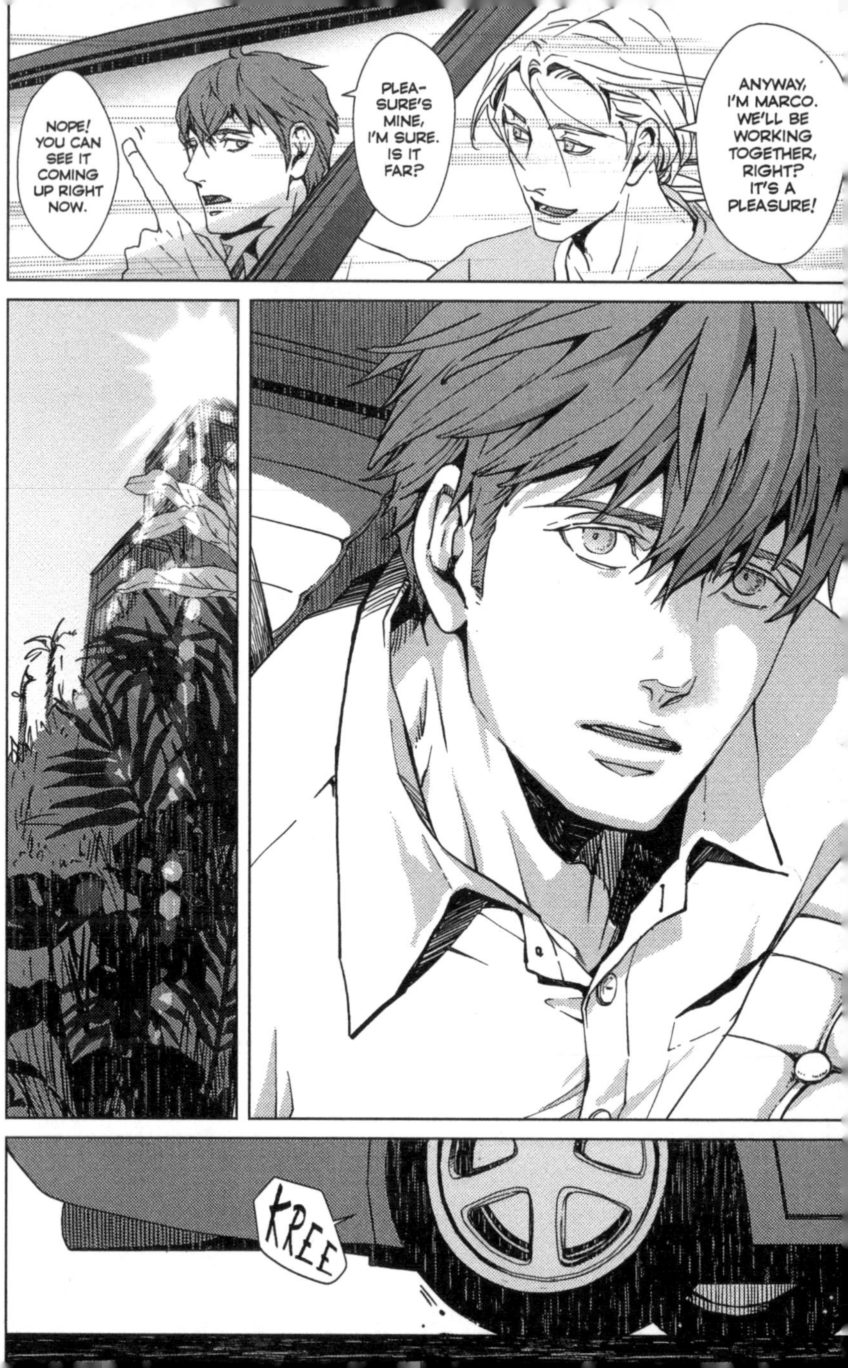
ANYWAY, I'M MARCO. WE'LL BE WORKING TOGETHER, RIGHT? IT'S A PLEASURE!
PLEA-SURE'S MINE, I'M SURE. IS IT FAR?
NOPE! YOU CAN SEE IT COMING UP RIGHT NOW.
KREE

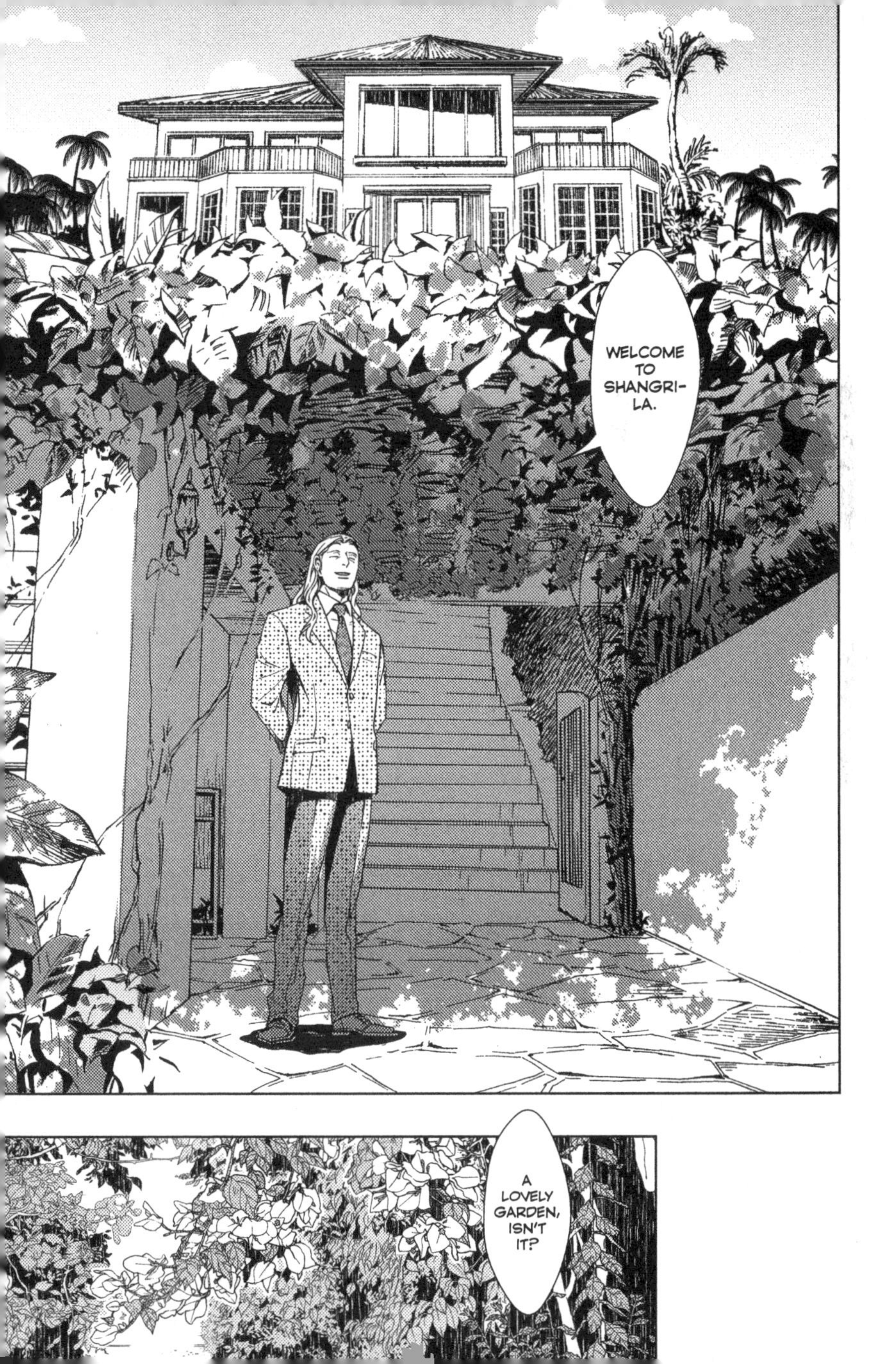
WELCOME TO SHANGRI-LA.
A LOVELY GARDEN, ISN'T IT?

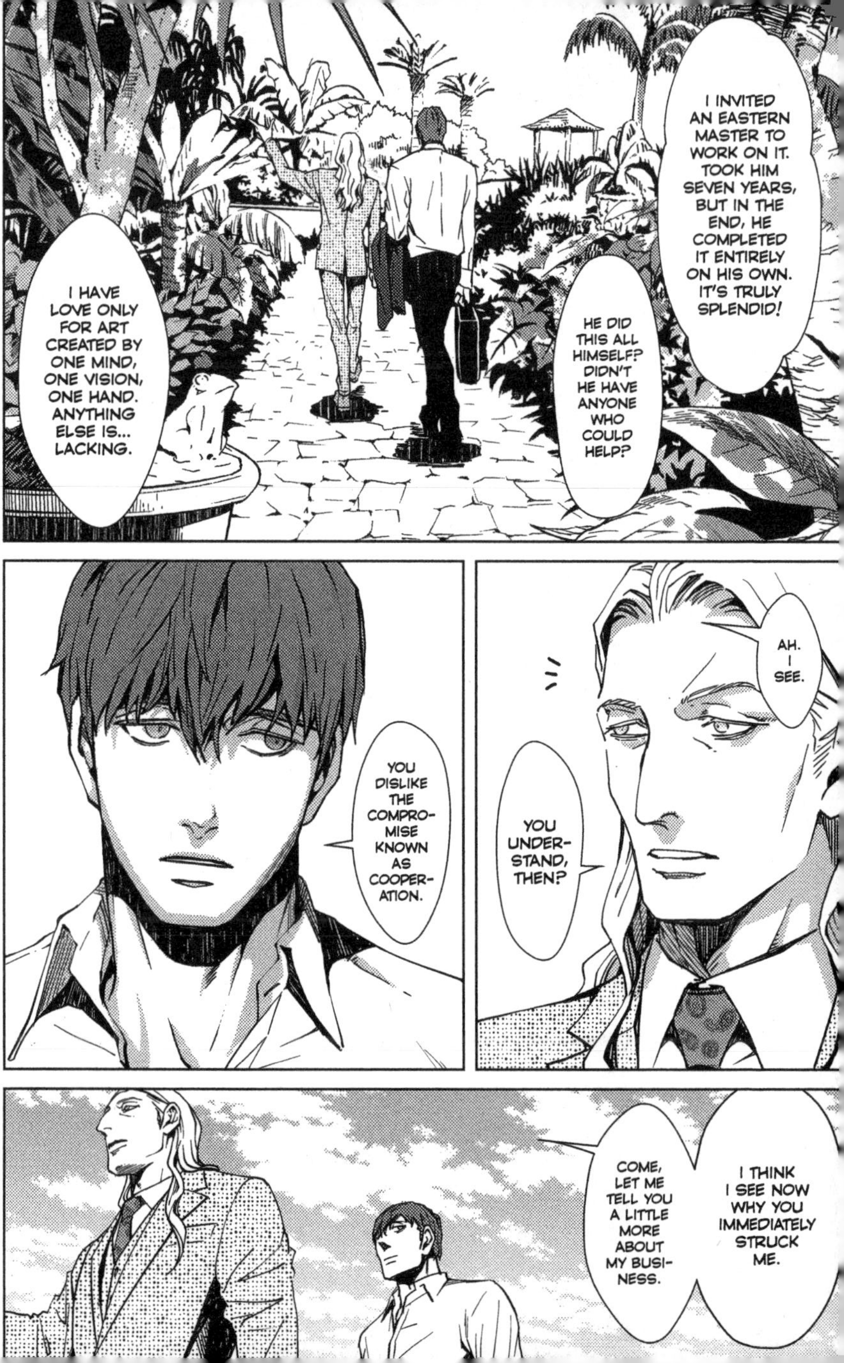
I INVITED AN EASTERN MASTER TO WORK ON IT. TOOK HIM SEVEN YEARS, BUT IN THE END, HE COMPLETED IT ENTIRELY ON HIS OWN. IT'S TRULY SPLENDID!
HE DID THIS ALL HIMSELF? DIDN'T HE HAVE ANYONE WHO COULD HELP?
I HAVE LOVE ONLY FOR ART CREATED BY ONE MIND, ONE VISION, ONE HAND. ANYTHING ELSE IS... LACKING.
AH. I SEE.
YOU UNDER-STAND, THEN?
YOU DISLIKE THE COMPRO-MISE KNOWN AS COOPER-ATION.
I THINK I SEE NOW WHY YOU IMMEDIATELY STRUCK ME.
COME, LET ME TELL YOU A LITTLE MORE ABOUT MY BUSI-NESS.

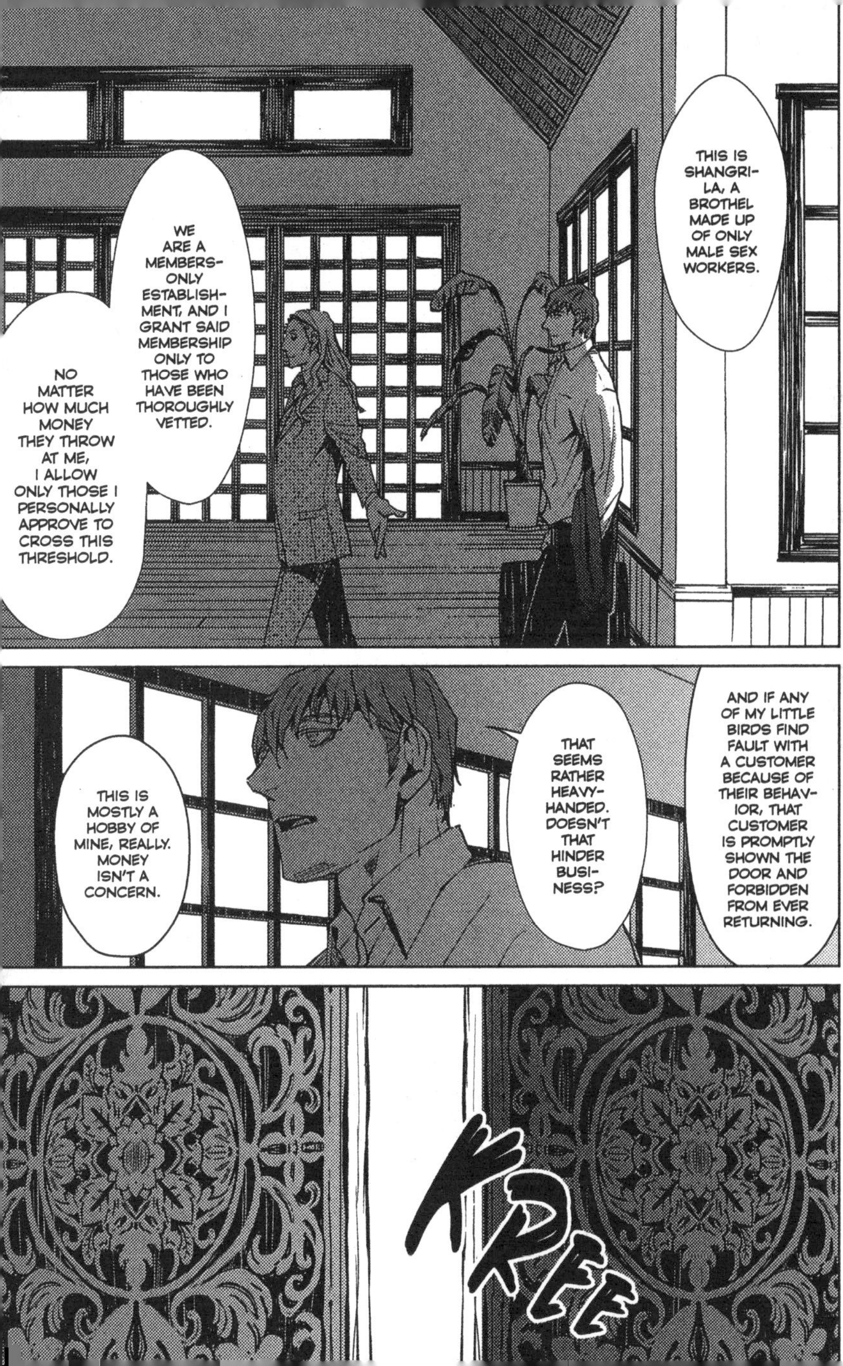
THIS IS SHANGRI-LA, A BROTHEL MADE UP OF ONLY MALE SEX WORKERS.
WE ARE A MEMBERS-ONLY ESTABLISHMENT, AND I GRANT SAID MEMBERSHIP ONLY TO THOSE WHO HAVE BEEN THOROUGHLY VETTED.
NO MATTER HOW MUCH MONEY THEY THROW AT ME, I ALLOW ONLY THOSE I PERSONALLY APPROVE TO CROSS THIS THRESHOLD.
AND IF ANY OF MY LITTLE BIRDS FIND FAULT WITH A CUSTOMER BECAUSE OF THEIR BEHAVIOR, THAT CUSTOMER IS PROMPTLY SHOWN THE DOOR AND FORBIDDEN FROM EVER RETURNING.
THAT SEEMS RATHER HEAVY-HANDED. DOESN'T THAT HINDER BUSINESS?
THIS IS MOSTLY A HOBBY OF MINE, REALLY. MONEY ISN'T A CONCERN.
KREE

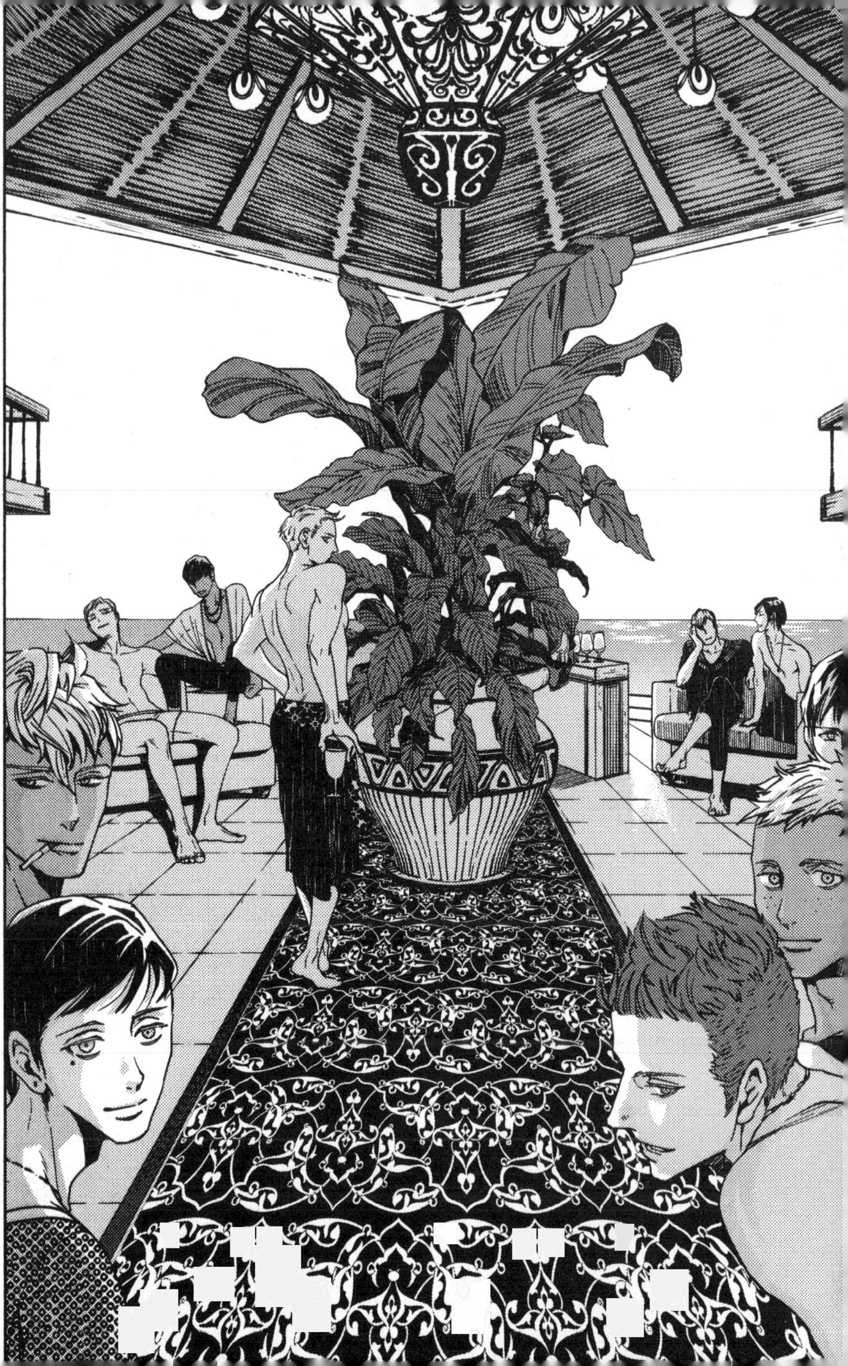

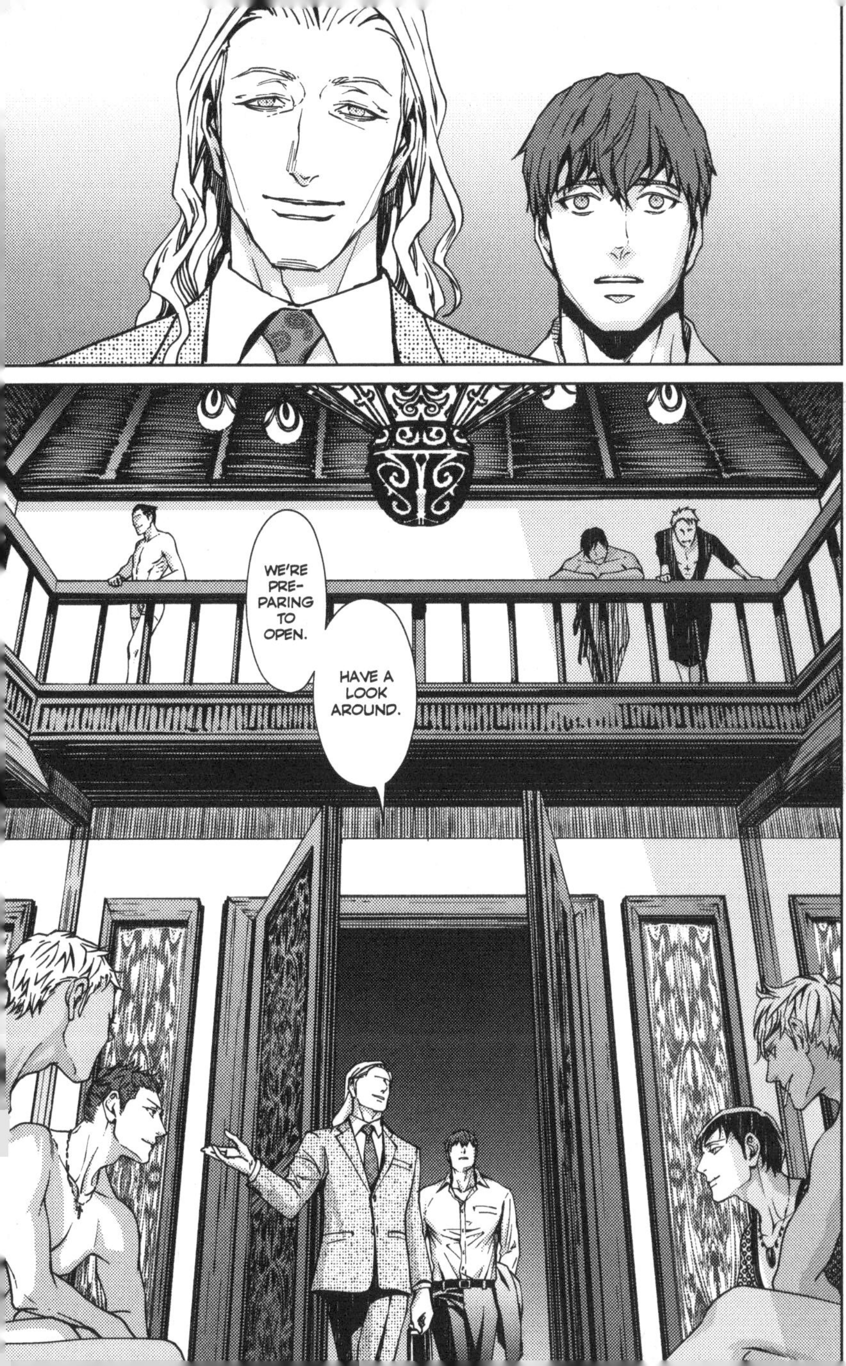
WE'RE PRE-PARING TO OPEN.
HAVE A LOOK AROUND.

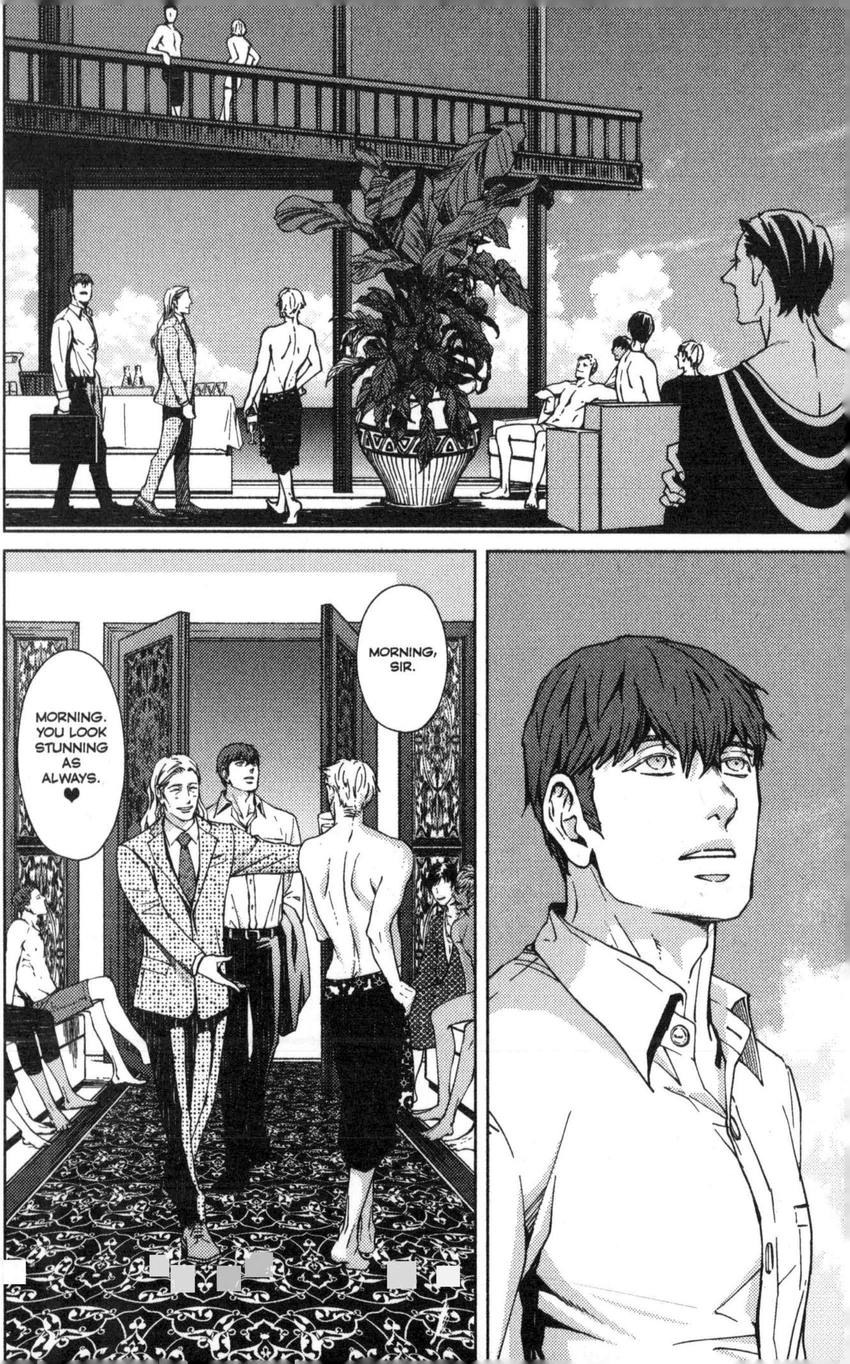
MORNING, SIR.
MORNING. YOU LOOK STUNNING AS ALWAYS. ❤

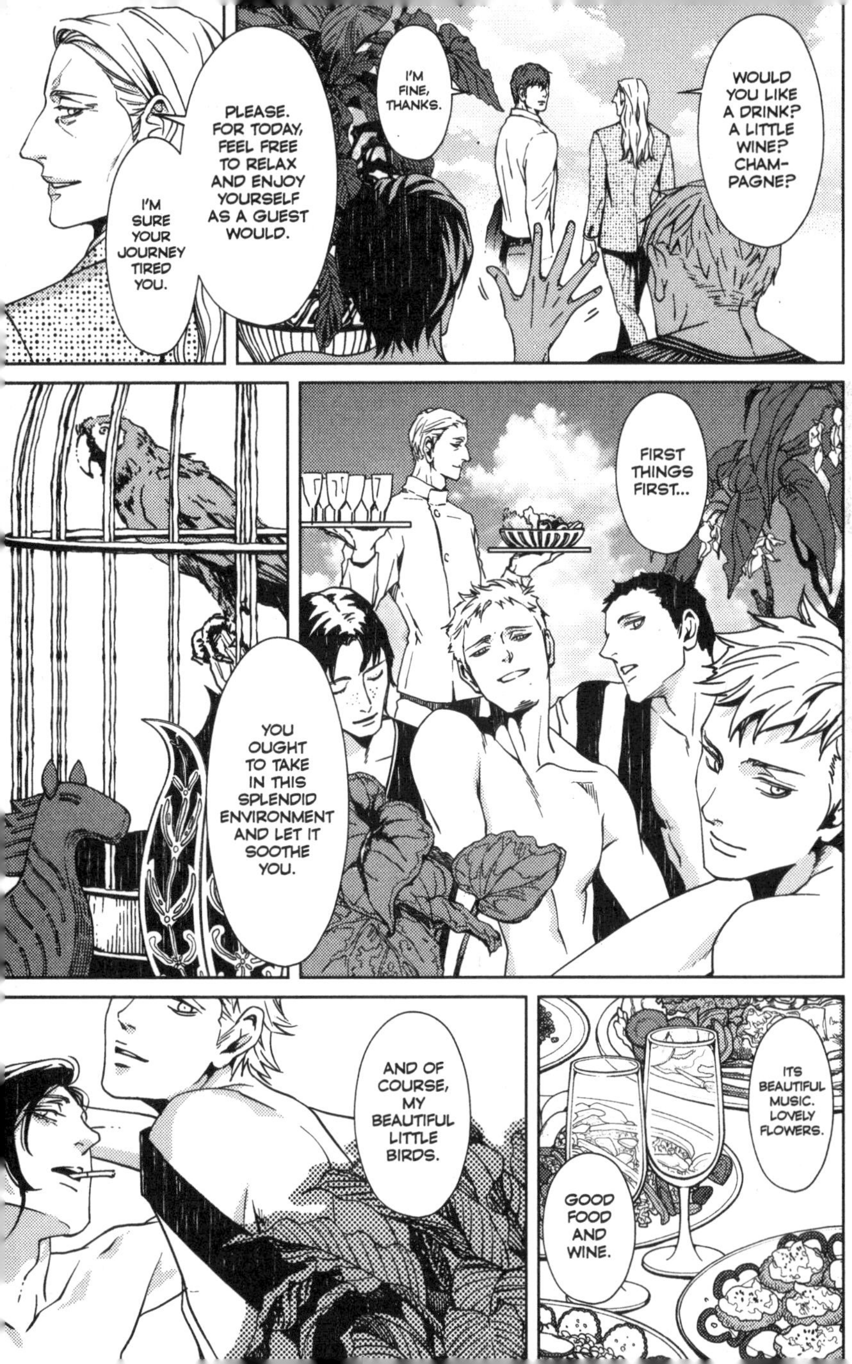
WOULD YOU LIKE A DRINK? A LITTLE WINE? CHAM-PAGNE?
I'M FINE, THANKS.
PLEASE. FOR TODAY, FEEL FREE TO RELAX AND ENJOY YOURSELF AS A GUEST WOULD.
I'M SURE YOUR JOURNEY TIRED YOU.
FIRST THINGS FIRST...
YOU OUGHT TO TAKE IN THIS SPLENDID ENVIRONMENT AND LET IT SOOTHE YOU.
ITS BEAUTIFUL MUSIC. LOVELY FLOWERS.
GOOD FOOD AND WINE.
AND OF COURSE, MY BEAUTIFUL LITTLE BIRDS.

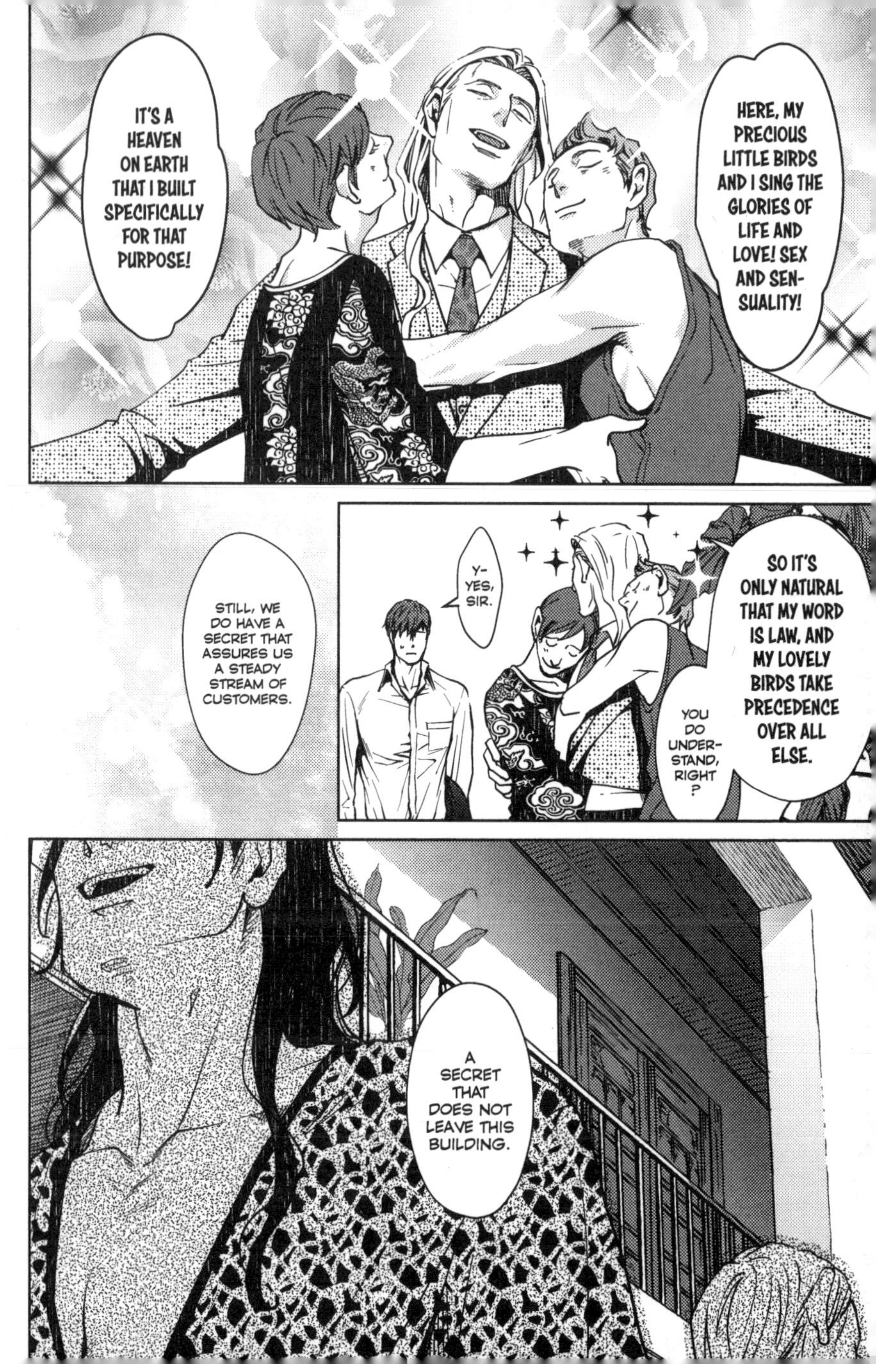
HERE, MY PRECIOUS LITTLE BIRDS AND I SING THE GLORIES OF LIFE AND LOVE! SEX AND SEN-SUALITY!
IT'S A HEAVEN ON EARTH THAT I BUILT SPECIFICALLY FOR THAT PURPOSE!
SO IT'S ONLY NATURAL THAT MY WORD IS LAW, AND MY LOVELY BIRDS TAKE PRECEDENCE OVER ALL ELSE.
YOU DO UNDER-STAND, RIGHT?
Y-YES, SIR.
STILL, WE DO HAVE A SECRET THAT ASSURES US A STEADY STREAM OF CUSTOMERS.
A SECRET THAT DOES NOT LEAVE THIS BUILDING.

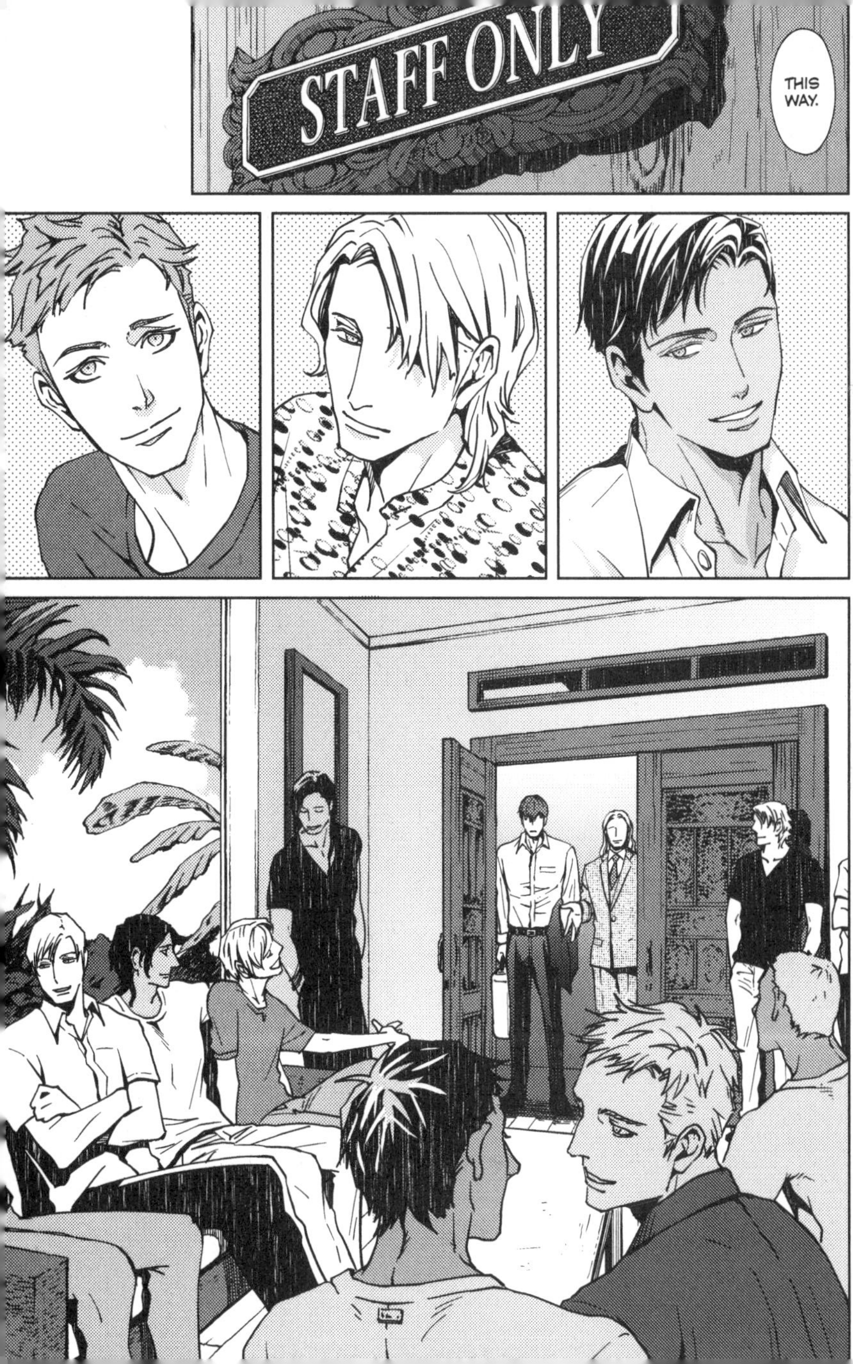
STAFF ONLY
THIS WAY.

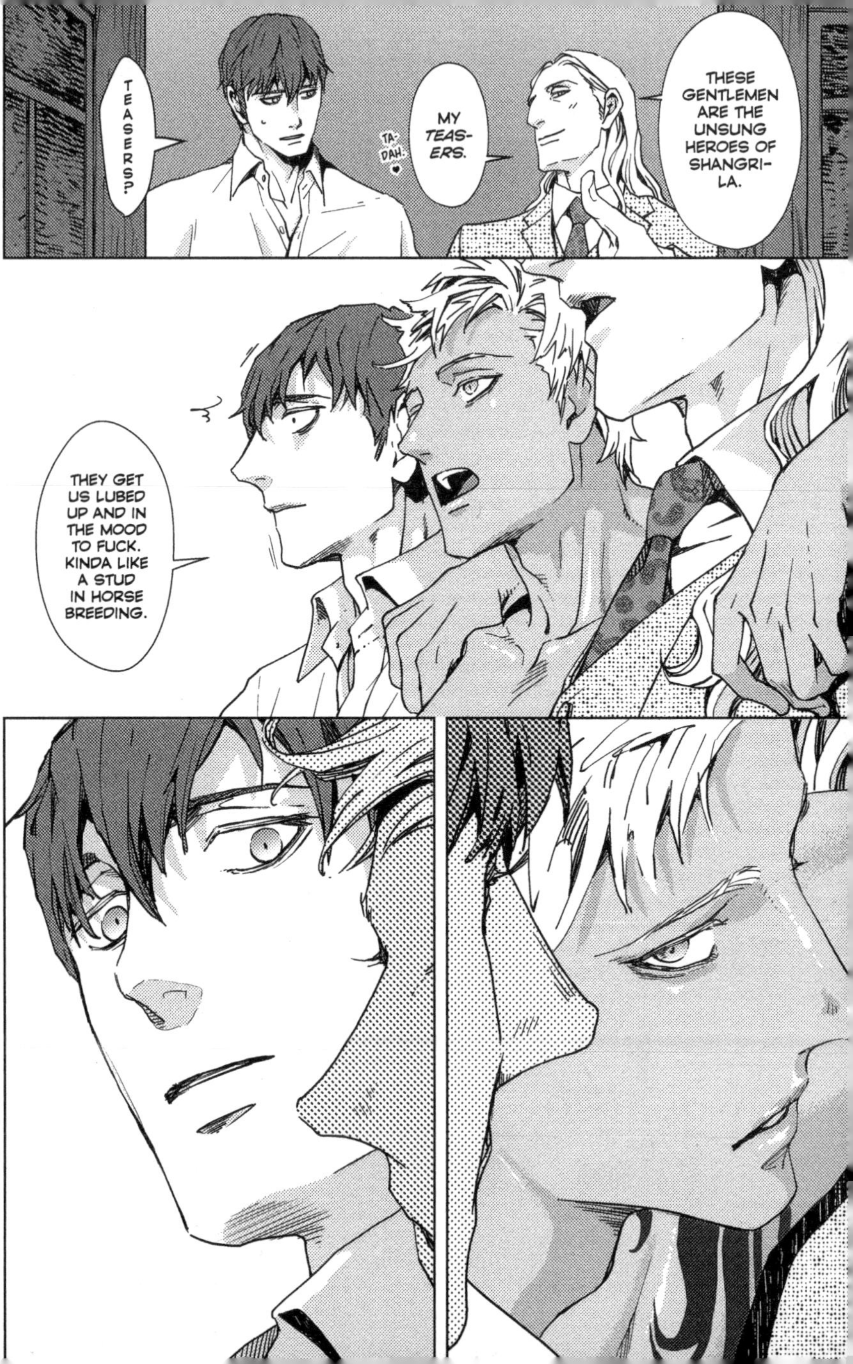
THESE GENTLEMEN ARE THE UNSUNG HEROES OF SHANGRI-LA.
MY TEASERS.
TA-DAH. ♥
TEASERS?
THEY GET US LUBED UP AND IN THE MOOD TO FUCK. KINDA LIKE A STUD IN HORSE BREEDING.

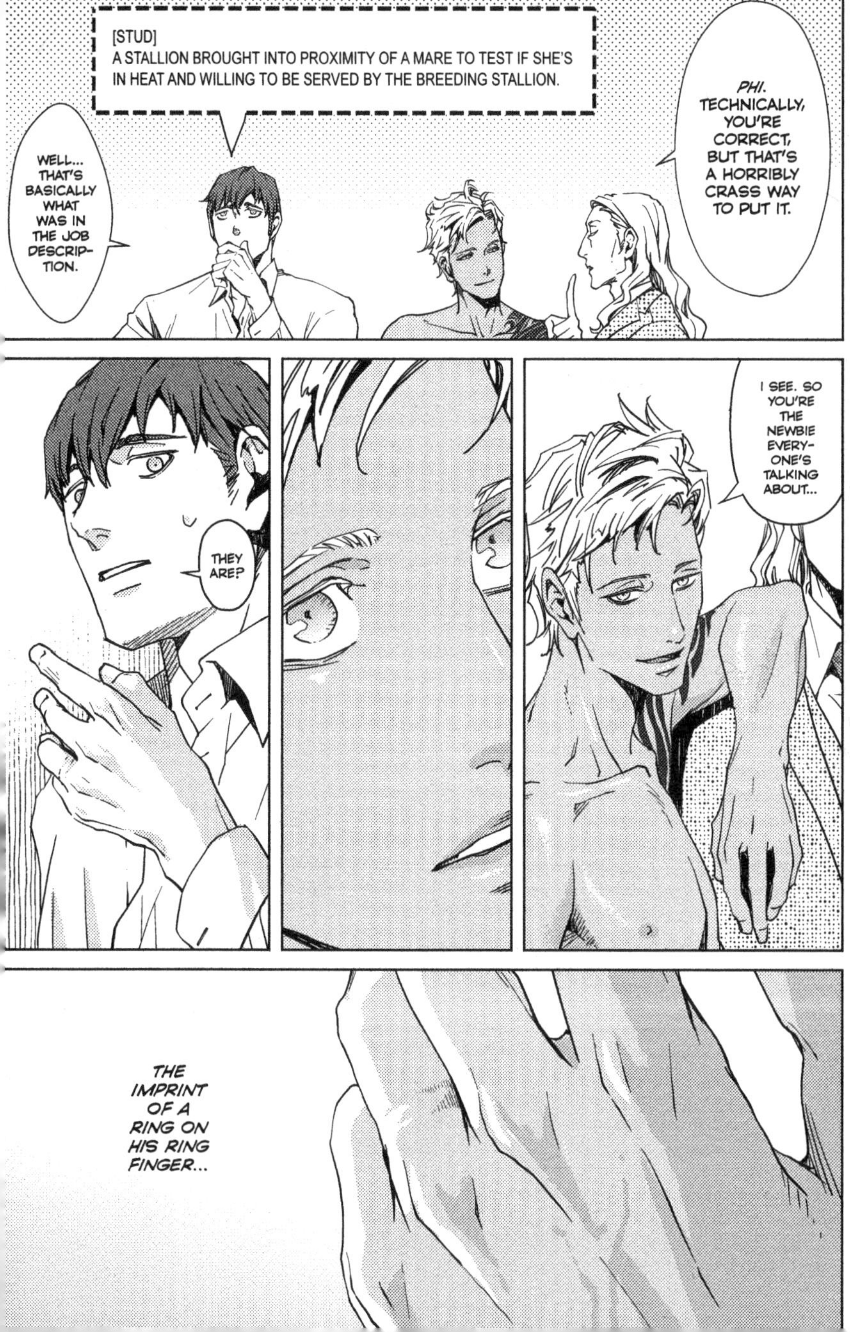
[STUD]
A STALLION BROUGHT INTO PROXIMITY OF A MARE TO TEST IF SHE'S IN HEAT AND WILLING TO BE SERVED BY THE BREEDING STALLION.
PHI. TECHNICALLY, YOU'RE CORRECT, BUT THAT'S A HORRIBLY CRASS WAY TO PUT IT.
WELL... THAT'S BASICALLY WHAT WAS IN THE JOB DESCRIP-TION.
I SEE. SO YOU'RE THE NEWBIE EVERY-ONE'S TALKING ABOUT...
THEY ARE?
THE IMPRINT OF A RING ON HIS RING FINGER...

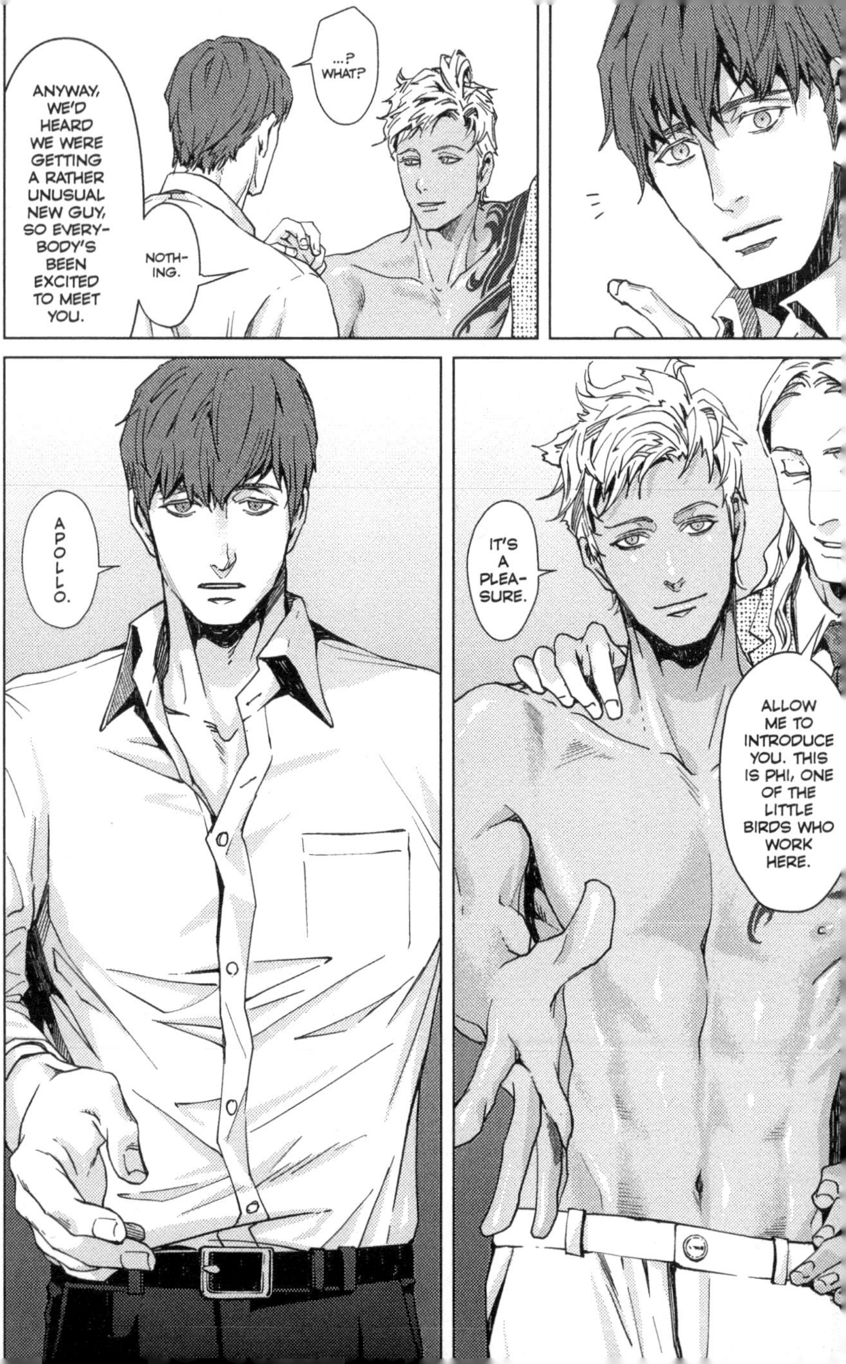
...? WHAT?
NOTHING.
ANYWAY, WE'D HEARD WE WERE GETTING A RATHER UNUSUAL NEW GUY, SO EVERYBODY'S BEEN EXCITED TO MEET YOU.
ALLOW ME TO INTRODUCE YOU. THIS IS PHI, ONE OF THE LITTLE BIRDS WHO WORK HERE.
IT'S A PLEASURE.
APOLLO.

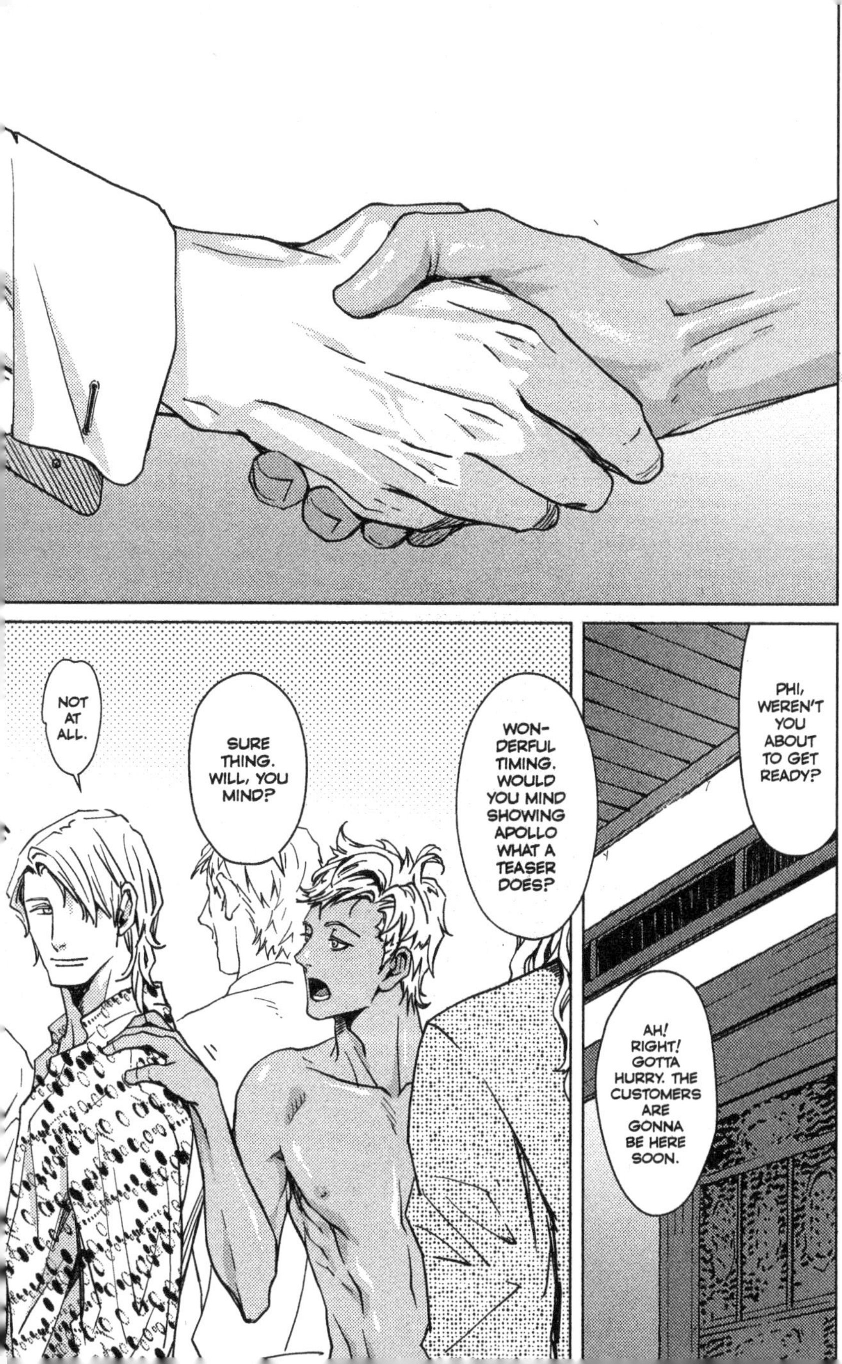
PHI, WEREN'T YOU ABOUT TO GET READY?
AH! RIGHT! GOTTA HURRY. THE CUSTOMERS ARE GONNA BE HERE SOON.
WON-DERFUL TIMING. WOULD YOU MIND SHOWING APOLLO WHAT A TEASER DOES?
SURE THING. WILL, YOU MIND?
NOT AT ALL.

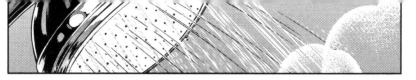

SO HOW WAS THAT CUSTOMER LAST NIGHT? HE DIDN'T DO ANYTHING UGLY, DID HE?

NOPE! HE WAS GREAT. BUT IT WAS OBVIOUS HE'D HAVE PREFERRED KARNA, NOT ME.

OH, HE WAS ONE OF KARNA'S REGULARS? POOR KARNA.

WHY DO YOU SAY THAT?

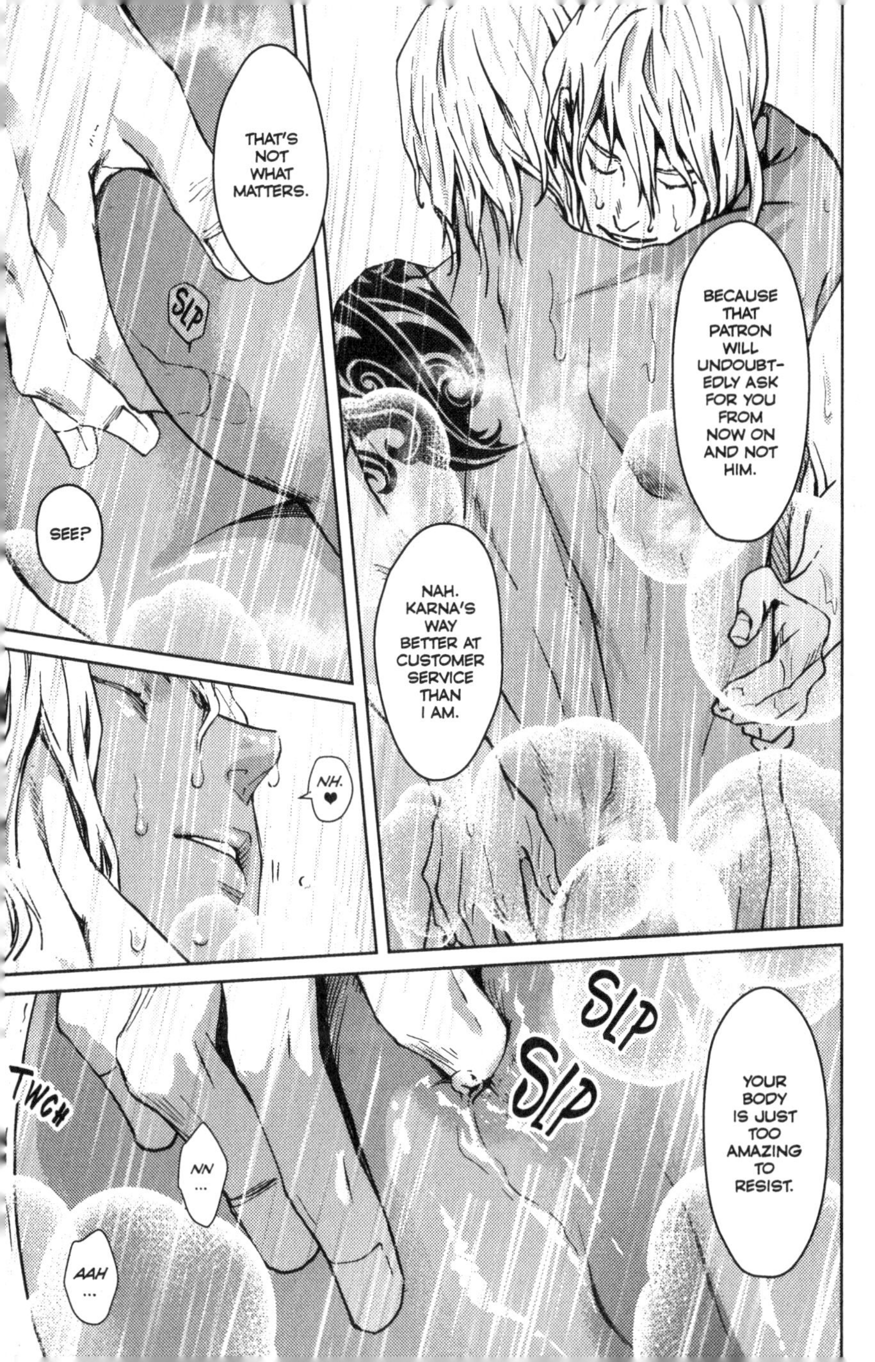
BECAUSE THAT PATRON WILL UNDOUBT-EDLY ASK FOR YOU FROM NOW ON AND NOT HIM.
NAH. KARNA'S WAY BETTER AT CUSTOMER SERVICE THAN I AM.
THAT'S NOT WHAT MATTERS.
SLIP
SEE?
NH. ♥
SLIP
SLIP
YOUR BODY IS JUST TOO AMAZING TO RESIST.
TWCH
NN ...
AAH ...

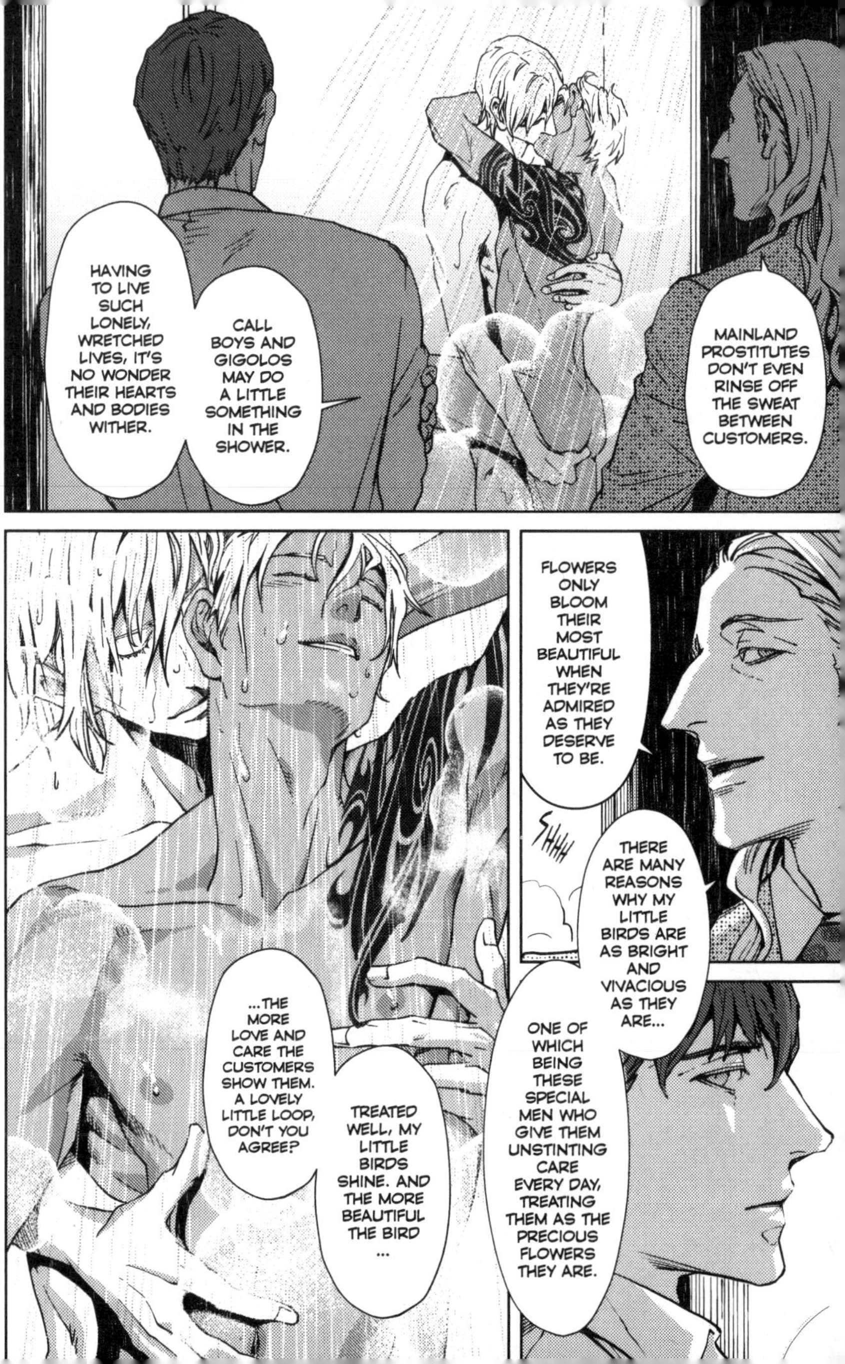
MAINLAND PROSTITUTES DON'T EVEN RINSE OFF THE SWEAT BETWEEN CUSTOMERS.
CALL BOYS AND GIGOLOS MAY DO A LITTLE SOMETHING IN THE SHOWER.
HAVING TO LIVE SUCH LONELY, WRETCHED LIVES, IT'S NO WONDER THEIR HEARTS AND BODIES WITHER.
FLOWERS ONLY BLOOM THEIR MOST BEAUTIFUL WHEN THEY'RE ADMIRED AS THEY DESERVE TO BE.
SHHH
THERE ARE MANY REASONS WHY MY LITTLE BIRDS ARE AS BRIGHT AND VIVACIOUS AS THEY ARE...
ONE OF WHICH BEING THESE SPECIAL MEN WHO GIVE THEM UNSTINTING CARE EVERY DAY, TREATING THEM AS THE PRECIOUS FLOWERS THEY ARE.
TREATED WELL, MY LITTLE BIRDS SHINE. AND THE MORE BEAUTIFUL THE BIRD ...
...THE MORE LOVE AND CARE THE CUSTOMERS SHOW THEM. A LOVELY LITTLE LOOP, DON'T YOU AGREE?

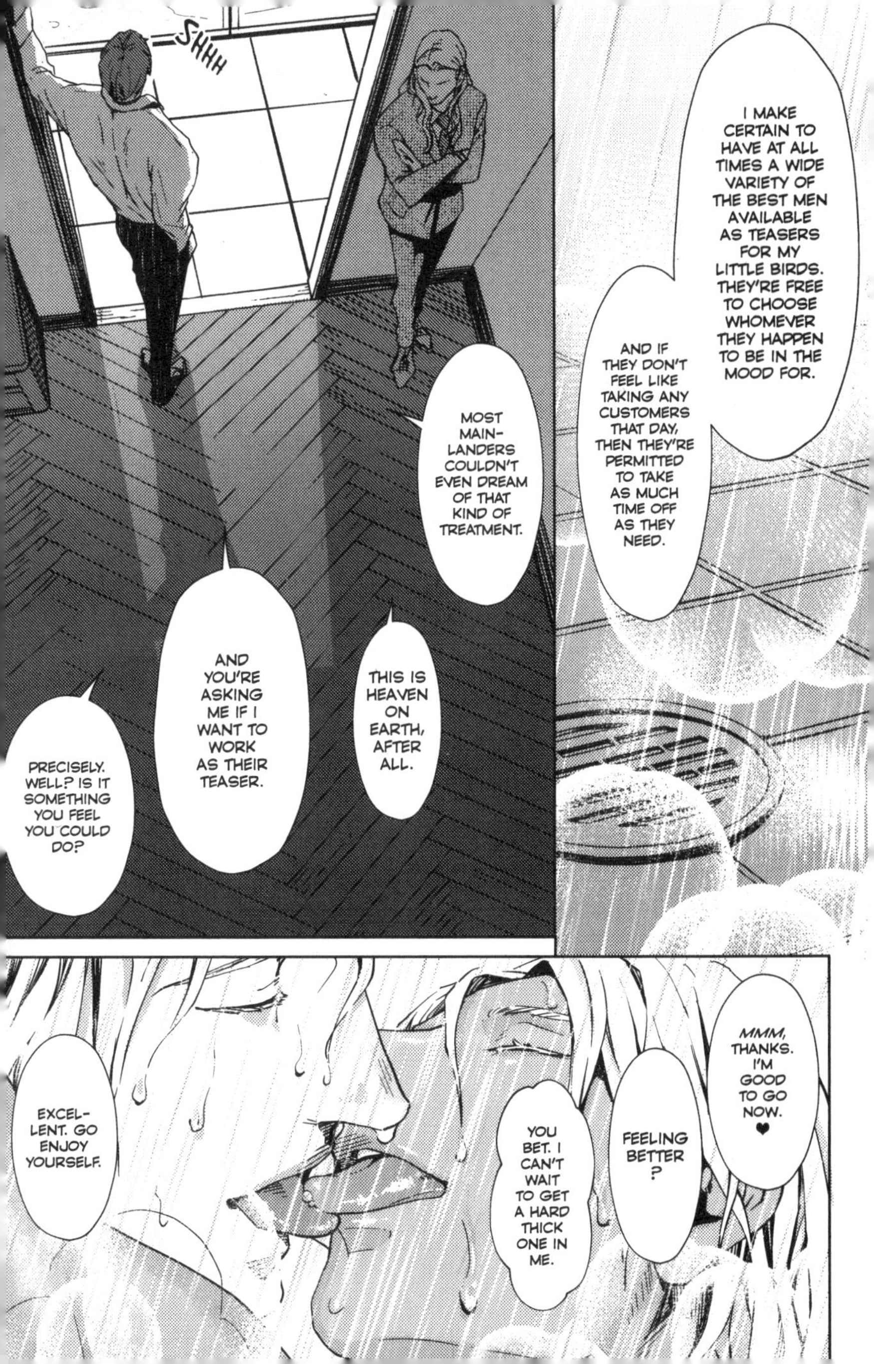
I MAKE CERTAIN TO HAVE AT ALL TIMES A WIDE VARIETY OF THE BEST MEN AVAILABLE AS TEASERS FOR MY LITTLE BIRDS. THEY'RE FREE TO CHOOSE WHOMEVER THEY HAPPEN TO BE IN THE MOOD FOR.
AND IF THEY DON'T FEEL LIKE TAKING ANY CUSTOMERS THAT DAY, THEN THEY'RE PERMITTED TO TAKE AS MUCH TIME OFF AS THEY NEED.
SHHH
MOST MAIN-LANDERS COULDN'T EVEN DREAM OF THAT KIND OF TREATMENT.
THIS IS HEAVEN ON EARTH, AFTER ALL.
AND YOU'RE ASKING ME IF I WANT TO WORK AS THEIR TEASER.
PRECISELY. WELL? IS IT SOMETHING YOU FEEL YOU COULD DO?
MMM, THANKS. I'M GOOD TO GO NOW. ❤
FEELING BETTER?
YOU BET. I CAN'T WAIT TO GET A HARD THICK ONE IN ME.
EXCEL-LENT. GO ENJOY YOURSELF.

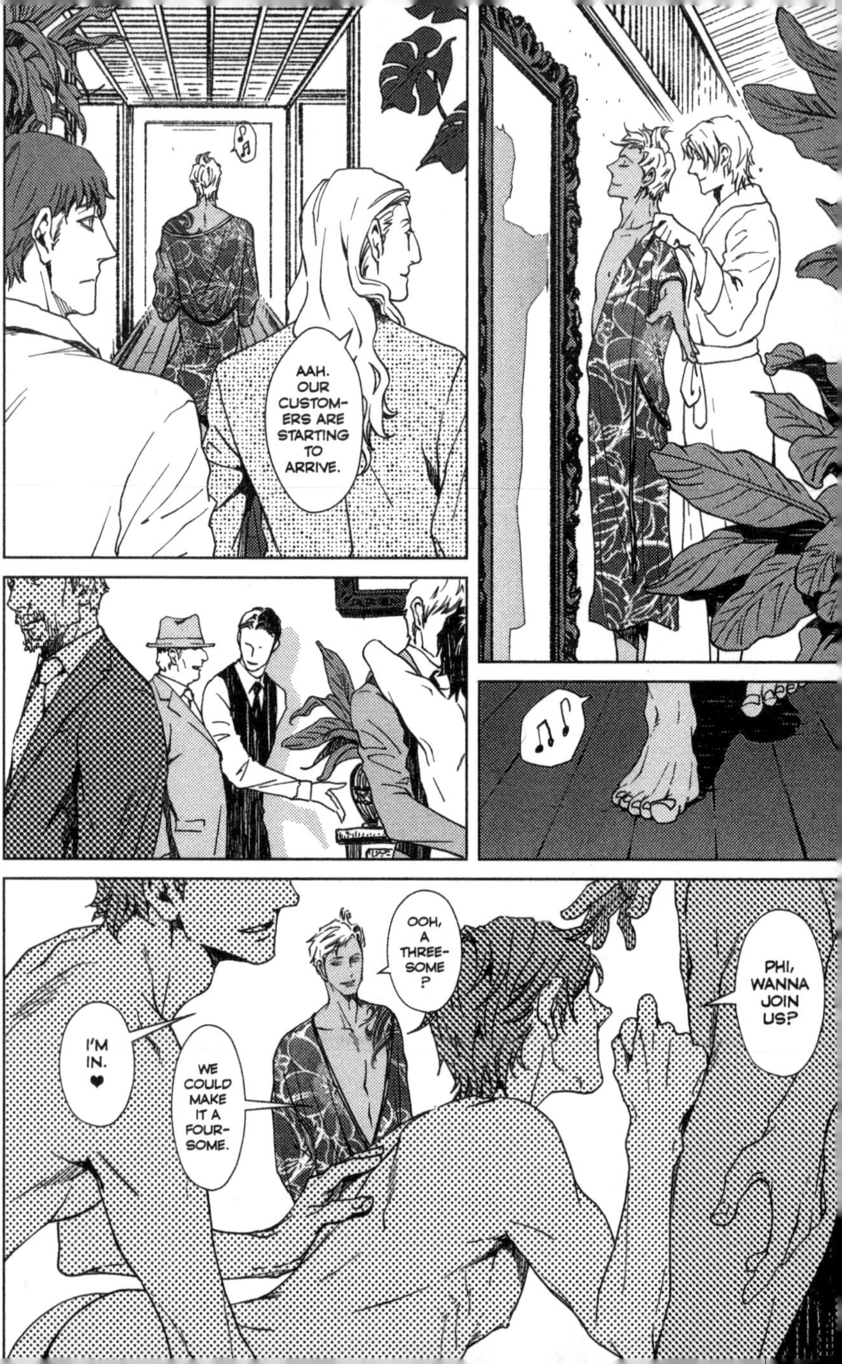
♪♫
AAH. OUR CUSTOMERS ARE STARTING TO ARRIVE.
♪♪
PHI, WANNA JOIN US?
OOH, A THREESOME?
I'M IN. ♥
WE COULD MAKE IT A FOURSOME.

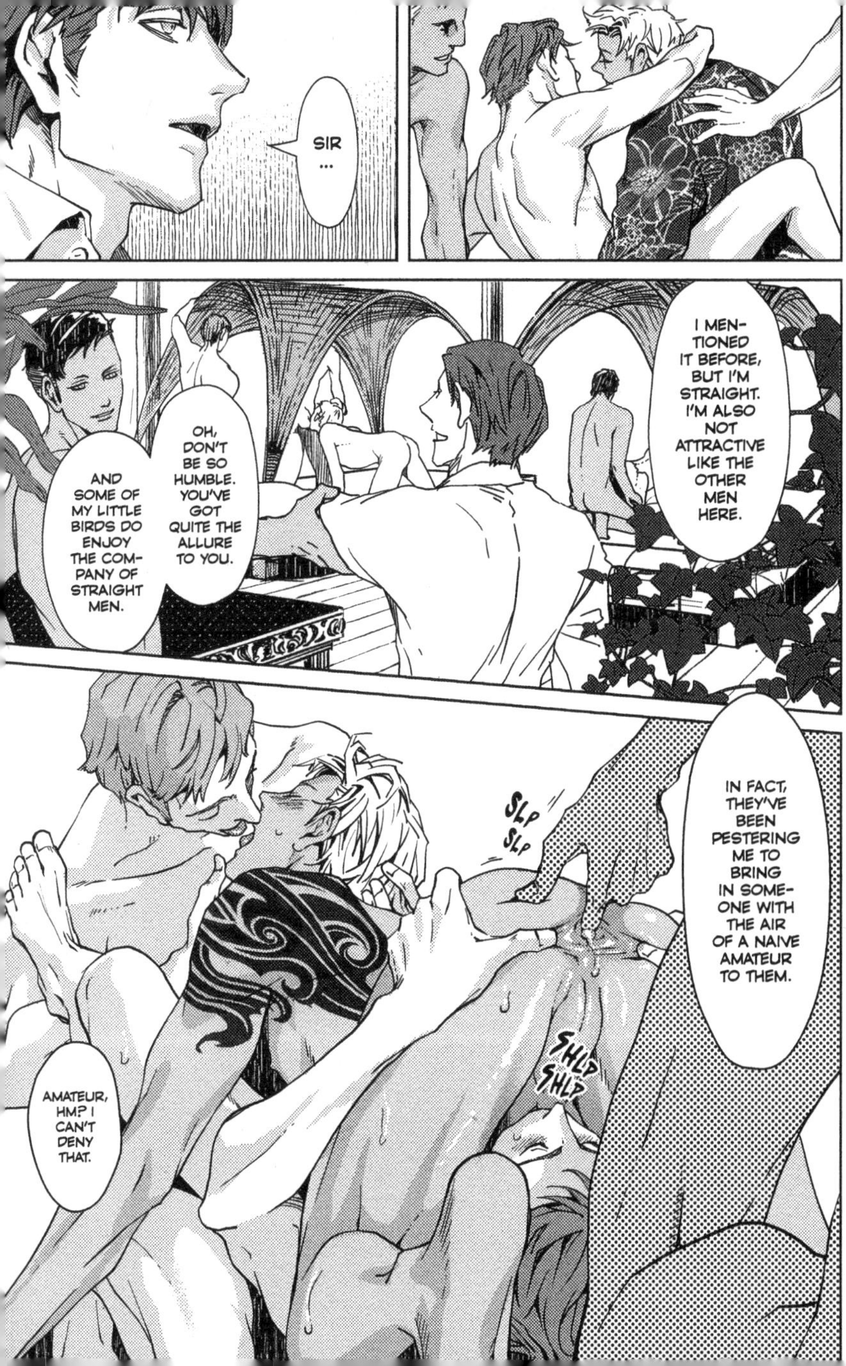
SIR ...
I MEN-TIONED IT BEFORE, BUT I'M STRAIGHT. I'M ALSO NOT ATTRACTIVE LIKE THE OTHER MEN HERE.
OH, DON'T BE SO HUMBLE. YOU'VE GOT QUITE THE ALLURE TO YOU.
AND SOME OF MY LITTLE BIRDS DO ENJOY THE COM-PANY OF STRAIGHT MEN.
IN FACT, THEY'VE BEEN PESTERING ME TO BRING IN SOME-ONE WITH THE AIR OF A NAIVE AMATEUR TO THEM.
SLP SLP
SHLP SHLP
AMATEUR, HM? I CAN'T DENY THAT.

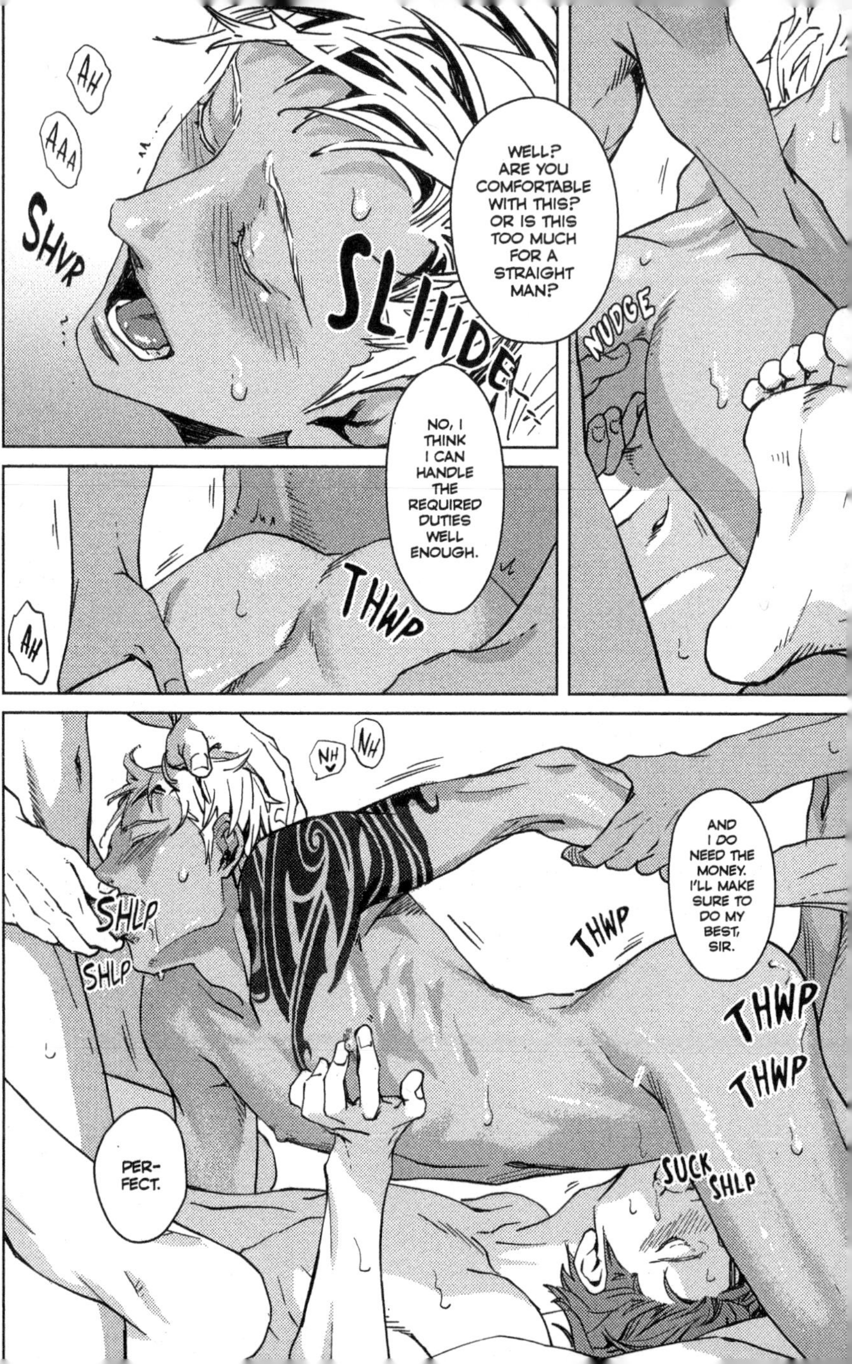
WELL? ARE YOU COMFORTABLE WITH THIS? OR IS THIS TOO MUCH FOR A STRAIGHT MAN?
NUDGE
AH
AAA
SHVR
SLIIIDE
NO, I THINK I CAN HANDLE THE REQUIRED DUTIES WELL ENOUGH.
THWP
AH
AND I DO NEED THE MONEY. I'LL MAKE SURE TO DO MY BEST, SIR.
NH
NH
THWP
THWP
THWP
SUCK
SHLP
SHLP
SHLP
PER-FECT.

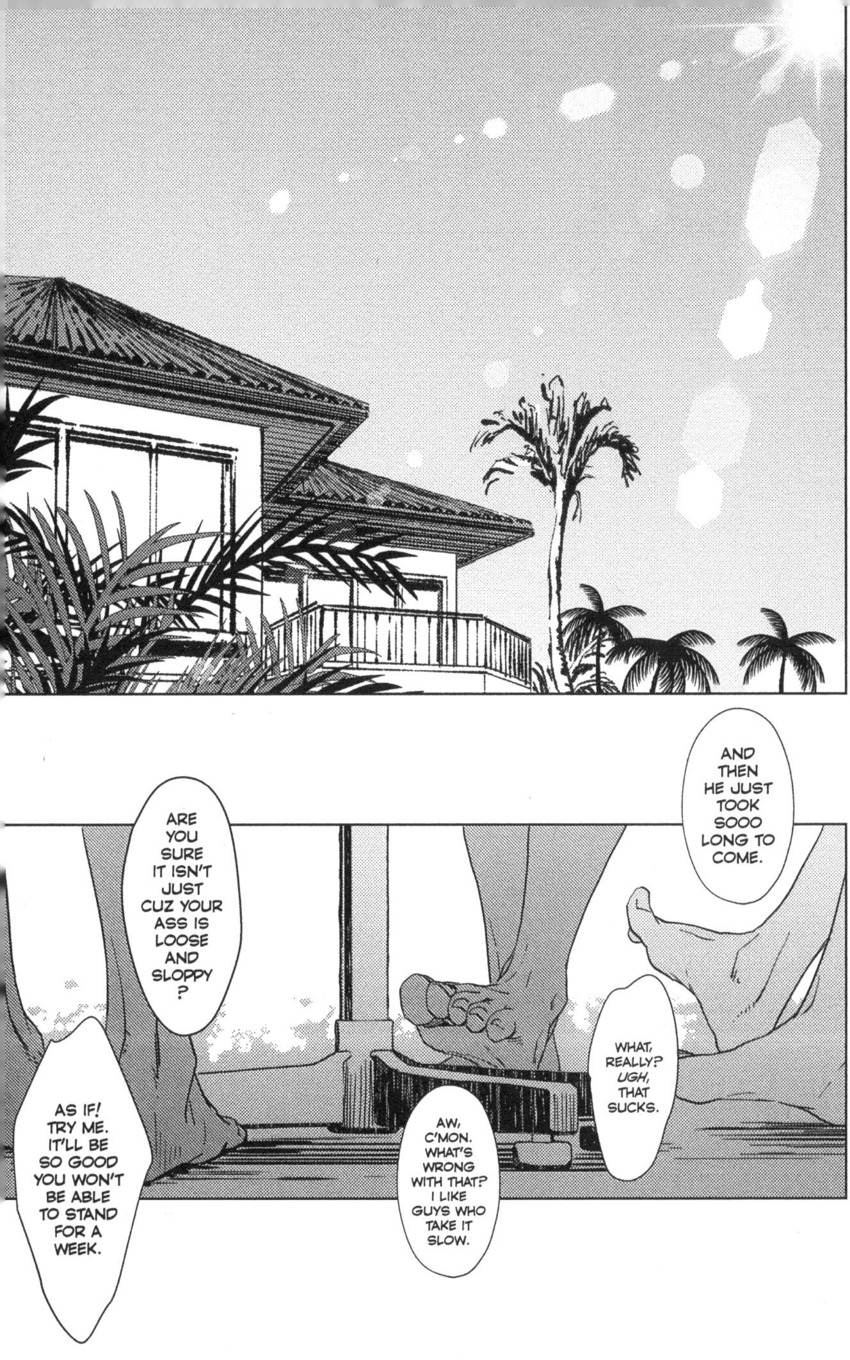
AND THEN HE JUST TOOK SOOO LONG TO COME.
WHAT, REALLY? *UGH*, THAT SUCKS.
AW, C'MON. WHAT'S WRONG WITH THAT? I LIKE GUYS WHO TAKE IT SLOW.
ARE YOU SURE IT ISN'T JUST CUZ YOUR ASS IS LOOSE AND SLOPPY?
AS IF! TRY ME. IT'LL BE SO GOOD YOU WON'T BE ABLE TO STAND FOR A WEEK.

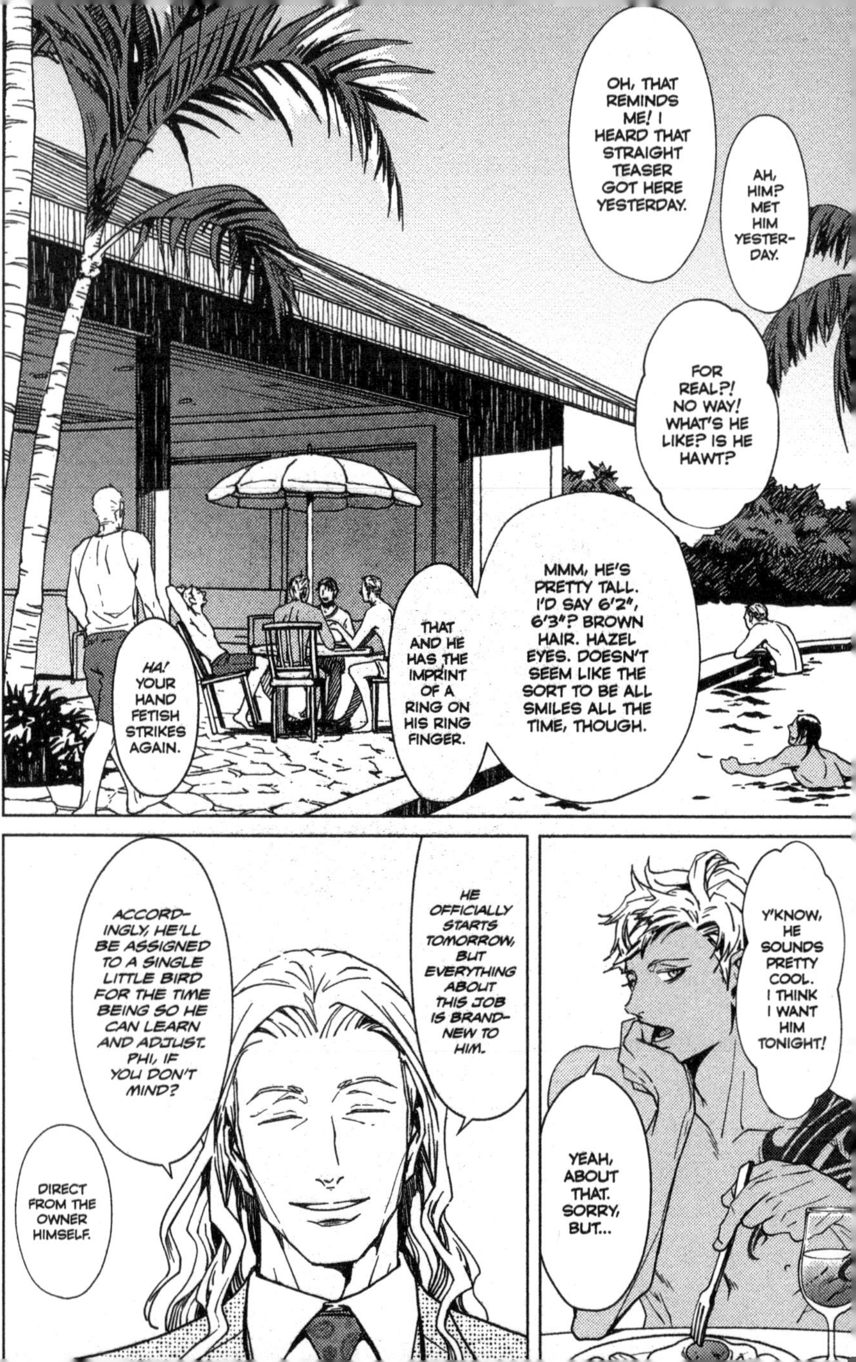
OH, THAT REMINDS ME! I HEARD THAT STRAIGHT TEASER GOT HERE YESTERDAY.
AH, HIM? MET HIM YESTER-DAY.
FOR REAL?! NO WAY! WHAT'S HE LIKE? IS HE HAWT?
MMM, HE'S PRETTY TALL. I'D SAY 6'2", 6'3"? BROWN HAIR. HAZEL EYES. DOESN'T SEEM LIKE THE SORT TO BE ALL SMILES ALL THE TIME, THOUGH.
THAT AND HE HAS THE IMPRINT OF A RING ON HIS RING FINGER.
HA! YOUR HAND FETISH STRIKES AGAIN.
Y'KNOW, HE SOUNDS PRETTY COOL. I THINK I WANT HIM TONIGHT!
YEAH, ABOUT THAT. SORRY, BUT...
HE OFFICIALLY STARTS TOMORROW, BUT EVERYTHING ABOUT THIS JOB IS BRAND-NEW TO HIM.
ACCORD-INGLY, HE'LL BE ASSIGNED TO A SINGLE LITTLE BIRD FOR THE TIME BEING SO HE CAN LEARN AND ADJUST. PHI, IF YOU DON'T MIND?
DIRECT FROM THE OWNER HIMSELF.

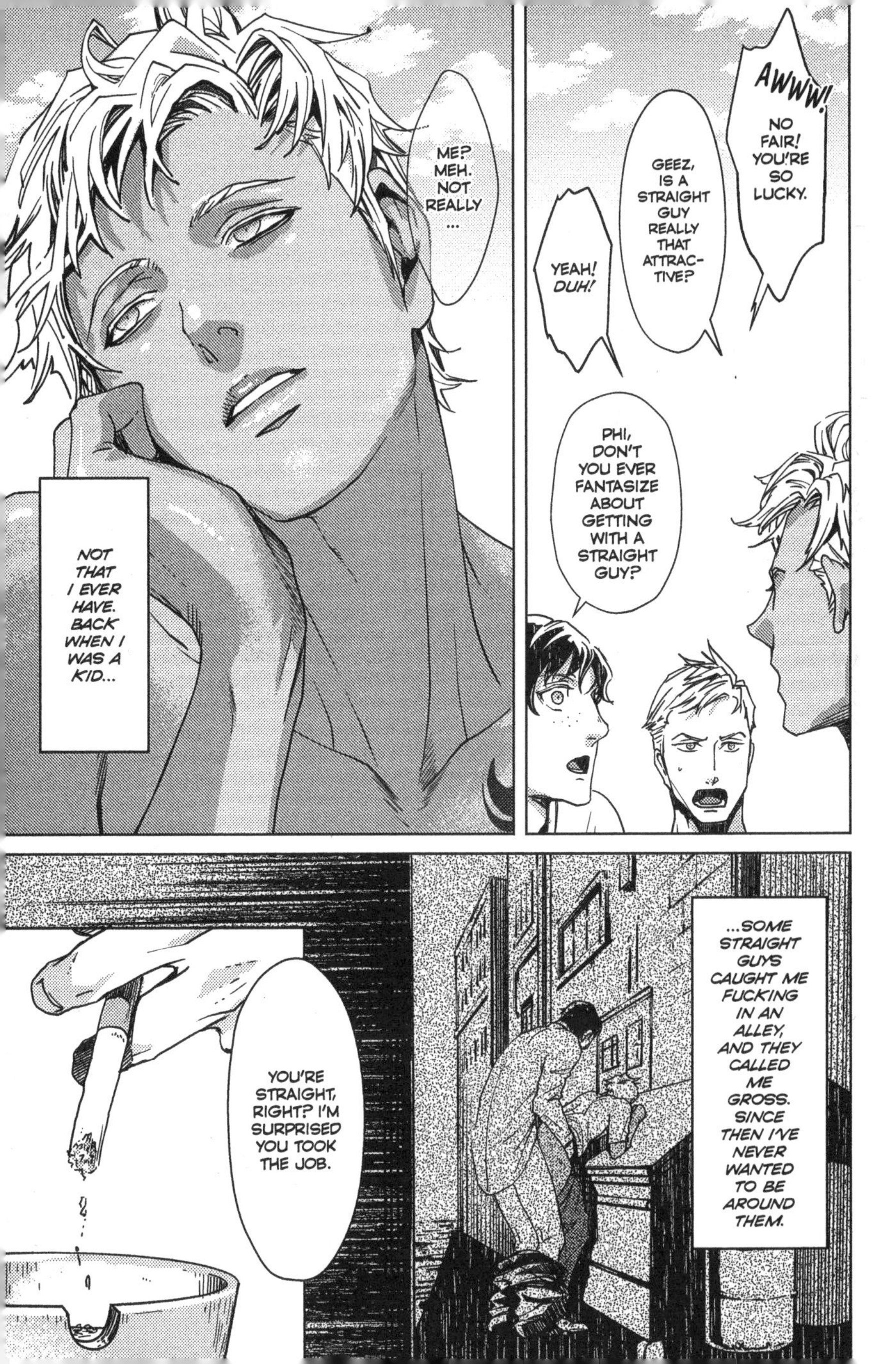
AWWW!
NO FAIR! YOU'RE SO LUCKY.
GEEZ, IS A STRAIGHT GUY REALLY THAT ATTRACTIVE?
YEAH! DUH!
PHI, DON'T YOU EVER FANTASIZE ABOUT GETTING WITH A STRAIGHT GUY?
ME? MEH. NOT REALLY ...
NOT THAT I EVER HAVE. BACK WHEN I WAS A KID...
...SOME STRAIGHT GUYS CAUGHT ME FUCKING IN AN ALLEY, AND THEY CALLED ME GROSS. SINCE THEN I'VE NEVER WANTED TO BE AROUND THEM.
YOU'RE STRAIGHT, RIGHT? I'M SURPRISED YOU TOOK THE JOB.

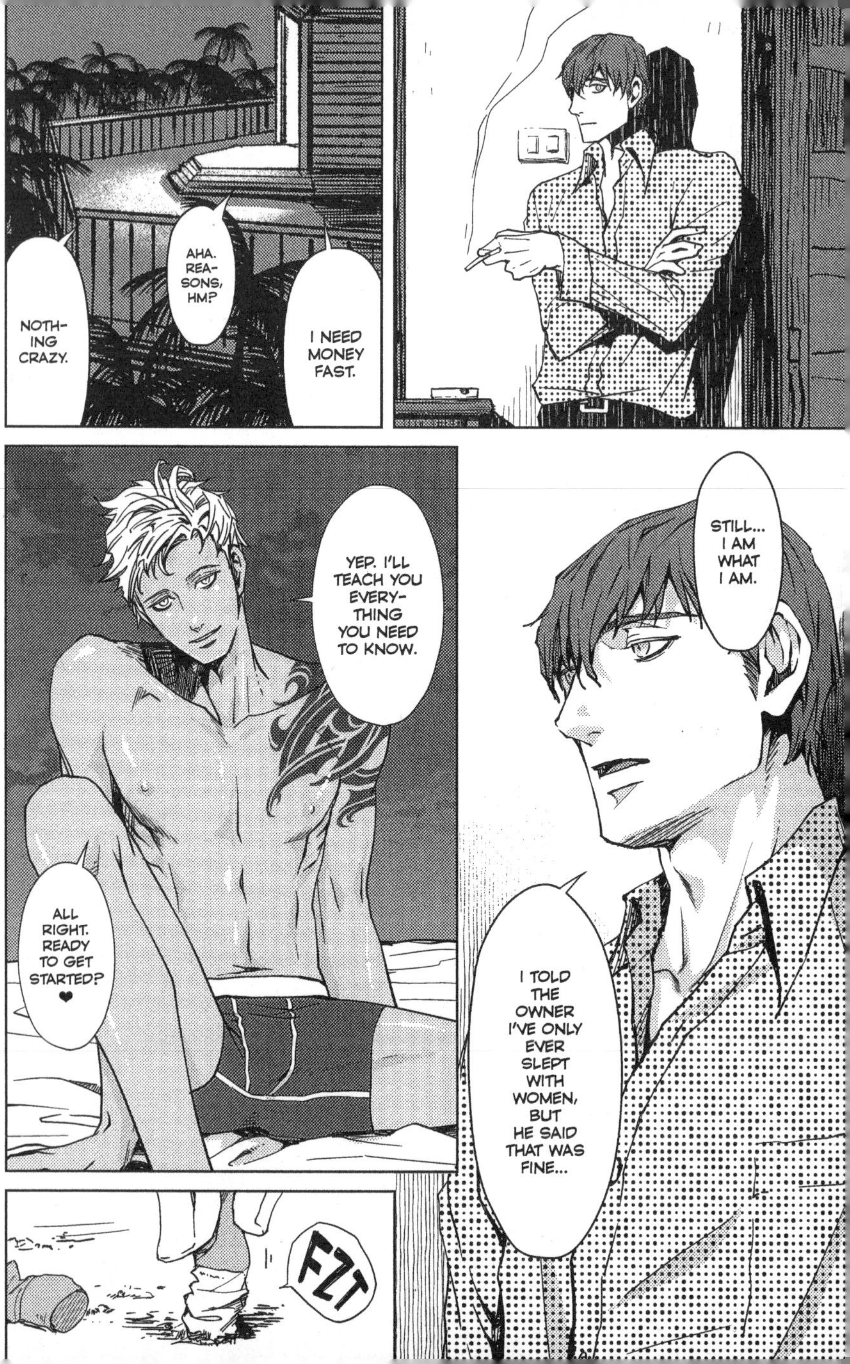
I NEED MONEY FAST.
AHA. REA-SONS, HM?
NOTH-ING CRAZY.
STILL... I AM WHAT I AM.
I TOLD THE OWNER I'VE ONLY EVER SLEPT WITH WOMEN, BUT HE SAID THAT WAS FINE...
YEP. I'LL TEACH YOU EVERY-THING YOU NEED TO KNOW.
ALL RIGHT. READY TO GET STARTED? ❤
FZT

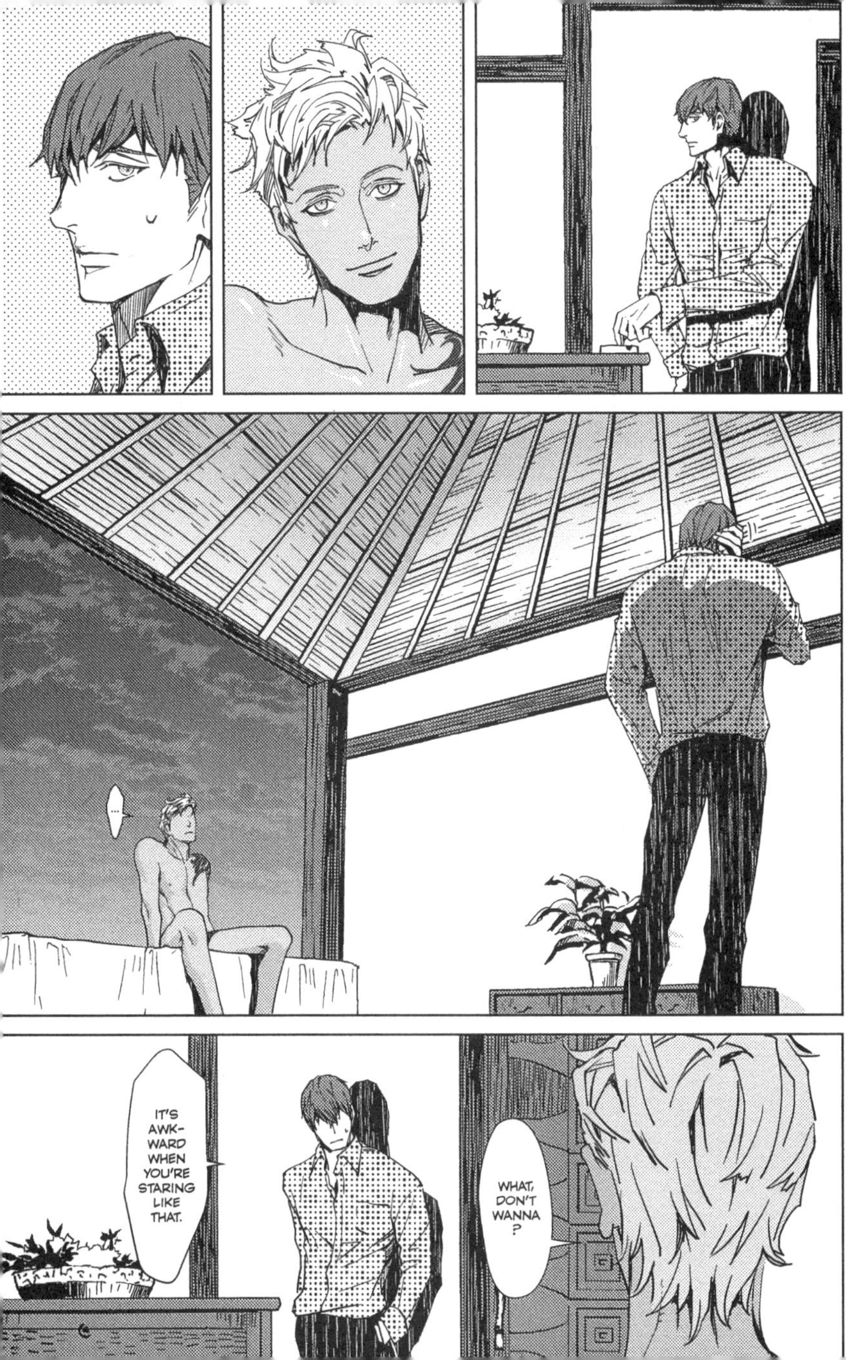
...
WHAT, DON'T WANNA?
IT'S AWKWARD WHEN YOU'RE STARING LIKE THAT.

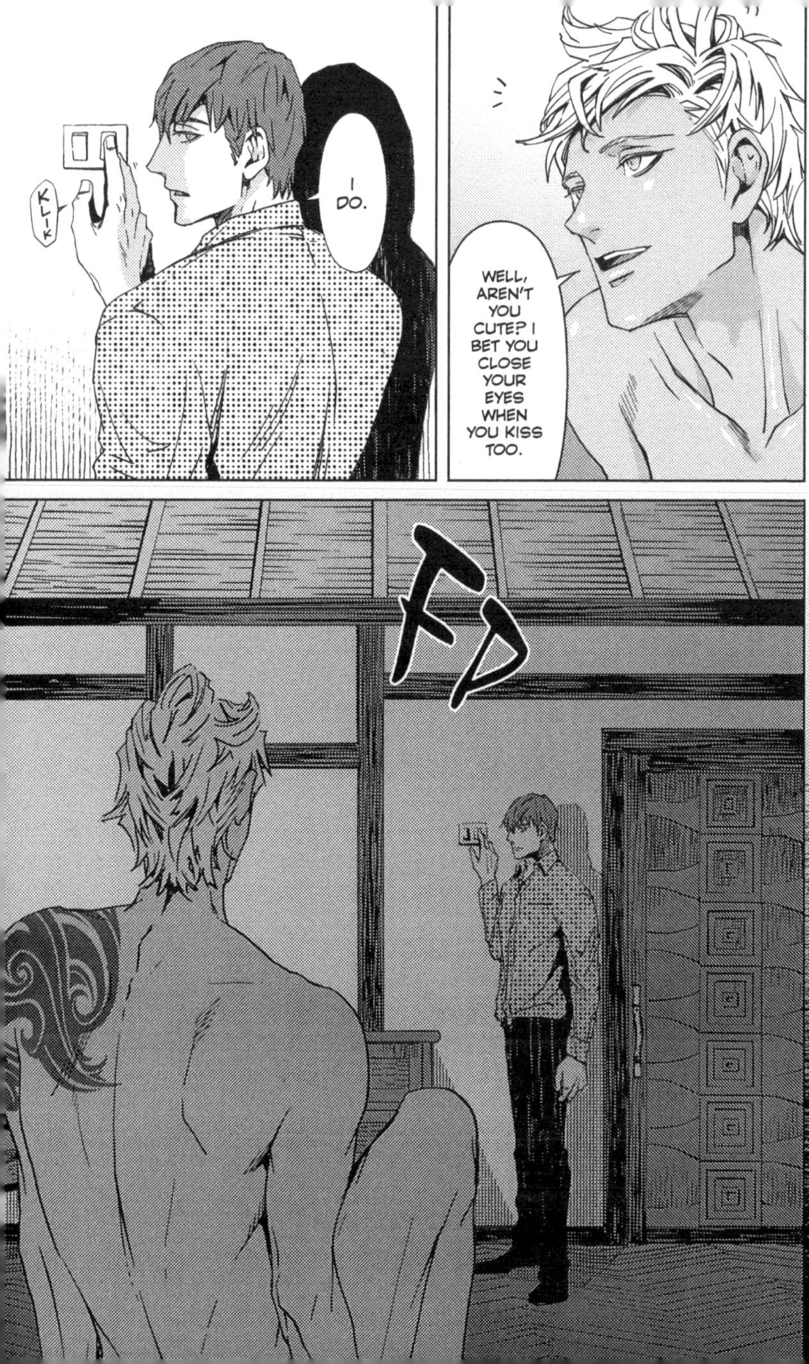
WELL, AREN'T YOU CUTE? I BET YOU CLOSE YOUR EYES WHEN YOU KISS TOO.
I DO.
KLIK

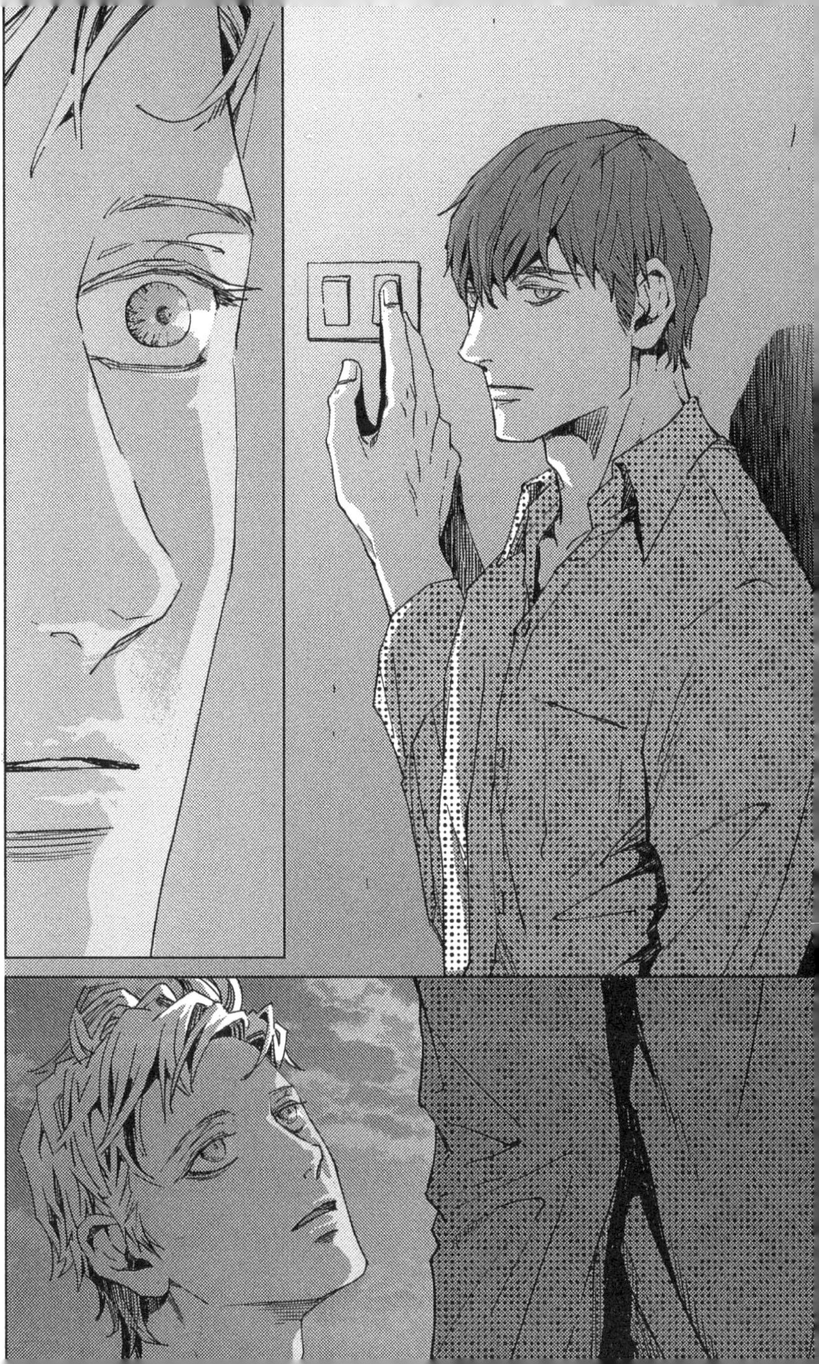

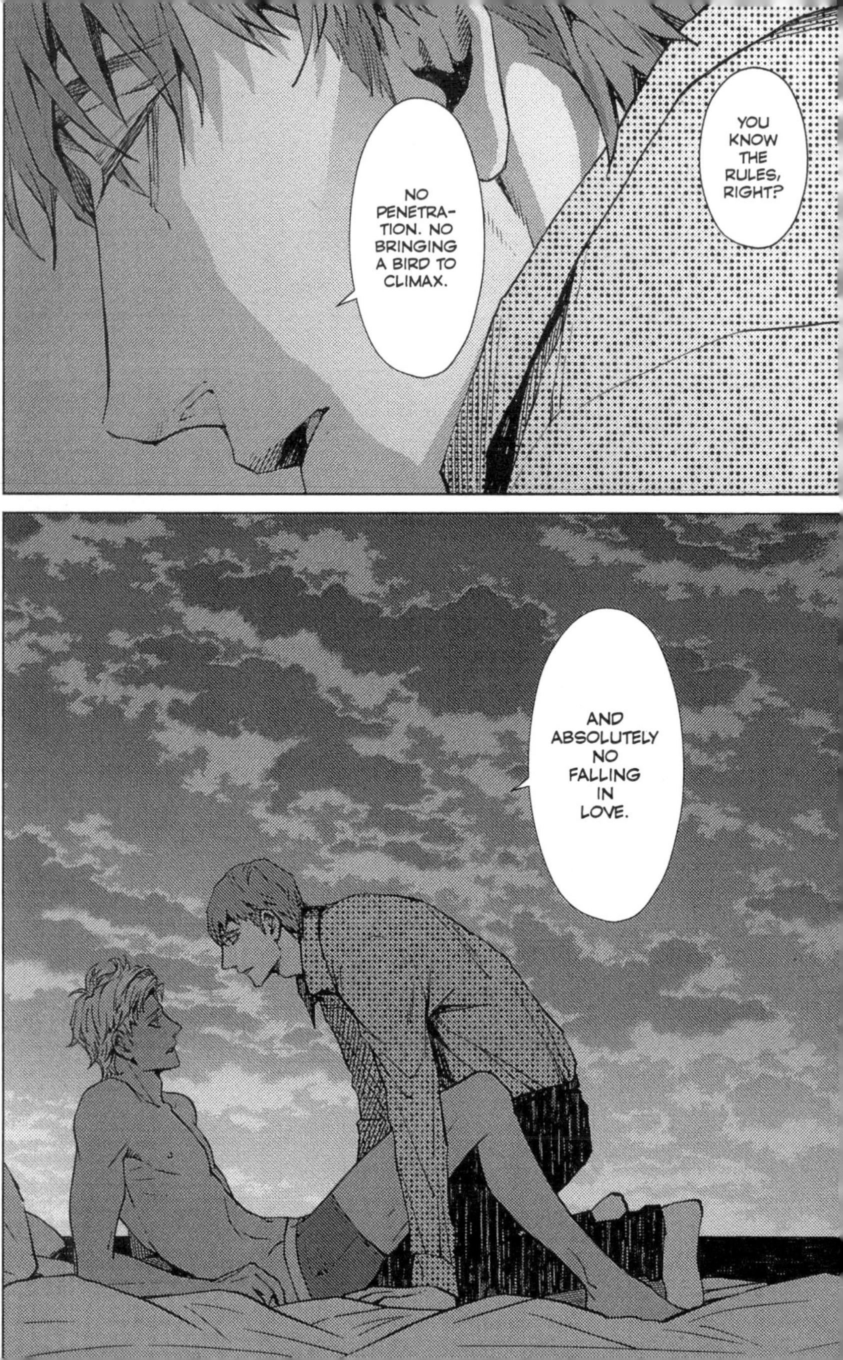
YOU KNOW THE RULES, RIGHT?
NO PENETRATION. NO BRINGING A BIRD TO CLIMAX.
AND ABSOLUTELY NO FALLING IN LOVE.

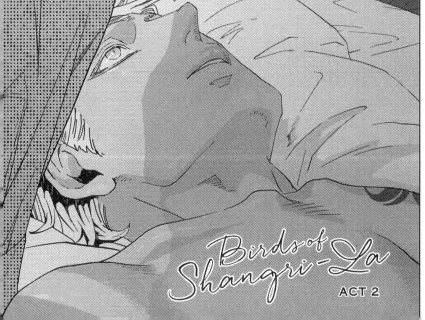

Birds of Shangri-La

ACT 2

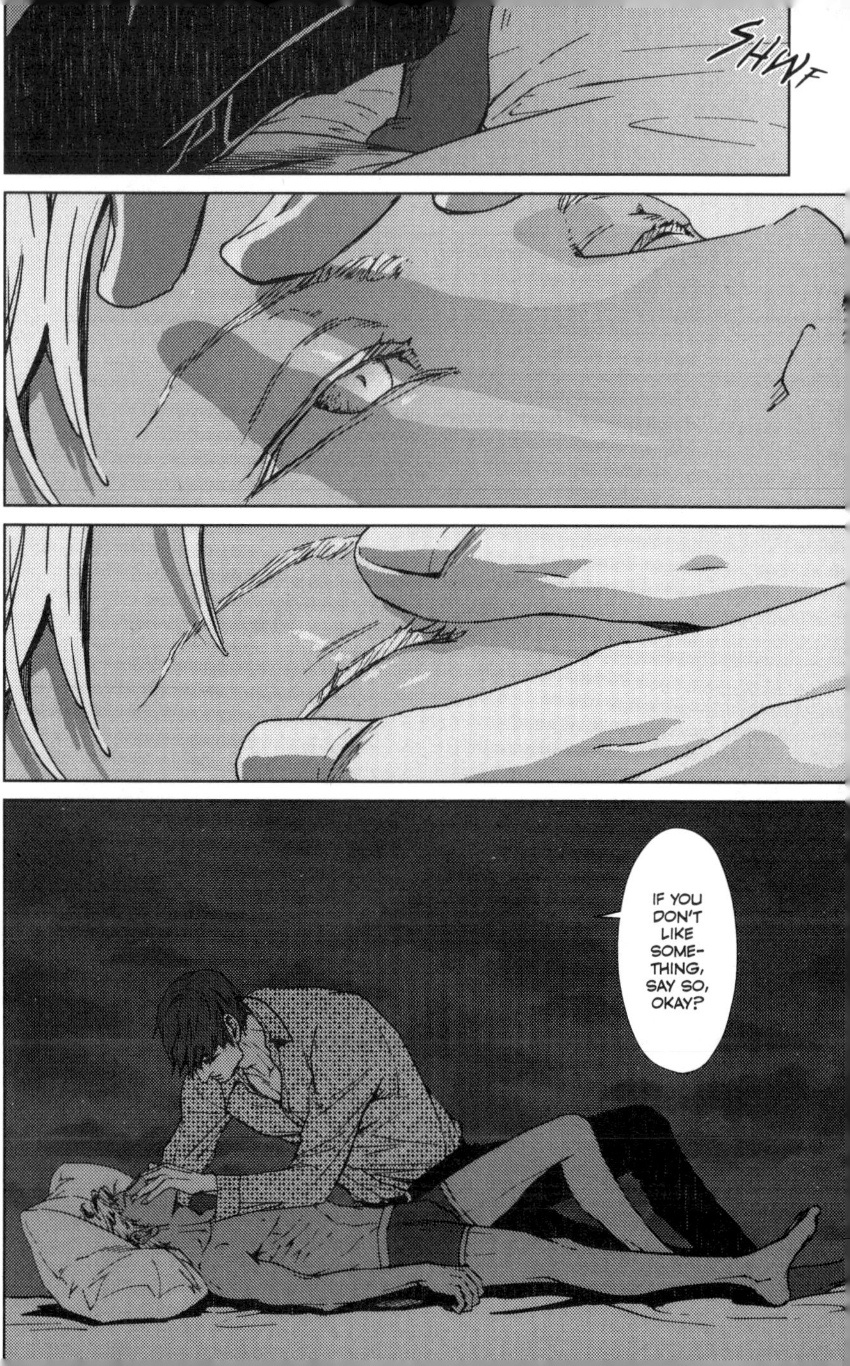
SHWF
IF YOU DON'T LIKE SOME-THING, SAY SO, OKAY?

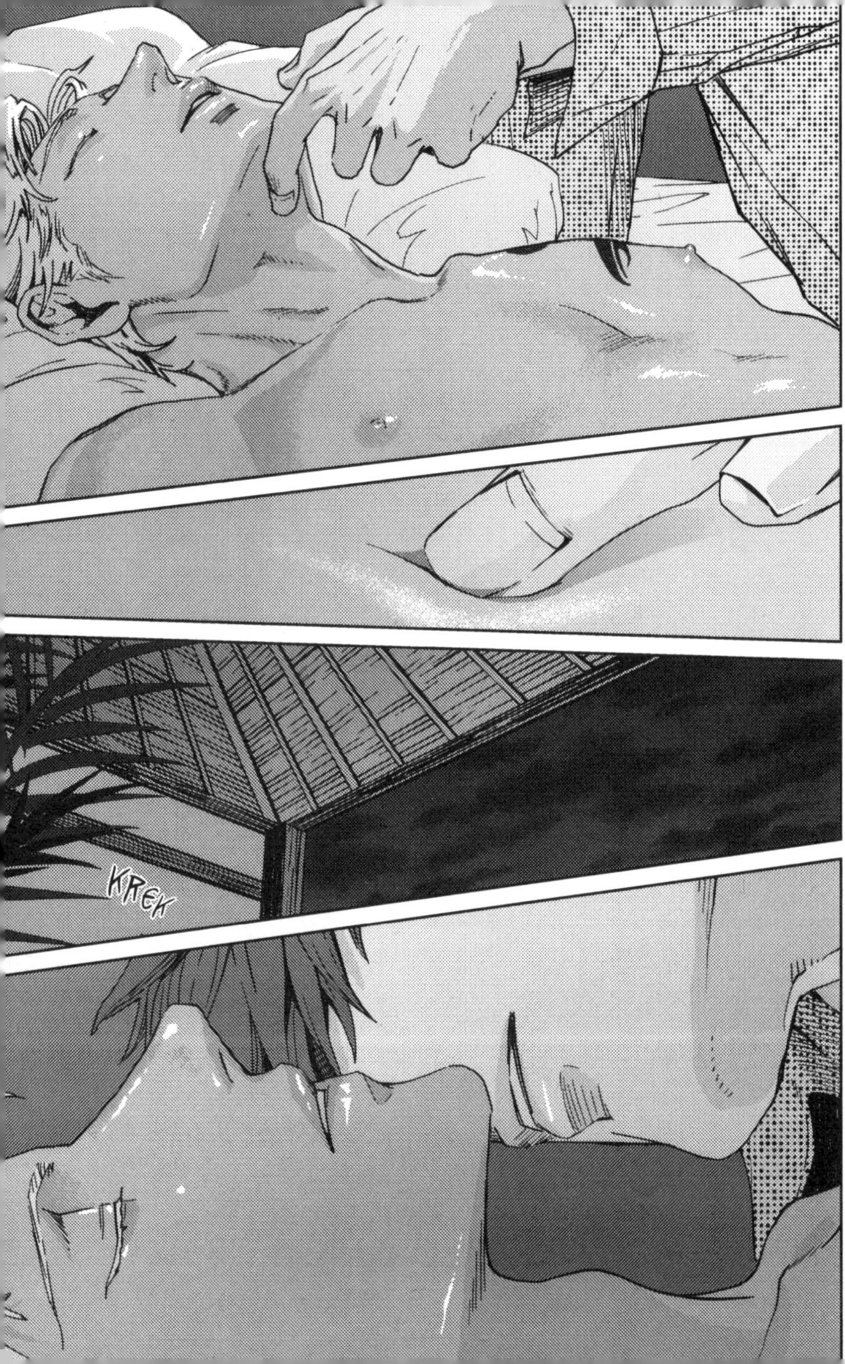
KREK

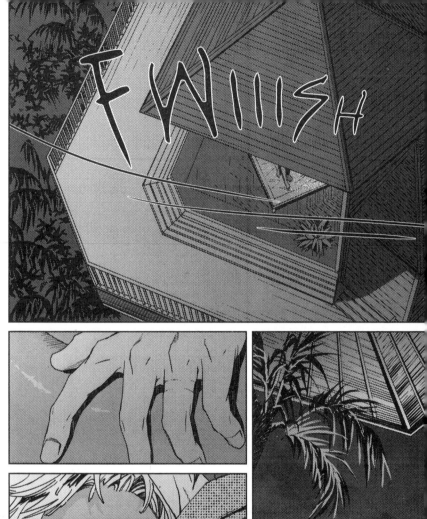

FWIIIISH

SWIFF

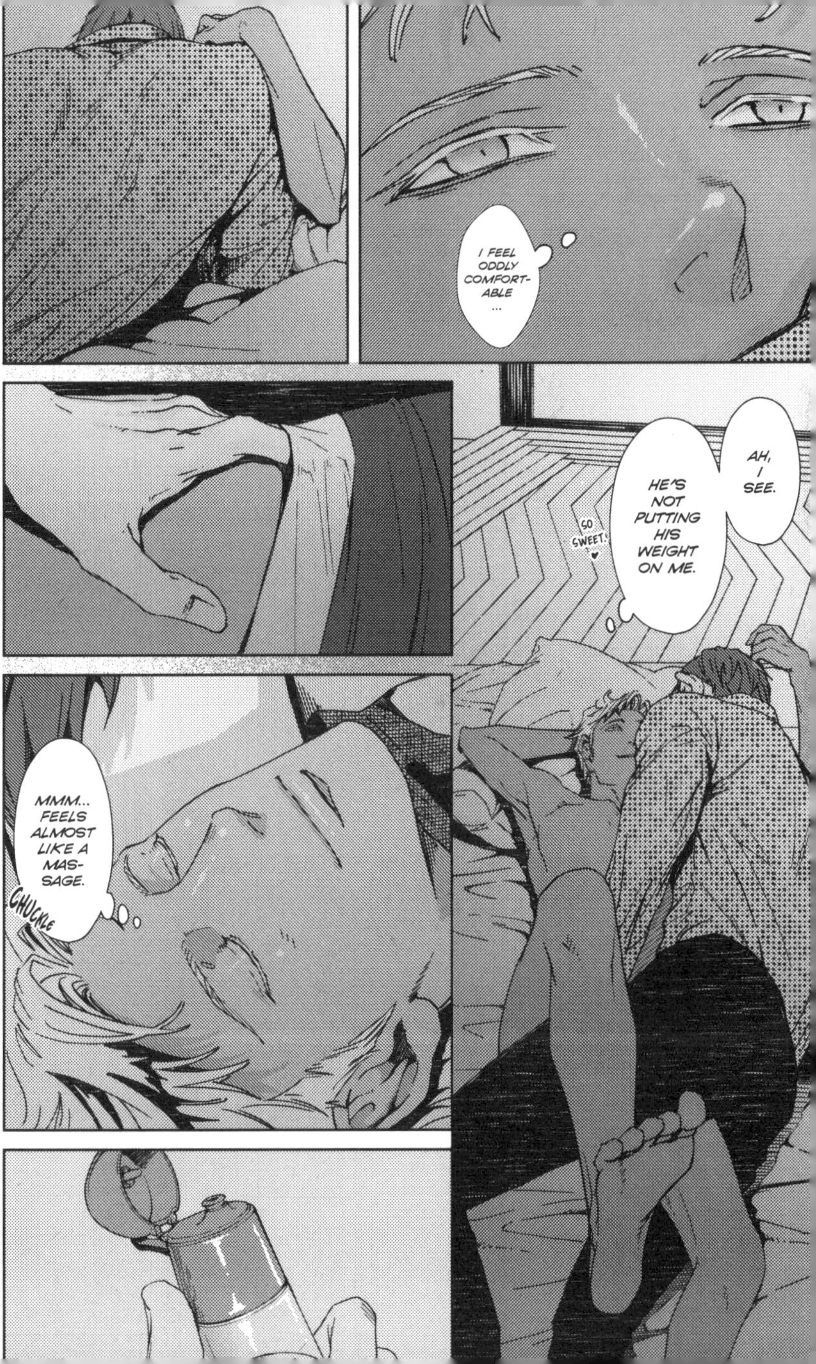
I FEEL ODDLY COMFORTABLE ...
AH, I SEE.
HE'S NOT PUTTING HIS WEIGHT ON ME.
SO SWEET.♥
MMM... FEELS ALMOST LIKE A MASSAGE.
CHUCKLE

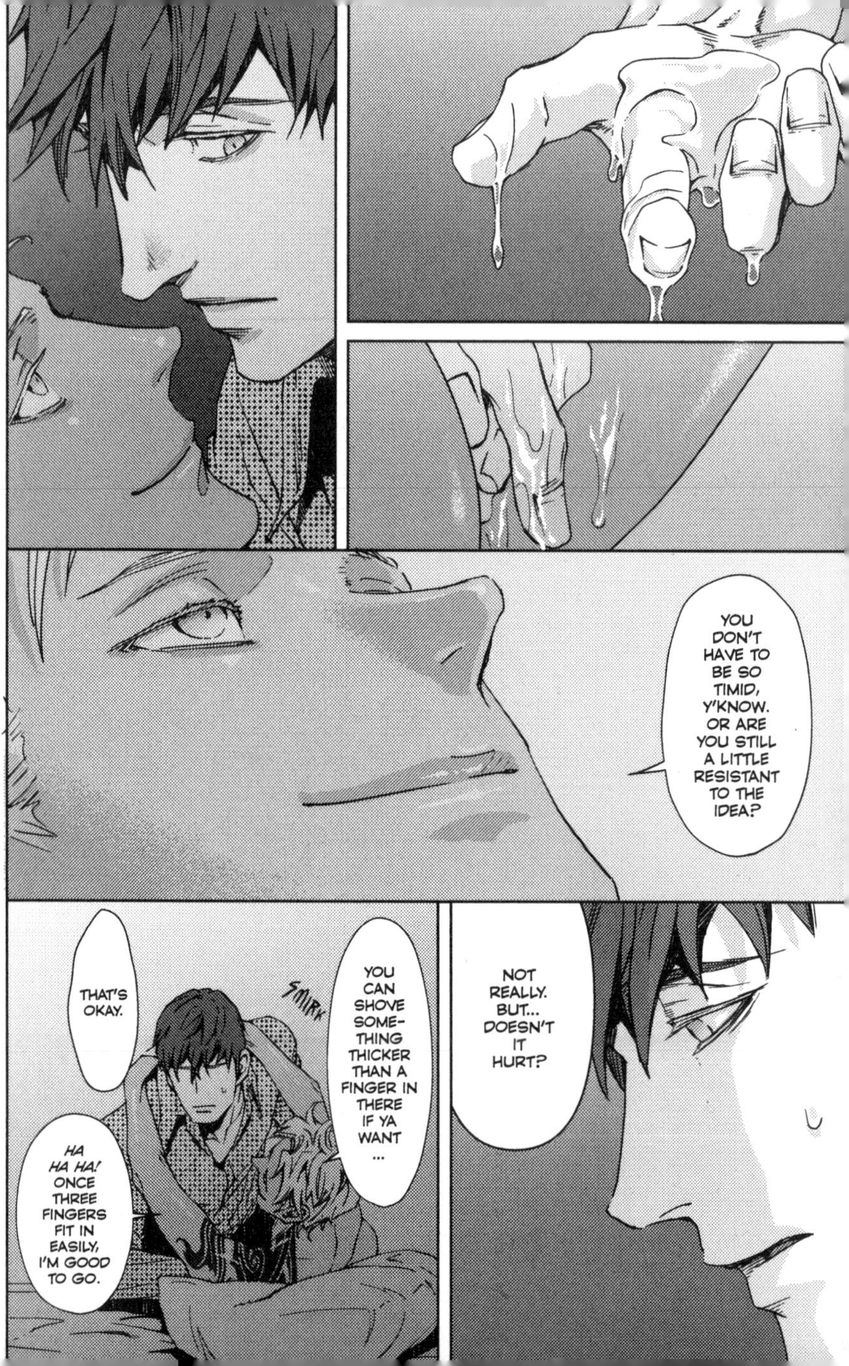
YOU DON'T HAVE TO BE SO TIMID, Y'KNOW. OR ARE YOU STILL A LITTLE RESISTANT TO THE IDEA?
NOT REALLY. BUT... DOESN'T IT HURT?
YOU CAN SHOVE SOME-THING THICKER THAN A FINGER IN THERE IF YA WANT ...
SMIRK
THAT'S OKAY.
HA HA HA! ONCE THREE FINGERS FIT IN EASILY, I'M GOOD TO GO.

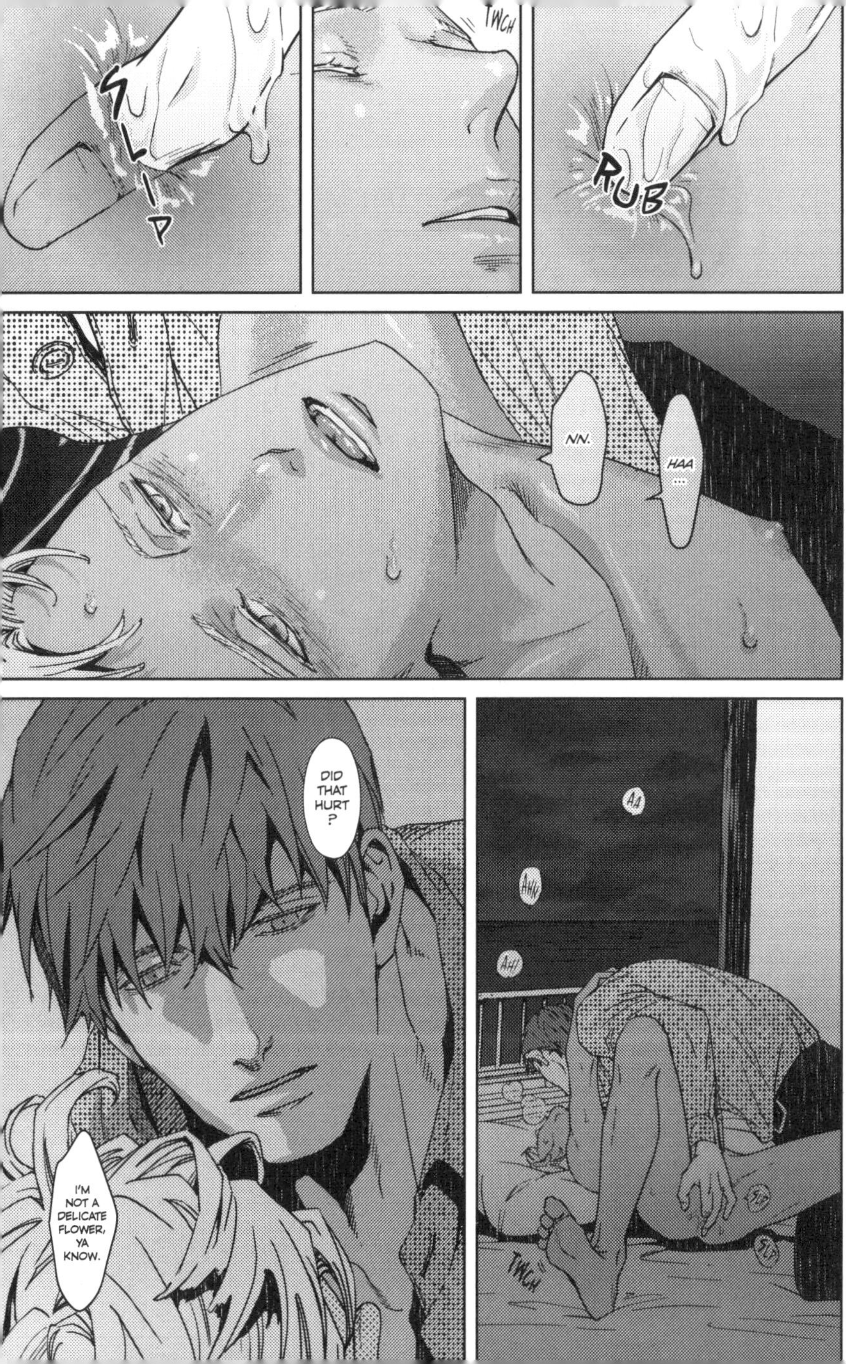
RUB
TWCH
SLIP
HAA...
NN.
AA
AHN
AH!
TWCH
DID THAT HURT?
I'M NOT A DELICATE FLOWER, YA KNOW.

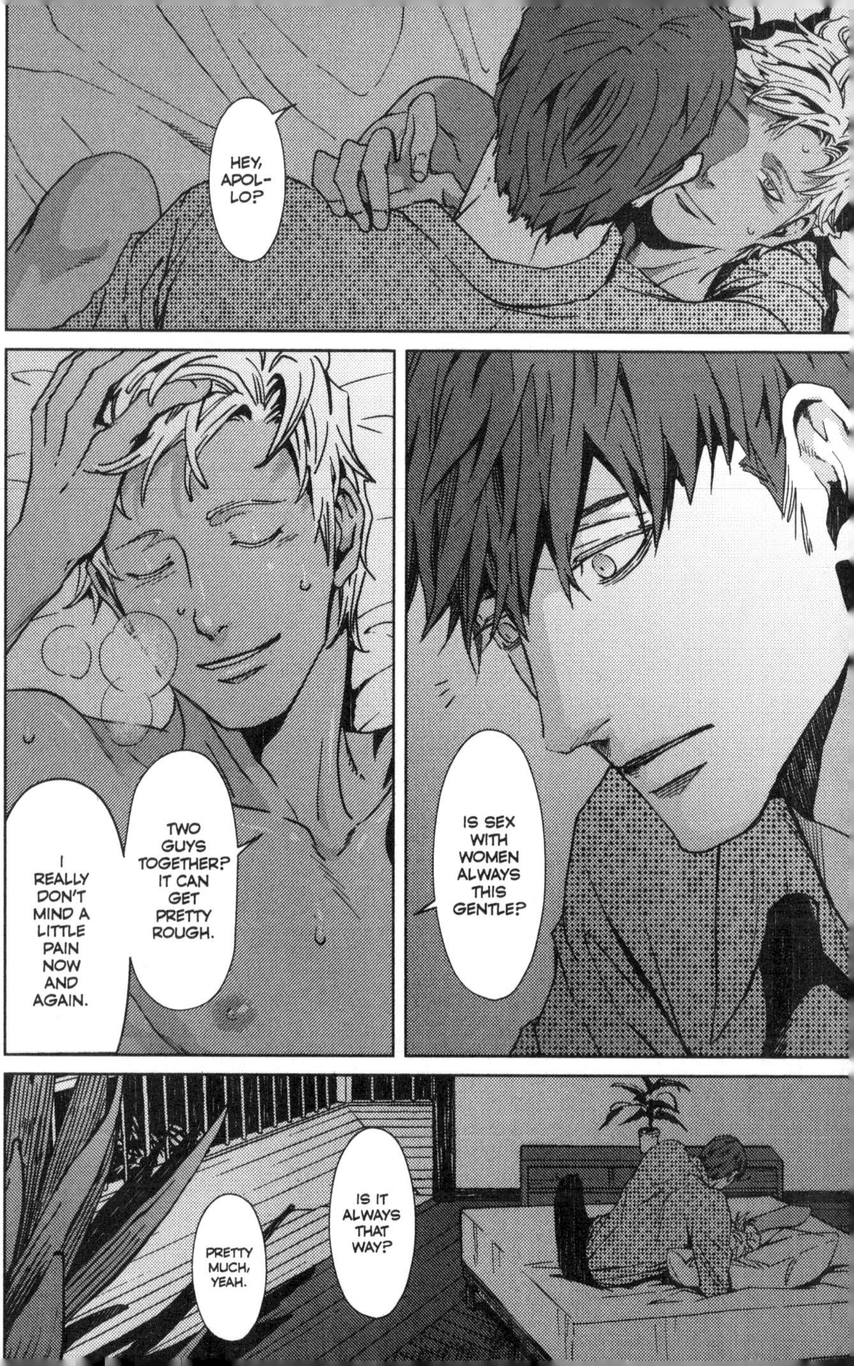
HEY, APOLLO?
IS SEX WITH WOMEN ALWAYS THIS GENTLE?
TWO GUYS TOGETHER? IT CAN GET PRETTY ROUGH.
I REALLY DON'T MIND A LITTLE PAIN NOW AND AGAIN.
IS IT ALWAYS THAT WAY?
PRETTY MUCH, YEAH.

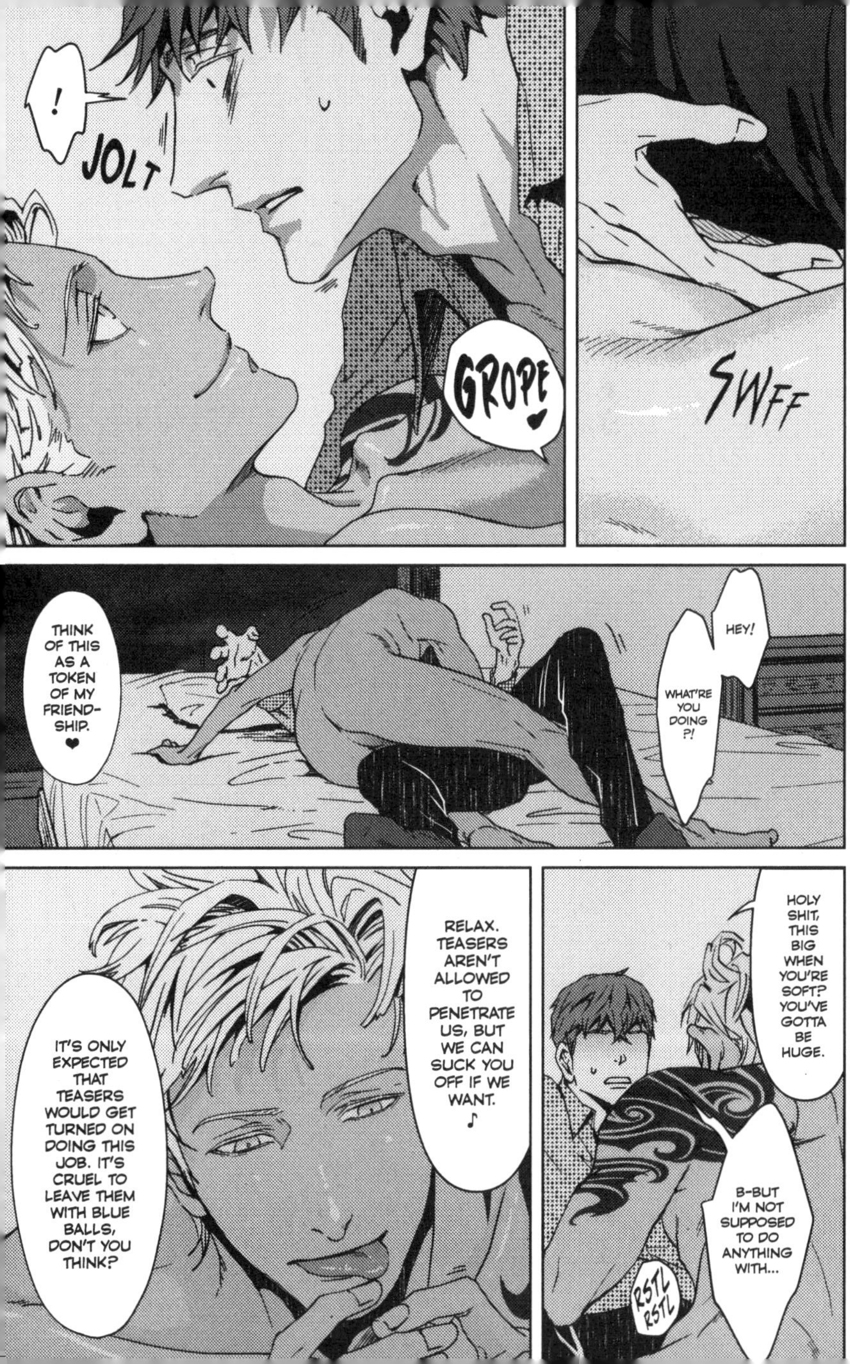
SWFF
!
JOLT
GROPE ❤
HEY!
WHAT'RE YOU DOING ?!
THINK OF THIS AS A TOKEN OF MY FRIEND-SHIP. ❤
HOLY SHIT, THIS BIG WHEN YOU'RE SOFT? YOU'VE GOTTA BE HUGE.
B-BUT I'M NOT SUPPOSED TO DO ANYTHING WITH...
RSTL RSTL
RELAX. TEASERS AREN'T ALLOWED TO PENETRATE US, BUT WE CAN SUCK YOU OFF IF WE WANT. ♪
IT'S ONLY EXPECTED THAT TEASERS WOULD GET TURNED ON DOING THIS JOB. IT'S CRUEL TO LEAVE THEM WITH BLUE BALLS, DON'T YOU THINK?

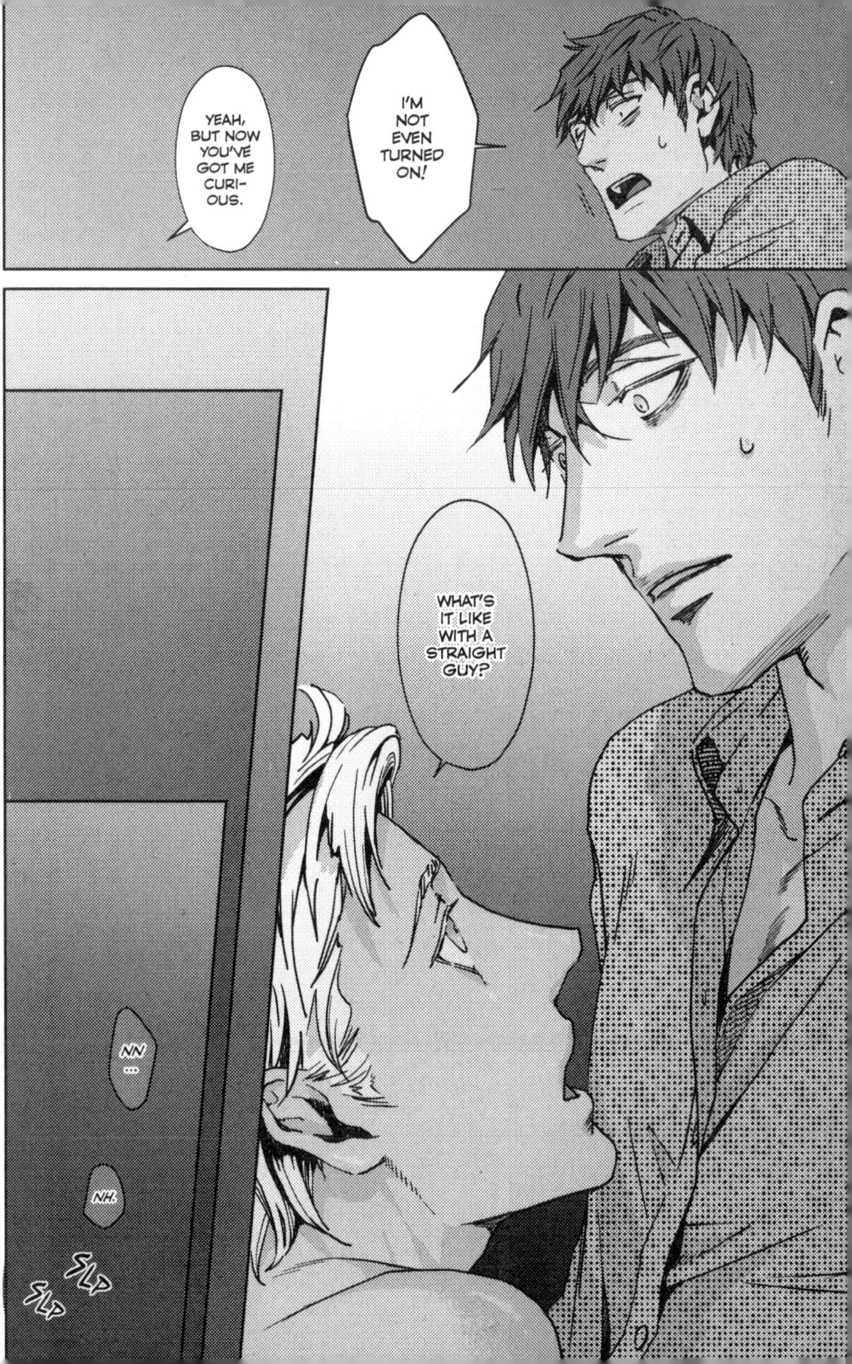
I'M NOT EVEN TURNED ON!
YEAH, BUT NOW YOU'VE GOT ME CURI-OUS.
WHAT'S IT LIKE WITH A STRAIGHT GUY?
NN ...
NH.
SLP
SLP

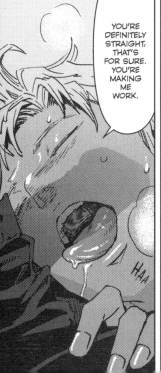

YOU'RE
DEFINITELY
STRAIGHT,
THAT'S
FOR SURE.
YOU'RE
MAKING
ME
WORK.

HAA

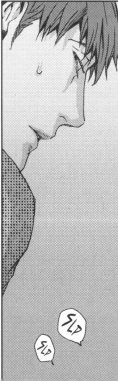

SLD

SLD

SUCK

SLP

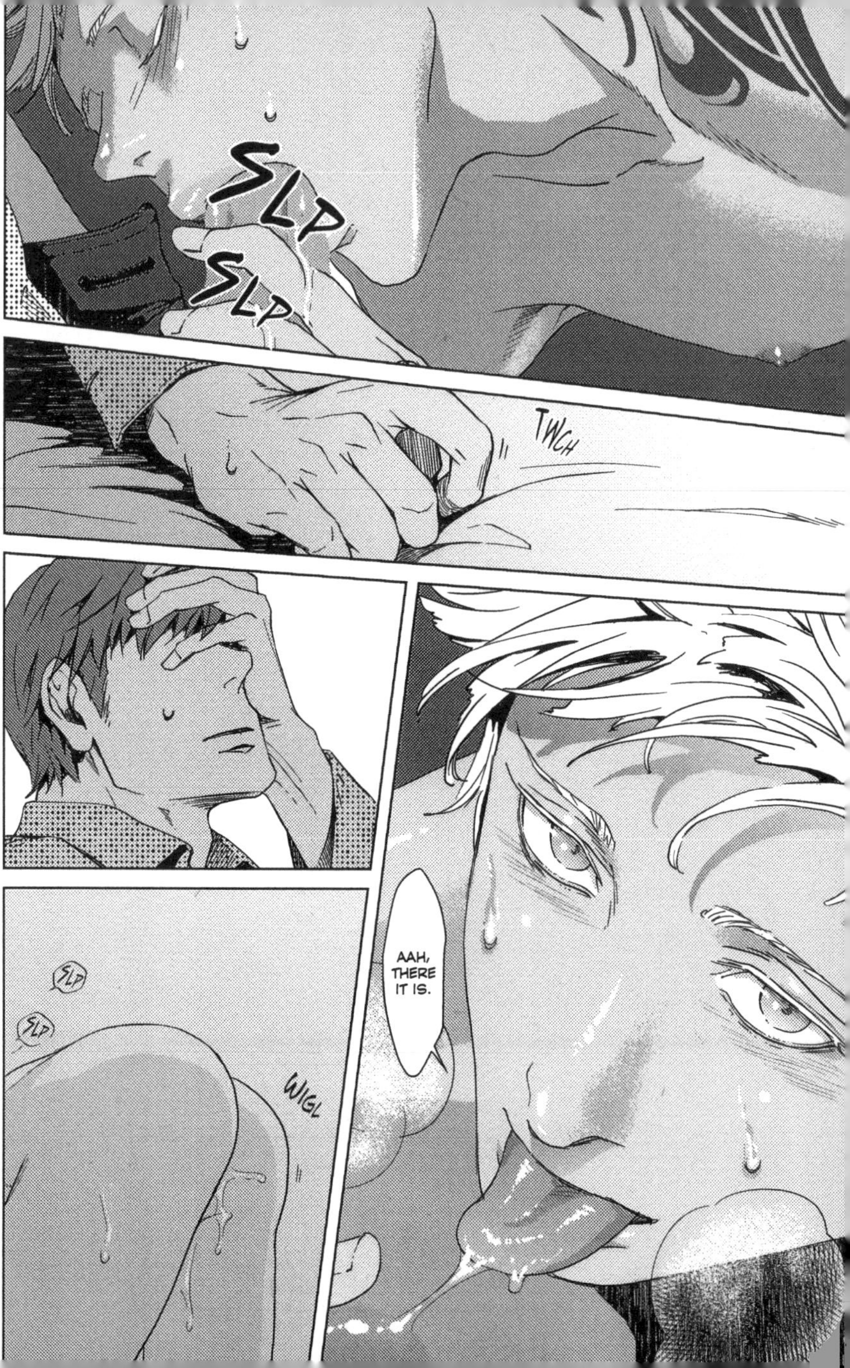
SLP
SLP
TWCH
AAH, THERE IT IS.
SLP
SLP
WIGL

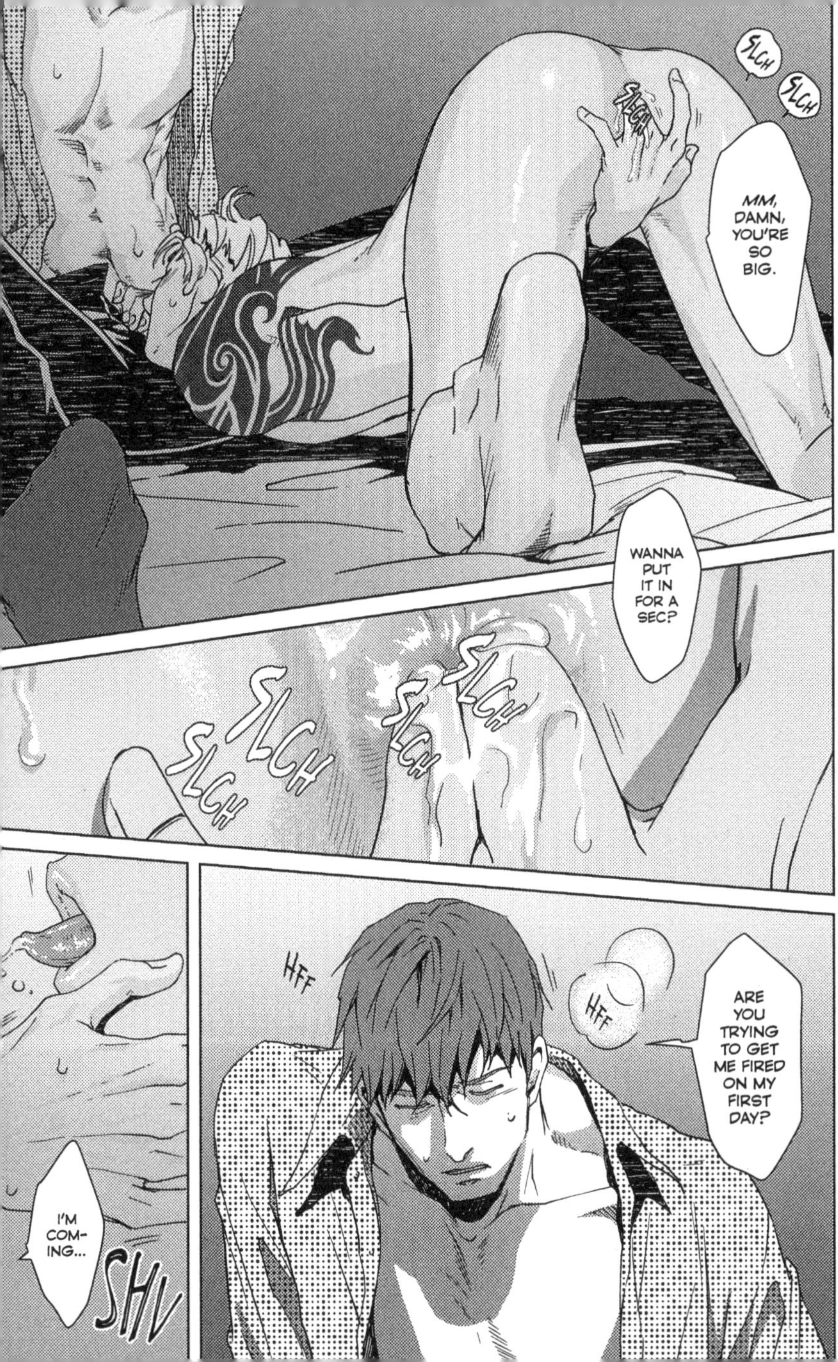
SLCH
SLCH
SLCH
MM, DAMN, YOU'RE SO BIG.
WANNA PUT IT IN FOR A SEC?
SLCH
SLCH
SLCH
SLCH
HFF
HFF
ARE YOU TRYING TO GET ME FIRED ON MY FIRST DAY?
I'M COMING...
SHV

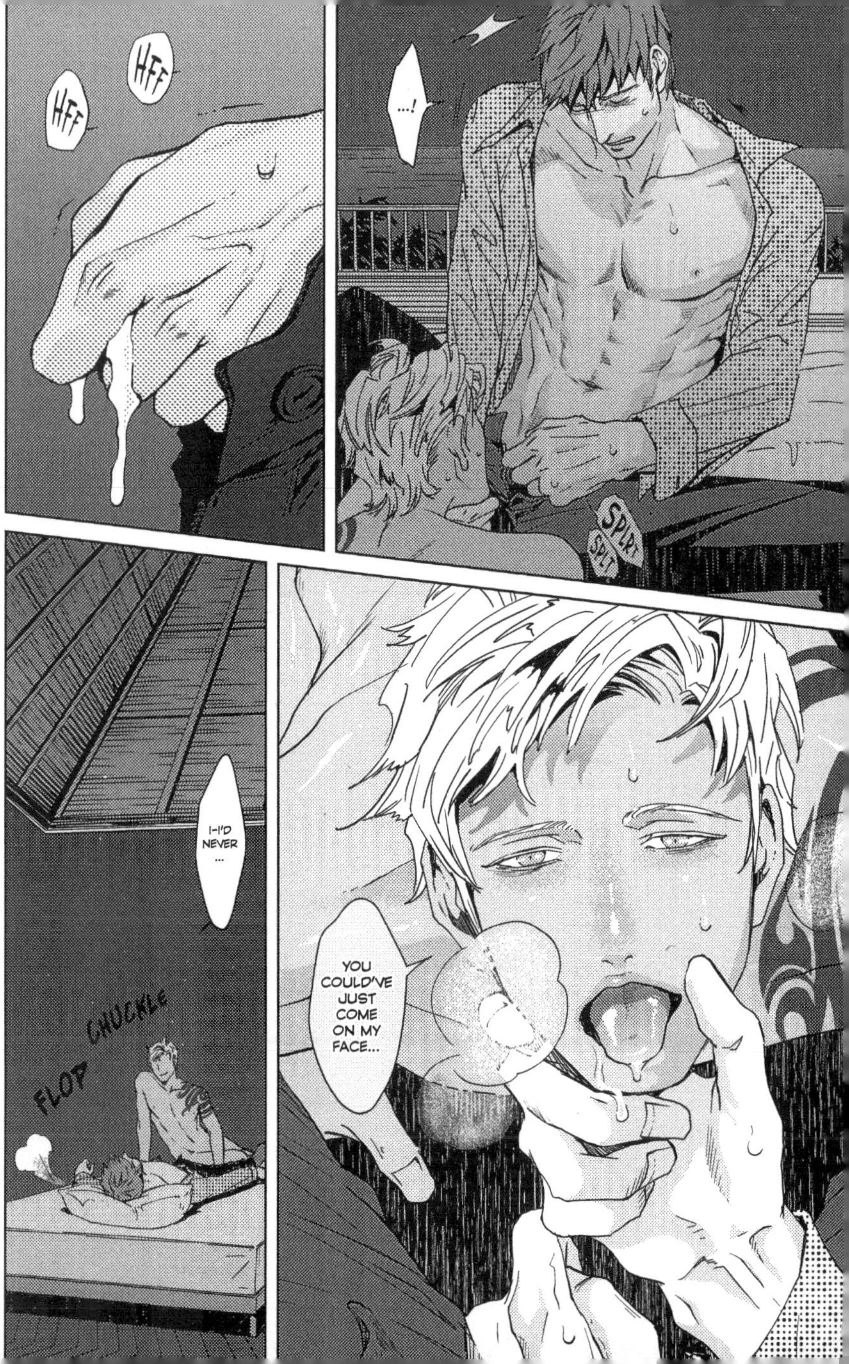
...!
SPLRT
SPLT
HFF
HFF
YOU COULD'VE JUST COME ON MY FACE...
I-I'D NEVER ...
CHUCKLE
FLOP

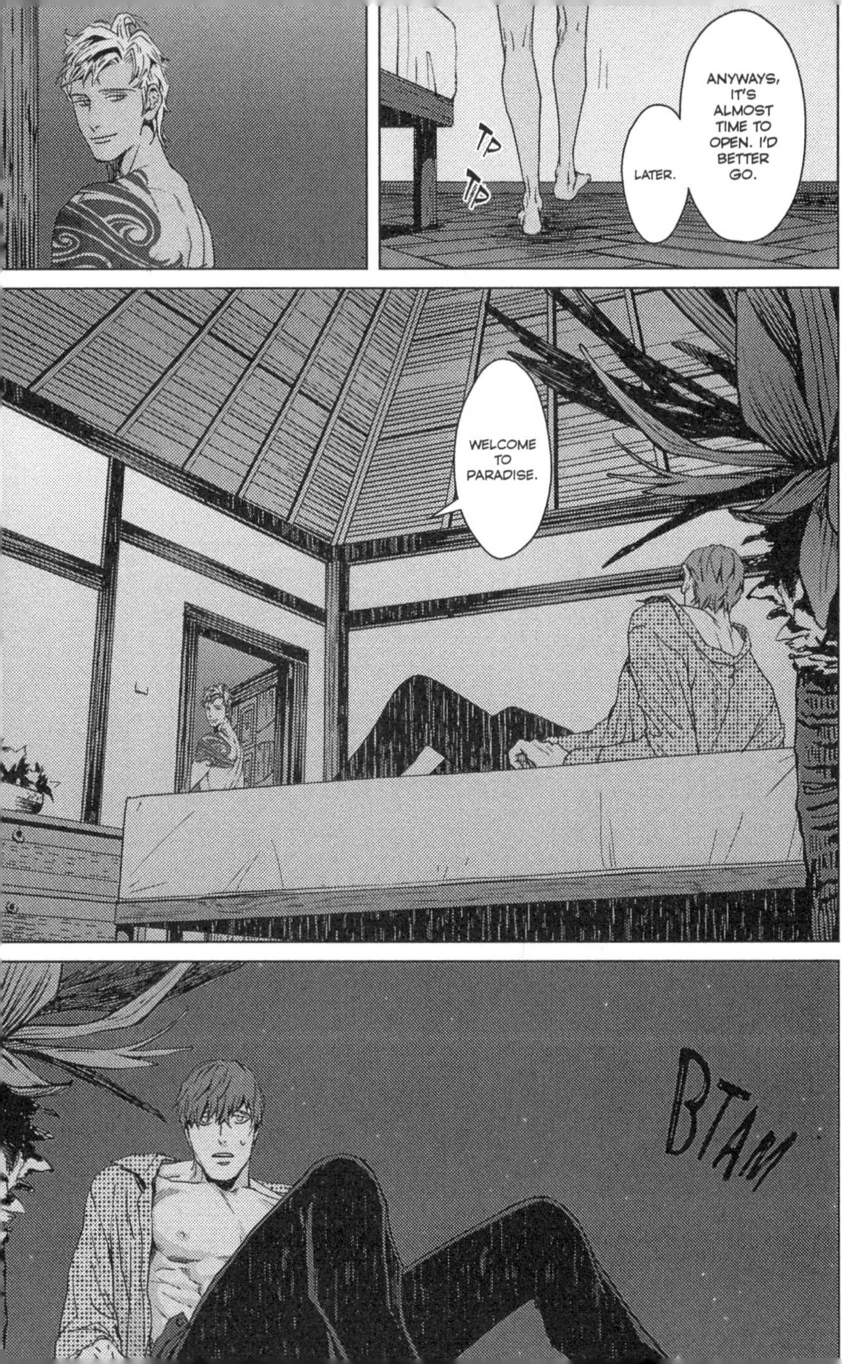
ANYWAYS, IT'S ALMOST TIME TO OPEN. I'D BETTER GO.
LATER.
TP
TP
WELCOME TO PARADISE.
BTAM

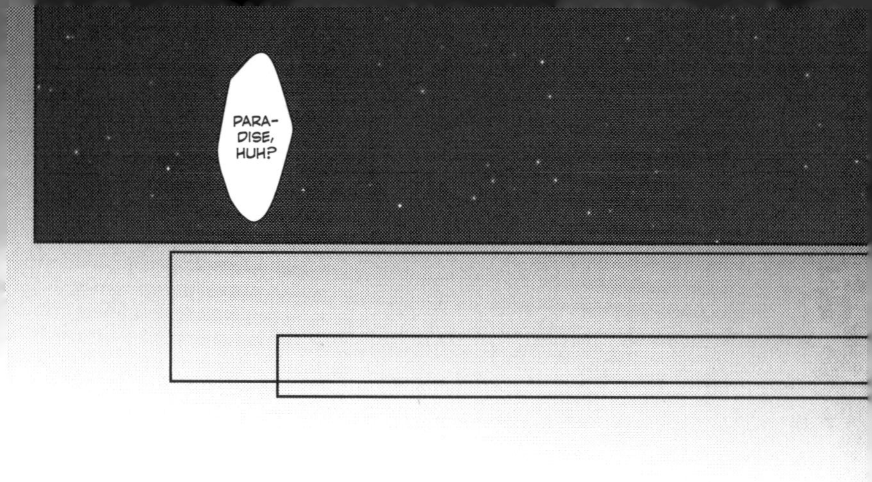
PARA-DISE, HUH?

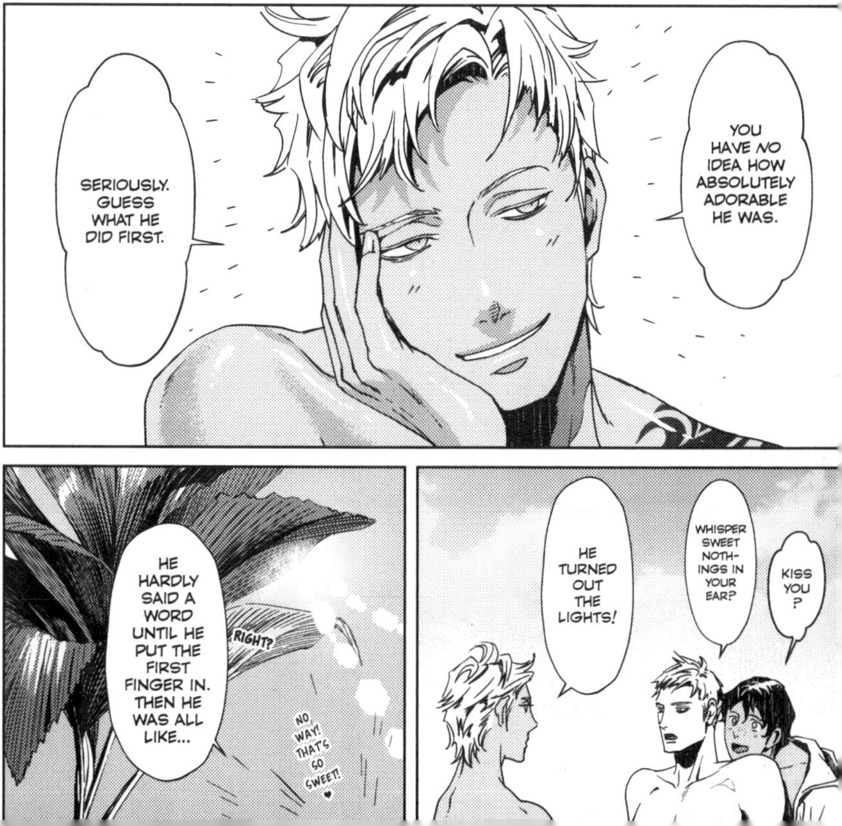
YOU HAVE *NO* IDEA HOW ABSOLUTELY ADORABLE HE WAS.
SERIOUSLY. GUESS WHAT HE DID FIRST.
KISS YOU?
WHISPER SWEET NOTH-INGS IN YOUR EAR?
HE TURNED OUT THE LIGHTS!
HE HARDLY SAID A WORD UNTIL HE PUT THE FIRST FINGER IN. THEN HE WAS ALL LIKE...
RIGHT?
NO WAY! THAT'S SO SWEET!

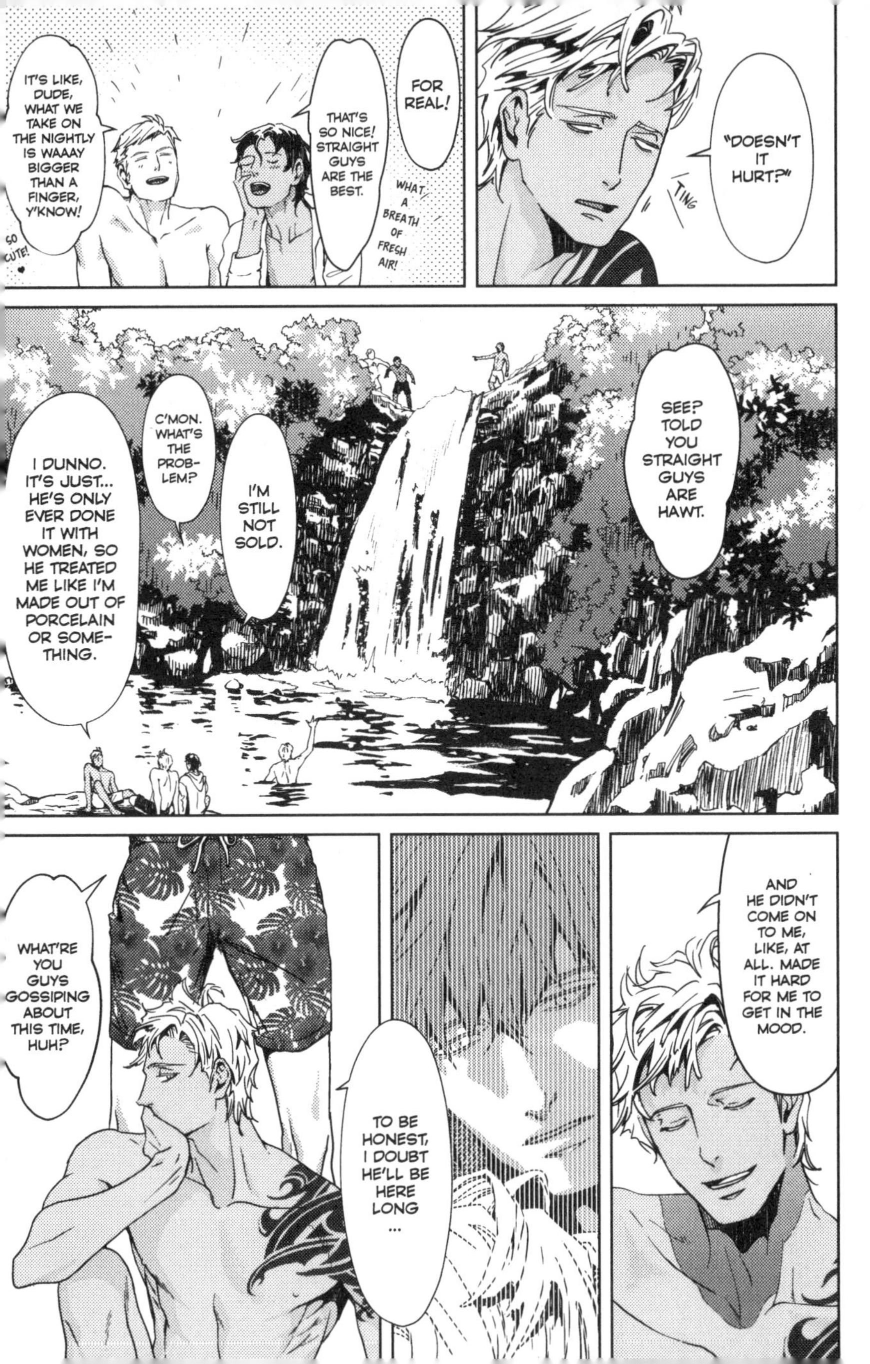
"DOESN'T IT HURT?"
TING
FOR REAL!
THAT'S SO NICE! STRAIGHT GUYS ARE THE BEST.
WHAT A BREATH OF FRESH AIR!
IT'S LIKE, DUDE, WHAT WE TAKE ON THE NIGHTLY IS WAAAY BIGGER THAN A FINGER, Y'KNOW!
SO CUTE! ♥
SEE? TOLD YOU STRAIGHT GUYS ARE HAWT.
I'M STILL NOT SOLD.
C'MON. WHAT'S THE PROB-LEM?
I DUNNO. IT'S JUST... HE'S ONLY EVER DONE IT WITH WOMEN, SO HE TREATED ME LIKE I'M MADE OUT OF PORCELAIN OR SOME-THING.
AND HE DIDN'T COME ON TO ME, LIKE, AT ALL. MADE IT HARD FOR ME TO GET IN THE MOOD.
TO BE HONEST, I DOUBT HE'LL BE HERE LONG ...
WHAT'RE YOU GUYS GOSSIPING ABOUT THIS TIME, HUH?

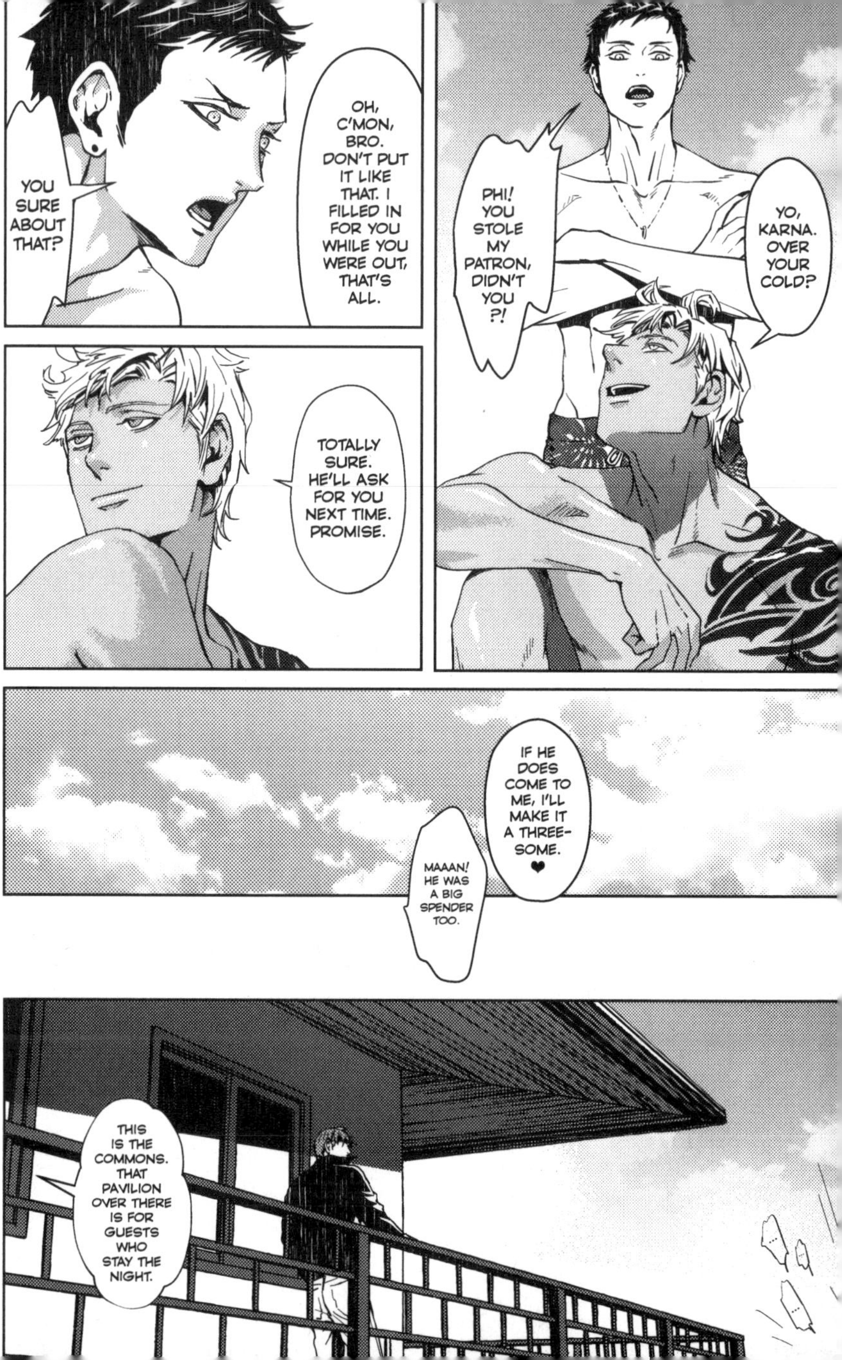
YO, KARNA. OVER YOUR COLD?
PHI! YOU STOLE MY PATRON, DIDN'T YOU ?!
OH, C'MON, BRO. DON'T PUT IT LIKE THAT. I FILLED IN FOR YOU WHILE YOU WERE OUT, THAT'S ALL.
YOU SURE ABOUT THAT?
TOTALLY SURE. HE'LL ASK FOR YOU NEXT TIME. PROMISE.
IF HE DOES COME TO ME, I'LL MAKE IT A THREE-SOME. ❤
MAAAN! HE WAS A BIG SPENDER TOO.
THIS IS THE COMMONS. THAT PAVILION OVER THERE IS FOR GUESTS WHO STAY THE NIGHT.

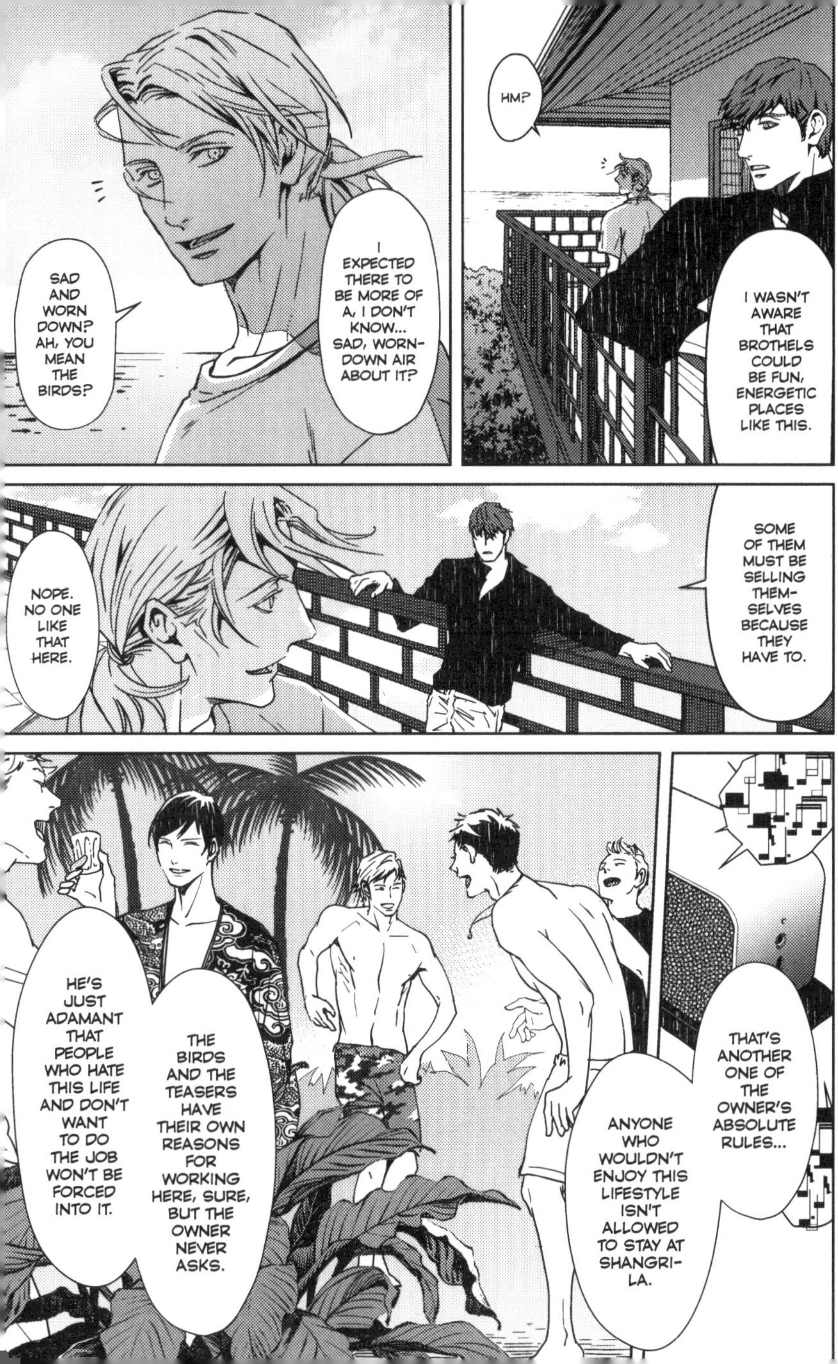
HM?
I WASN'T AWARE THAT BROTHELS COULD BE FUN, ENERGETIC PLACES LIKE THIS.
I EXPECTED THERE TO BE MORE OF A, I DON'T KNOW... SAD, WORN-DOWN AIR ABOUT IT?
SAD AND WORN DOWN? AH, YOU MEAN THE BIRDS?
SOME OF THEM MUST BE SELLING THEM-SELVES BECAUSE THEY HAVE TO.
NOPE. NO ONE LIKE THAT HERE.
THAT'S ANOTHER ONE OF THE OWNER'S ABSOLUTE RULES...
ANYONE WHO WOULDN'T ENJOY THIS LIFESTYLE ISN'T ALLOWED TO STAY AT SHANGRI-LA.
THE BIRDS AND THE TEASERS HAVE THEIR OWN REASONS FOR WORKING HERE, SURE, BUT THE OWNER NEVER ASKS.
HE'S JUST ADAMANT THAT PEOPLE WHO HATE THIS LIFE AND DON'T WANT TO DO THE JOB WON'T BE FORCED INTO IT.

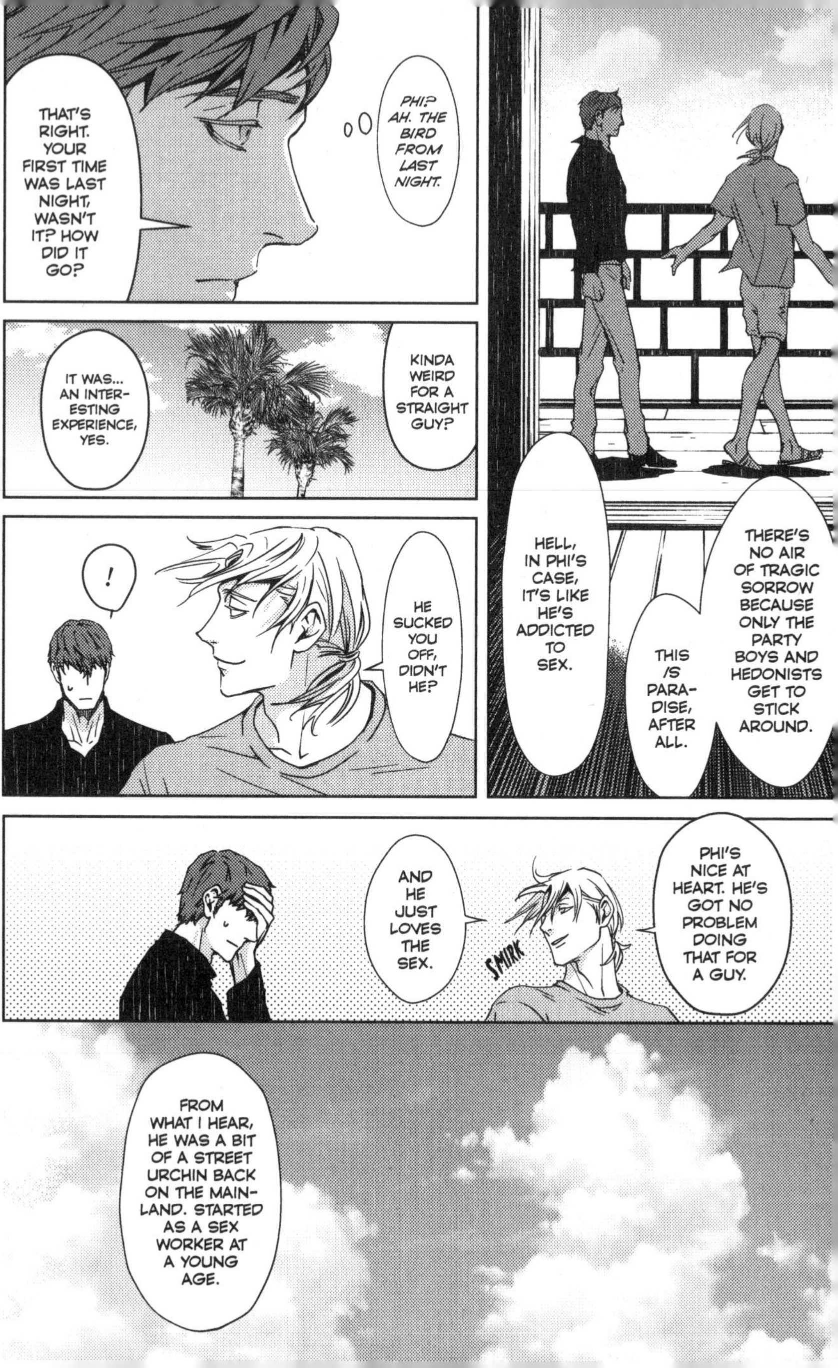
THERE'S NO AIR OF TRAGIC SORROW BECAUSE ONLY THE PARTY BOYS AND HEDONISTS GET TO STICK AROUND.
THIS *IS* PARADISE, AFTER ALL.
HELL, IN PHI'S CASE, IT'S LIKE HE'S ADDICTED TO SEX.
THAT'S RIGHT. YOUR FIRST TIME WAS LAST NIGHT, WASN'T IT? HOW DID IT GO?
PHI? AH. THE BIRD FROM LAST NIGHT.
KINDA WEIRD FOR A STRAIGHT GUY?
IT WAS... AN INTER-ESTING EXPERIENCE, YES.
HE SUCKED YOU OFF, DIDN'T HE?
!
PHI'S NICE AT HEART. HE'S GOT NO PROBLEM DOING THAT FOR A GUY.
SMIRK
AND HE JUST LOVES THE SEX.
FROM WHAT I HEAR, HE WAS A BIT OF A STREET URCHIN BACK ON THE MAIN-LAND. STARTED AS A SEX WORKER AT A YOUNG AGE.

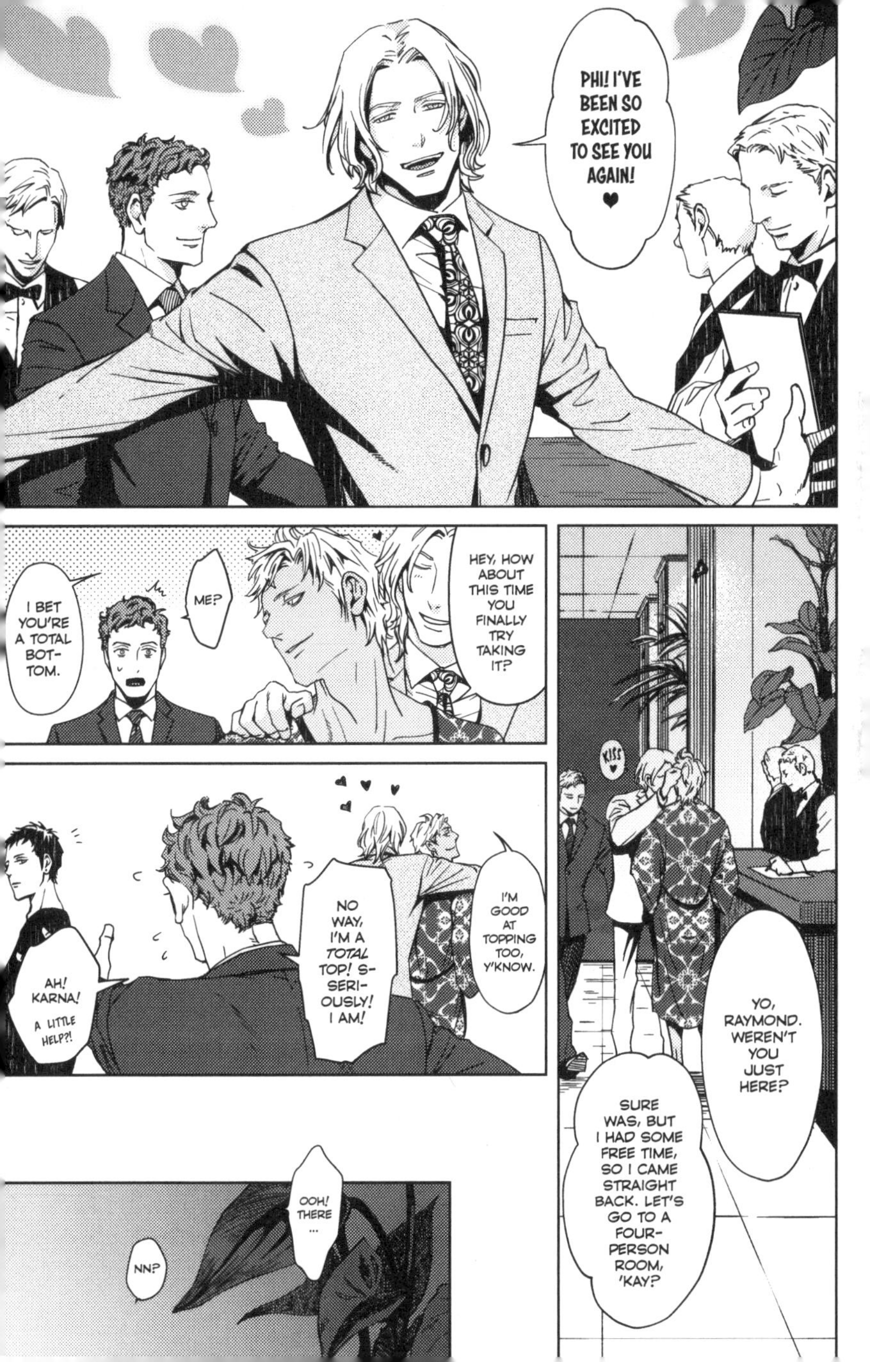
PHI! I'VE BEEN SO EXCITED TO SEE YOU AGAIN! ♥
YO, RAYMOND. WEREN'T YOU JUST HERE?
KISS ♥
SURE WAS, BUT I HAD SOME FREE TIME, SO I CAME STRAIGHT BACK. LET'S GO TO A FOUR-PERSON ROOM, 'KAY?
HEY, HOW ABOUT THIS TIME YOU FINALLY TRY TAKING IT?
ME?
I BET YOU'RE A TOTAL BOT-TOM.
I'M GOOD AT TOPPING TOO, Y'KNOW.
NO WAY, I'M A *TOTAL* TOP! S-SERI-OUSLY! I AM!
AH! KARNA! A LITTLE HELP?!
OOH! THERE ...
NN?

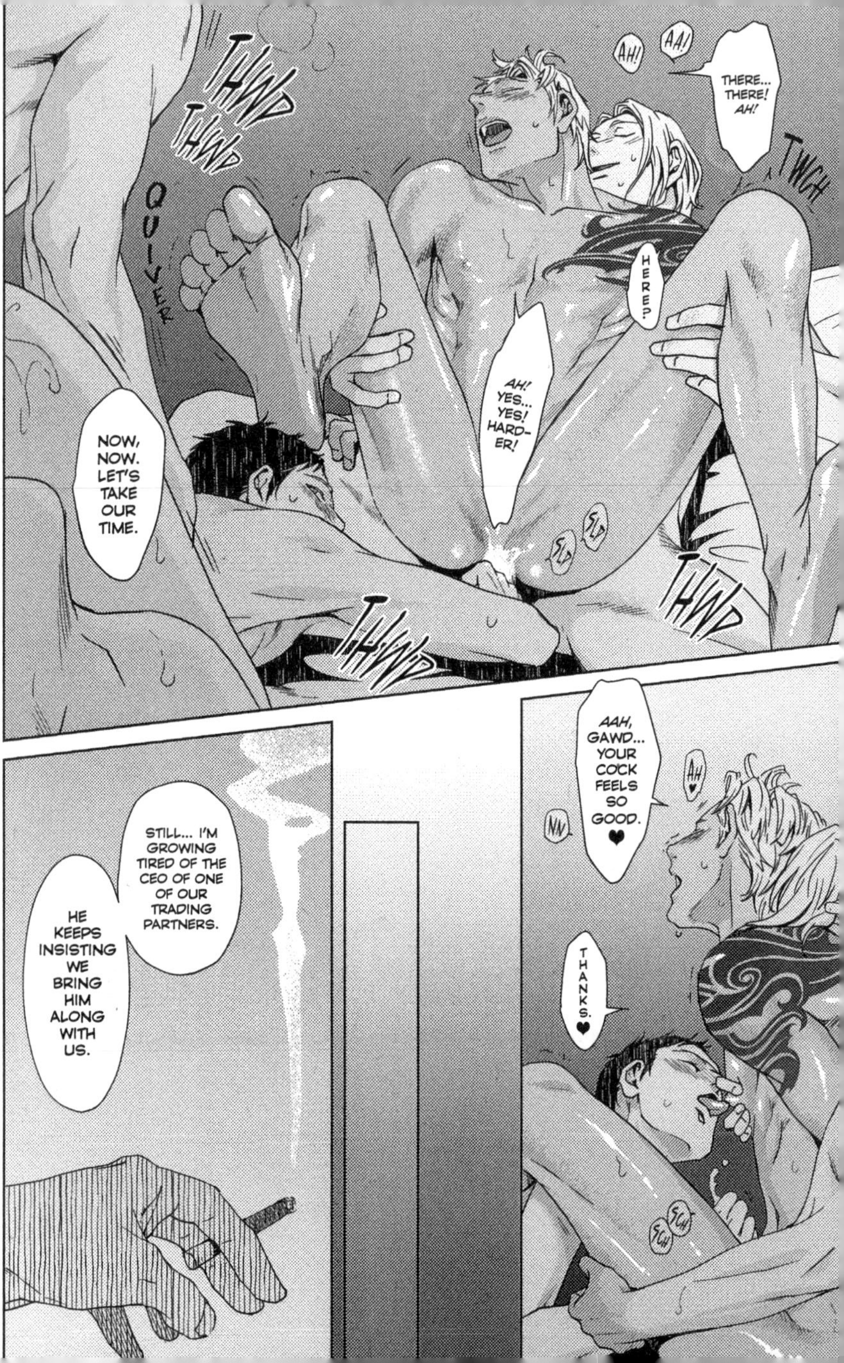
AA!
AH!
THERE... THERE! AH!
TWCH
THWD
THWD
HERE?
QUIVER
AH! YES... YES! HARDER!
NOW, NOW. LET'S TAKE OUR TIME.
SCH
SCH
THWD
THWD
AAH, GAWD... YOUR COCK FEELS SO GOOD. ♥
AH ♥
NN
THANKS. ♥
SCH
SCH
STILL... I'M GROWING TIRED OF THE CEO OF ONE OF OUR TRADING PARTNERS.
HE KEEPS INSISTING WE BRING HIM ALONG WITH US.

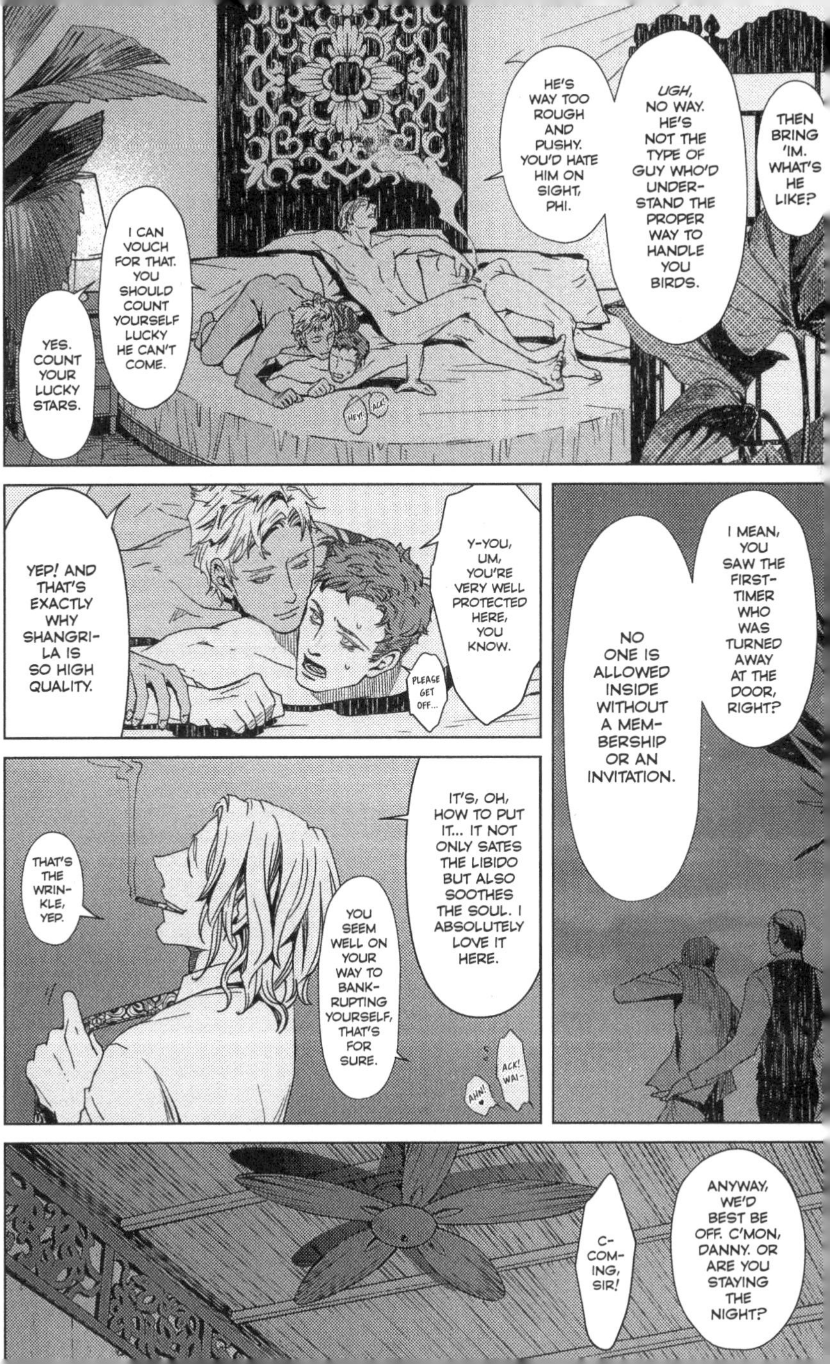
THEN BRING 'IM. WHAT'S HE LIKE?
UGH, NO WAY. HE'S NOT THE TYPE OF GUY WHO'D UNDERSTAND THE PROPER WAY TO HANDLE YOU BIRDS.
HE'S WAY TOO ROUGH AND PUSHY. YOU'D HATE HIM ON SIGHT, PHI.
I CAN VOUCH FOR THAT. YOU SHOULD COUNT YOURSELF LUCKY HE CAN'T COME.
ACK!
HEY!
YES. COUNT YOUR LUCKY STARS.
I MEAN, YOU SAW THE FIRST-TIMER WHO WAS TURNED AWAY AT THE DOOR, RIGHT?
NO ONE IS ALLOWED INSIDE WITHOUT A MEMBERSHIP OR AN INVITATION.
Y-YOU, UM, YOU'RE VERY WELL PROTECTED HERE, YOU KNOW.
PLEASE GET OFF...
YEP! AND THAT'S EXACTLY WHY SHANGRI-LA IS SO HIGH QUALITY.
IT'S, OH, HOW TO PUT IT... IT NOT ONLY SATES THE LIBIDO BUT ALSO SOOTHES THE SOUL. I ABSOLUTELY LOVE IT HERE.
ACK! WAI-
AHN! ♥
YOU SEEM WELL ON YOUR WAY TO BANKRUPTING YOURSELF, THAT'S FOR SURE.
THAT'S THE WRINKLE, YEP.
ANYWAY, WE'D BEST BE OFF. C'MON, DANNY. OR ARE YOU STAYING THE NIGHT?
C-COMING, SIR!

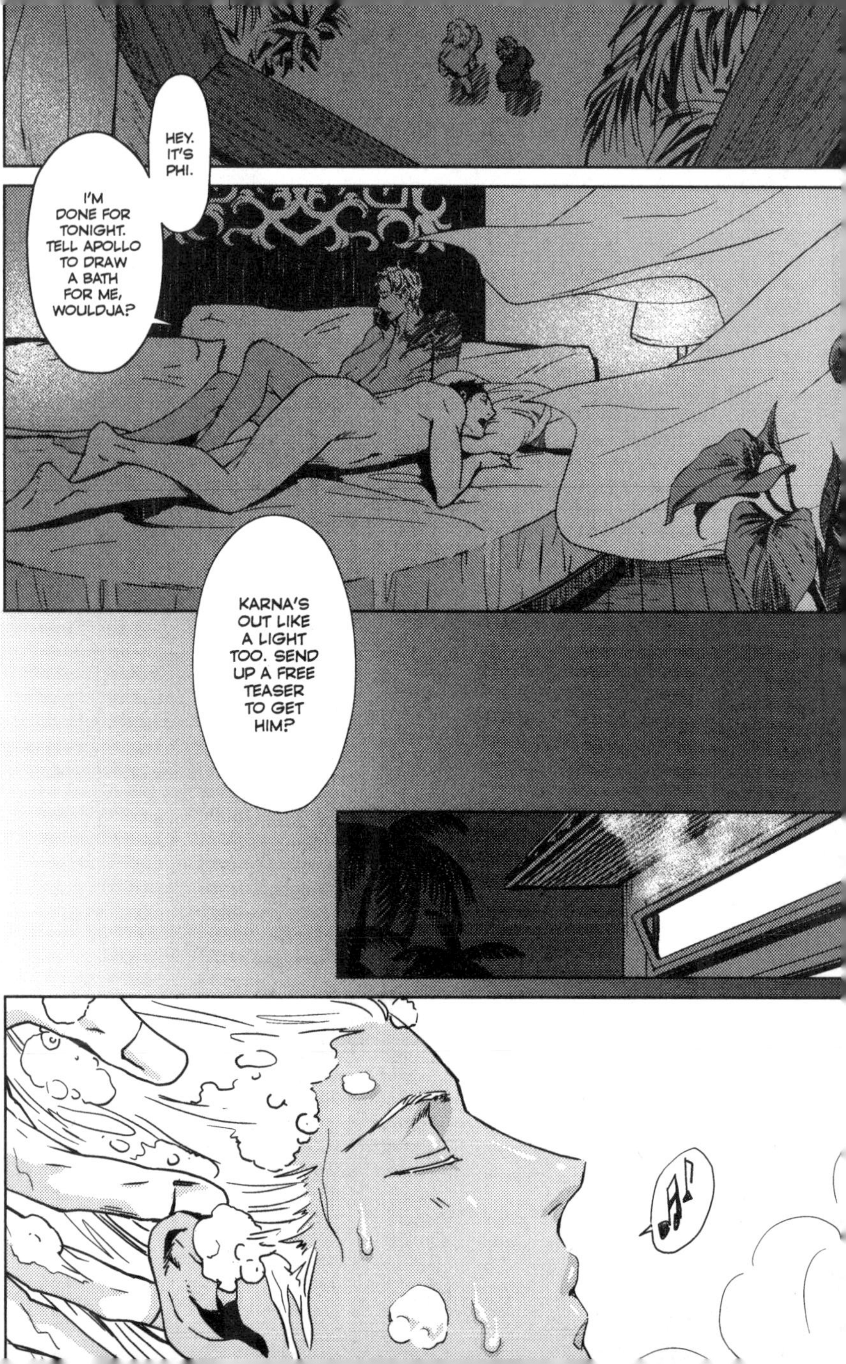
HEY. IT'S PHI.
I'M DONE FOR TONIGHT. TELL APOLLO TO DRAW A BATH FOR ME, WOULDJA?
KARNA'S OUT LIKE A LIGHT TOO. SEND UP A FREE TEASER TO GET HIM?

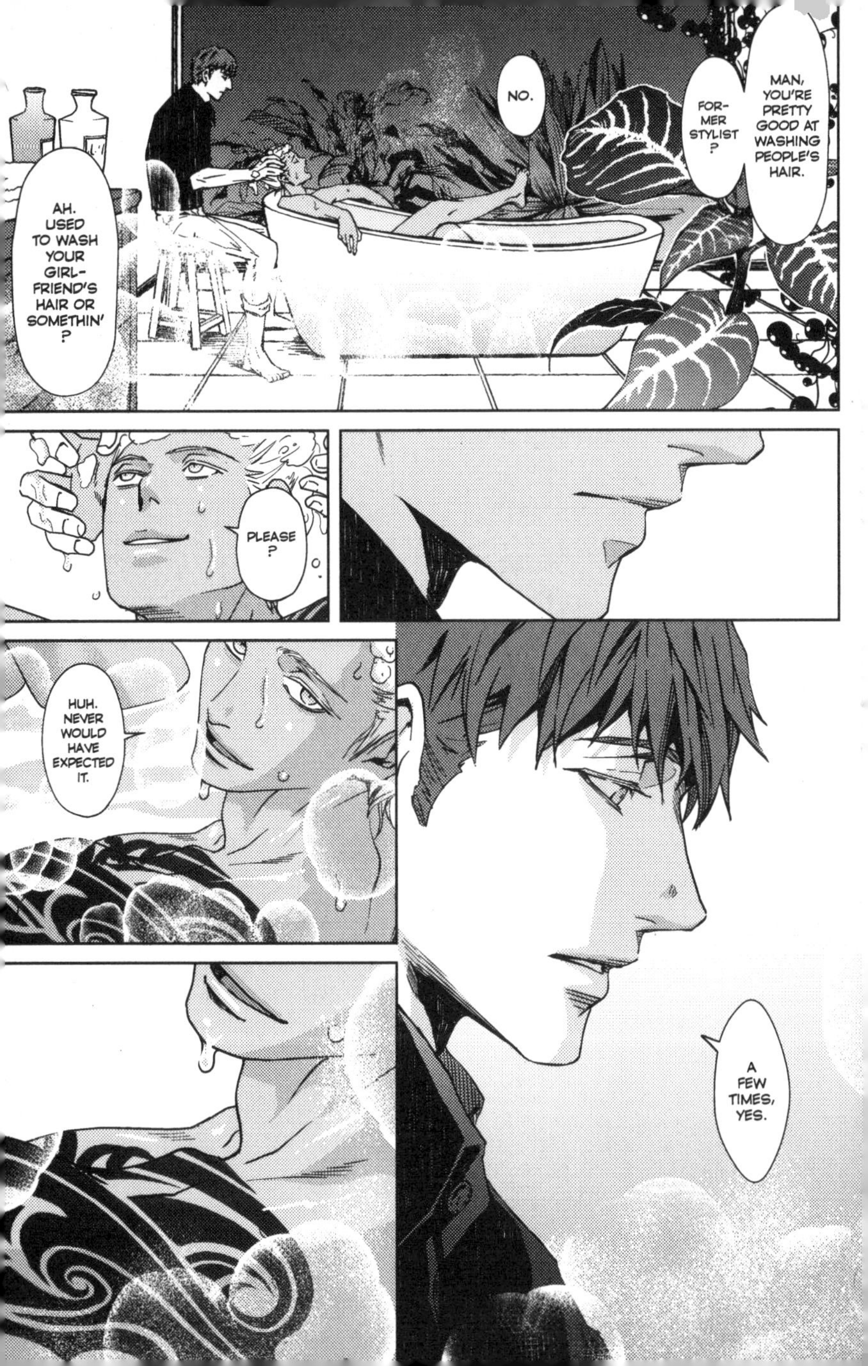
MAN, YOU'RE PRETTY GOOD AT WASHING PEOPLE'S HAIR.
FORMER STYLIST?
NO.
AH. USED TO WASH YOUR GIRLFRIEND'S HAIR OR SOMETHIN'?
PLEASE?
A FEW TIMES, YES.
HUH. NEVER WOULD HAVE EXPECTED IT.

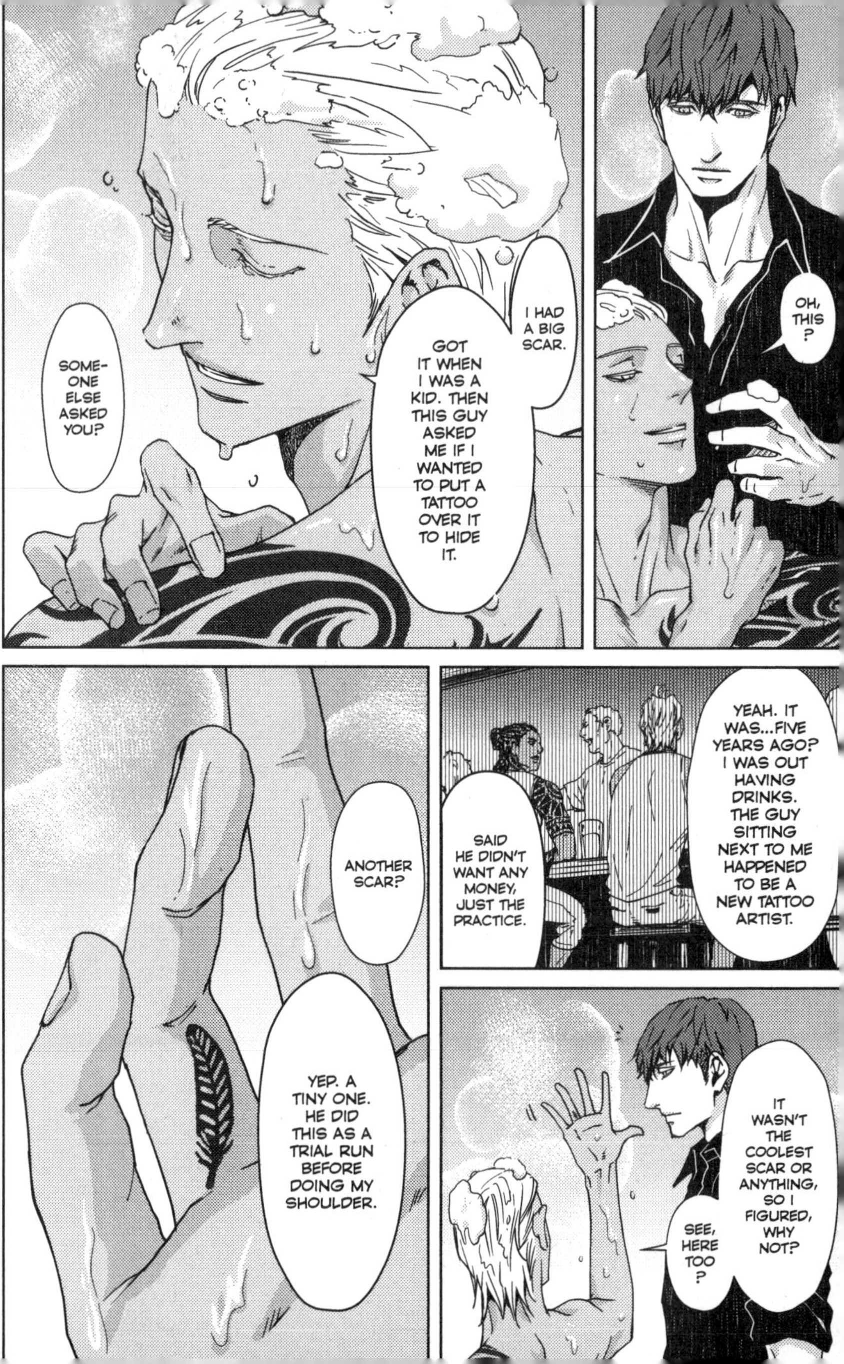
OH, THIS?
I HAD A BIG SCAR.
GOT IT WHEN I WAS A KID. THEN THIS GUY ASKED ME IF I WANTED TO PUT A TATTOO OVER IT TO HIDE IT.
SOME-ONE ELSE ASKED YOU?
YEAH. IT WAS...FIVE YEARS AGO? I WAS OUT HAVING DRINKS. THE GUY SITTING NEXT TO ME HAPPENED TO BE A NEW TATTOO ARTIST.
SAID HE DIDN'T WANT ANY MONEY, JUST THE PRACTICE.
IT WASN'T THE COOLEST SCAR OR ANYTHING, SO I FIGURED, WHY NOT?
SEE, HERE TOO?
ANOTHER SCAR?
YEP. A TINY ONE. HE DID THIS AS A TRIAL RUN BEFORE DOING MY SHOULDER.

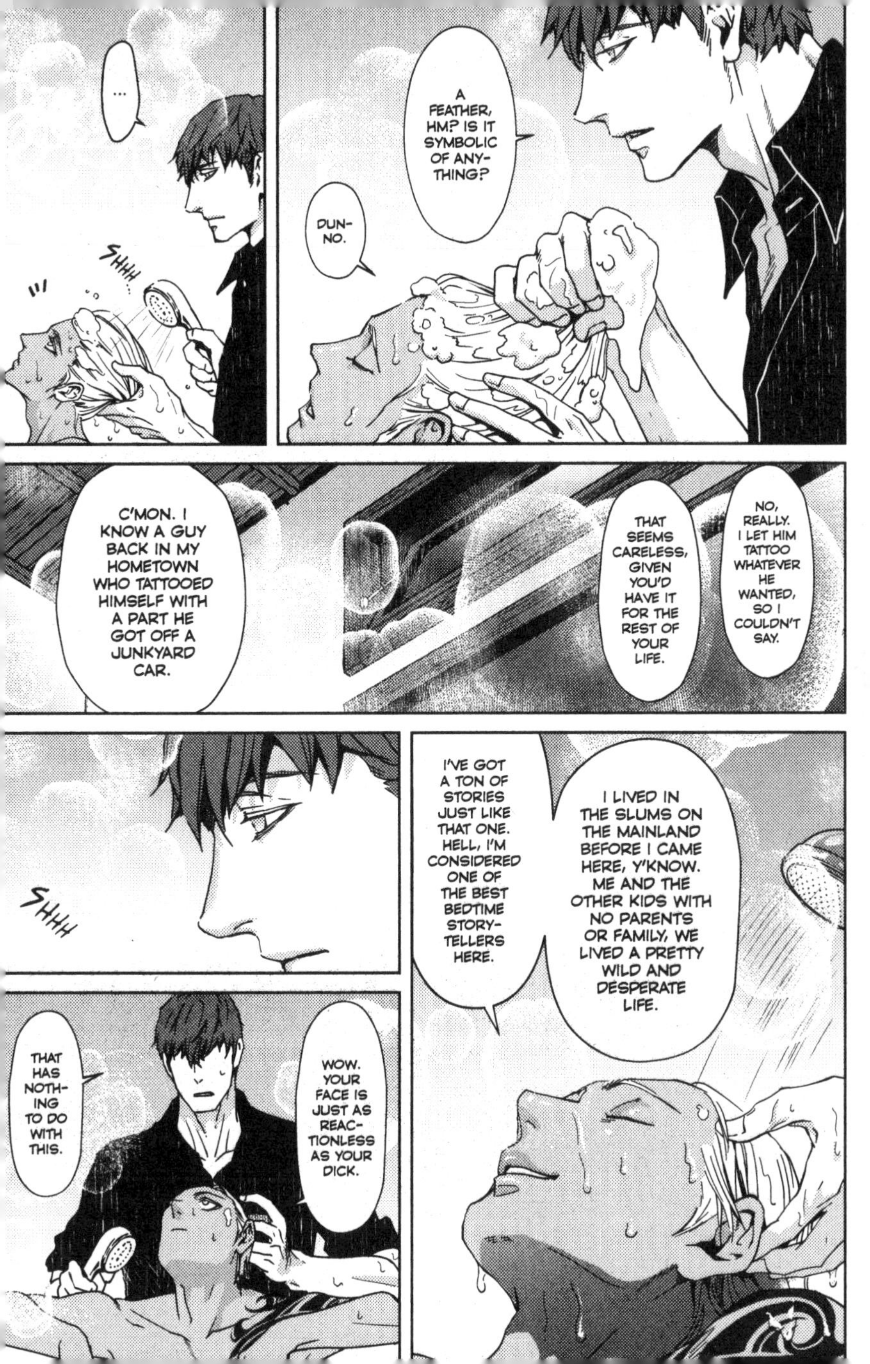
A FEATHER, HM? IS IT SYMBOLIC OF ANY-THING?
DUN-NO.
...
SHHH...
NO, REALLY. I LET HIM TATTOO WHATEVER HE WANTED, SO I COULDN'T SAY.
THAT SEEMS CARELESS, GIVEN YOU'D HAVE IT FOR THE REST OF YOUR LIFE.
C'MON. I KNOW A GUY BACK IN MY HOMETOWN WHO TATTOOED HIMSELF WITH A PART HE GOT OFF A JUNKYARD CAR.
I LIVED IN THE SLUMS ON THE MAINLAND BEFORE I CAME HERE, Y'KNOW. ME AND THE OTHER KIDS WITH NO PARENTS OR FAMILY, WE LIVED A PRETTY WILD AND DESPERATE LIFE.
I'VE GOT A TON OF STORIES JUST LIKE THAT ONE. HELL, I'M CONSIDERED ONE OF THE BEST BEDTIME STORY-TELLERS HERE.
SHHH
WOW. YOUR FACE IS JUST AS REAC-TIONLESS AS YOUR DICK.
THAT HAS NOTH-ING TO DO WITH THIS.

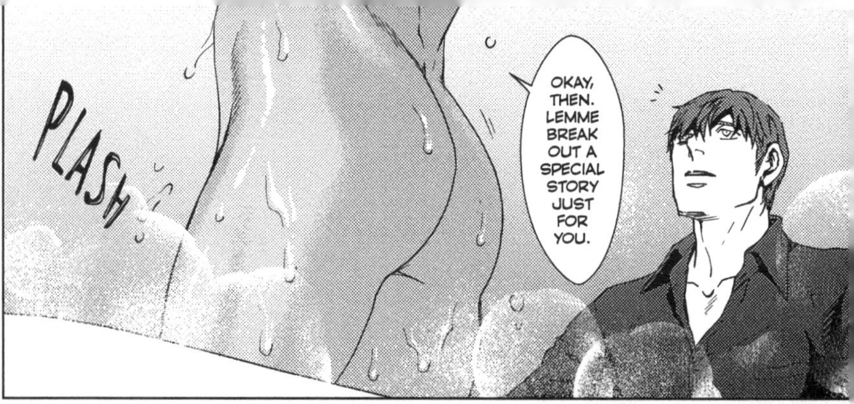
OKAY, THEN. LEMME BREAK OUT A SPECIAL STORY JUST FOR YOU.
PLASH

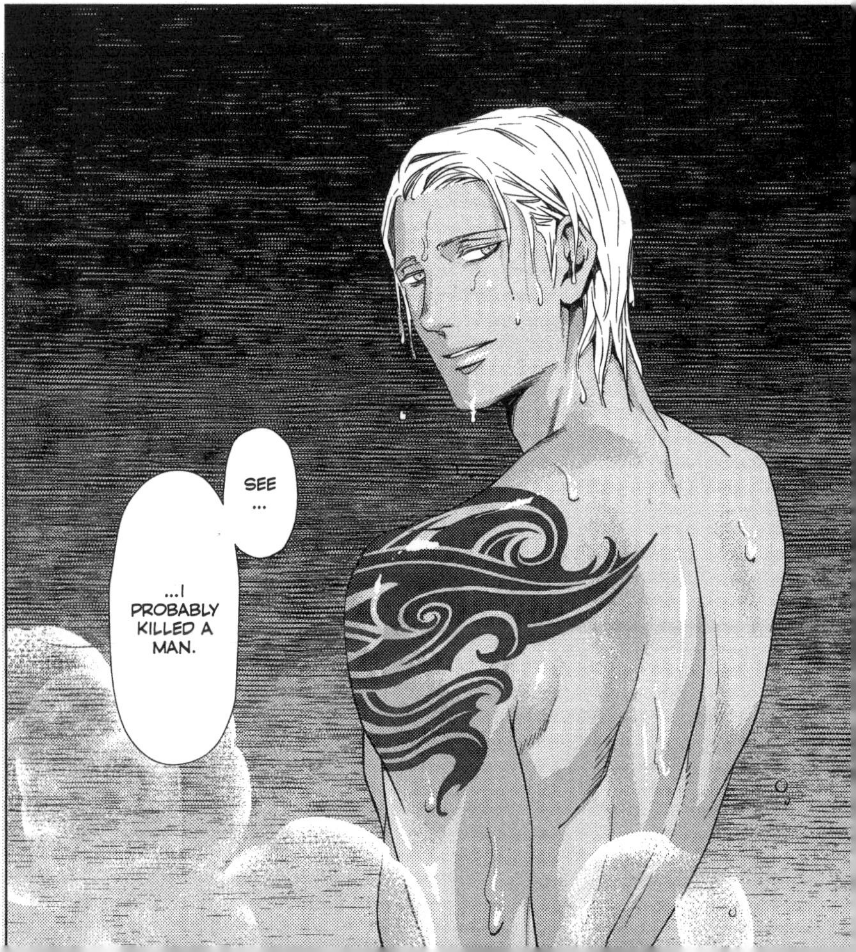
SEE ...
...I PROBABLY KILLED A MAN.

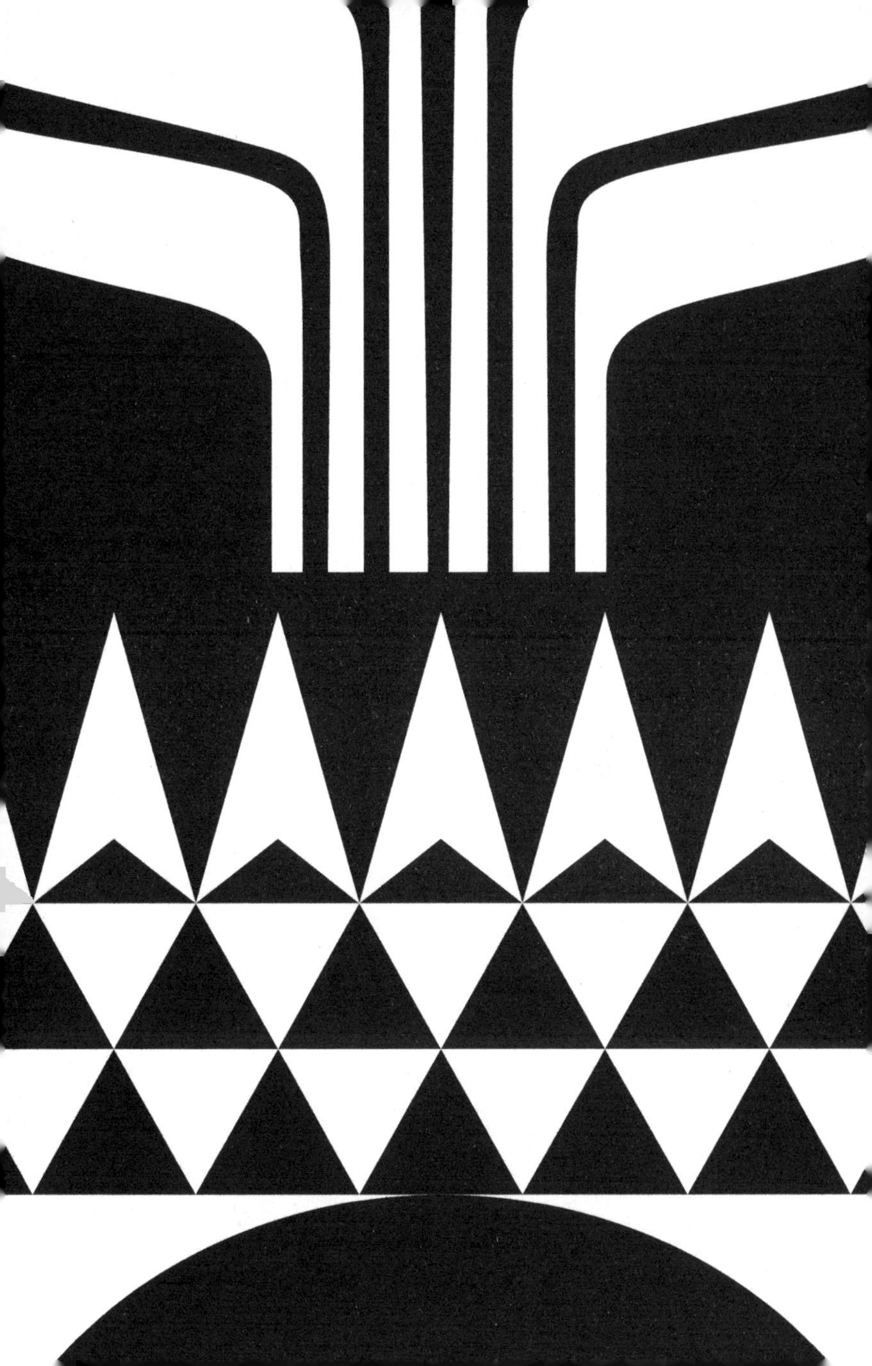

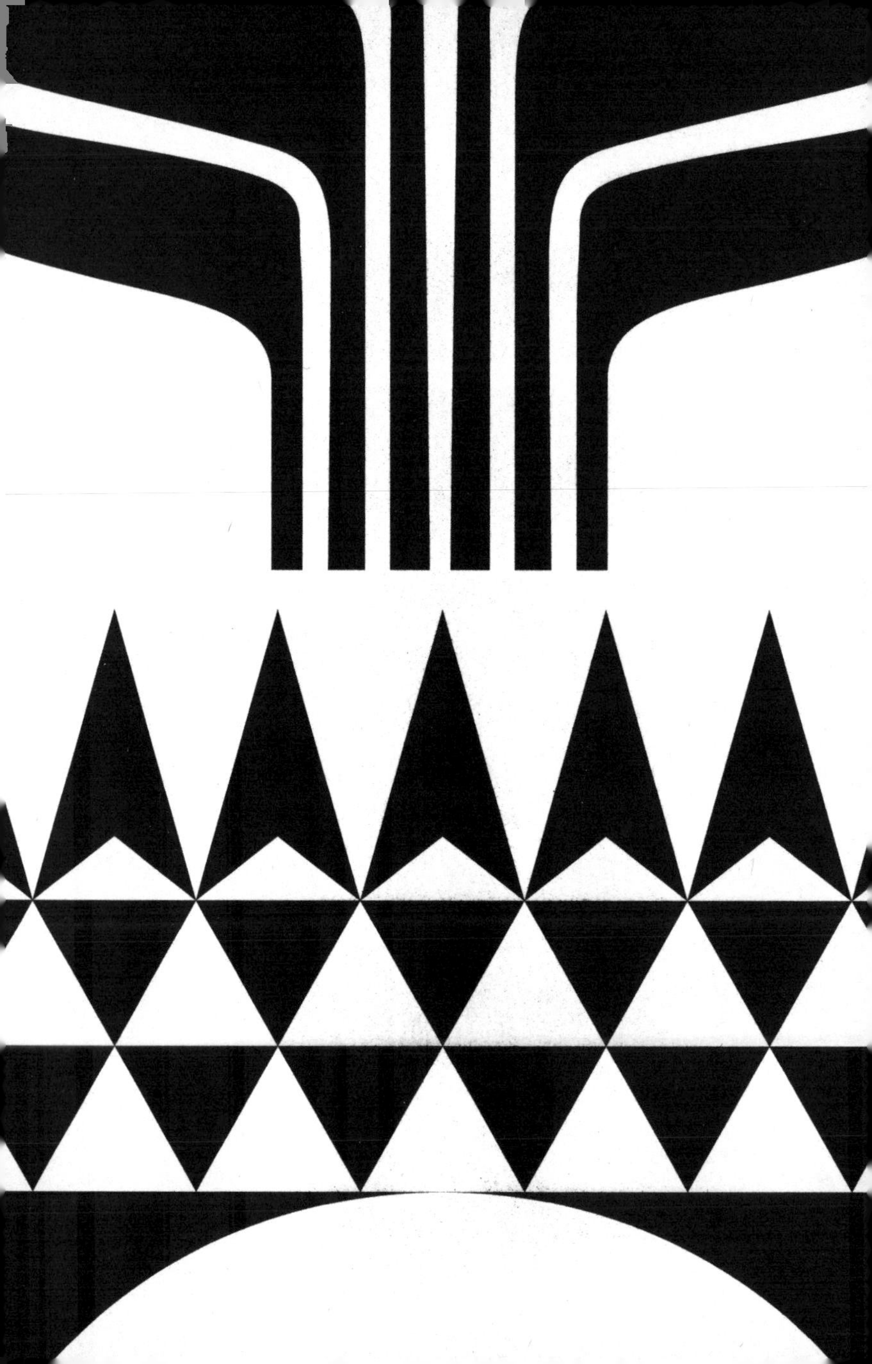

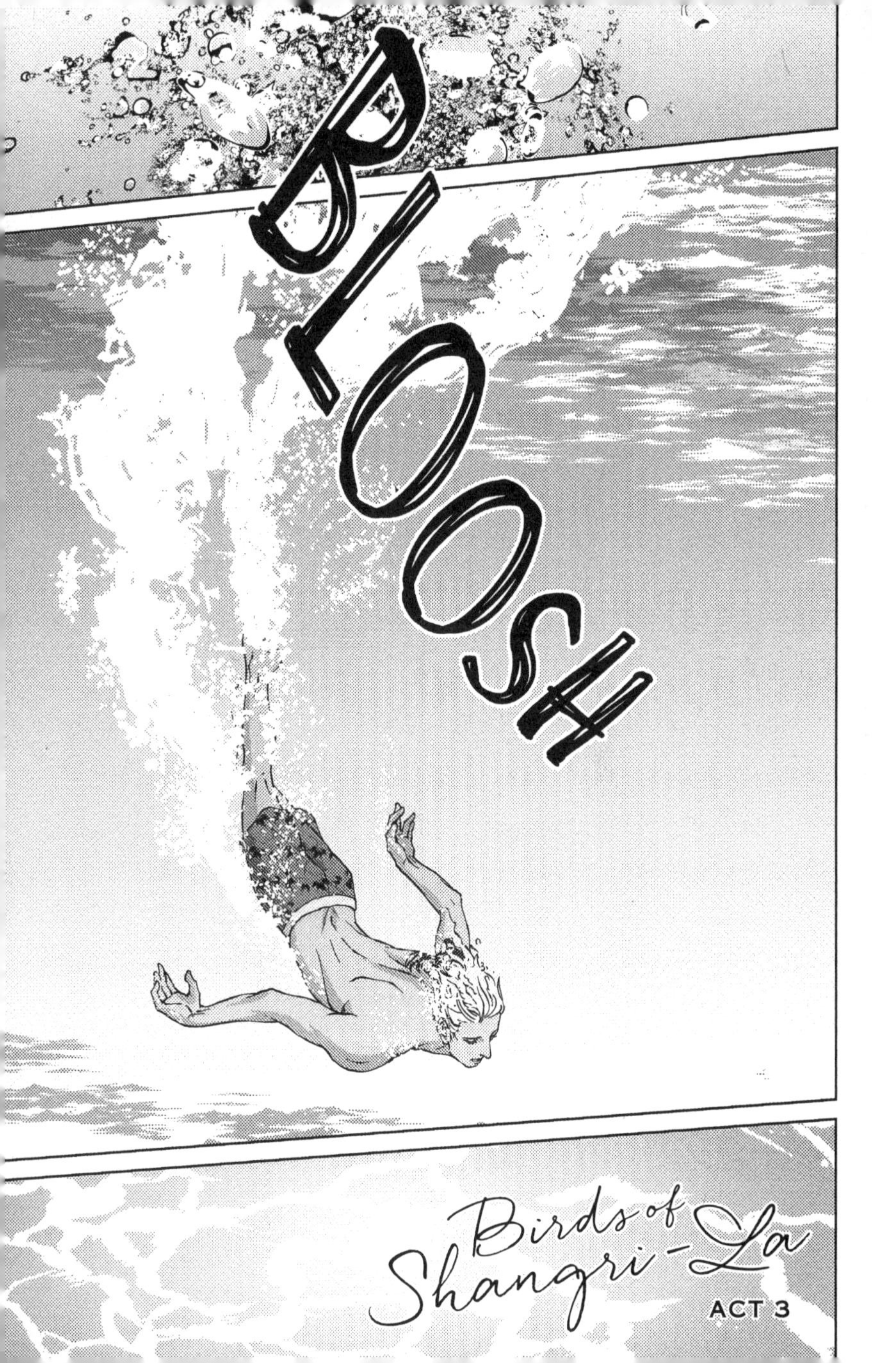
BLOOSH
Birds of Shangri-La
ACT 3

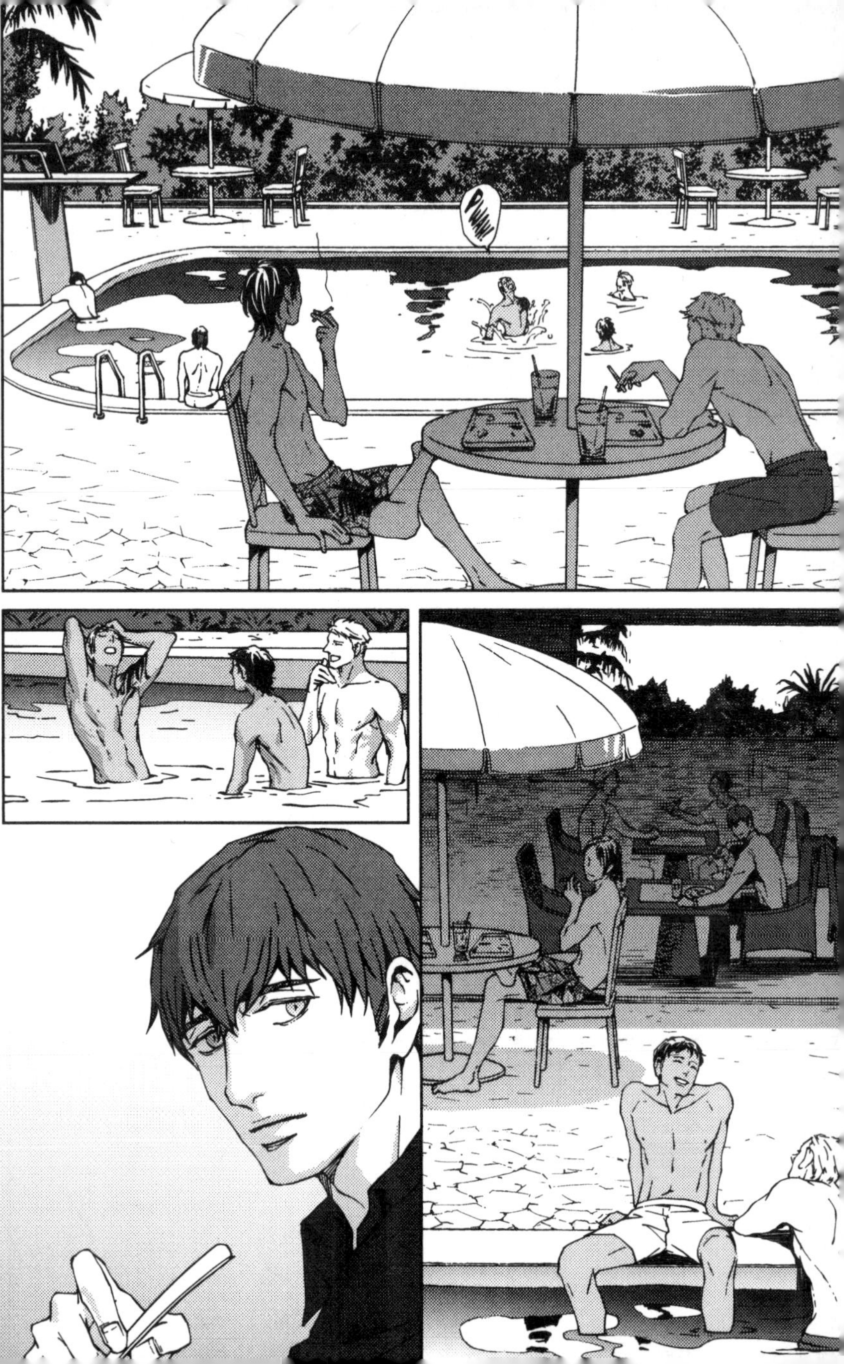
PWAH!

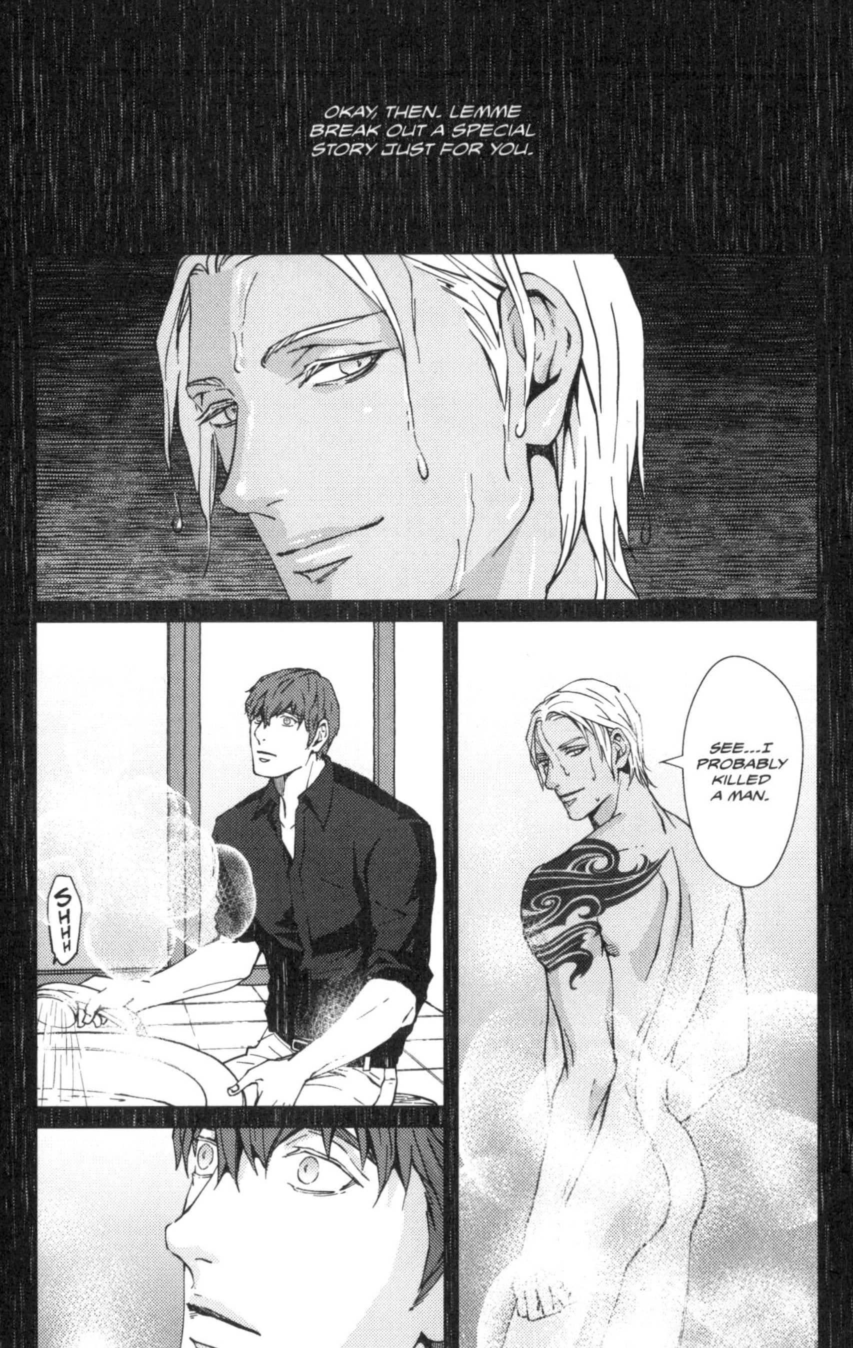
OKAY, THEN. LEMME BREAK OUT A SPECIAL STORY JUST FOR YOU.
SEE...I PROBABLY KILLED A MAN.
SHHH

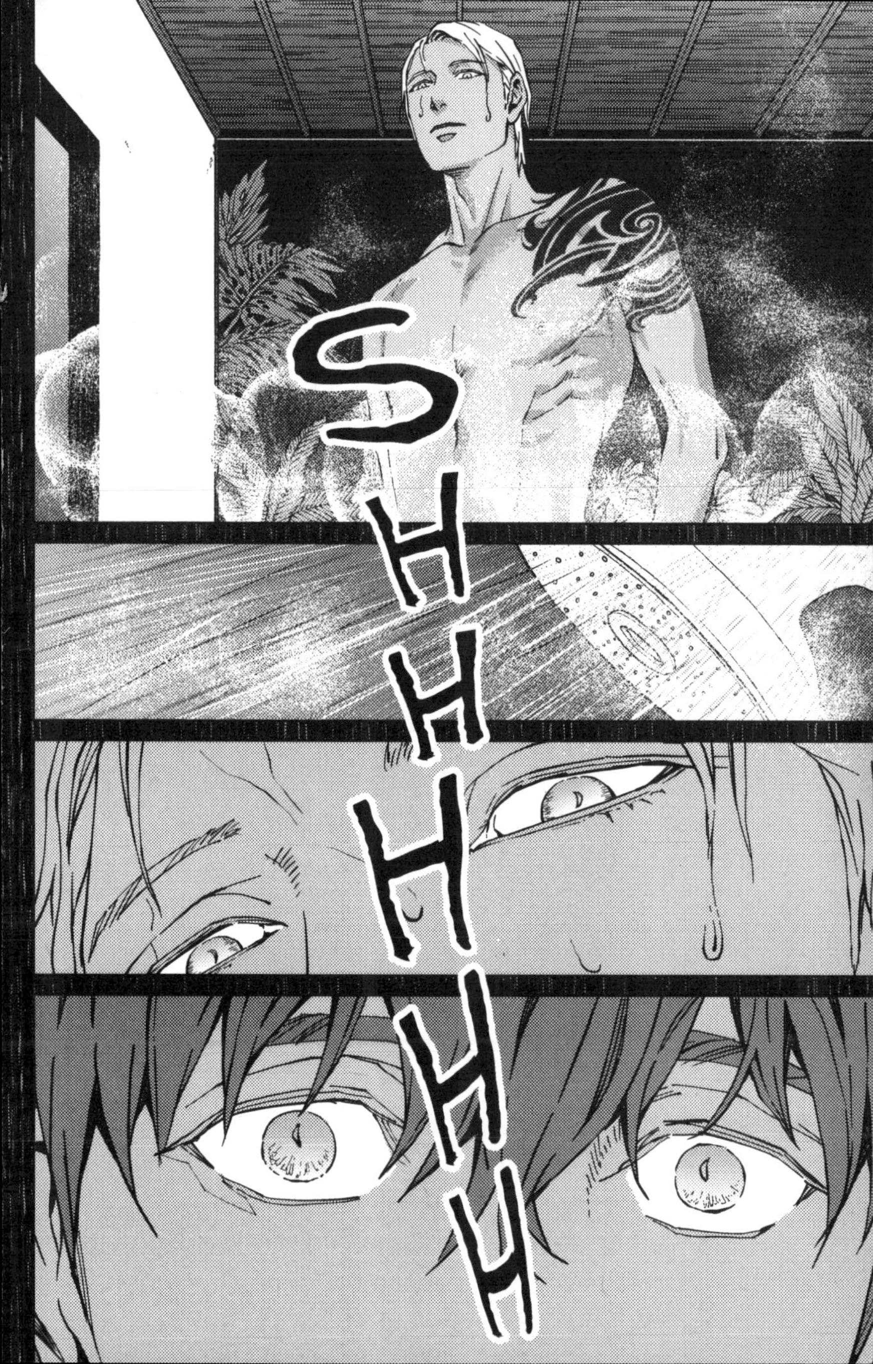
SHHHHHHH

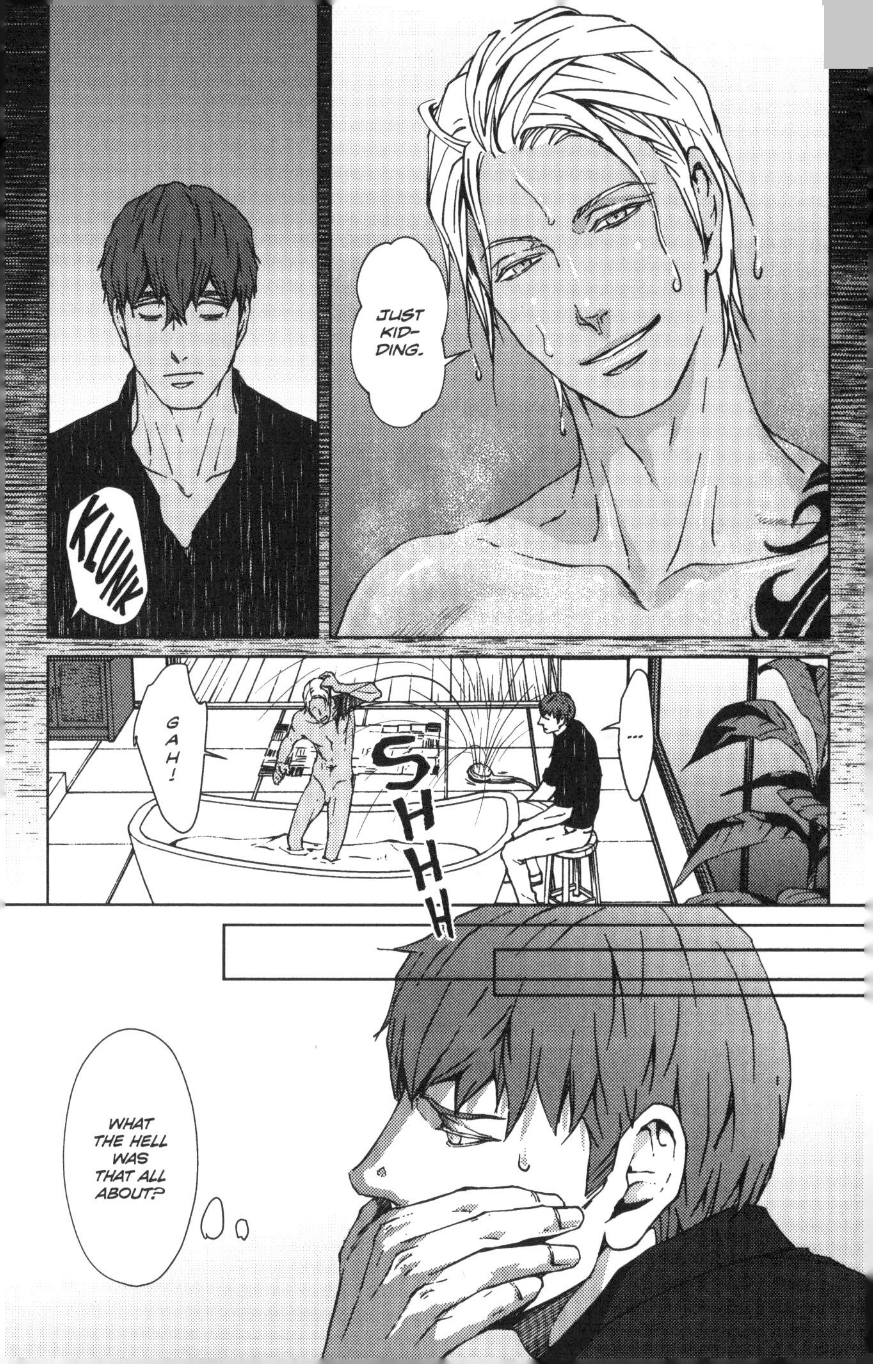
JUST KID-DING.
KLUNK
...
GAH!
SHHH
WHAT THE HELL WAS THAT ALL ABOUT?

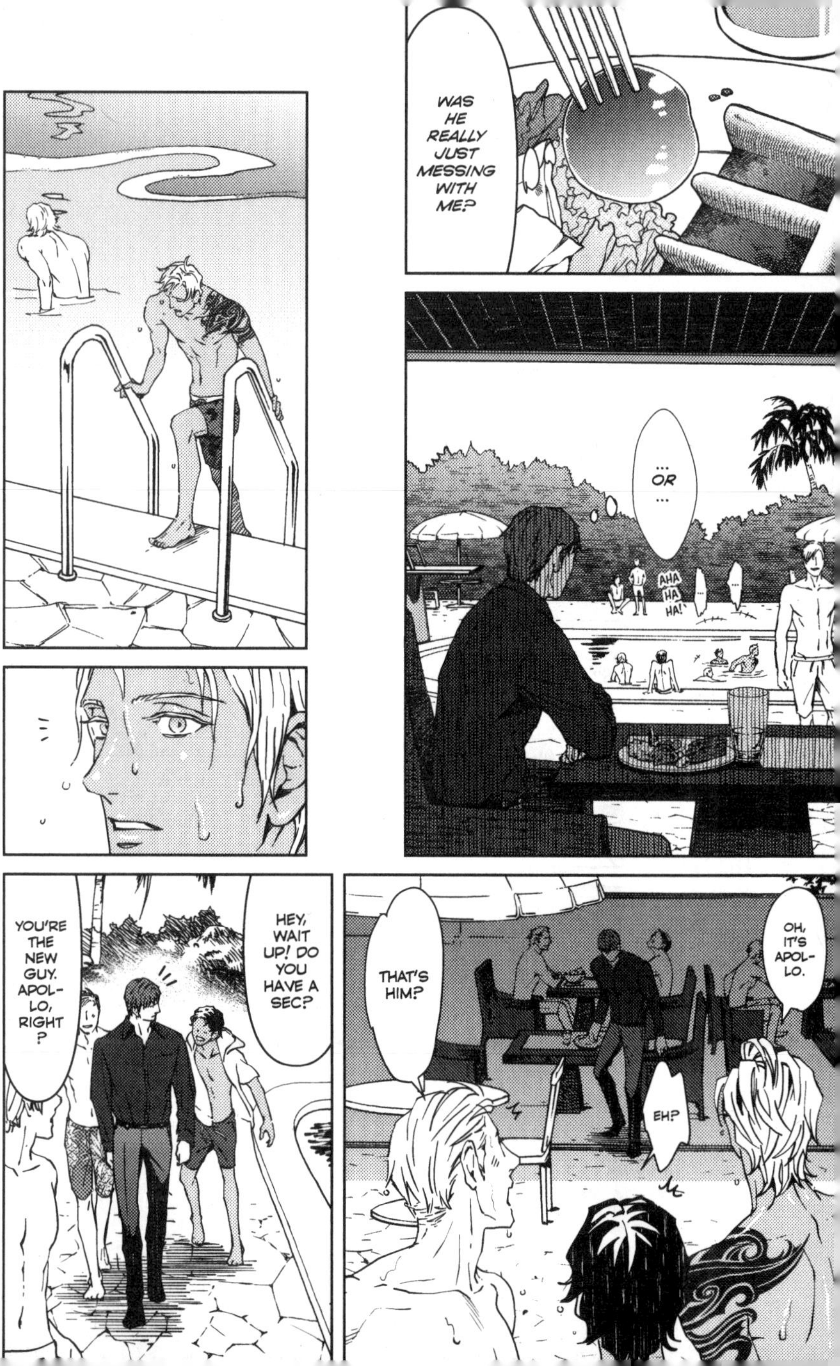
WAS HE REALLY JUST MESSING WITH ME?
... OR ...
AHA HA HA!
OH, IT'S APOLLO.
THAT'S HIM?
EH?
HEY, WAIT UP! DO YOU HAVE A SEC?
YOU'RE THE NEW GUY. APOLLO, RIGHT?

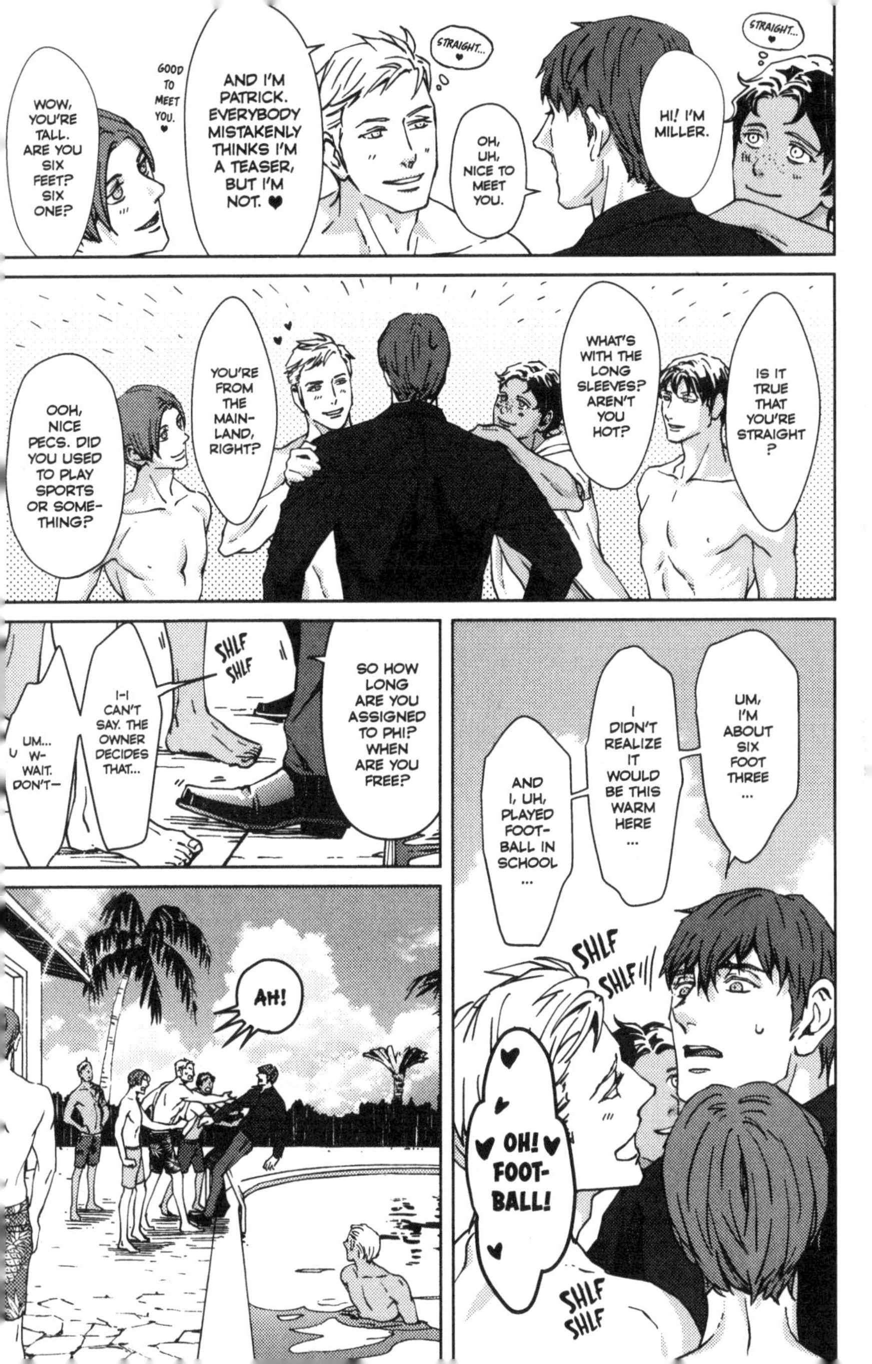
STRAIGHT... ♥
HI! I'M MILLER.
STRAIGHT... ♥
OH, UH, NICE TO MEET YOU.
AND I'M PATRICK. EVERYBODY MISTAKENLY THINKS I'M A TEASER, BUT I'M NOT. ♥
GOOD TO MEET YOU. ♥
WOW, YOU'RE TALL. ARE YOU SIX FEET? SIX ONE?
IS IT TRUE THAT YOU'RE STRAIGHT?
WHAT'S WITH THE LONG SLEEVES? AREN'T YOU HOT?
YOU'RE FROM THE MAINLAND, RIGHT?
OOH, NICE PECS. DID YOU USED TO PLAY SPORTS OR SOMETHING?
UM, I'M ABOUT SIX FOOT THREE...
I DIDN'T REALIZE IT WOULD BE THIS WARM HERE...
AND I, UH, PLAYED FOOTBALL IN SCHOOL...
SHLF SHLF
OH! FOOTBALL!
SHLF SHLF
SO HOW LONG ARE YOU ASSIGNED TO PHI? WHEN ARE YOU FREE?
SHLF SHLF
I-I CAN'T SAY. THE OWNER DECIDES THAT...
UM... W-WAIT. DON'T—
AH!

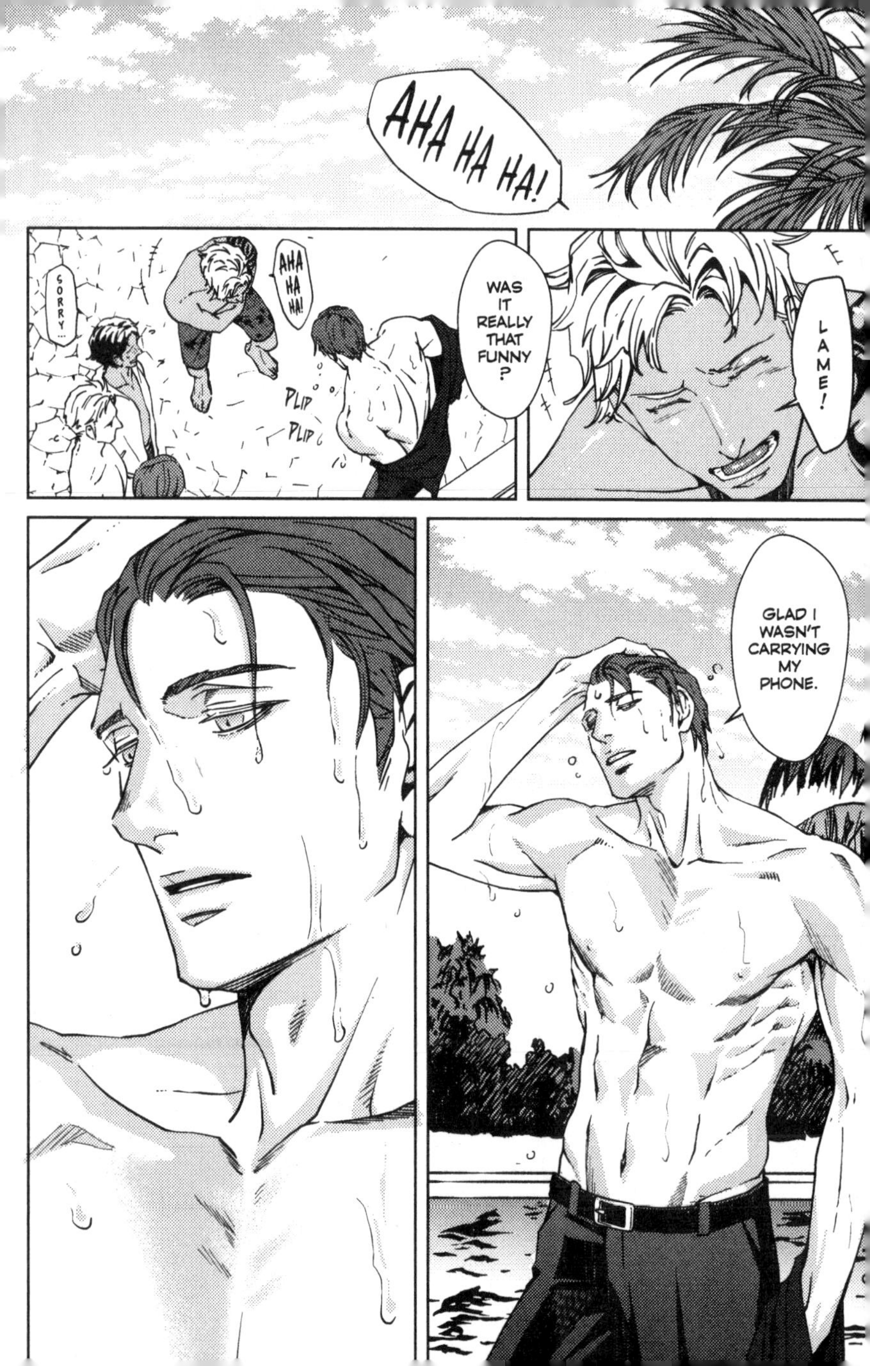
AHA HA HA!
LAME!
WAS IT REALLY THAT FUNNY?
AHA HA HA!
SORRY...
PLIP PLIP
GLAD I WASN'T CARRYING MY PHONE.

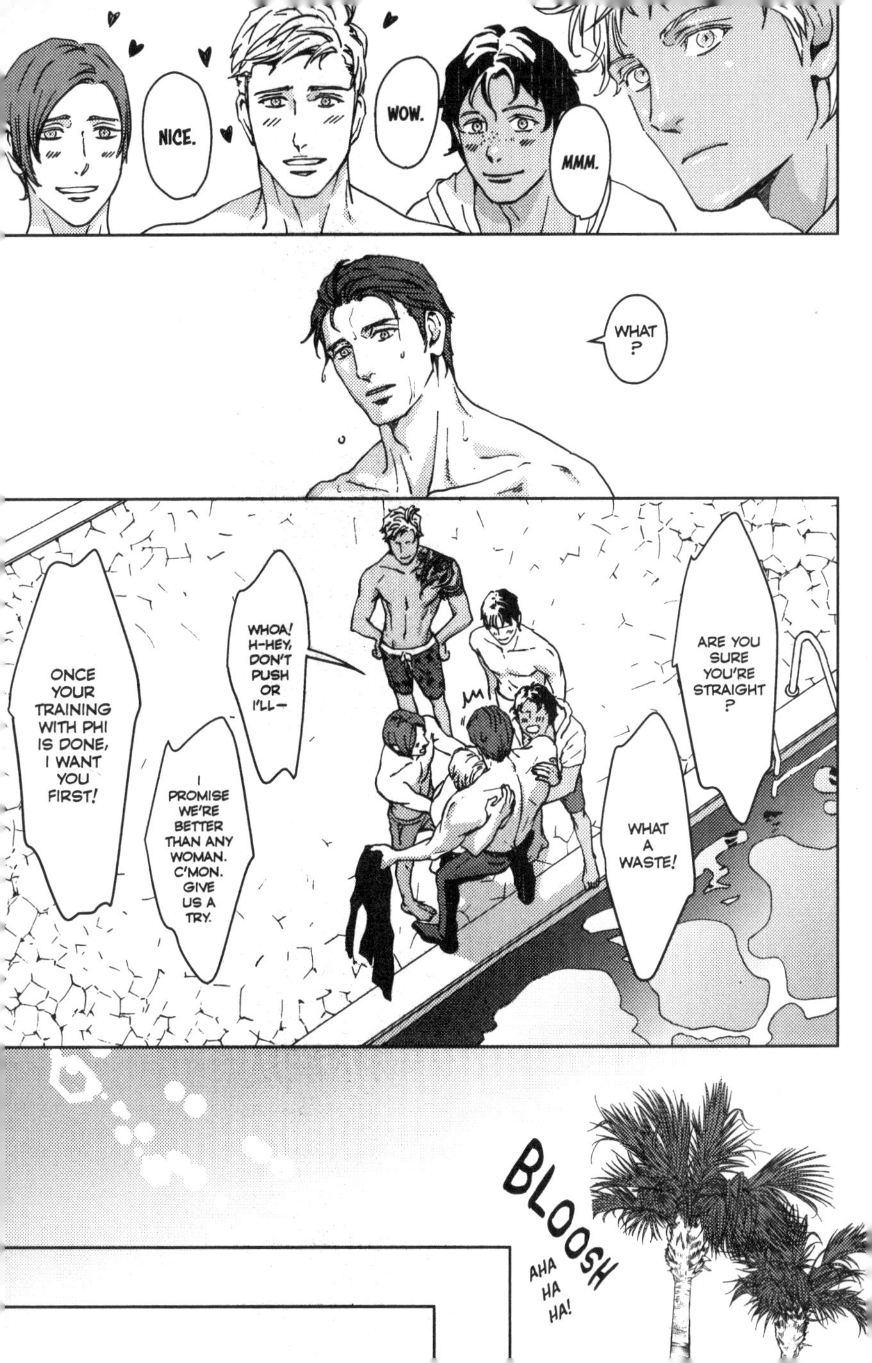
MMM.
WOW.
NICE.
WHAT?
ARE YOU SURE YOU'RE STRAIGHT?
WHAT A WASTE!
WHOA! H-HEY, DON'T PUSH OR I'LL—
ONCE YOUR TRAINING WITH PHI IS DONE, I WANT YOU FIRST!
I PROMISE WE'RE BETTER THAN ANY WOMAN. C'MON. GIVE US A TRY.
BLOOSH
AHA HA HA!

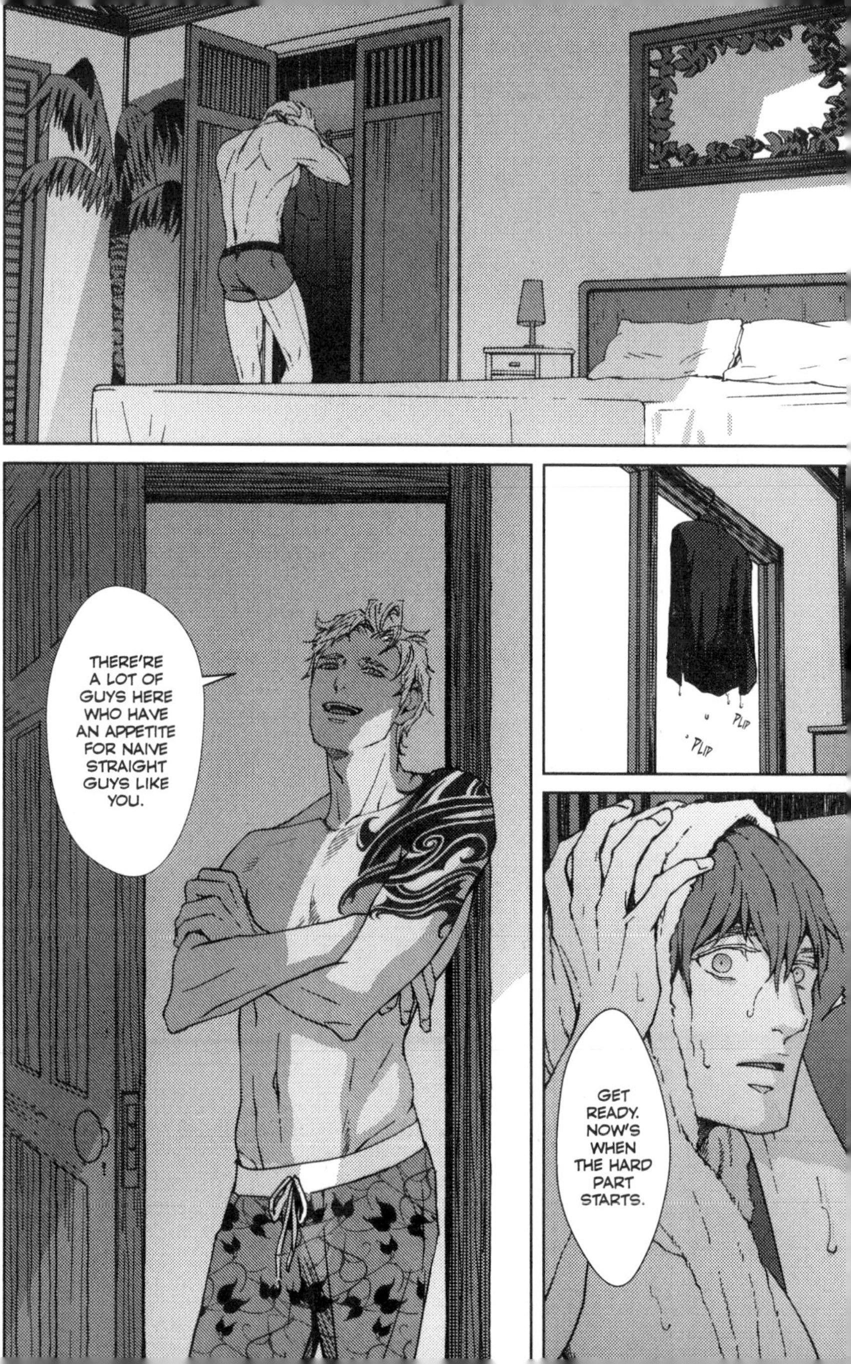
PLIP
PLIP
GET READY. NOW'S WHEN THE HARD PART STARTS.
THERE'RE A LOT OF GUYS HERE WHO HAVE AN APPETITE FOR NAIVE STRAIGHT GUYS LIKE YOU.

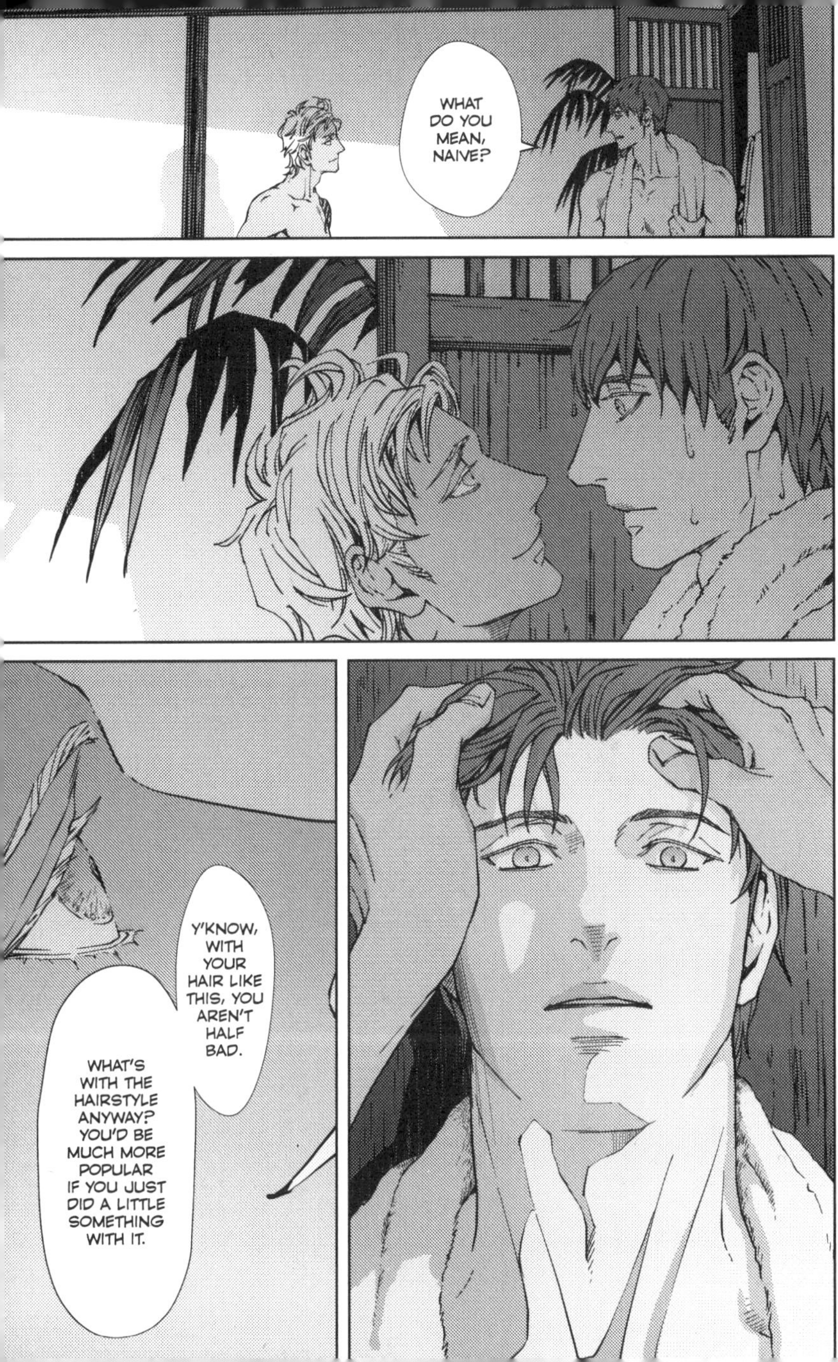
WHAT DO YOU MEAN, NAIVE?
Y'KNOW, WITH YOUR HAIR LIKE THIS, YOU AREN'T HALF BAD.
WHAT'S WITH THE HAIRSTYLE ANYWAY? YOU'D BE MUCH MORE POPULAR IF YOU JUST DID A LITTLE SOMETHING WITH IT.

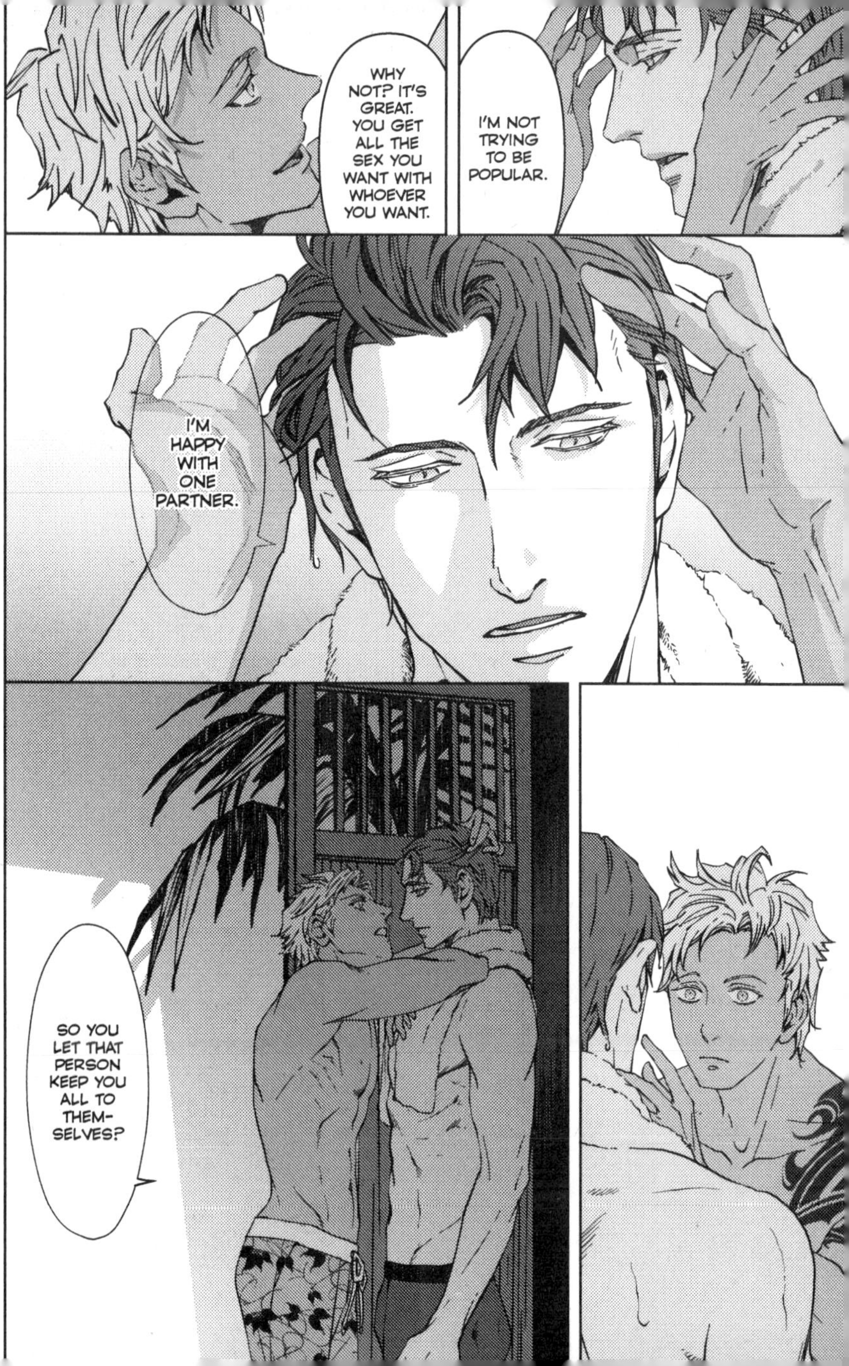
I'M NOT TRYING TO BE POPULAR.
WHY NOT? IT'S GREAT. YOU GET ALL THE SEX YOU WANT WITH WHOEVER YOU WANT.
I'M HAPPY WITH ONE PARTNER.
SO YOU LET THAT PERSON KEEP YOU ALL TO THEM-SELVES?

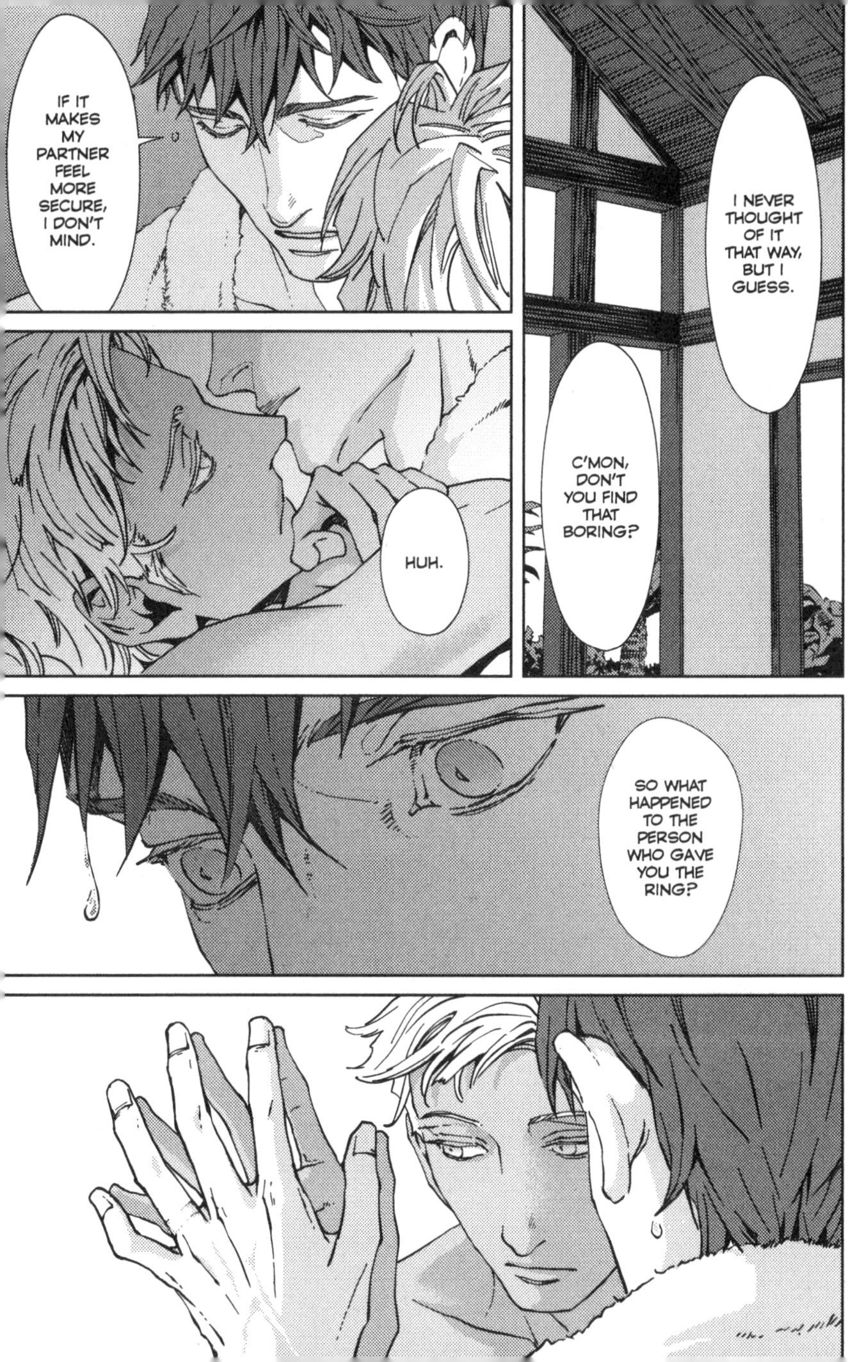
I NEVER THOUGHT OF IT THAT WAY, BUT I GUESS.
C'MON, DON'T YOU FIND THAT BORING?
IF IT MAKES MY PARTNER FEEL MORE SECURE, I DON'T MIND.
HUH.
SO WHAT HAPPENED TO THE PERSON WHO GAVE YOU THE RING?

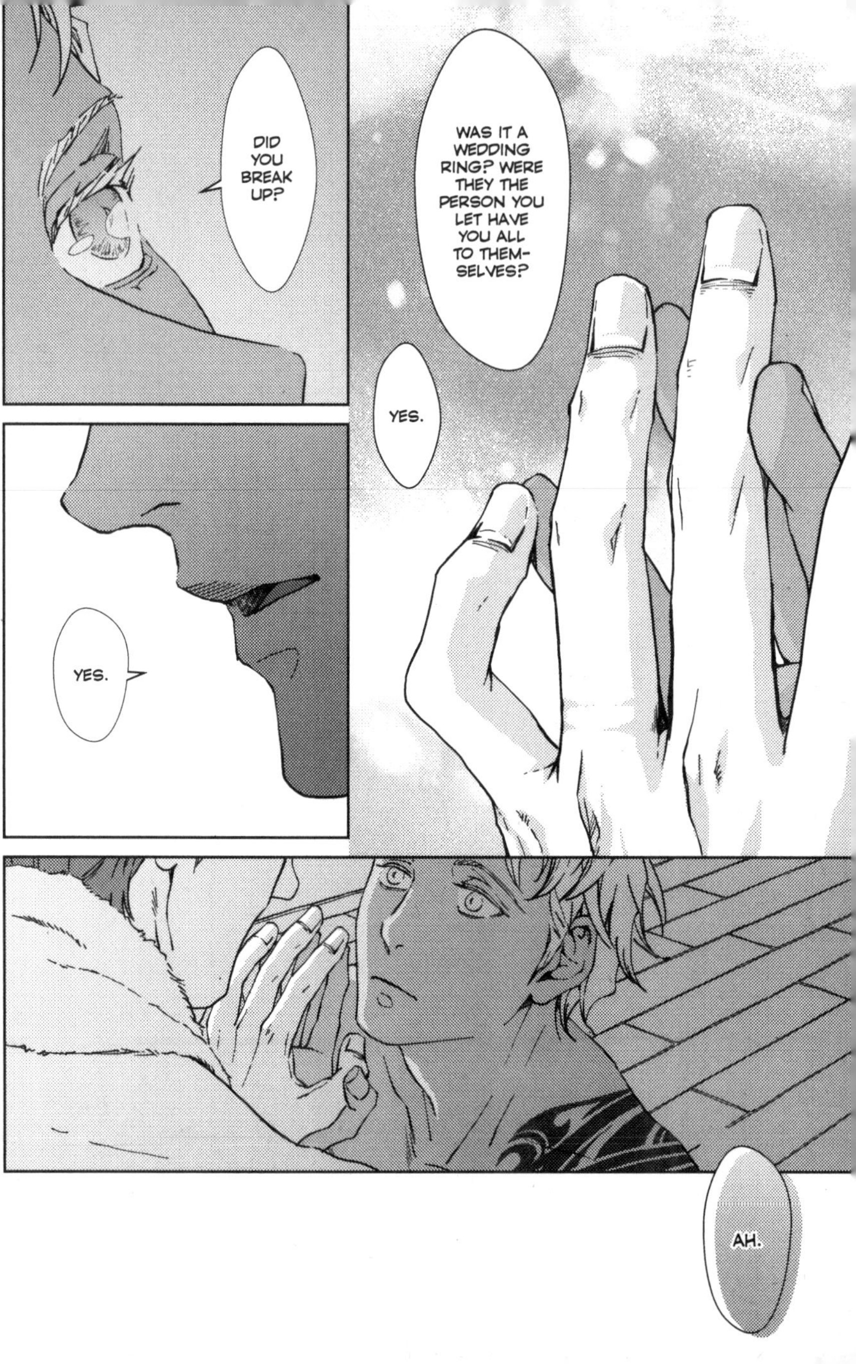
WAS IT A WEDDING RING? WERE THEY THE PERSON YOU LET HAVE YOU ALL TO THEM-SELVES?
YES.
DID YOU BREAK UP?
YES.
AH.

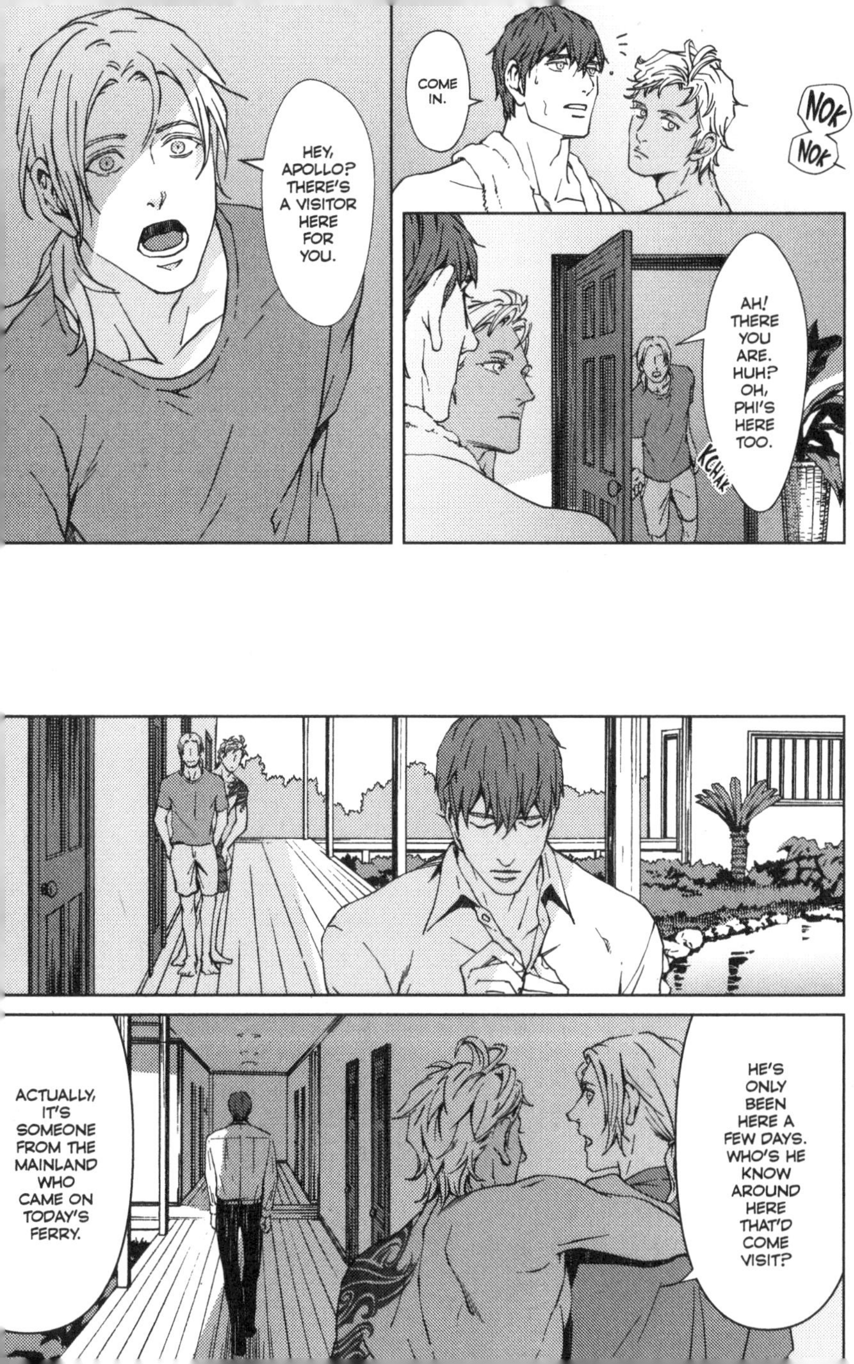
NOK NOK
COME IN.
AH! THERE YOU ARE. HUH? OH, PHI'S HERE TOO.
KCHAK
HEY, APOLLO? THERE'S A VISITOR HERE FOR YOU.
HE'S ONLY BEEN HERE A FEW DAYS. WHO'S HE KNOW AROUND HERE THAT'D COME VISIT?
ACTUALLY, IT'S SOMEONE FROM THE MAINLAND WHO CAME ON TODAY'S FERRY.

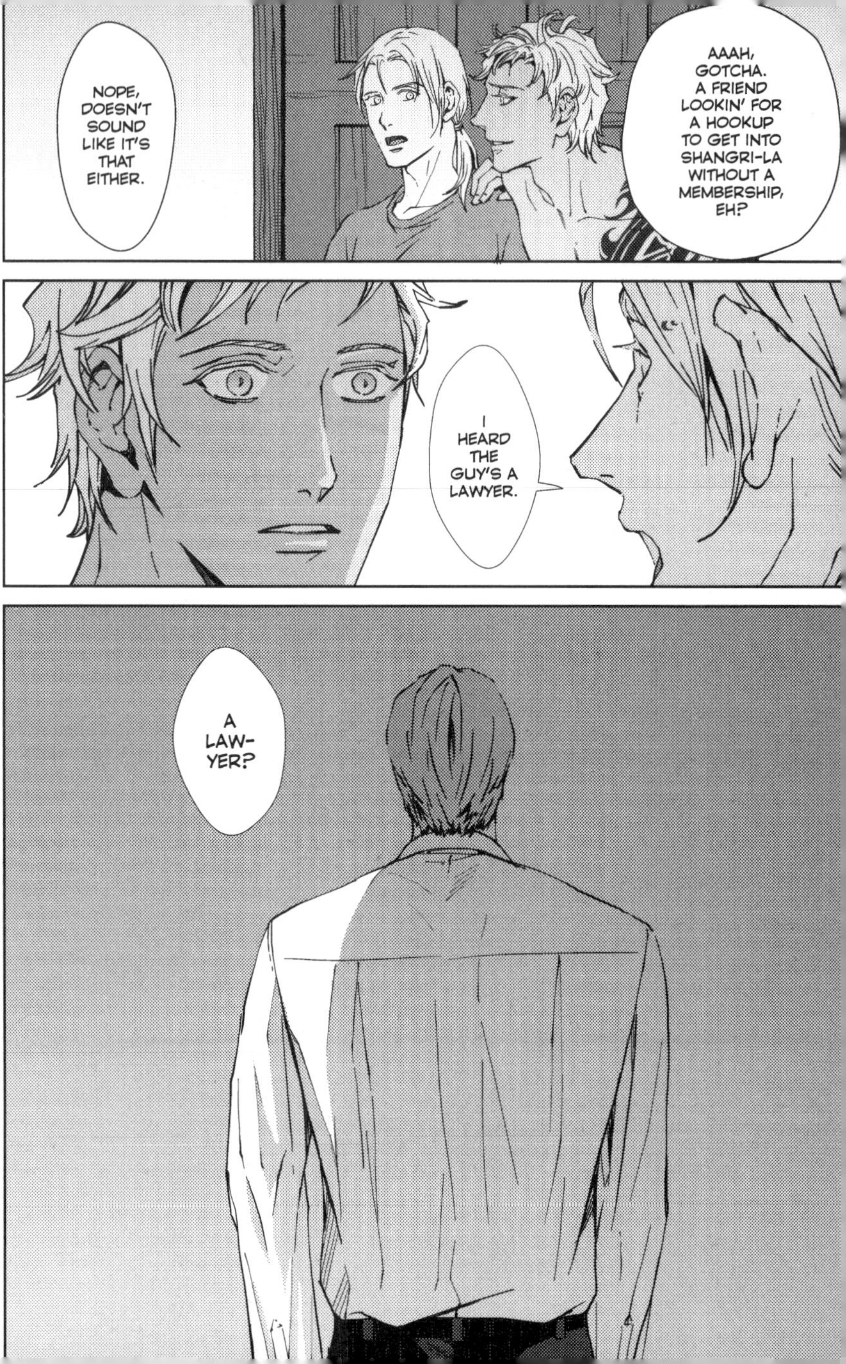
AAAH, GOTCHA. A FRIEND LOOKIN' FOR A HOOKUP TO GET INTO SHANGRI-LA WITHOUT A MEMBERSHIP, EH?
NOPE, DOESN'T SOUND LIKE IT'S THAT EITHER.
I HEARD THE GUY'S A LAWYER.
A LAW-YER?

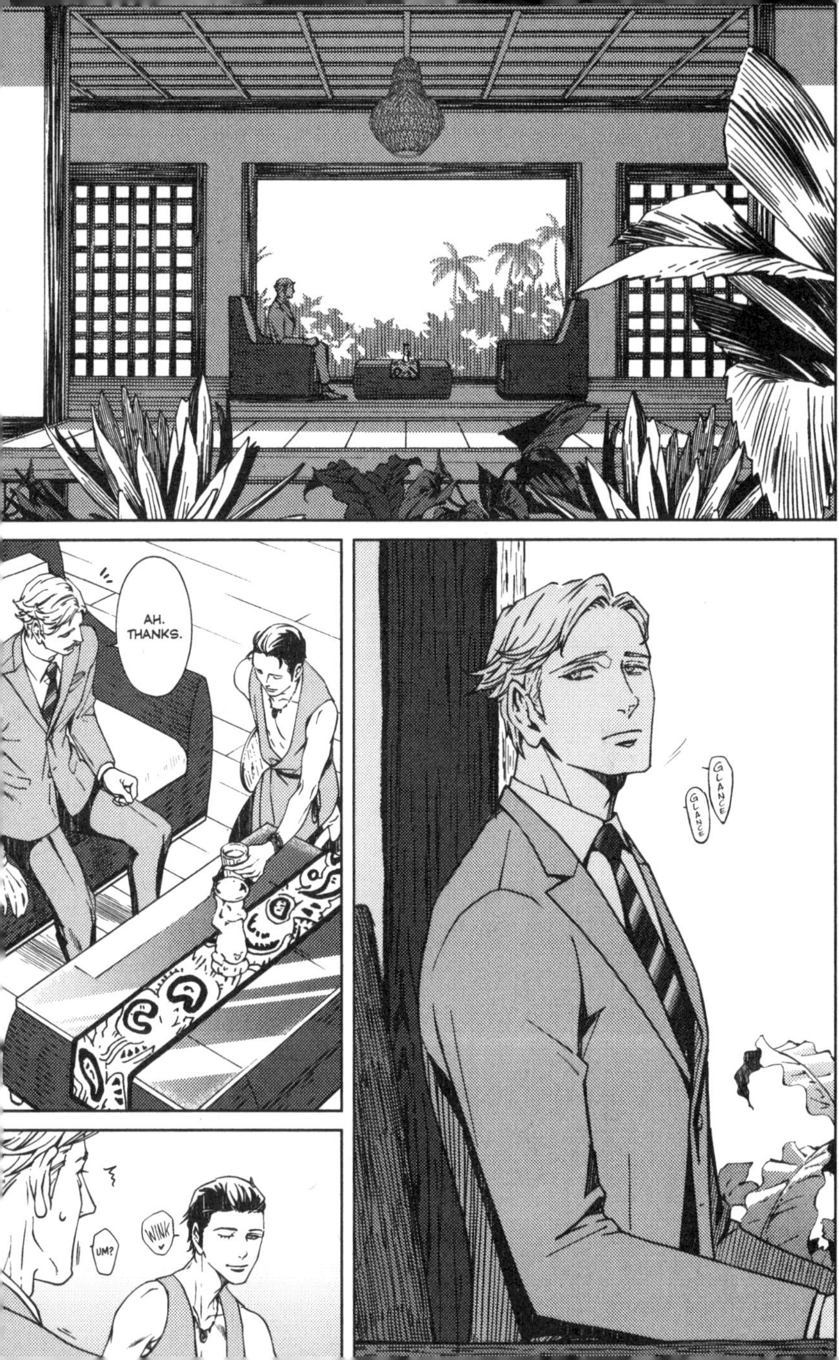
GLANCE
GLANCE
AH. THANKS.
WINK
UM?

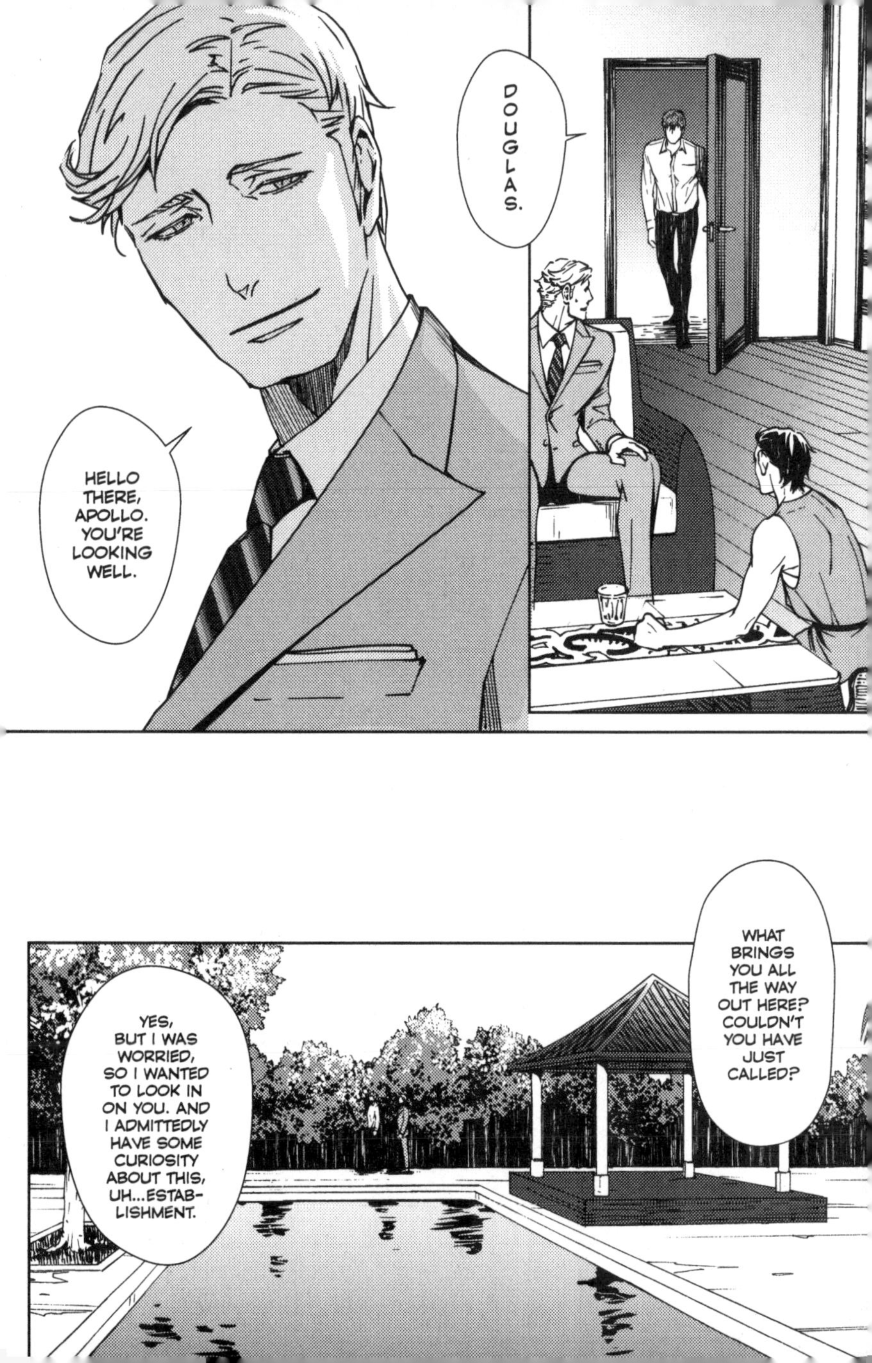
DOUGLAS.
HELLO THERE, APOLLO. YOU'RE LOOKING WELL.
WHAT BRINGS YOU ALL THE WAY OUT HERE? COULDN'T YOU HAVE JUST CALLED?
YES, BUT I WAS WORRIED, SO I WANTED TO LOOK IN ON YOU. AND I ADMITTEDLY HAVE SOME CURIOSITY ABOUT THIS, UH...ESTAB-LISHMENT.

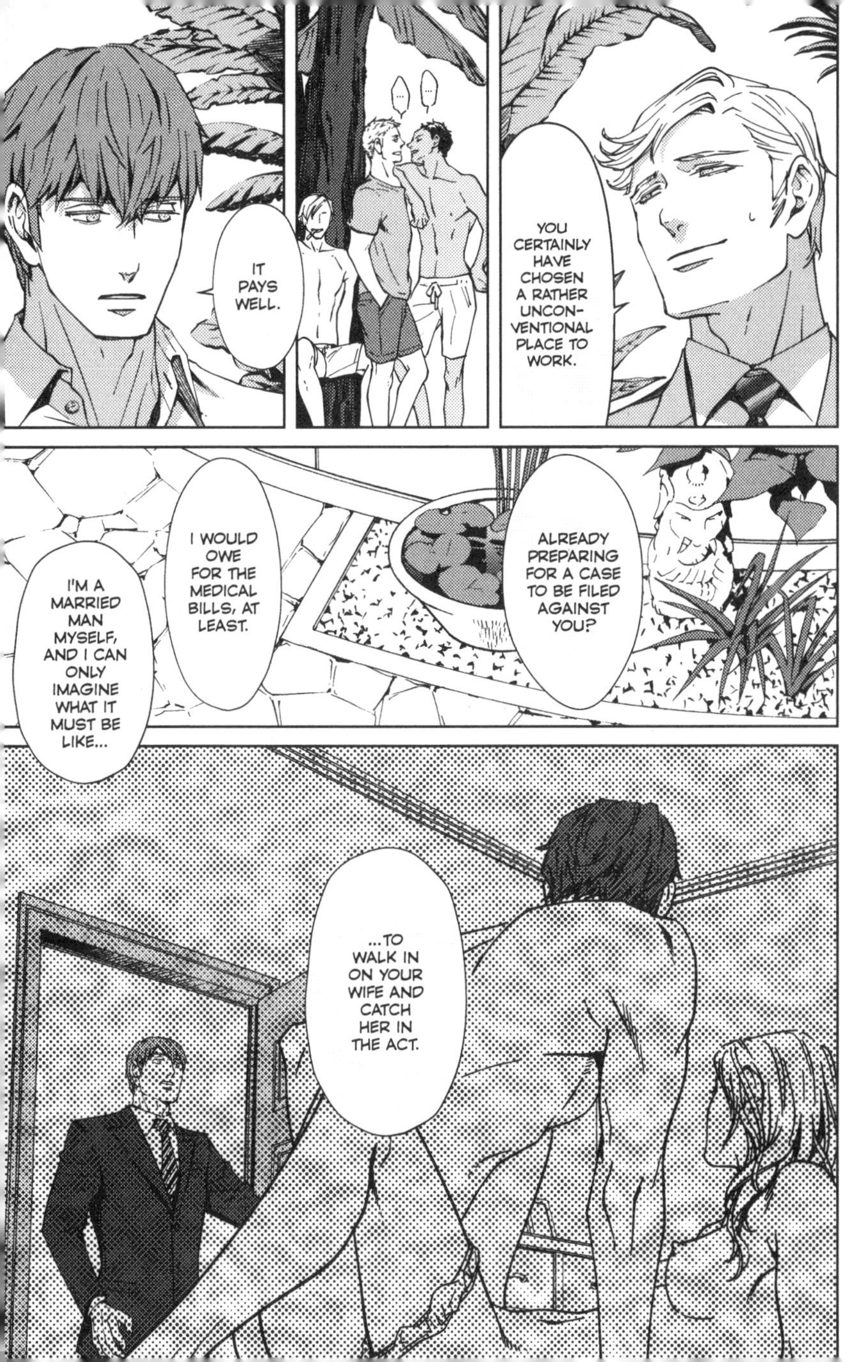
YOU CERTAINLY HAVE CHOSEN A RATHER UNCONVENTIONAL PLACE TO WORK.
...
...
IT PAYS WELL.
ALREADY PREPARING FOR A CASE TO BE FILED AGAINST YOU?
I WOULD OWE FOR THE MEDICAL BILLS, AT LEAST.
I'M A MARRIED MAN MYSELF, AND I CAN ONLY IMAGINE WHAT IT MUST BE LIKE...
...TO WALK IN ON YOUR WIFE AND CATCH HER IN THE ACT.

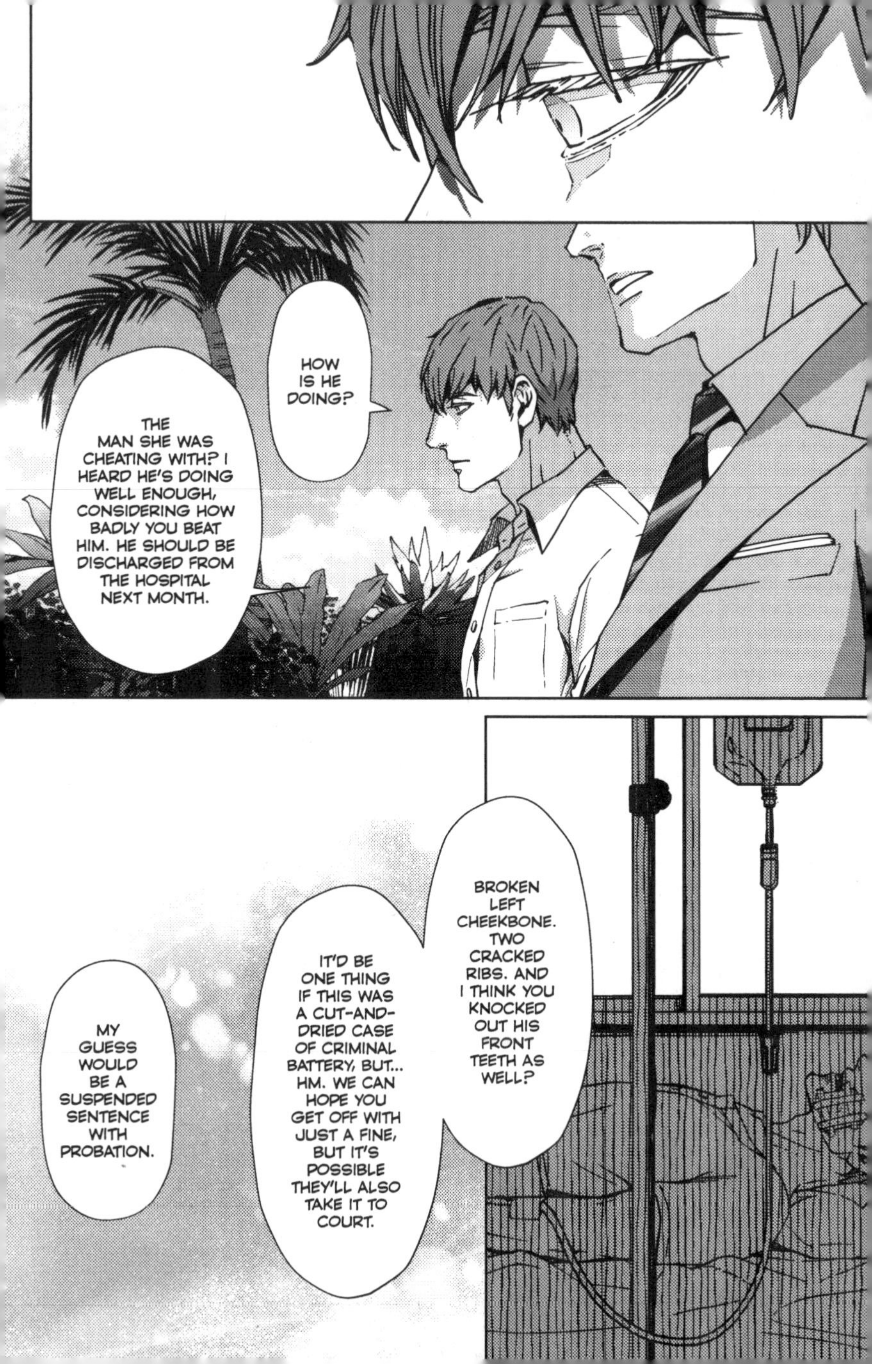
HOW IS HE DOING?
THE MAN SHE WAS CHEATING WITH? I HEARD HE'S DOING WELL ENOUGH, CONSIDERING HOW BADLY YOU BEAT HIM. HE SHOULD BE DISCHARGED FROM THE HOSPITAL NEXT MONTH.
BROKEN LEFT CHEEKBONE. TWO CRACKED RIBS. AND I THINK YOU KNOCKED OUT HIS FRONT TEETH AS WELL?
IT'D BE ONE THING IF THIS WAS A CUT-AND-DRIED CASE OF CRIMINAL BATTERY, BUT... HM. WE CAN HOPE YOU GET OFF WITH JUST A FINE, BUT IT'S POSSIBLE THEY'LL ALSO TAKE IT TO COURT.
MY GUESS WOULD BE A SUSPENDED SENTENCE WITH PROBATION.

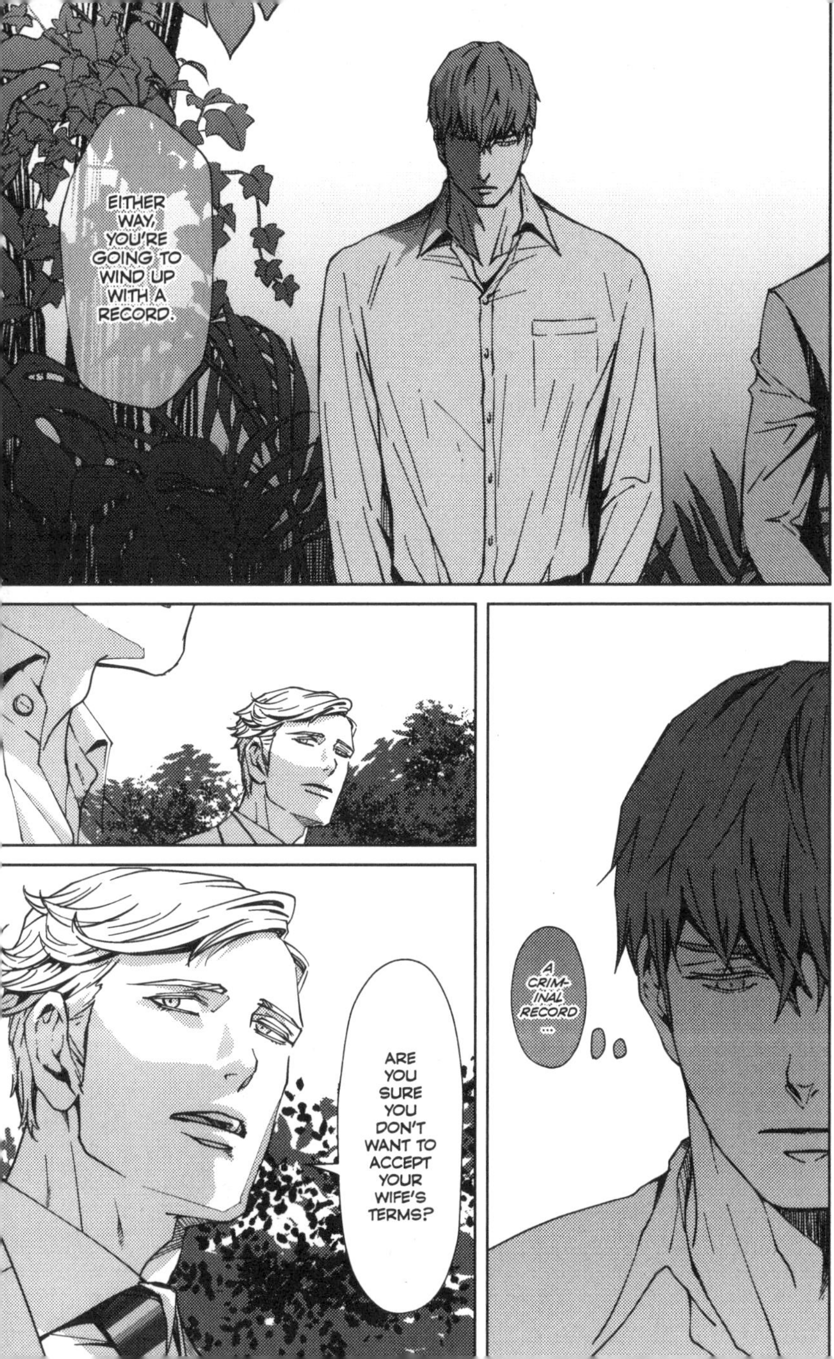
EITHER WAY, YOU'RE GOING TO WIND UP WITH A RECORD.
A CRIMINAL RECORD...
ARE YOU SURE YOU DON'T WANT TO ACCEPT YOUR WIFE'S TERMS?

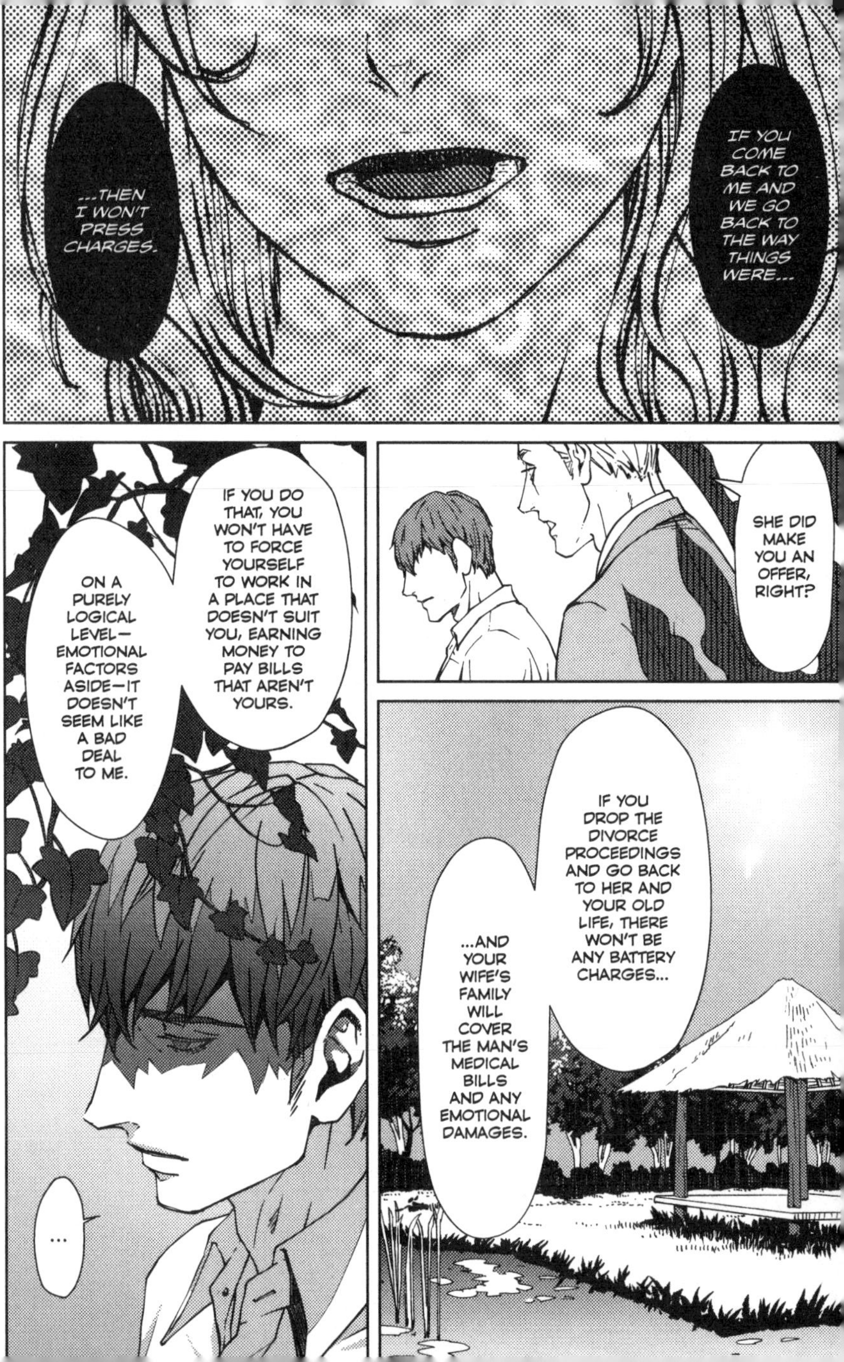
IF YOU COME BACK TO ME AND WE GO BACK TO THE WAY THINGS WERE...
...THEN I WON'T PRESS CHARGES.
SHE DID MAKE YOU AN OFFER, RIGHT?
IF YOU DROP THE DIVORCE PROCEEDINGS AND GO BACK TO HER AND YOUR OLD LIFE, THERE WON'T BE ANY BATTERY CHARGES...
...AND YOUR WIFE'S FAMILY WILL COVER THE MAN'S MEDICAL BILLS AND ANY EMOTIONAL DAMAGES.
IF YOU DO THAT, YOU WON'T HAVE TO FORCE YOURSELF TO WORK IN A PLACE THAT DOESN'T SUIT YOU, EARNING MONEY TO PAY BILLS THAT AREN'T YOURS.
ON A PURELY LOGICAL LEVEL—EMOTIONAL FACTORS ASIDE—IT DOESN'T SEEM LIKE A BAD DEAL TO ME.
...

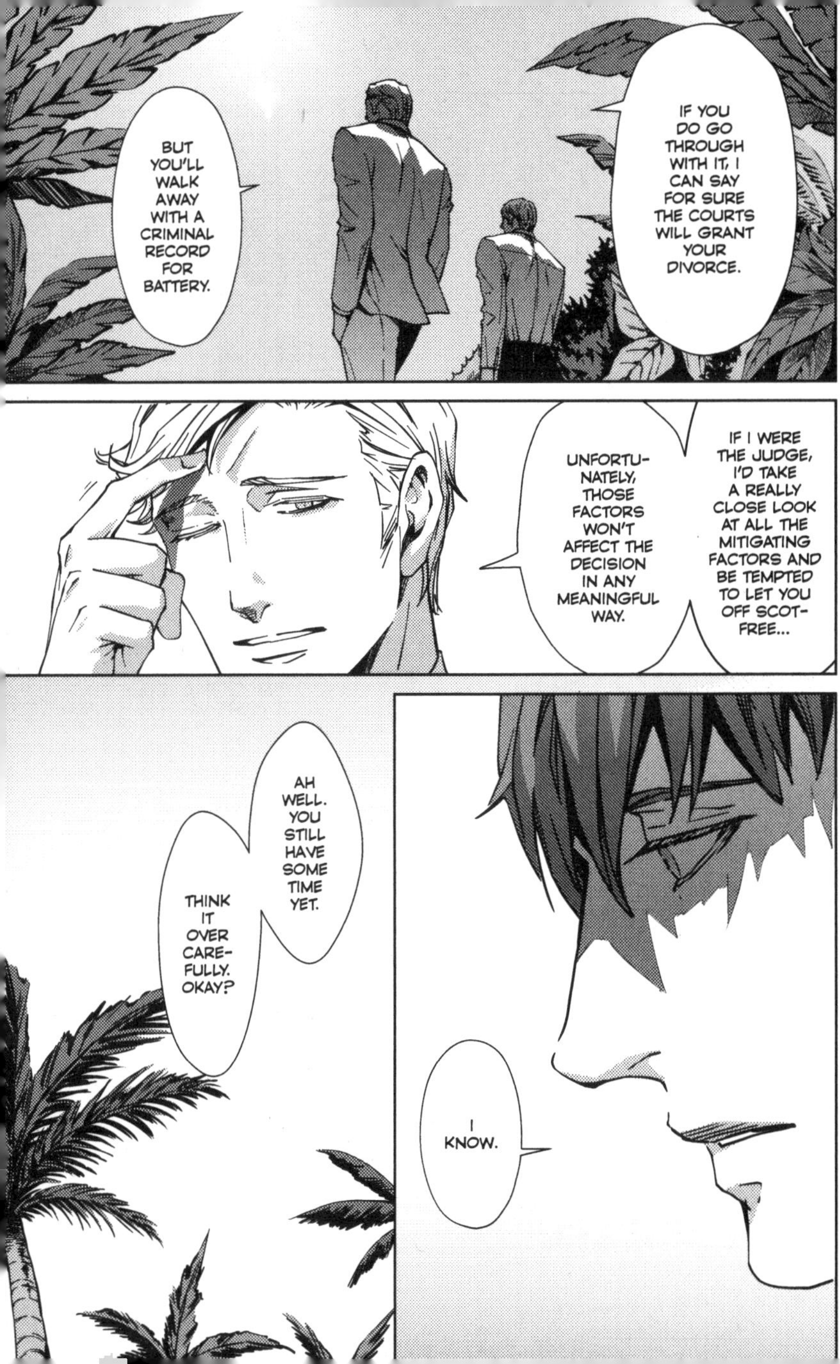
IF YOU DO GO THROUGH WITH IT, I CAN SAY FOR SURE THE COURTS WILL GRANT YOUR DIVORCE.
BUT YOU'LL WALK AWAY WITH A CRIMINAL RECORD FOR BATTERY.
IF I WERE THE JUDGE, I'D TAKE A REALLY CLOSE LOOK AT ALL THE MITIGATING FACTORS AND BE TEMPTED TO LET YOU OFF SCOT-FREE...
UNFORTU-NATELY, THOSE FACTORS WON'T AFFECT THE DECISION IN ANY MEANINGFUL WAY.
I KNOW.
AH WELL. YOU STILL HAVE SOME TIME YET.
THINK IT OVER CARE-FULLY. OKAY?

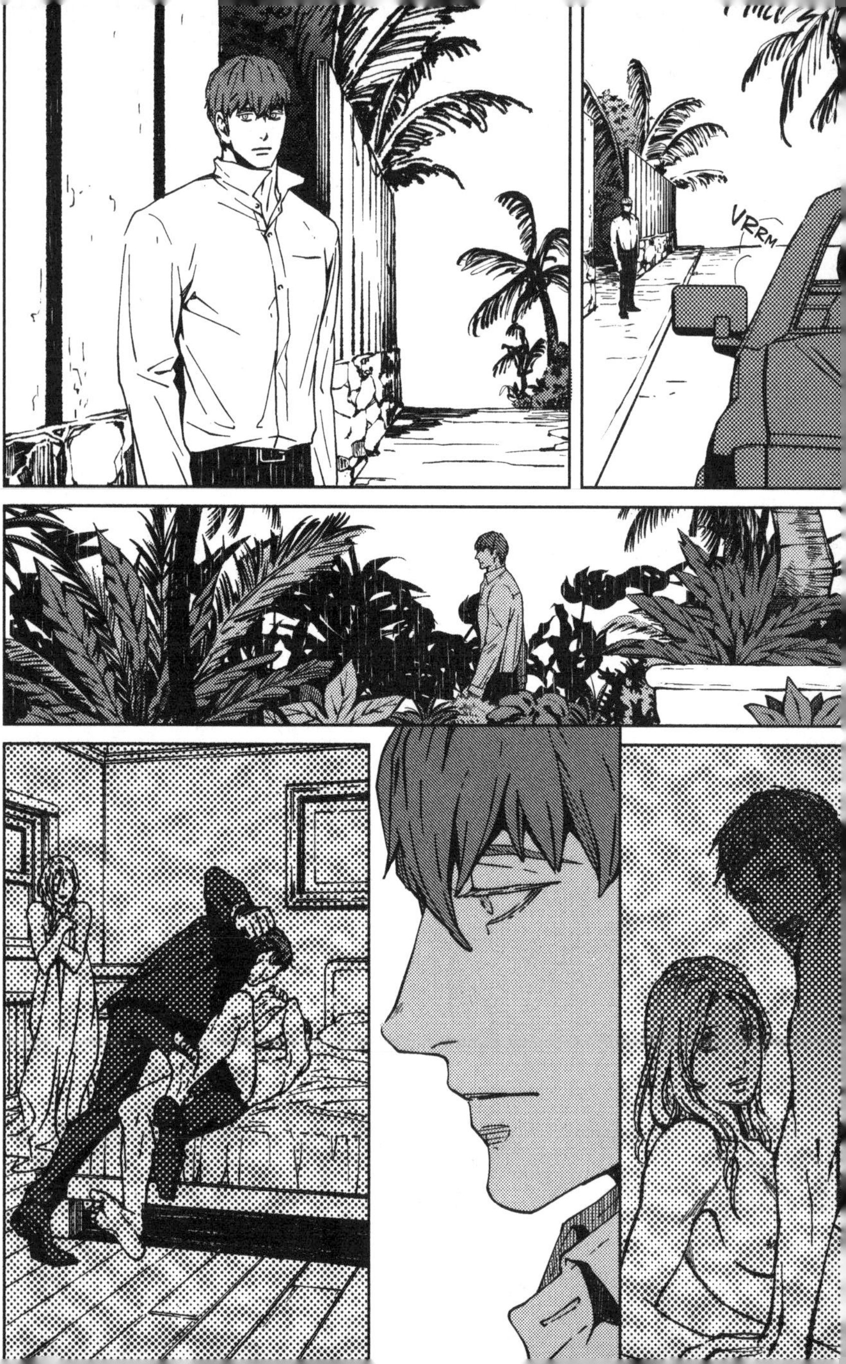
VRRM

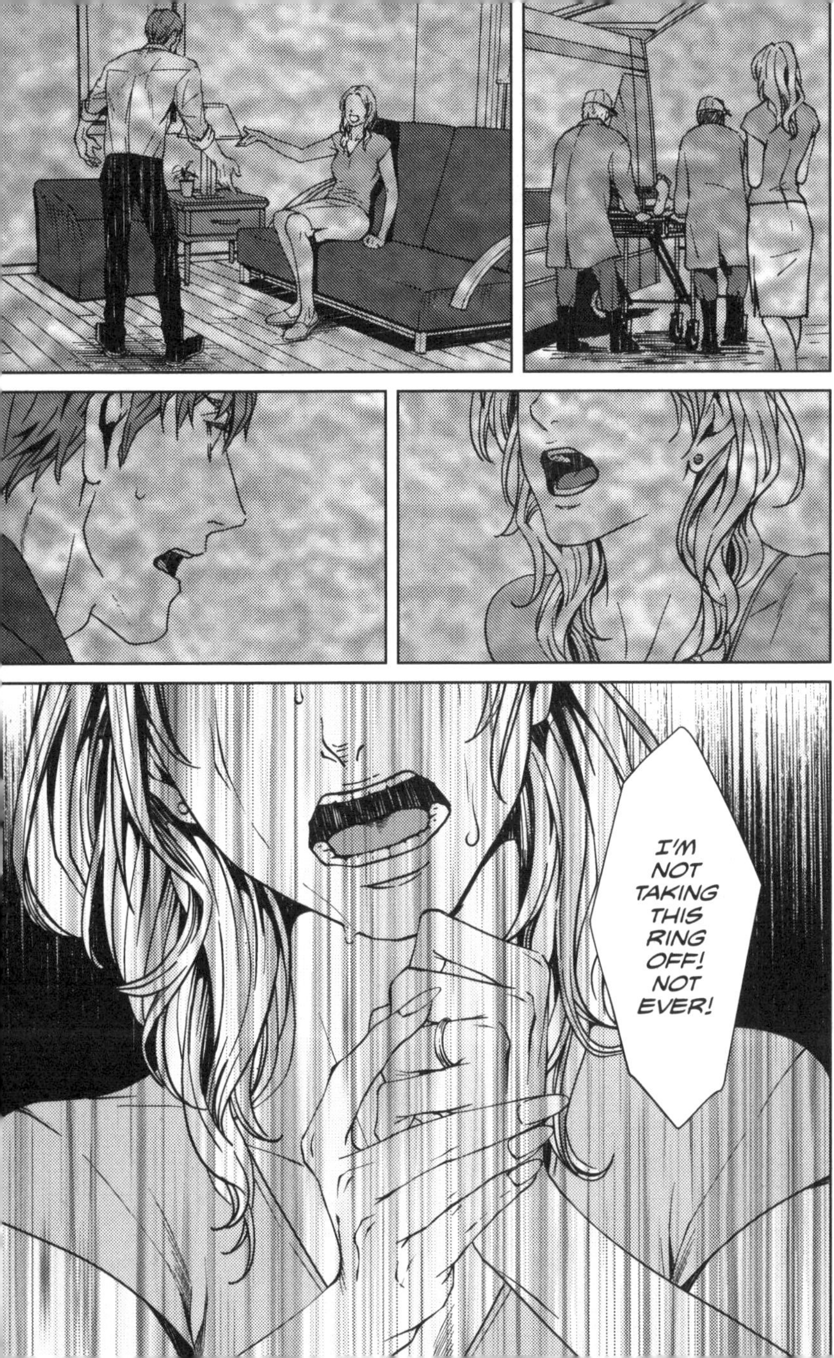
I'M NOT TAKING THIS RING OFF! NOT EVER!

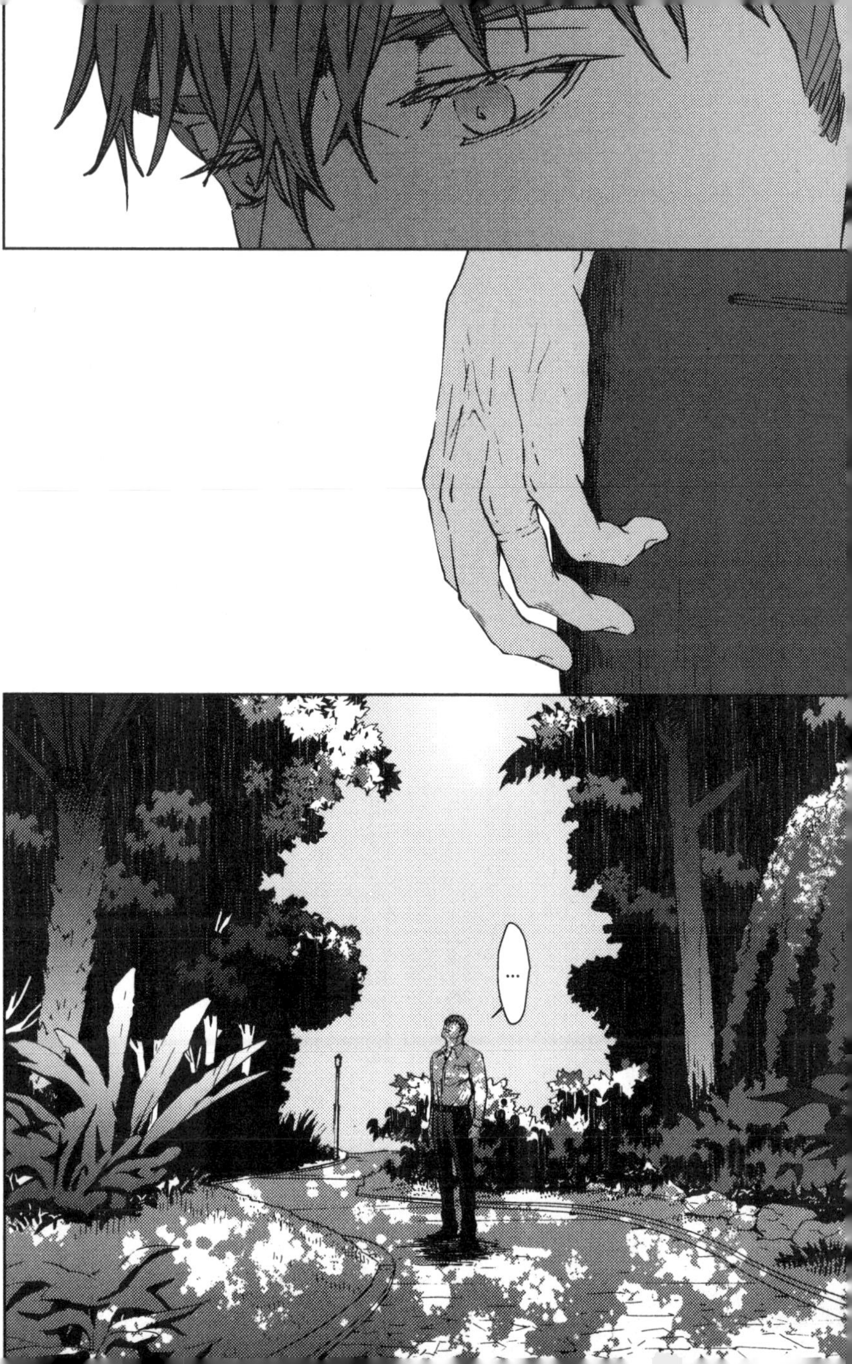
...

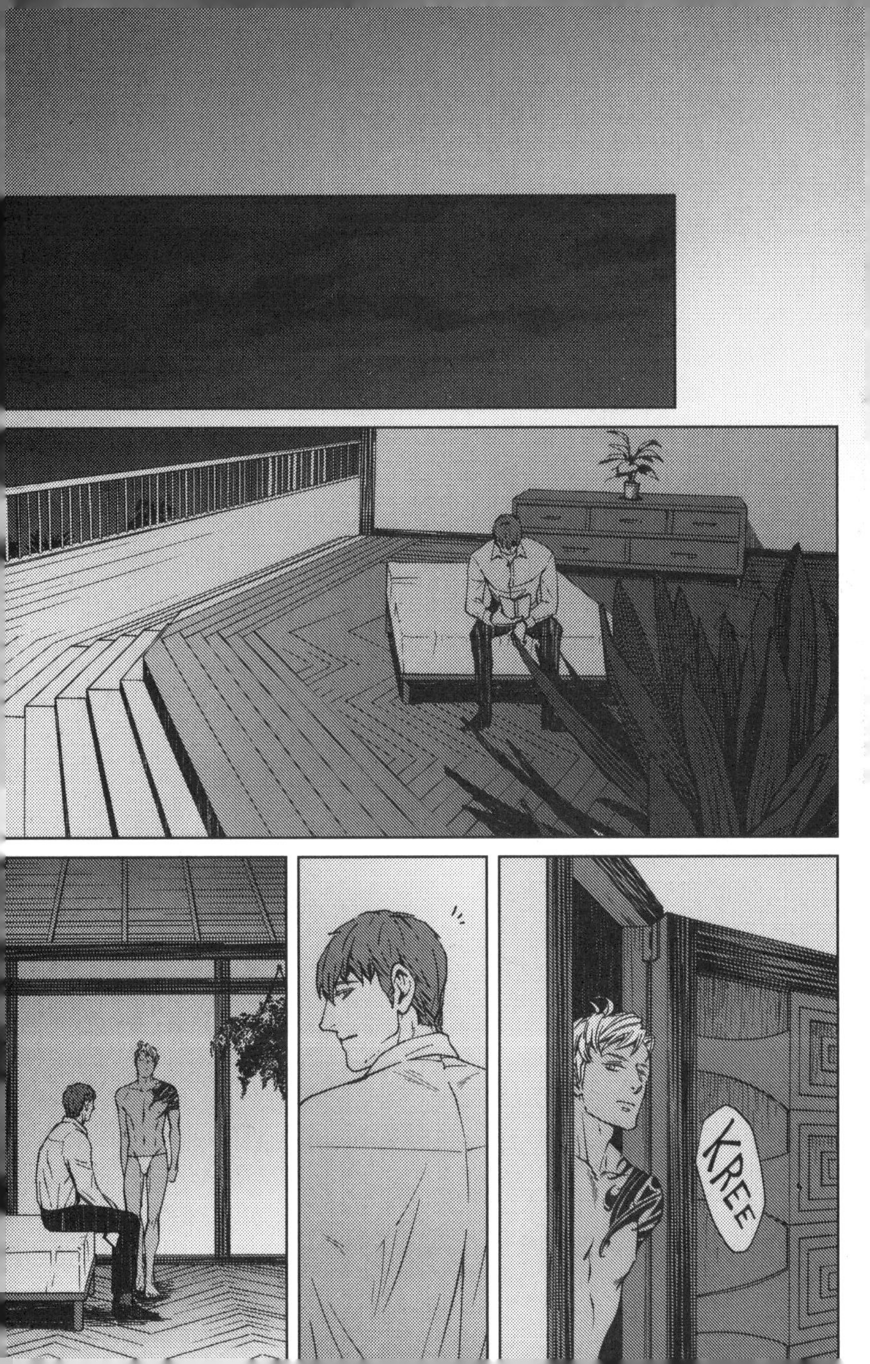
KREE

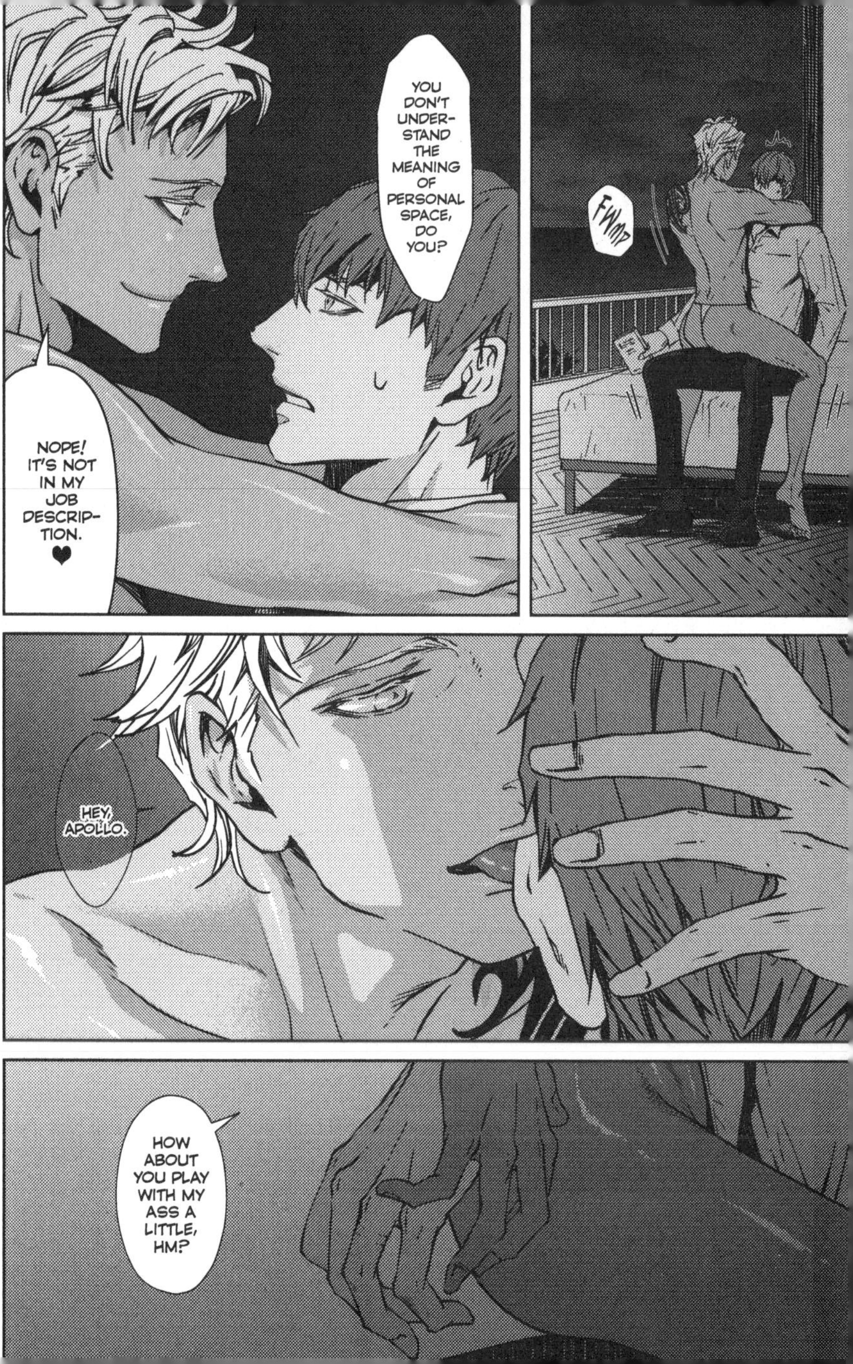
FWMP?
YOU DON'T UNDER-STAND THE MEANING OF PERSONAL SPACE, DO YOU?
NOPE! IT'S NOT IN MY JOB DESCRIP-TION. ♥
HEY, APOLLO.
HOW ABOUT YOU PLAY WITH MY ASS A LITTLE, HM?

FWMP
AAH ...
SLP
SLP
SLP
SLP

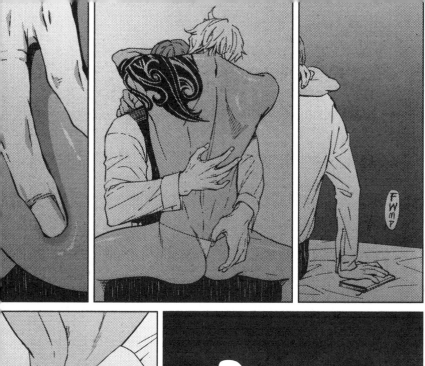

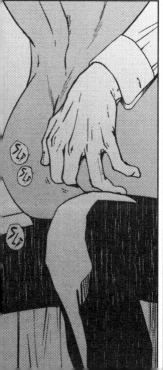

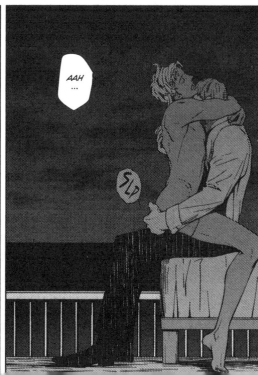

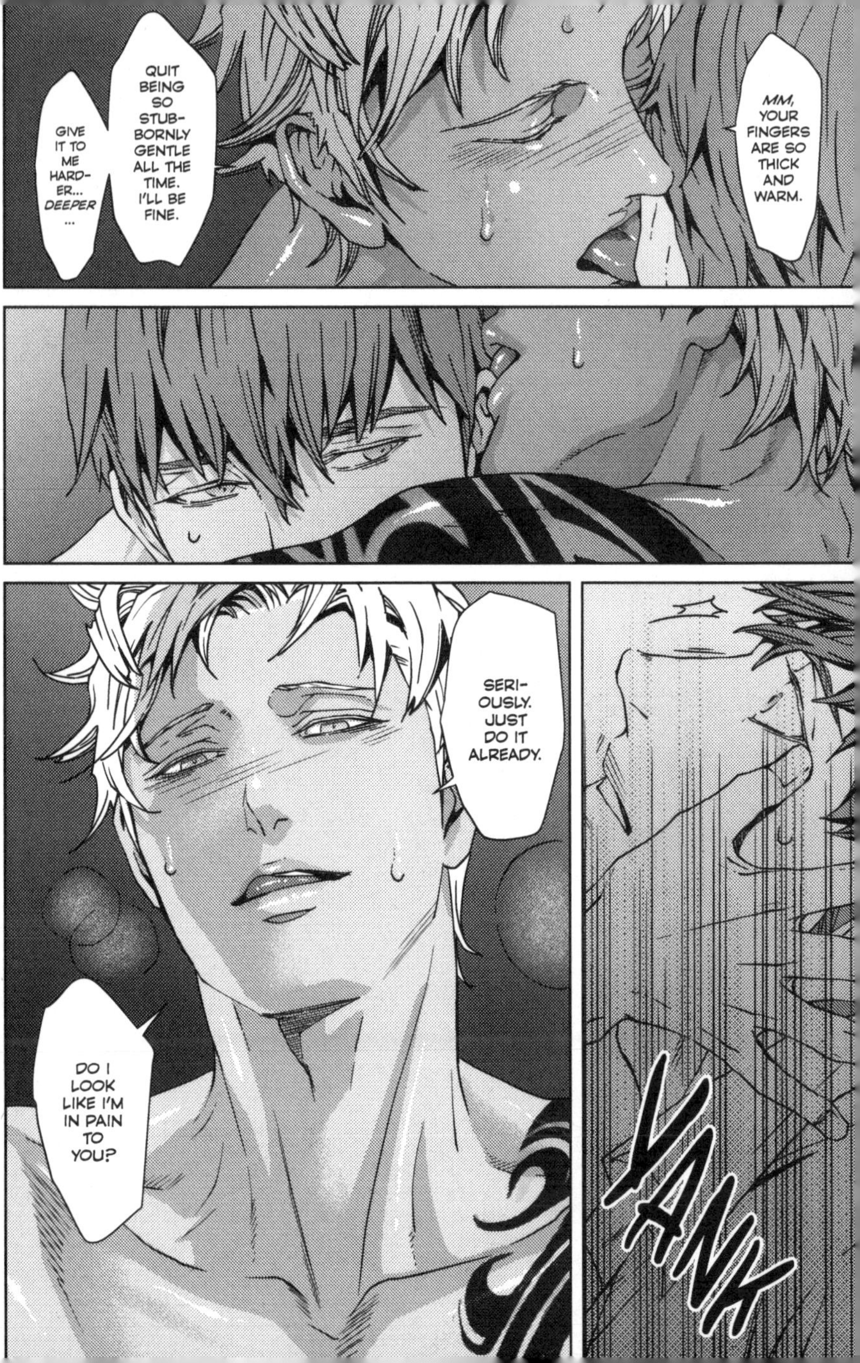
MM, YOUR FINGERS ARE SO THICK AND WARM.
QUIT BEING SO STUBBORNLY GENTLE ALL THE TIME. I'LL BE FINE.
GIVE IT TO ME HARDER... *DEEPER*...
YANK
SERIOUSLY. JUST DO IT ALREADY.
DO I LOOK LIKE I'M IN PAIN TO YOU?

S L U P

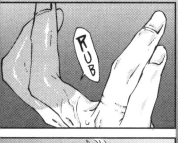

RUB

NN...
GOOD
BOY. ❤

NOW
SPREAD
YOUR
FINGERS
A LITTLE
AND
REALLY
GIVE
IT TO
ME...

AH!
NNH
•••

HAA
•••

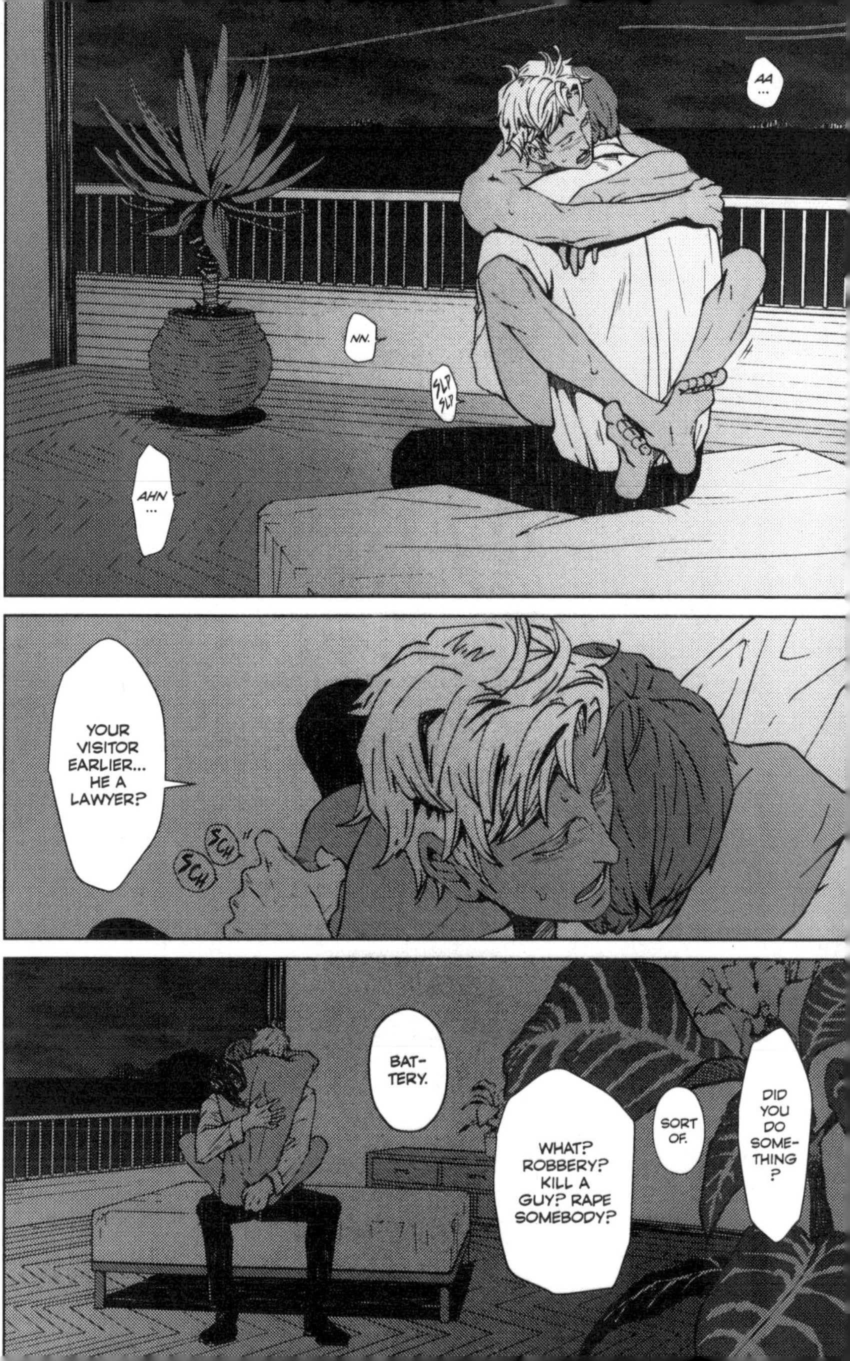
AA...
NN.
SLP SLP
AHN...
YOUR VISITOR EARLIER... HE A LAWYER?
SCH SCH
DID YOU DO SOME-THING?
SORT OF.
WHAT? ROBBERY? KILL A GUY? RAPE SOMEBODY?
BAT-TERY.

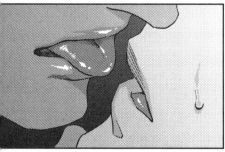

OH MY...

SO EVEN A GUY WITH HANDS AS GENTLE AND KIND AS YOURS WILL PUNCH A GUY, HM?

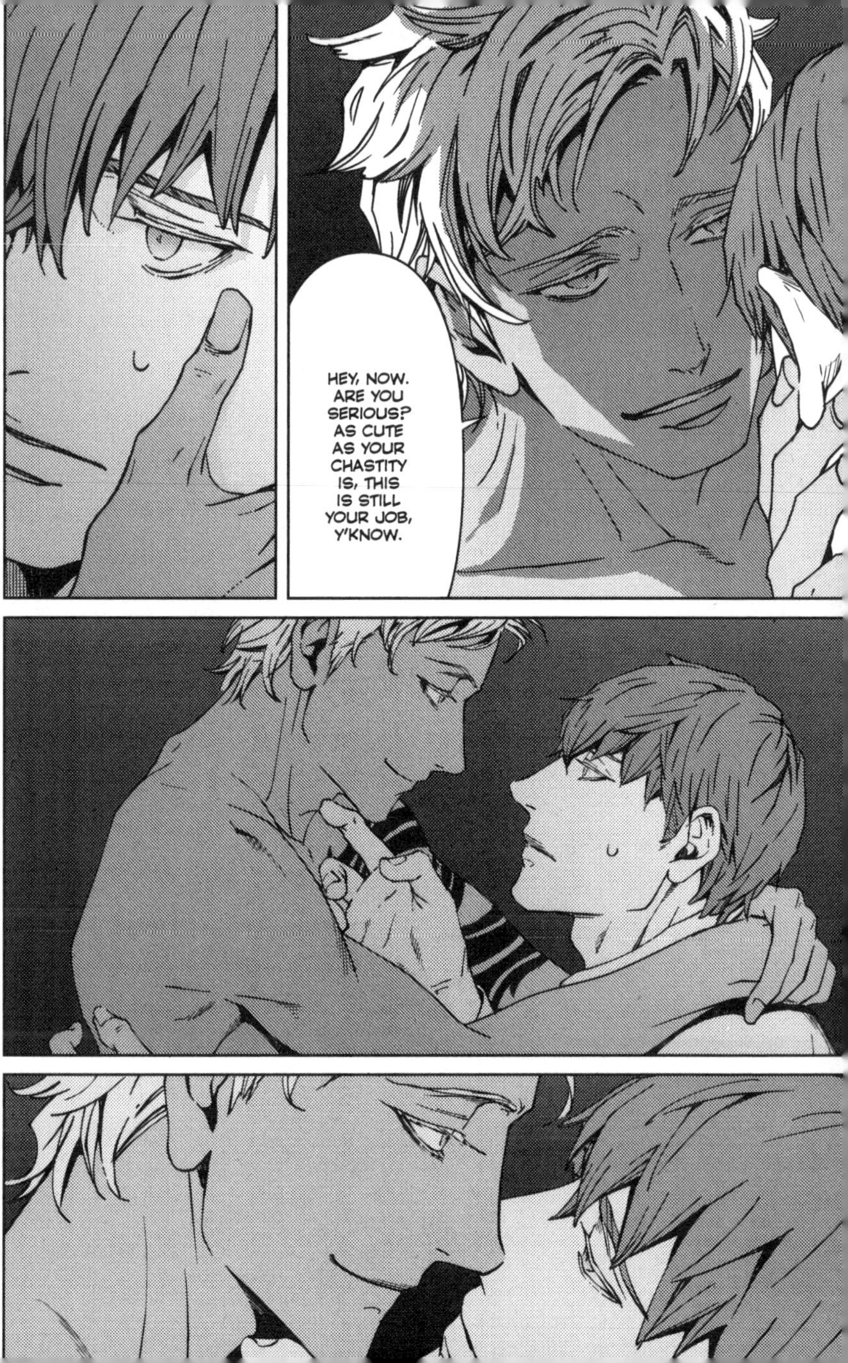
HEY, NOW. ARE YOU SERIOUS? AS CUTE AS YOUR CHASTITY IS, THIS IS STILL YOUR JOB, Y'KNOW.

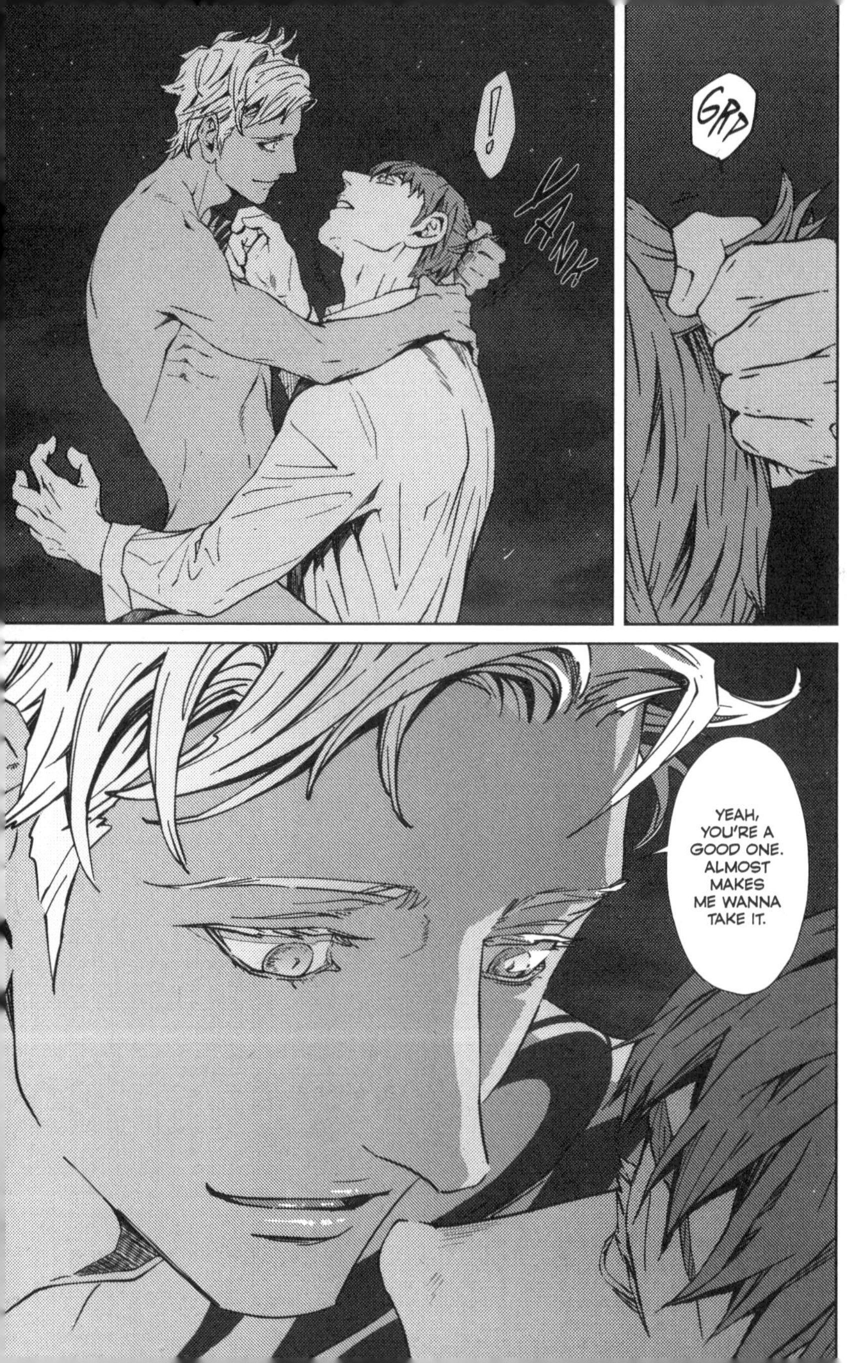
GRP
!
YANK
YEAH, YOU'RE A GOOD ONE. ALMOST MAKES ME WANNA TAKE IT.

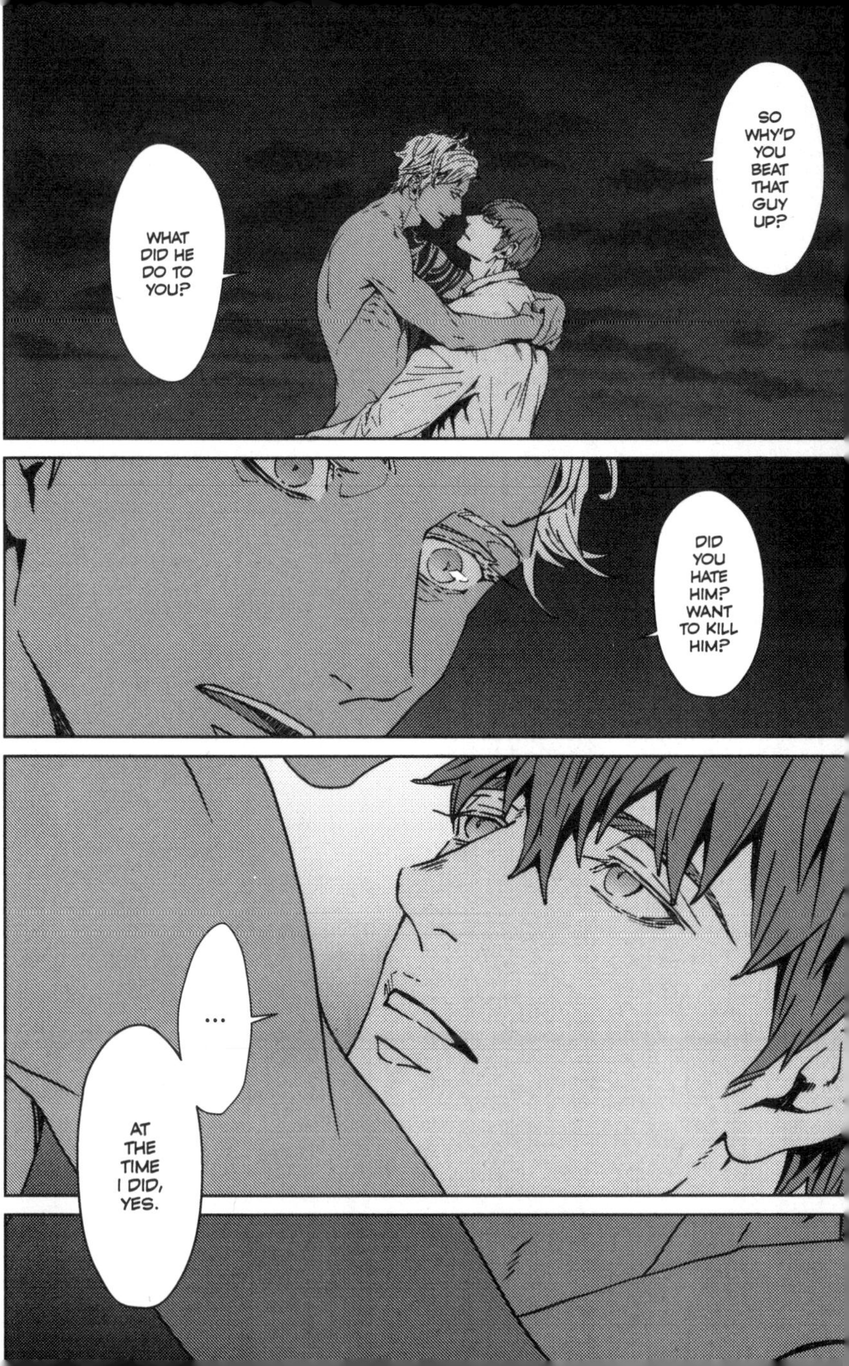
SO WHY'D YOU BEAT THAT GUY UP?
WHAT DID HE DO TO YOU?
DID YOU HATE HIM? WANT TO KILL HIM?
...
AT THE TIME I DID, YES.

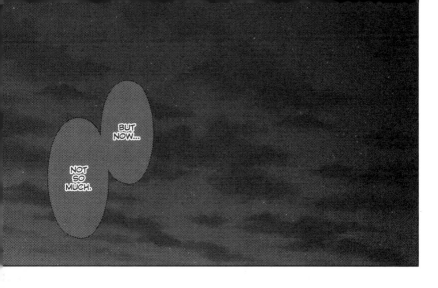

BUT NOW...

NOT SO MUCH.

FWISH

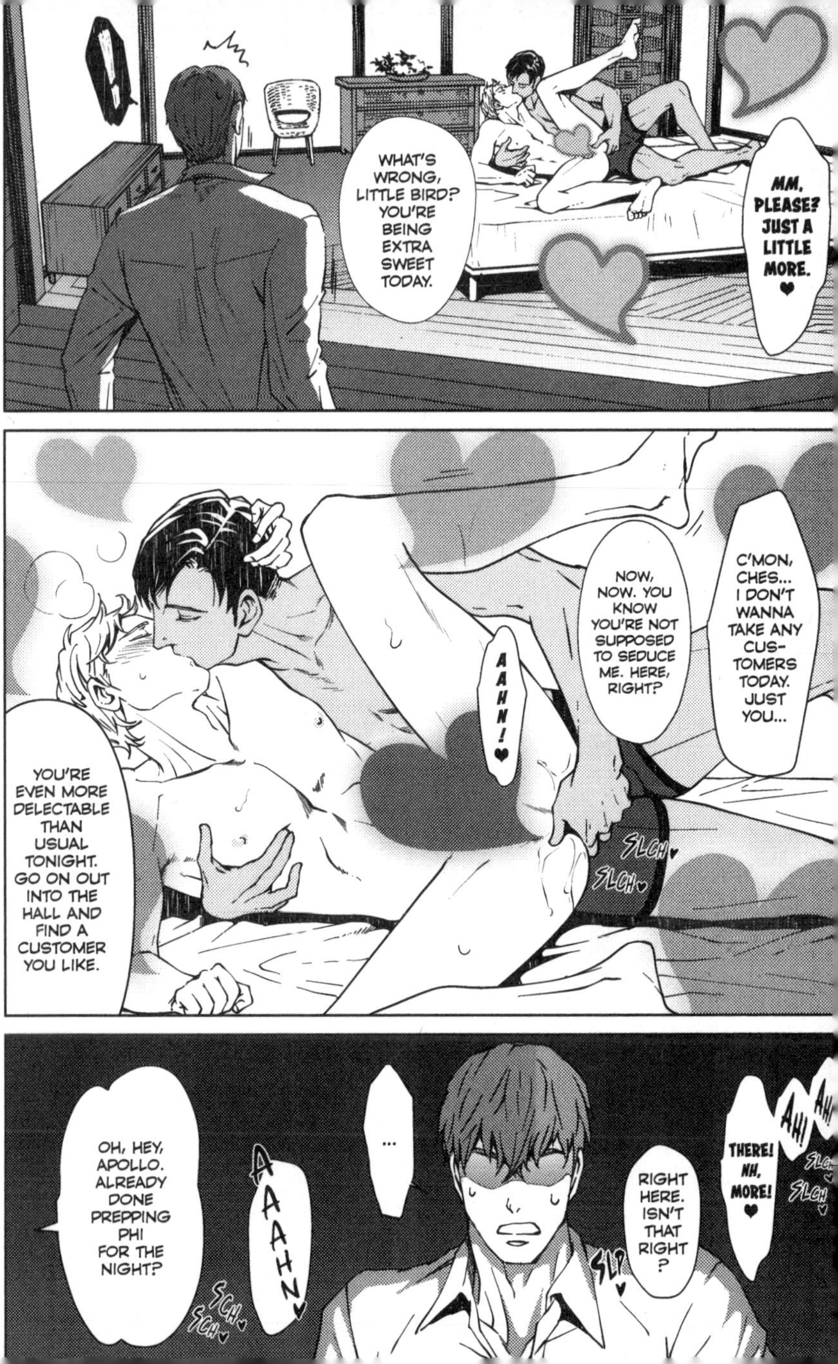
MM, PLEASE? JUST A LITTLE MORE. ♥
WHAT'S WRONG, LITTLE BIRD? YOU'RE BEING EXTRA SWEET TODAY.
C'MON, CHES... I DON'T WANNA TAKE ANY CUS-TOMERS TODAY. JUST YOU...
NOW, NOW. YOU KNOW YOU'RE NOT SUPPOSED TO SEDUCE ME. HERE, RIGHT?
AAHN! ♥
SLCH♥
SLCH♥
YOU'RE EVEN MORE DELECTABLE THAN USUAL TONIGHT. GO ON OUT INTO THE HALL AND FIND A CUSTOMER YOU LIKE.
AH! AH!
THERE! NH, MORE! ♥
SLCH SLCH
RIGHT HERE. ISN'T THAT RIGHT?
SLP♥
...
AAAHN♥
SCH SCH♥
OH, HEY, APOLLO. ALREADY DONE PREPPING PHI FOR THE NIGHT?

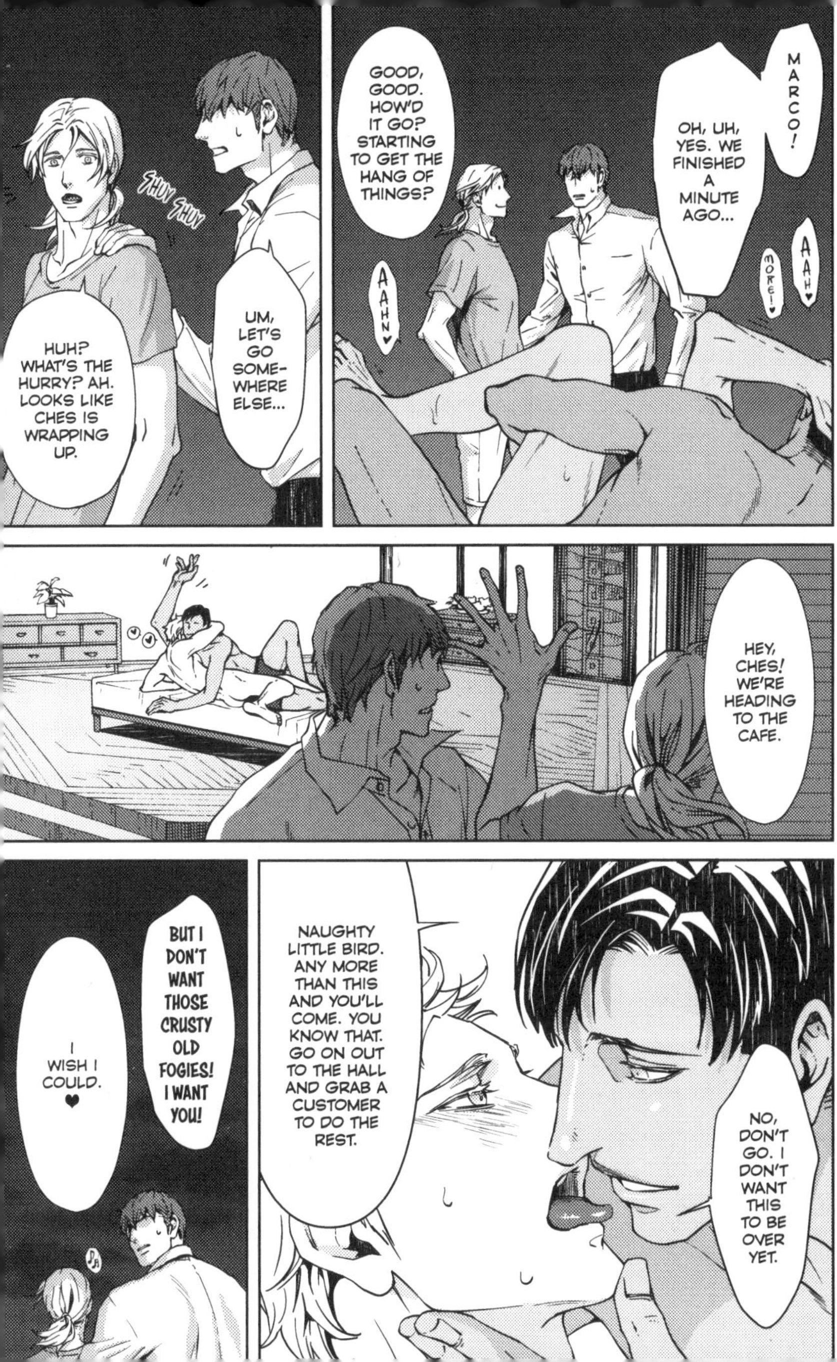
MARCO!
OH, UH, YES. WE FINISHED A MINUTE AGO...
AAH♥
MORE!
GOOD, GOOD. HOW'D IT GO? STARTING TO GET THE HANG OF THINGS?
AAHN♥
UM, LET'S GO SOME-WHERE ELSE...
SHUY SHUY
HUH? WHAT'S THE HURRY? AH. LOOKS LIKE CHES IS WRAPPING UP.
HEY, CHES! WE'RE HEADING TO THE CAFE.
NO, DON'T GO. I DON'T WANT THIS TO BE OVER YET.
NAUGHTY LITTLE BIRD. ANY MORE THAN THIS AND YOU'LL COME. YOU KNOW THAT. GO ON OUT TO THE HALL AND GRAB A CUSTOMER TO DO THE REST.
BUT I DON'T WANT THOSE CRUSTY OLD FOGIES! I WANT YOU!
I WISH I COULD. ♥

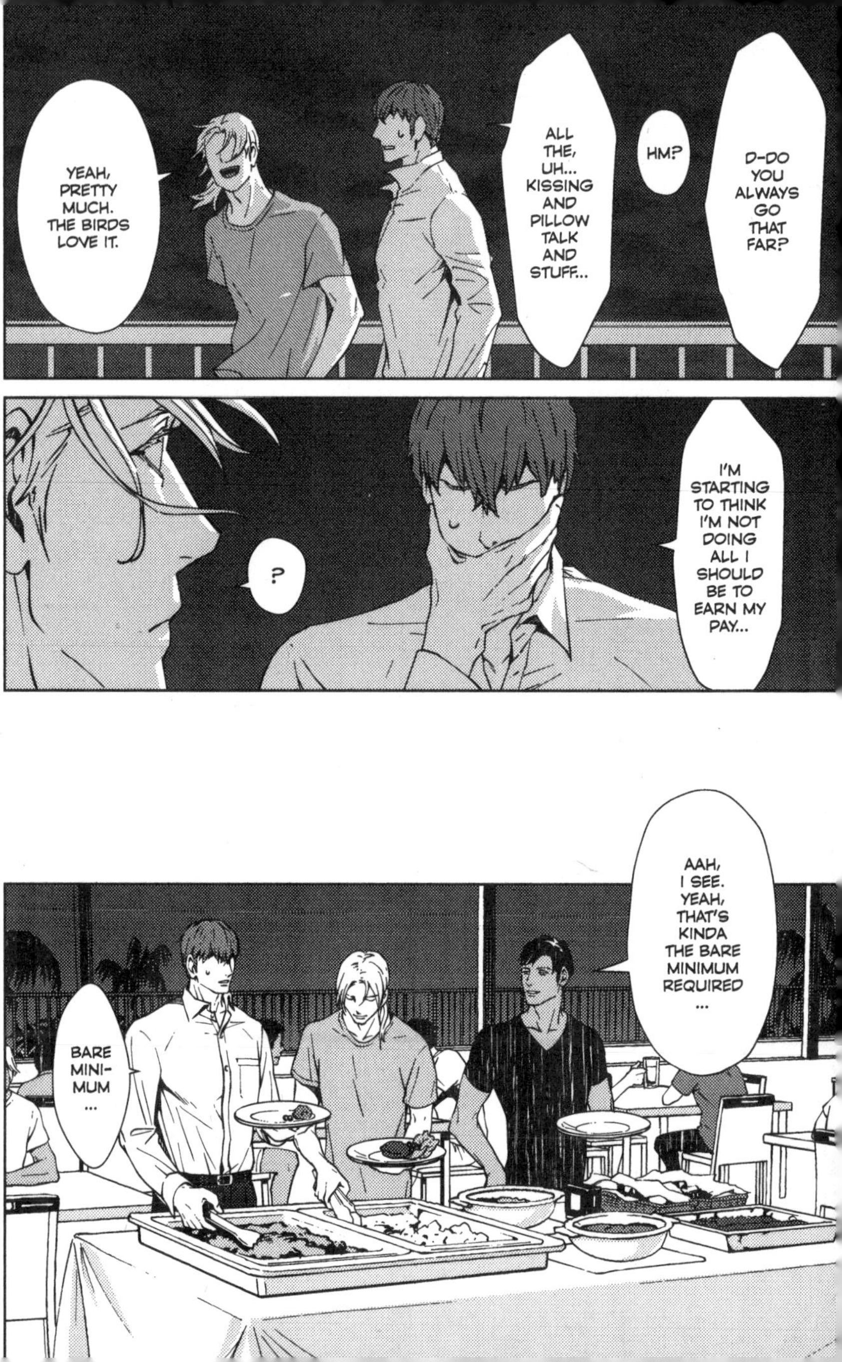
D-DO YOU ALWAYS GO THAT FAR?
HM?
ALL THE, UH... KISSING AND PILLOW TALK AND STUFF...
YEAH, PRETTY MUCH. THE BIRDS LOVE IT.
I'M STARTING TO THINK I'M NOT DOING ALL I SHOULD BE TO EARN MY PAY...
?
AAH, I SEE. YEAH, THAT'S KINDA THE BARE MINIMUM REQUIRED...
BARE MINI-MUM...

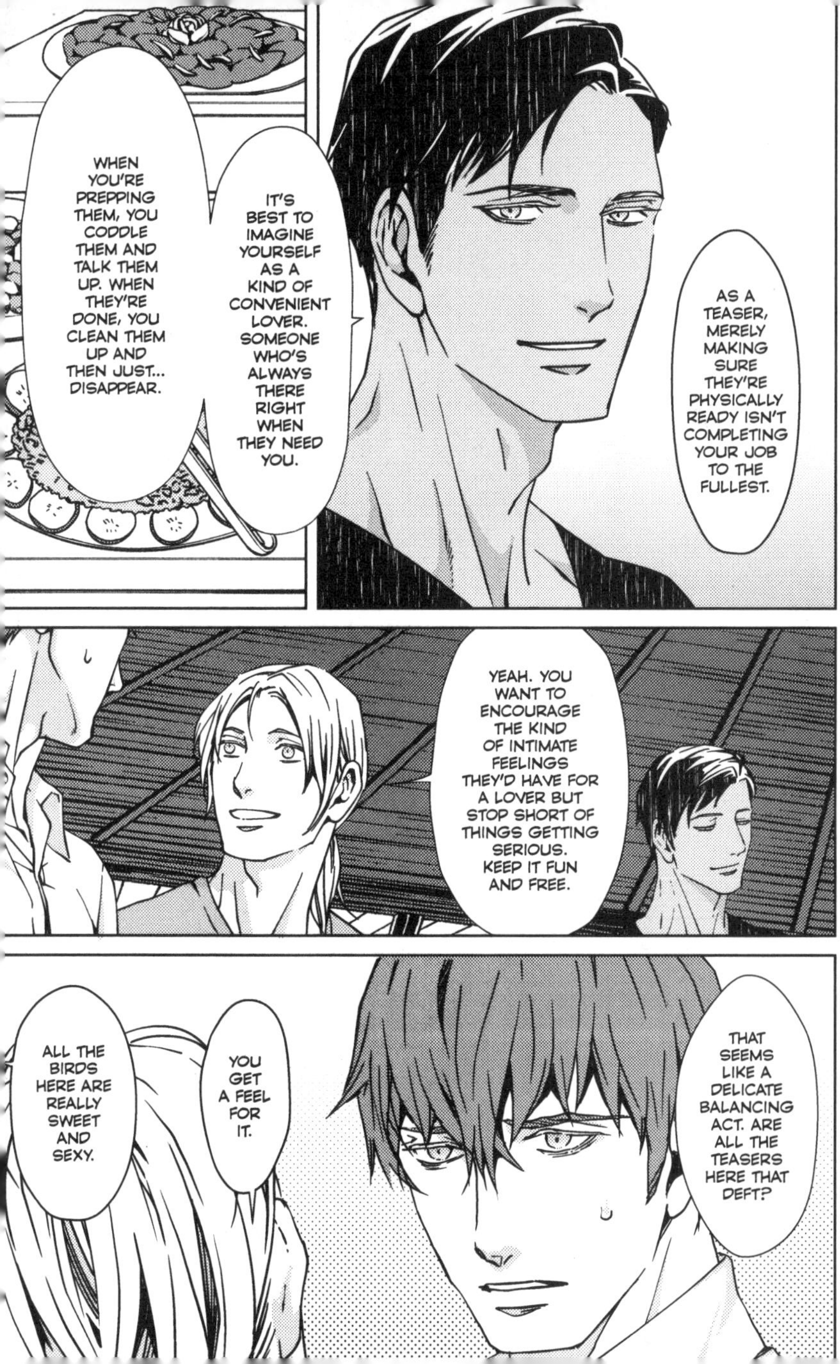
AS A TEASER, MERELY MAKING SURE THEY'RE PHYSICALLY READY ISN'T COMPLETING YOUR JOB TO THE FULLEST.
IT'S BEST TO IMAGINE YOURSELF AS A KIND OF CONVENIENT LOVER. SOMEONE WHO'S ALWAYS THERE RIGHT WHEN THEY NEED YOU.
WHEN YOU'RE PREPPING THEM, YOU CODDLE THEM AND TALK THEM UP. WHEN THEY'RE DONE, YOU CLEAN THEM UP AND THEN JUST... DISAPPEAR.
YEAH. YOU WANT TO ENCOURAGE THE KIND OF INTIMATE FEELINGS THEY'D HAVE FOR A LOVER BUT STOP SHORT OF THINGS GETTING SERIOUS. KEEP IT FUN AND FREE.
THAT SEEMS LIKE A DELICATE BALANCING ACT. ARE ALL THE TEASERS HERE THAT DEFT?
YOU GET A FEEL FOR IT.
ALL THE BIRDS HERE ARE REALLY SWEET AND SEXY.

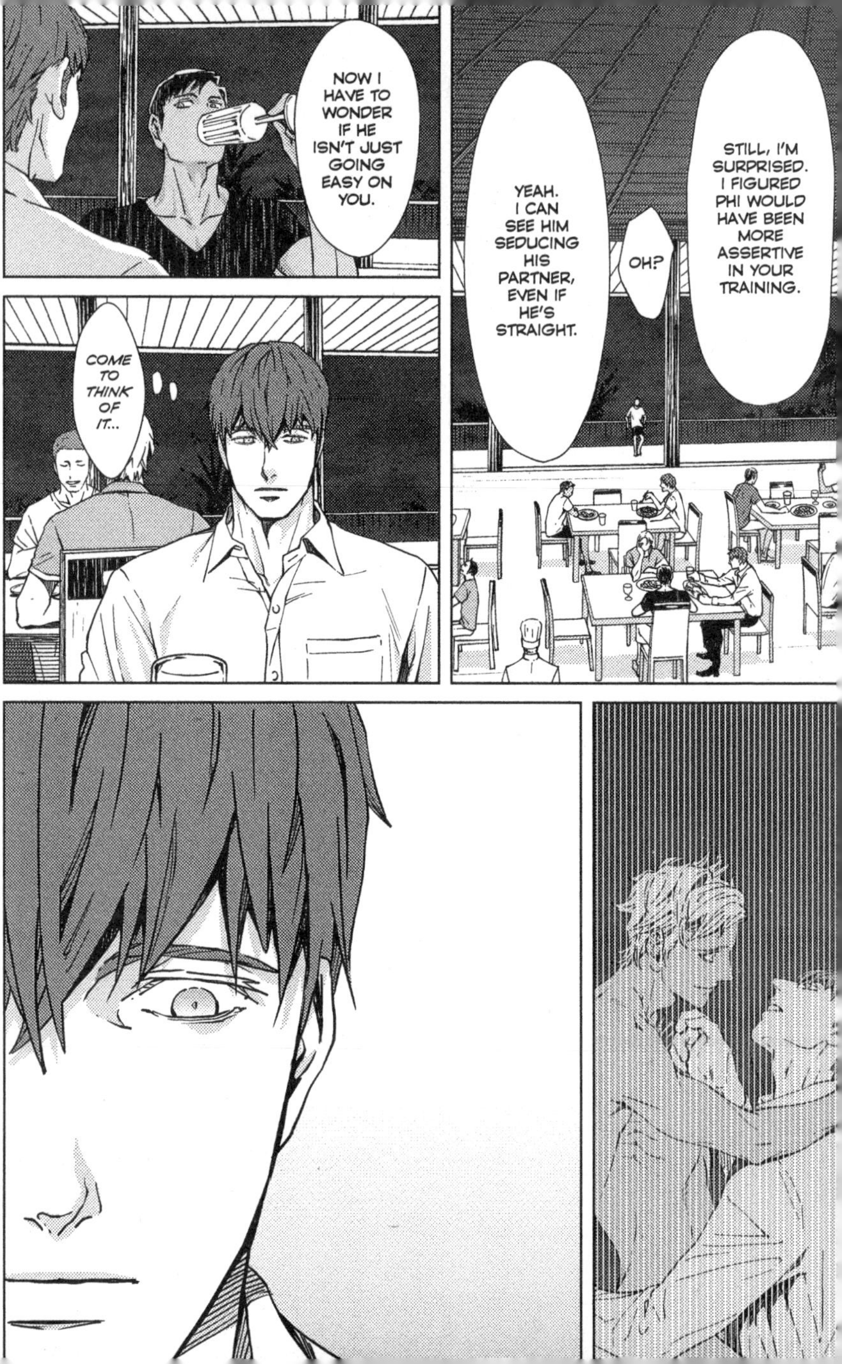
STILL, I'M SURPRISED. I FIGURED PHI WOULD HAVE BEEN MORE ASSERTIVE IN YOUR TRAINING.
OH?
YEAH. I CAN SEE HIM SEDUCING HIS PARTNER, EVEN IF HE'S STRAIGHT.
NOW I HAVE TO WONDER IF HE ISN'T JUST GOING EASY ON YOU.
COME TO THINK OF IT...

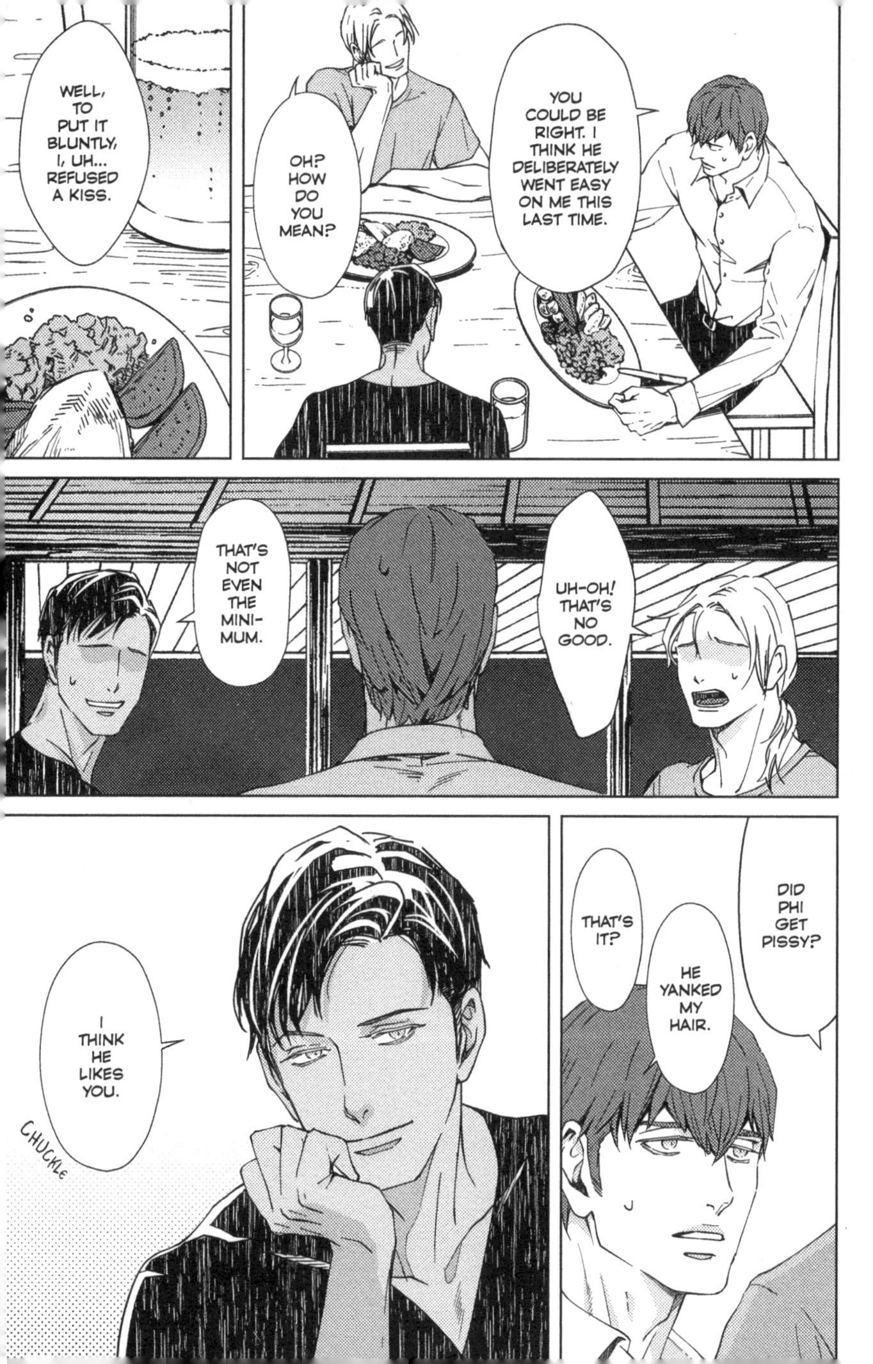
YOU COULD BE RIGHT. I THINK HE DELIBERATELY WENT EASY ON ME THIS LAST TIME.
OH? HOW DO YOU MEAN?
WELL, TO PUT IT BLUNTLY, I, UH... REFUSED A KISS.
UH-OH! THAT'S NO GOOD.
THAT'S NOT EVEN THE MINI-MUM.
DID PHI GET PISSY?
HE YANKED MY HAIR.
THAT'S IT?
I THINK HE LIKES YOU.
CHUCKLE

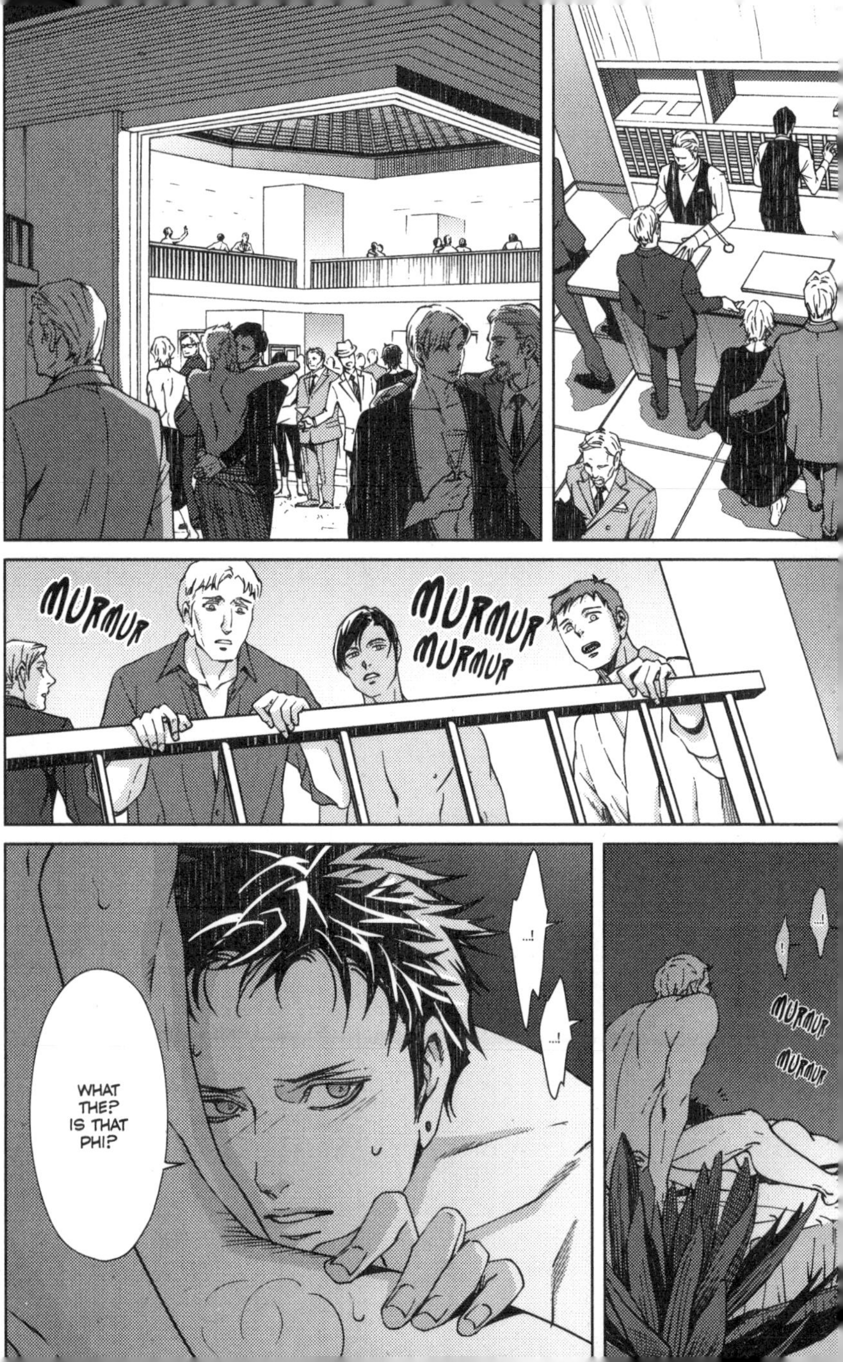
MURMUR
MURMUR
MURMUR
...!
!
MURMUR
MURMUR
...!
...!
WHAT THE? IS THAT PHI?

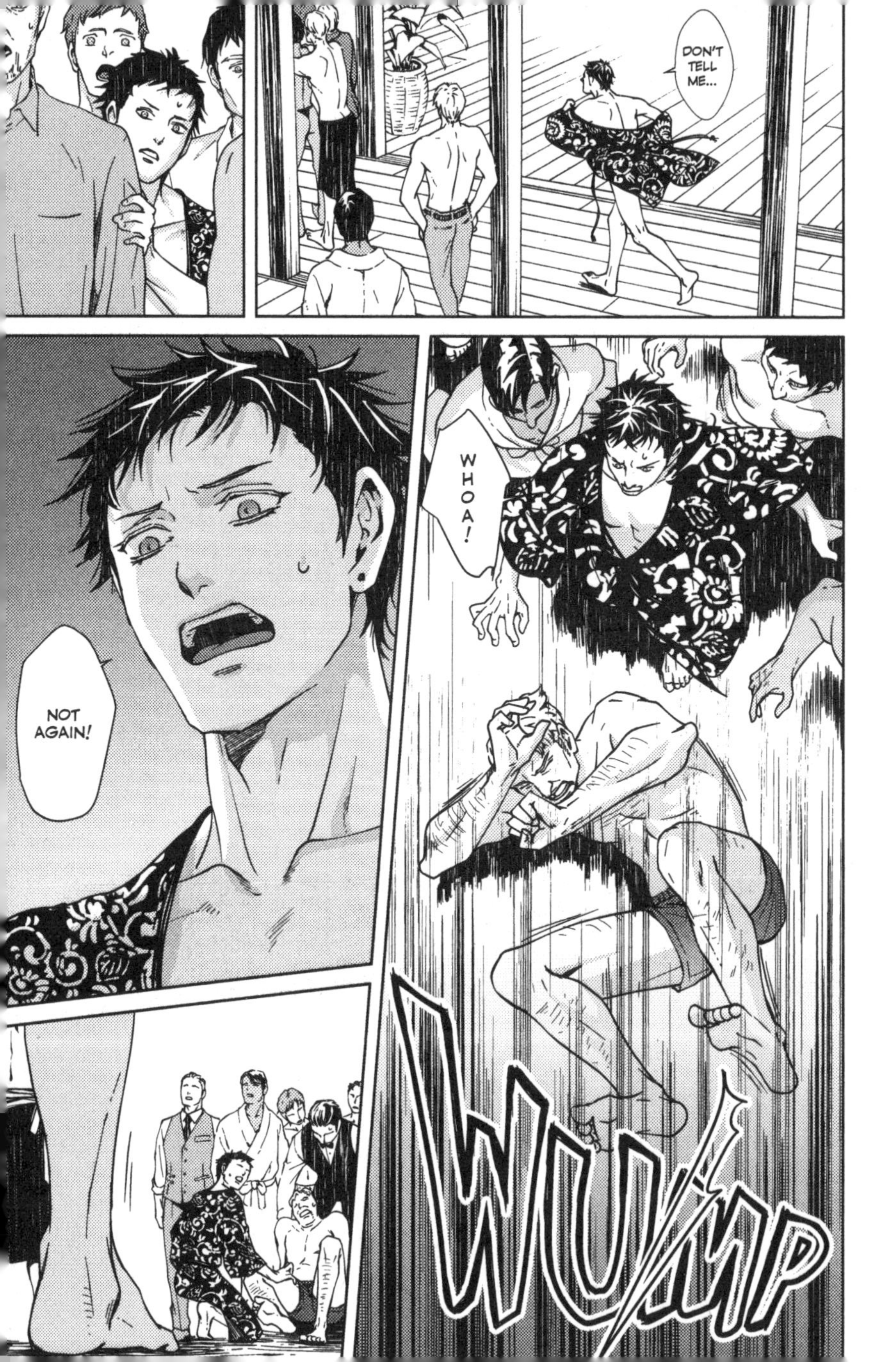
DON'T TELL ME...
WHOA!
WUMP
NOT AGAIN!

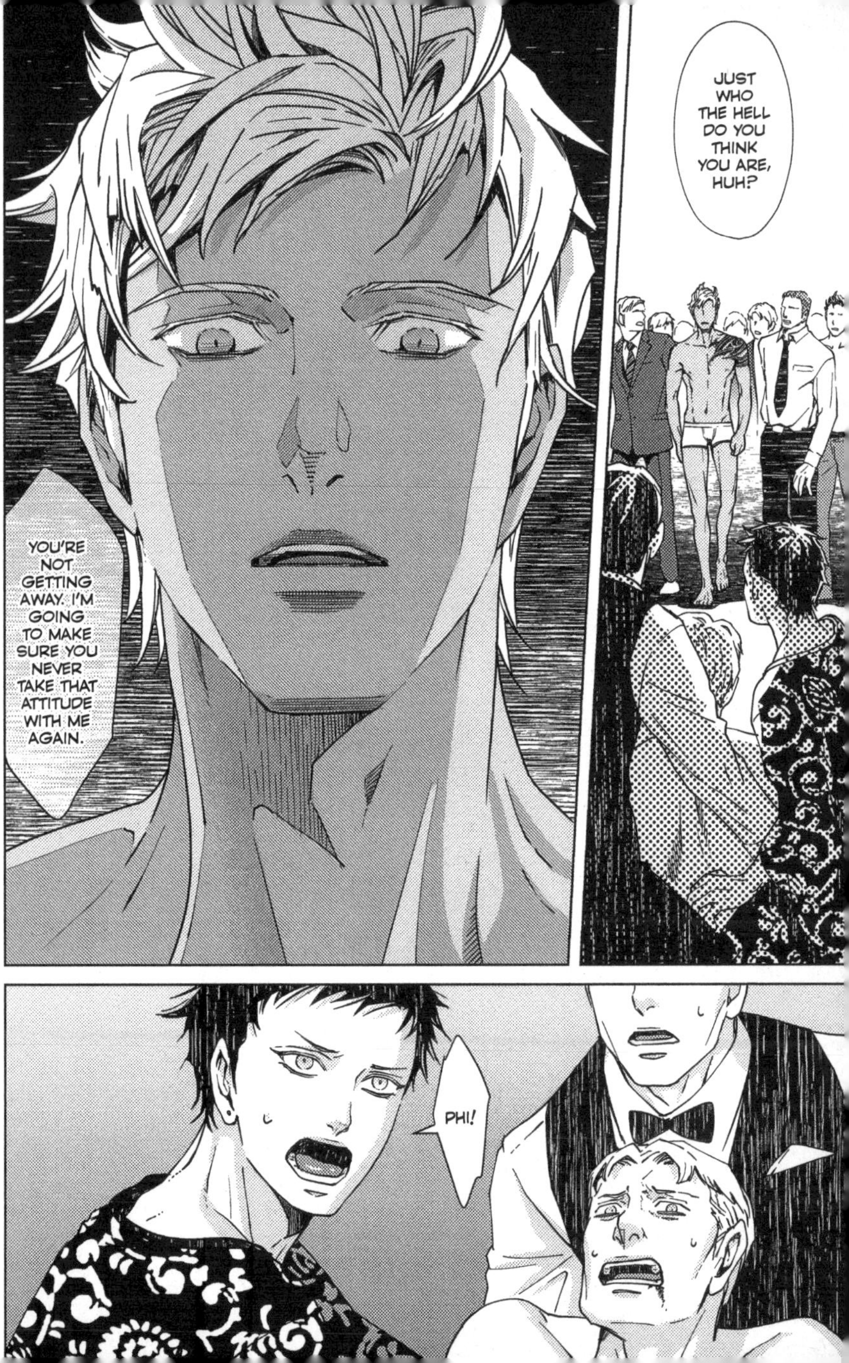
JUST WHO THE HELL DO YOU THINK YOU ARE, HUH?
YOU'RE NOT GETTING AWAY. I'M GOING TO MAKE SURE YOU NEVER TAKE THAT ATTITUDE WITH ME AGAIN.
PHI!

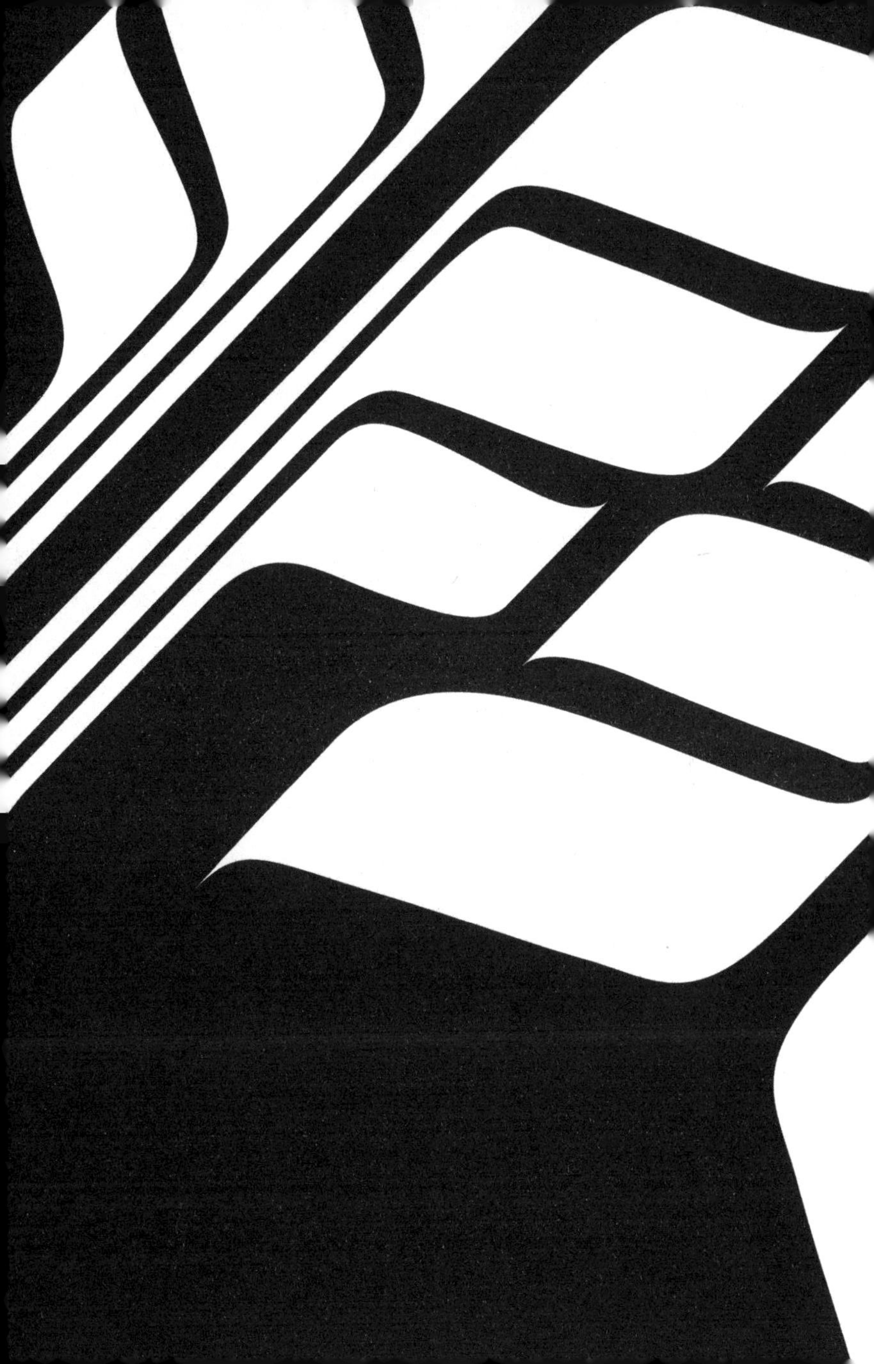

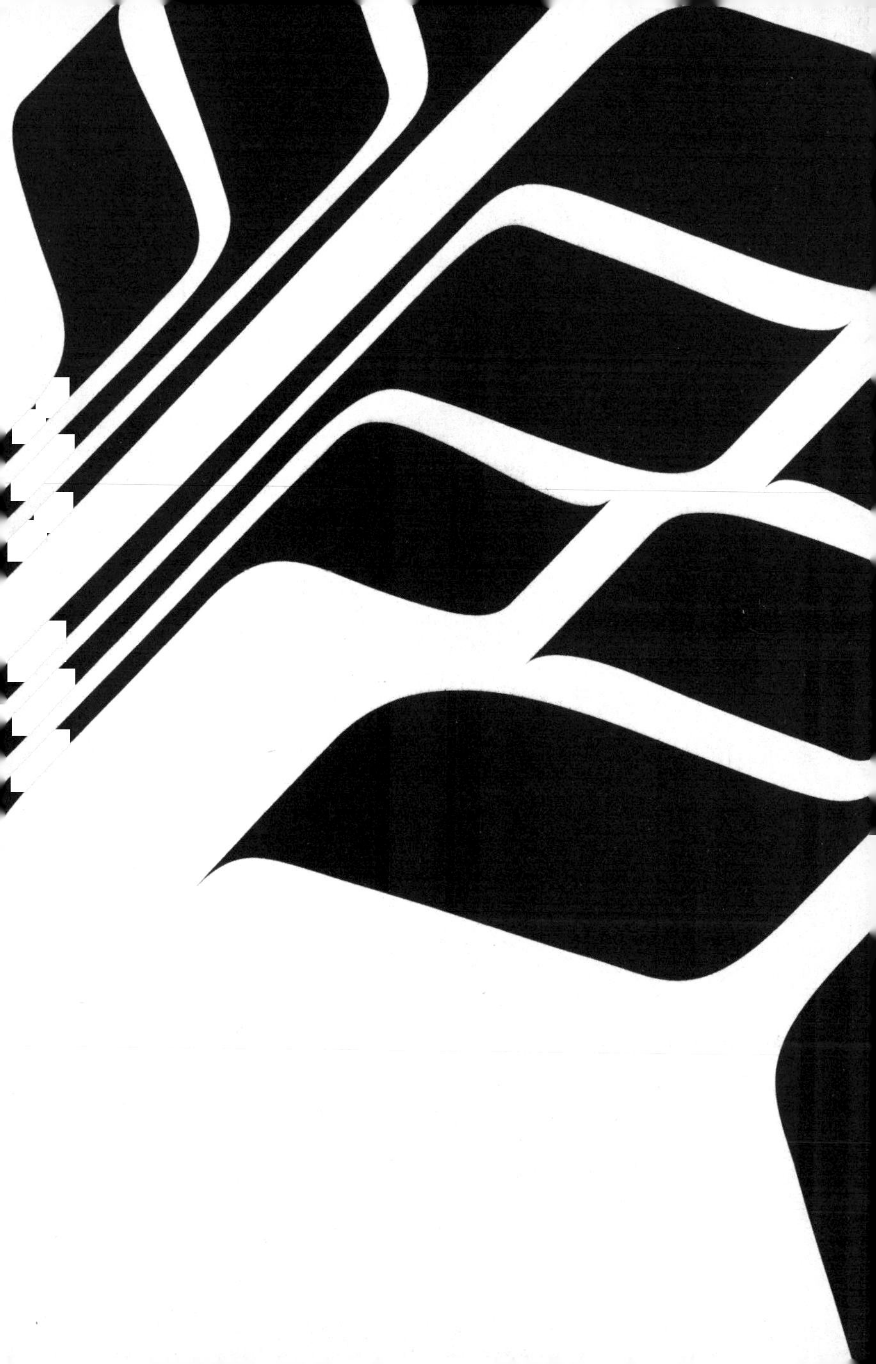

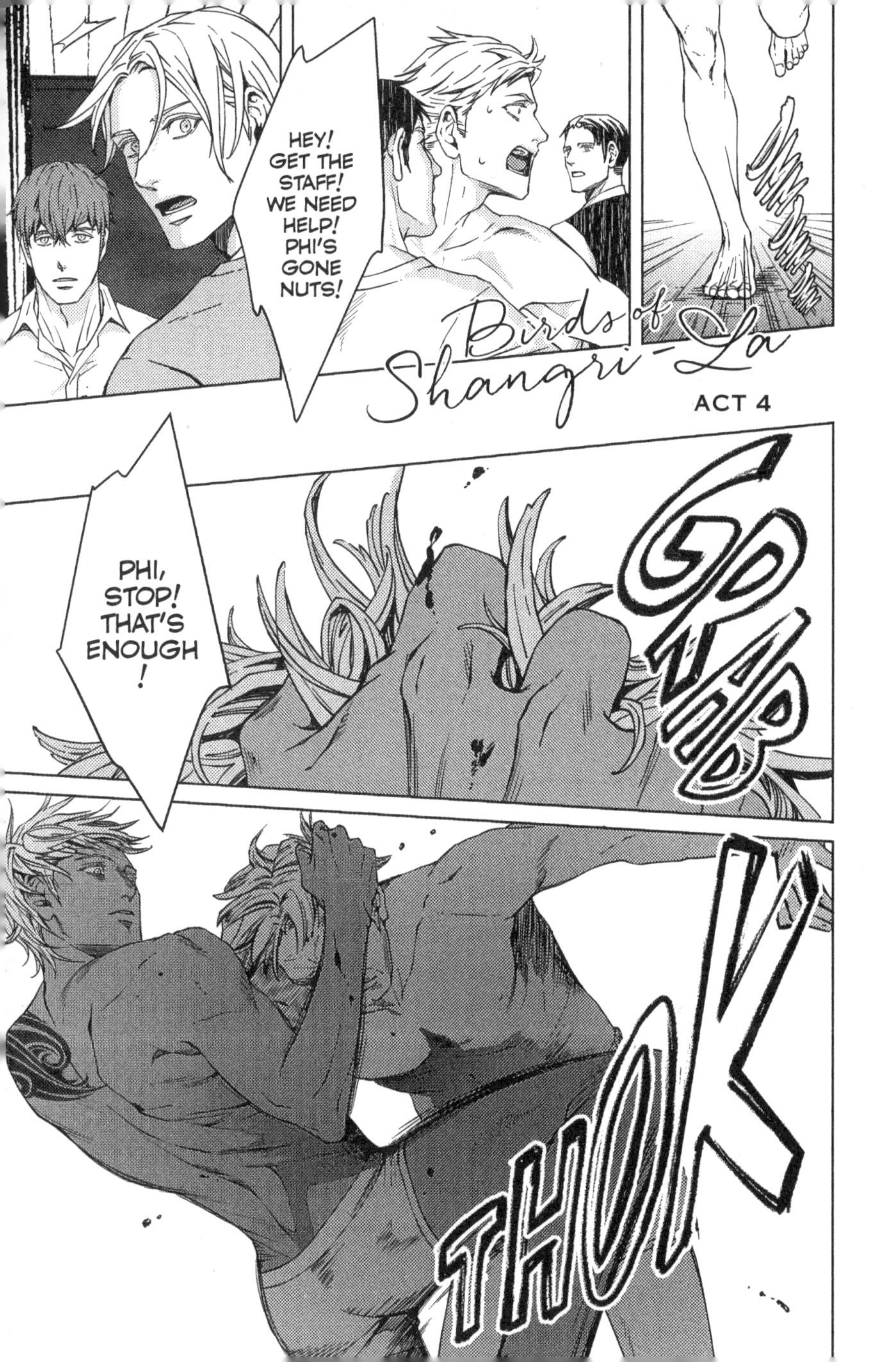
HEY! GET THE STAFF! WE NEED HELP! PHI'S GONE NUTS!
Birds of Shangri-La
ACT 4
PHI, STOP! THAT'S ENOUGH!
GRAB
THOK

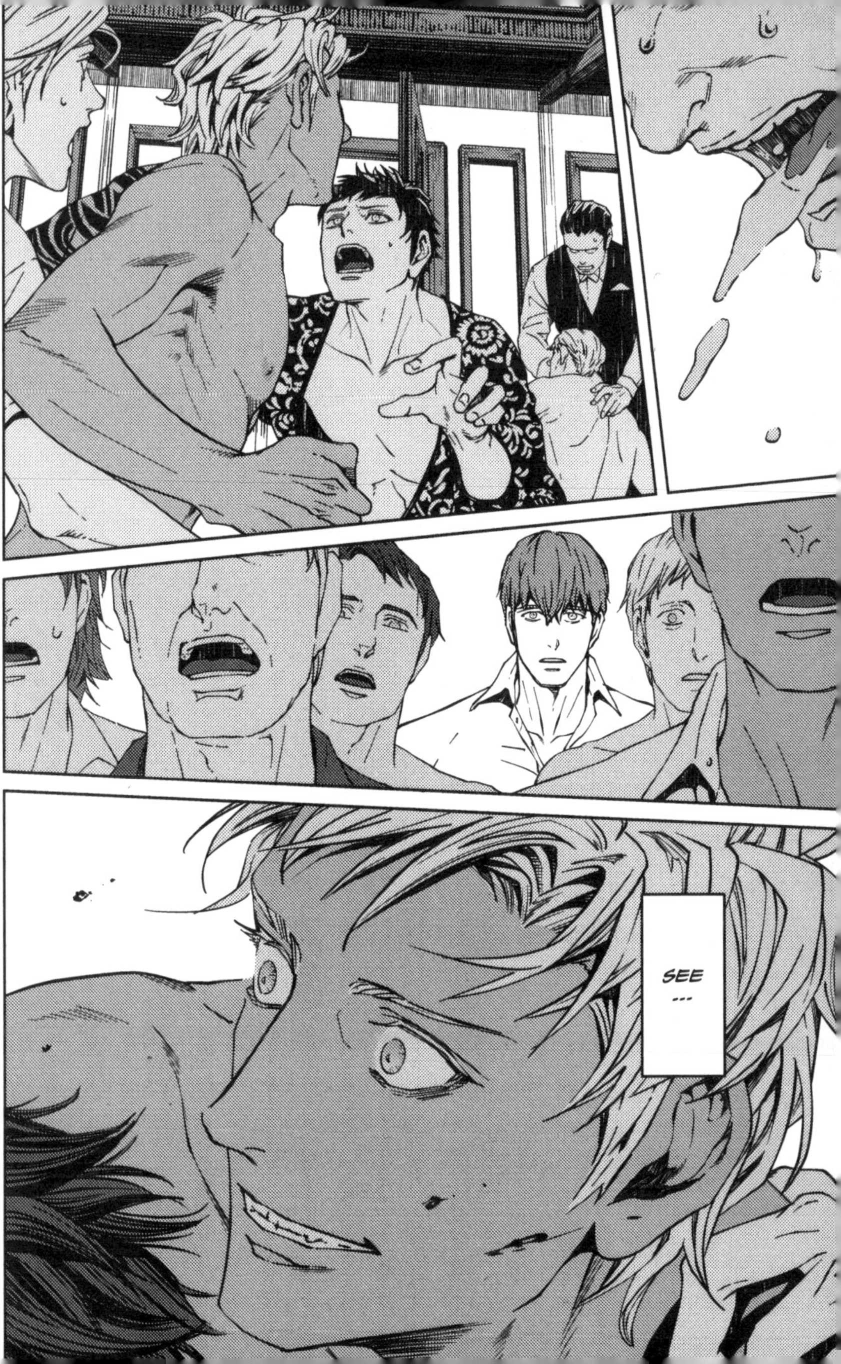
SEE ...

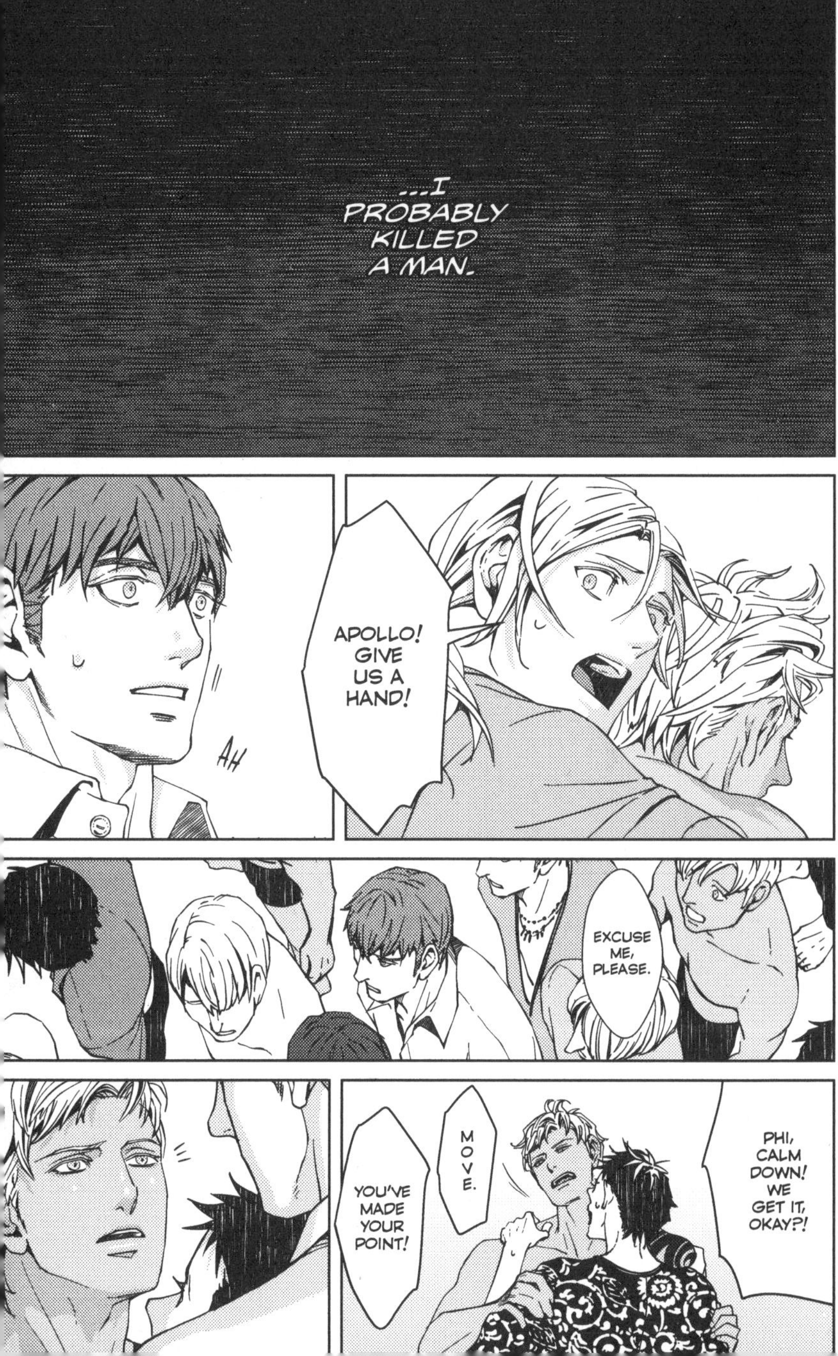
...I PROBABLY KILLED A MAN.
APOLLO! GIVE US A HAND!
AH
EXCUSE ME, PLEASE.
PHI, CALM DOWN! WE GET IT, OKAY?!
MOVE.
YOU'VE MADE YOUR POINT!

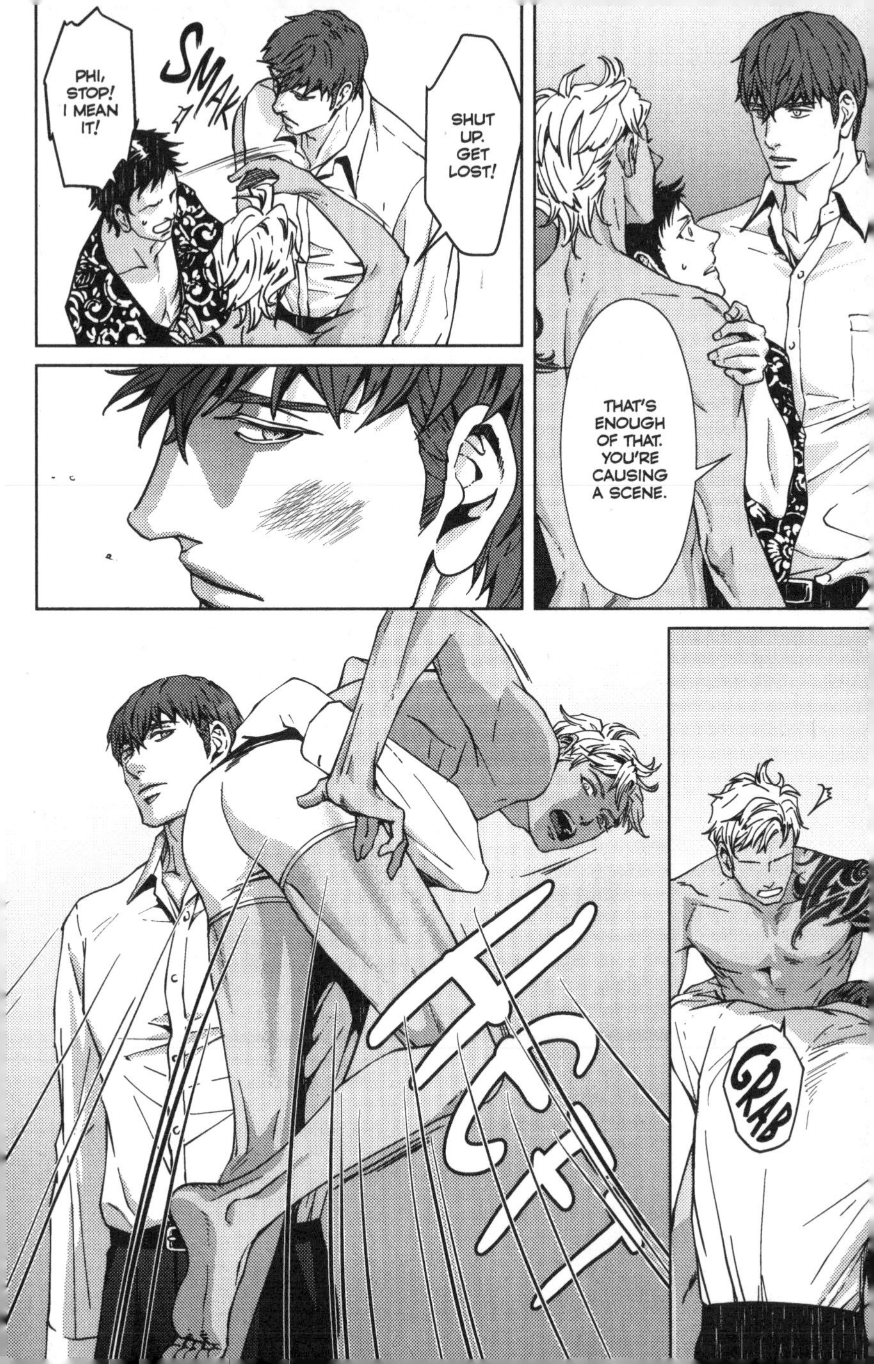
THAT'S ENOUGH OF THAT. YOU'RE CAUSING A SCENE.
SHUT UP. GET LOST!
SMAK
PHI, STOP! I MEAN IT!
GRAB

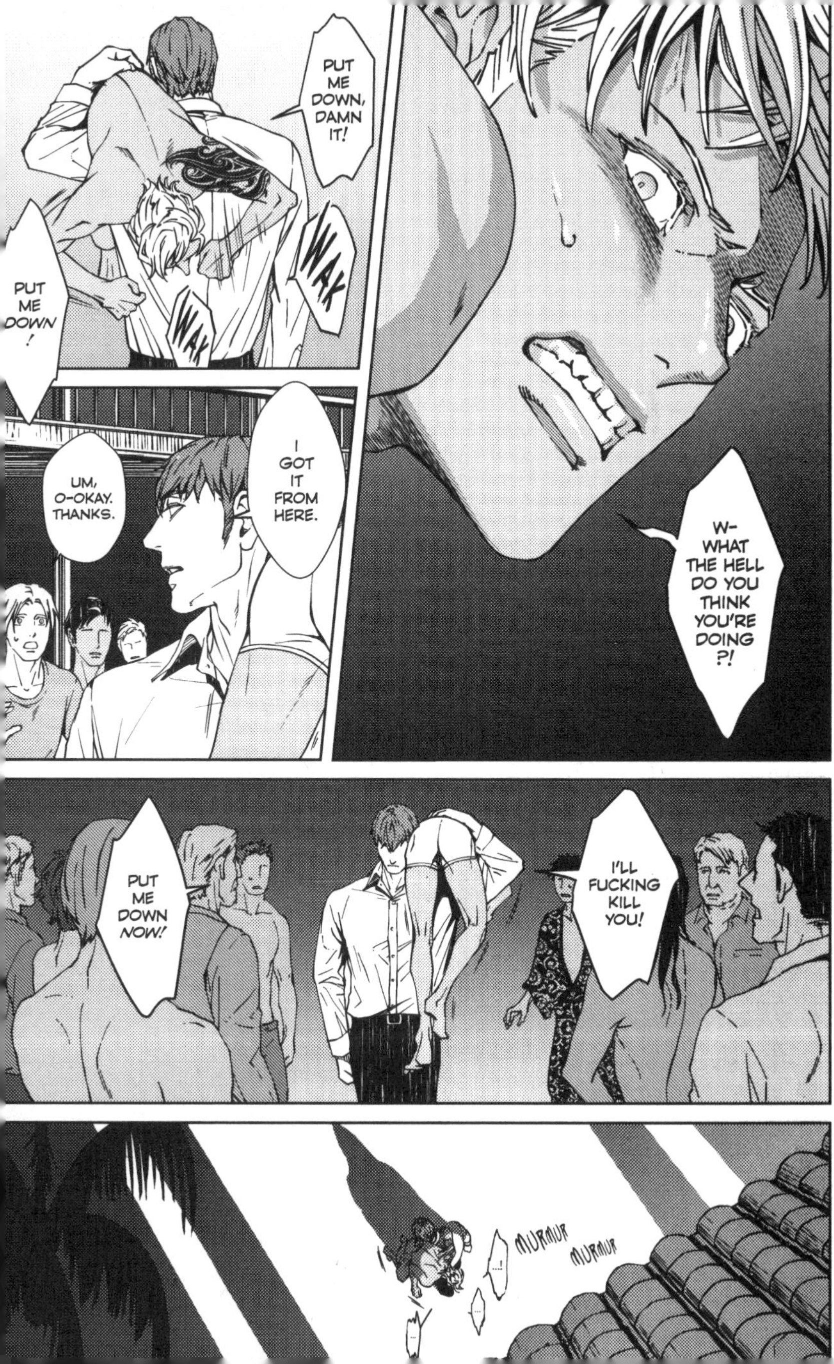
W-WHAT THE HELL DO YOU THINK YOU'RE DOING?!
PUT ME DOWN, DAMN IT!
WAK
WAK
PUT ME DOWN!
I GOT IT FROM HERE.
UM, O-OKAY. THANKS.
I'LL FUCKING KILL YOU!
PUT ME DOWN NOW!
MURMUR
MURMUR
...!
...
...

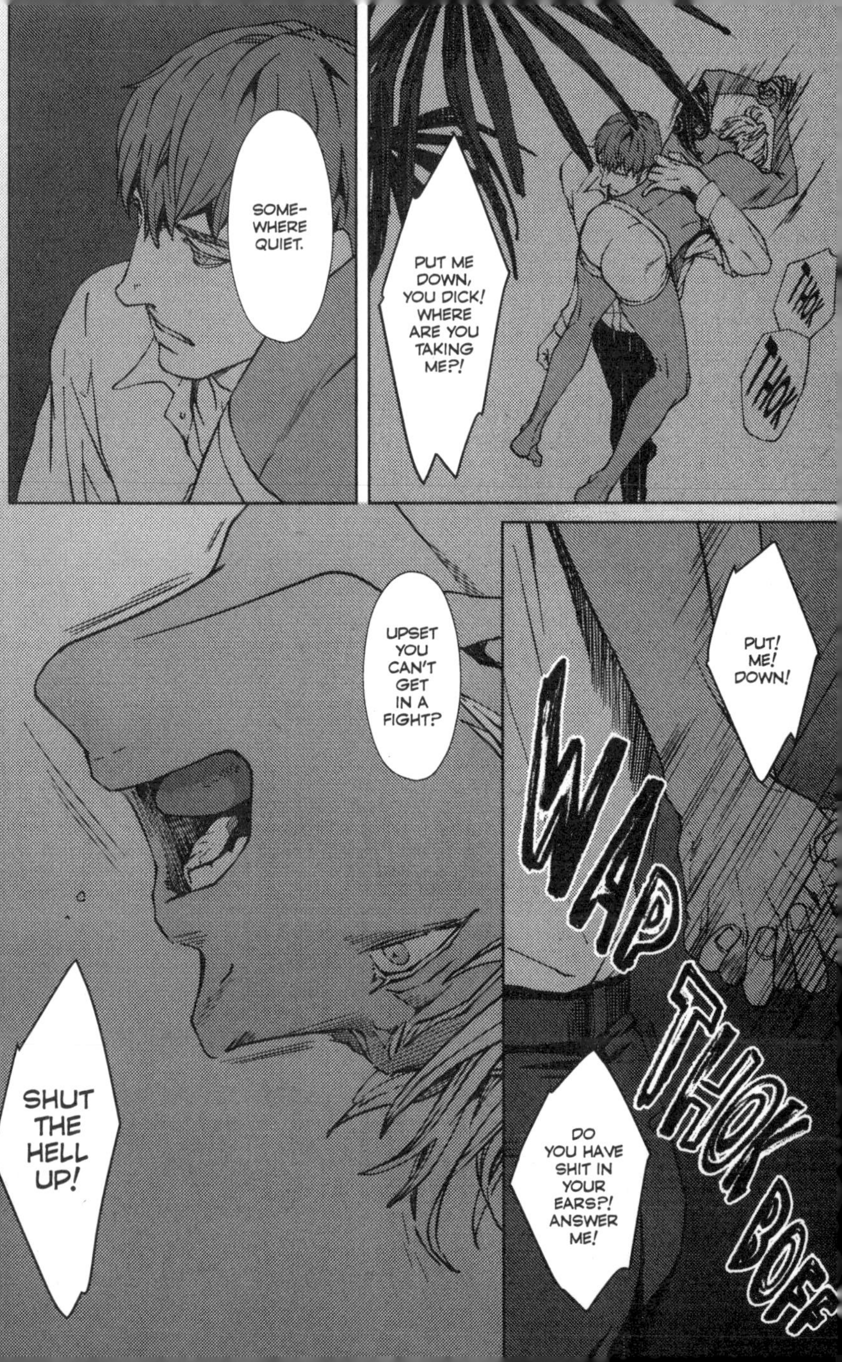
PUT ME DOWN, YOU DICK! WHERE ARE YOU TAKING ME?!
THOK
THOK
SOME-WHERE QUIET.
PUT! ME! DOWN!
WAP THOK BOFF
DO YOU HAVE SHIT IN YOUR EARS?! ANSWER ME!
UPSET YOU CAN'T GET IN A FIGHT?
SHUT THE HELL UP!

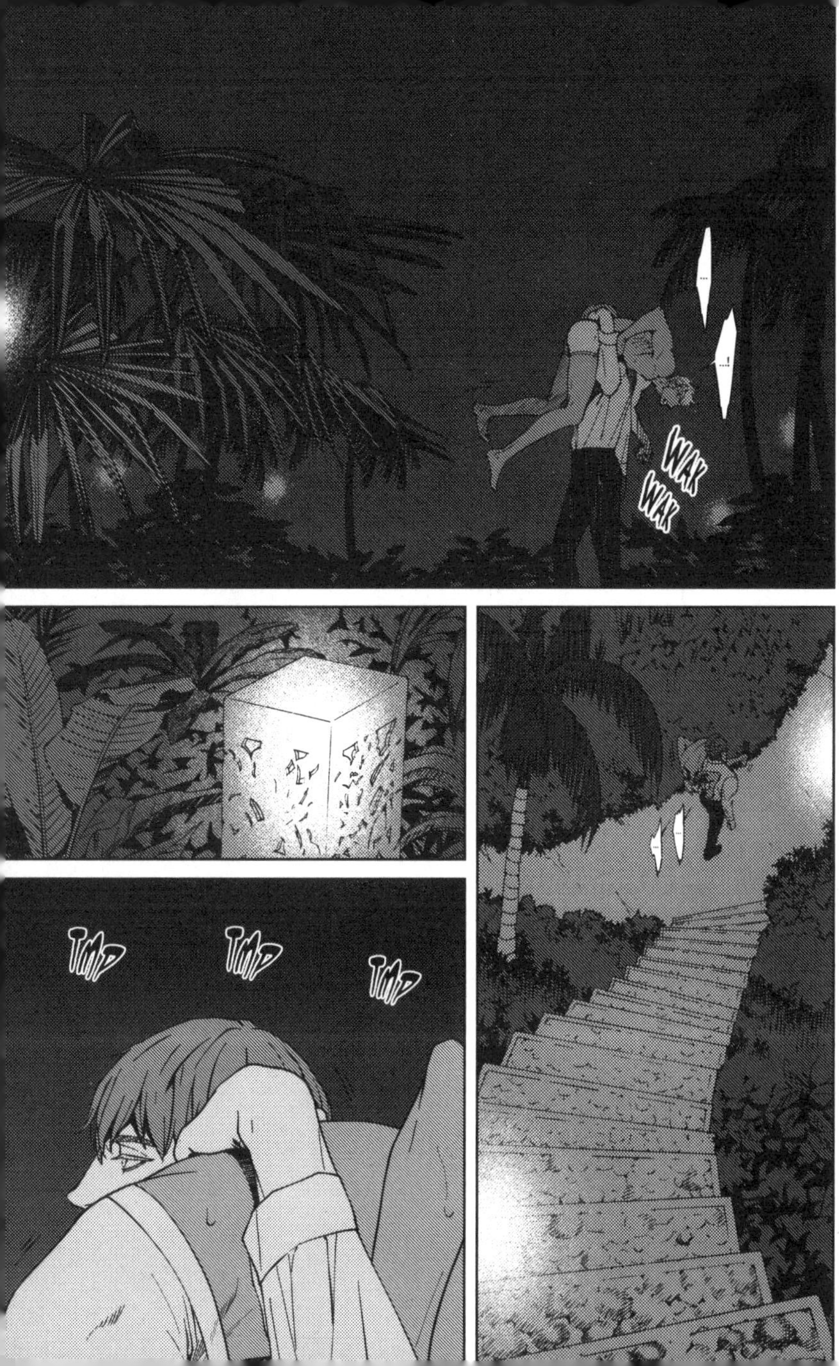
...
...!
WAK WAK
...
...
TMP
TMP
TMP

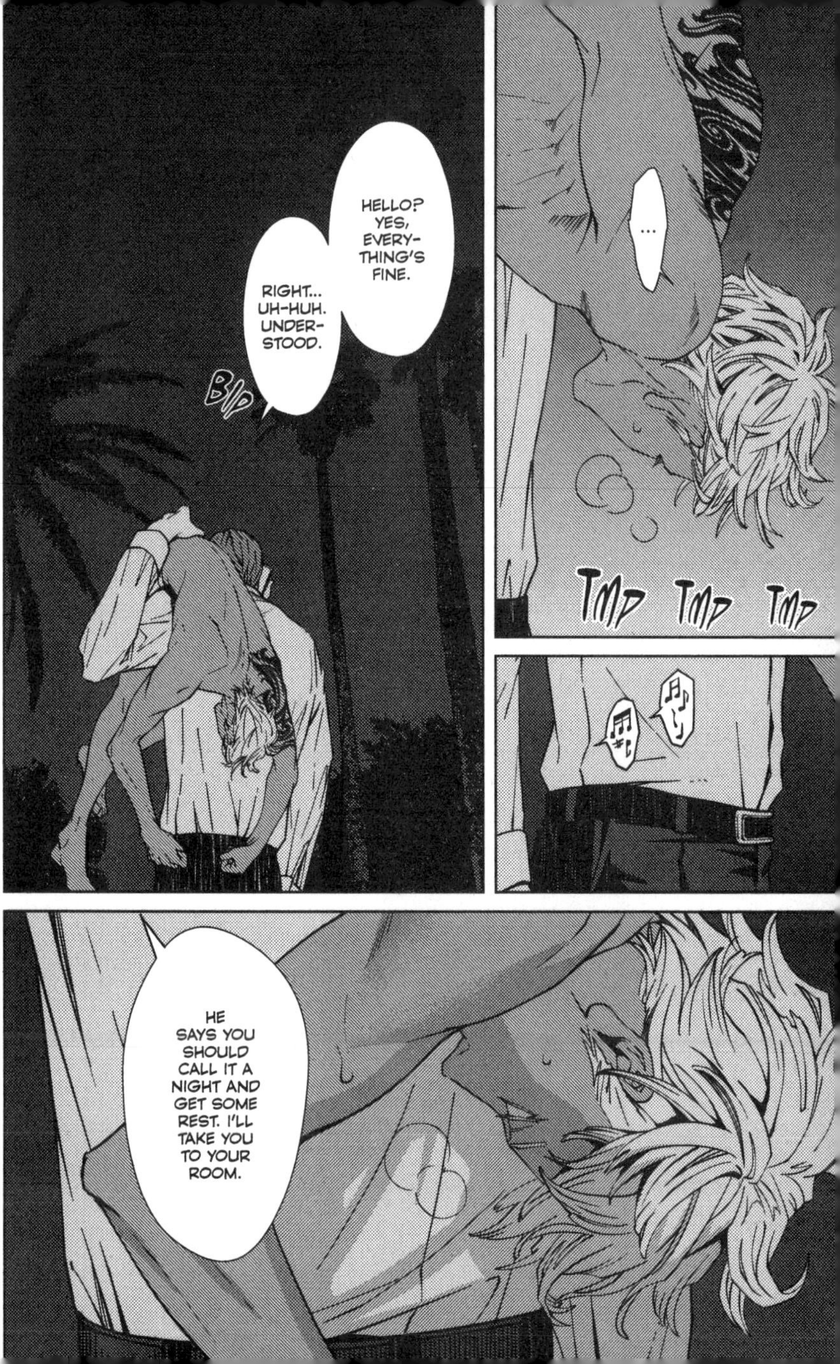
...
TMP TMP TMP
HELLO? YES, EVERY-THING'S FINE.
RIGHT... UH-HUH. UNDER-STOOD.
BIP
HE SAYS YOU SHOULD CALL IT A NIGHT AND GET SOME REST. I'LL TAKE YOU TO YOUR ROOM.

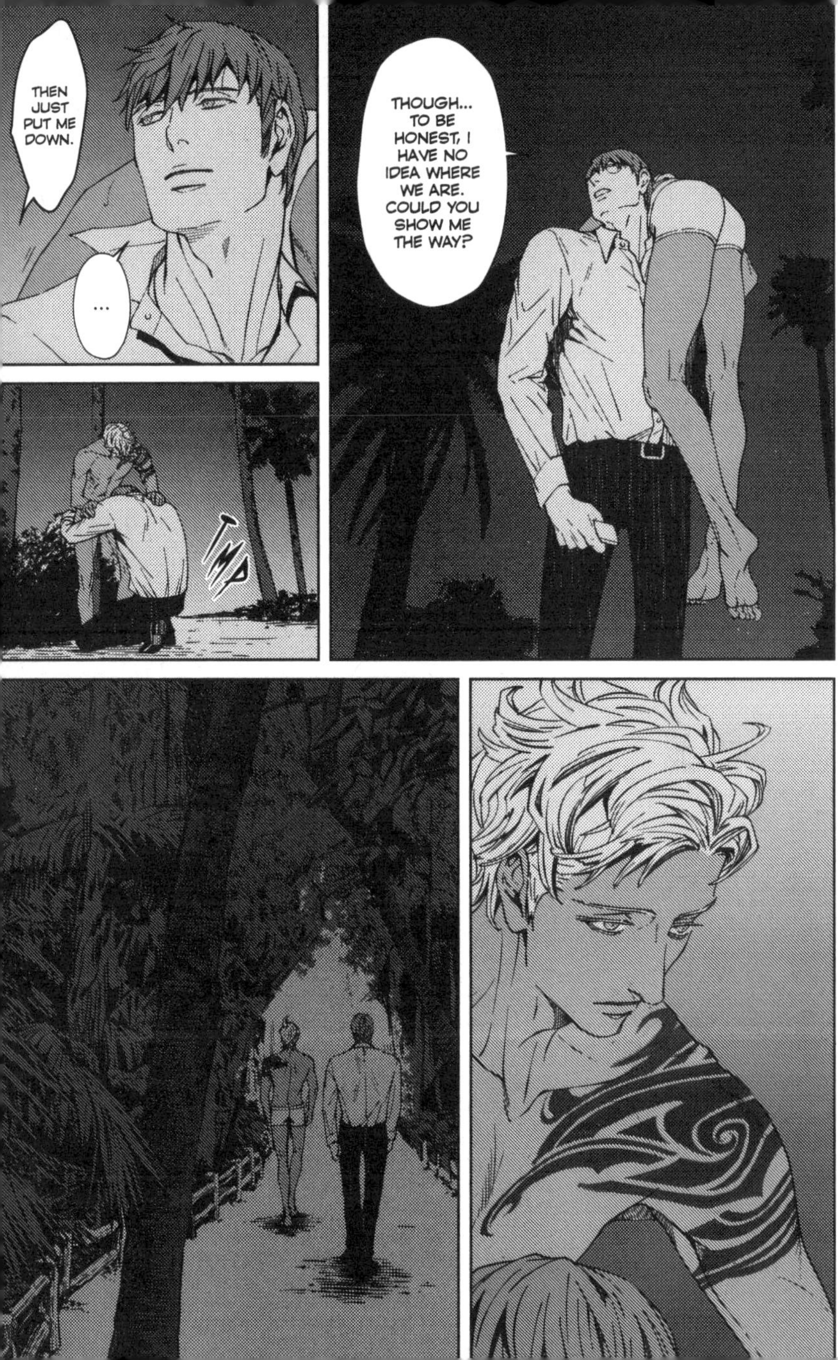
THOUGH... TO BE HONEST, I HAVE NO IDEA WHERE WE ARE. COULD YOU SHOW ME THE WAY?
THEN JUST PUT ME DOWN.
...
TMP

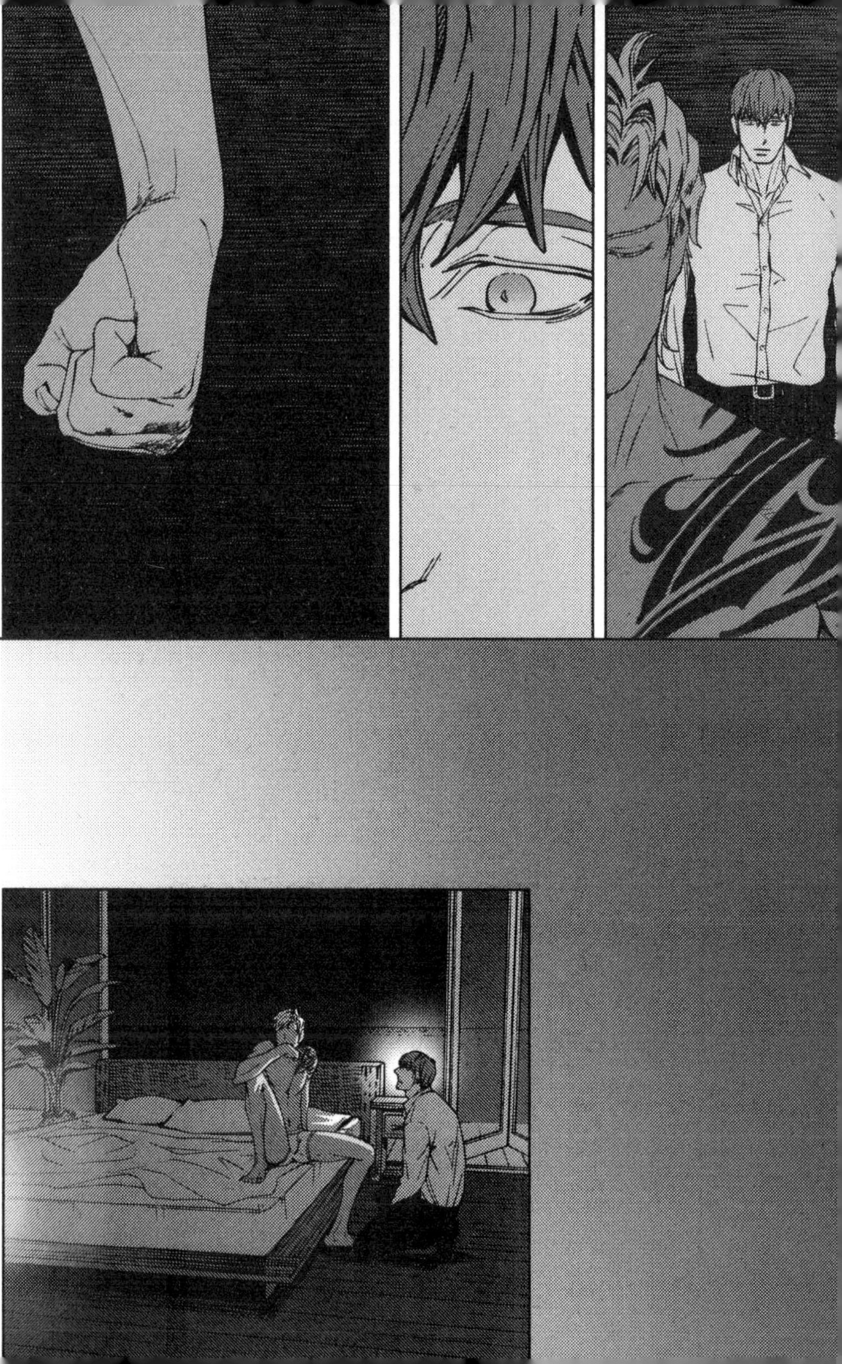

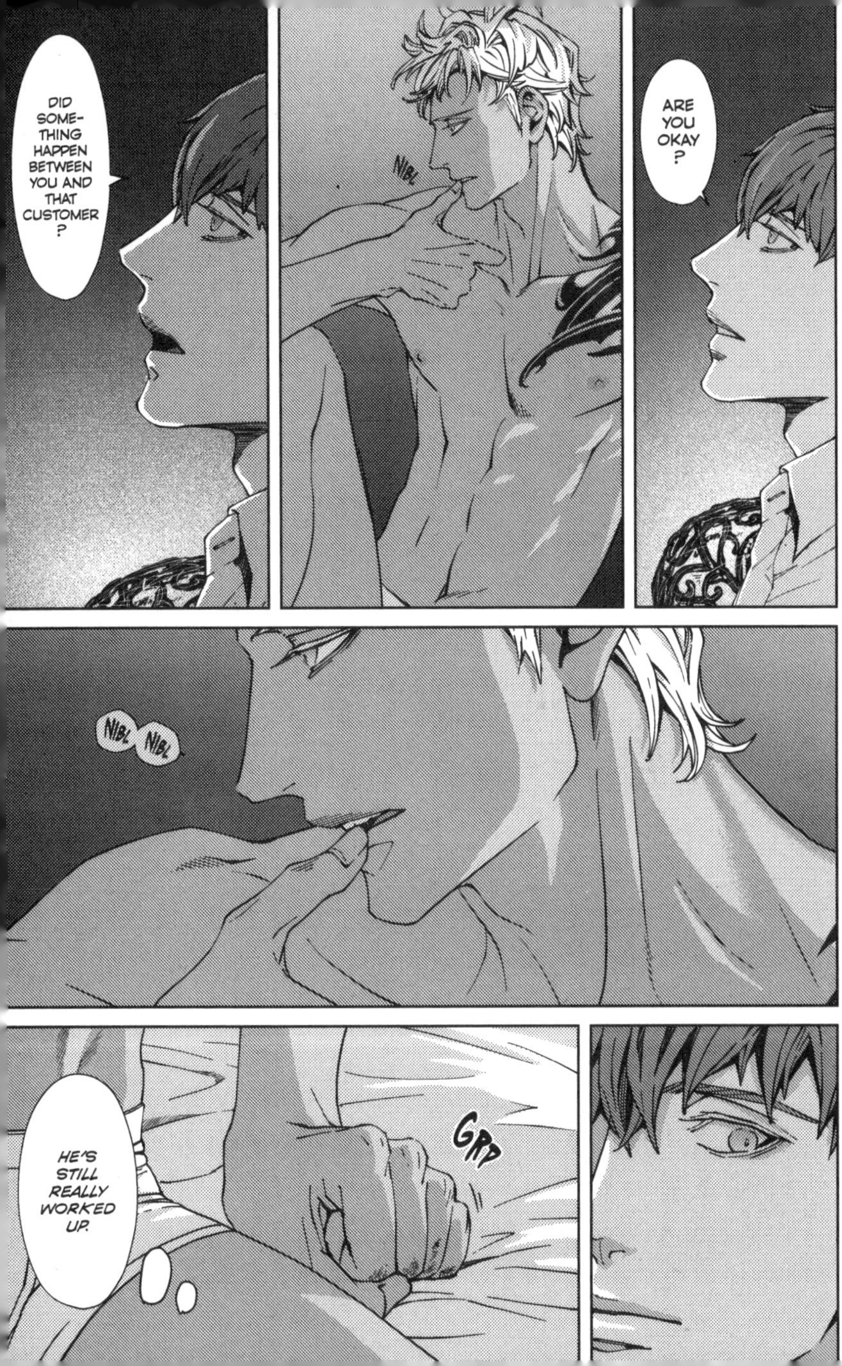
ARE YOU OKAY?
NIBL
DID SOMETHING HAPPEN BETWEEN YOU AND THAT CUSTOMER?
NIBL NIBL
GRP
HE'S STILL REALLY WORKED UP.

YANK

LET ME GET YOU SOME-THING TO DRINK.

WHAT DO YOU USUALLY HAVE? WINE? BEE—

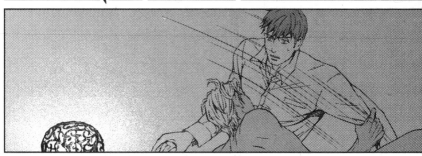

I DON'T WANT BOOZE. I WANT YOU...

TO WHAT?

SHWE

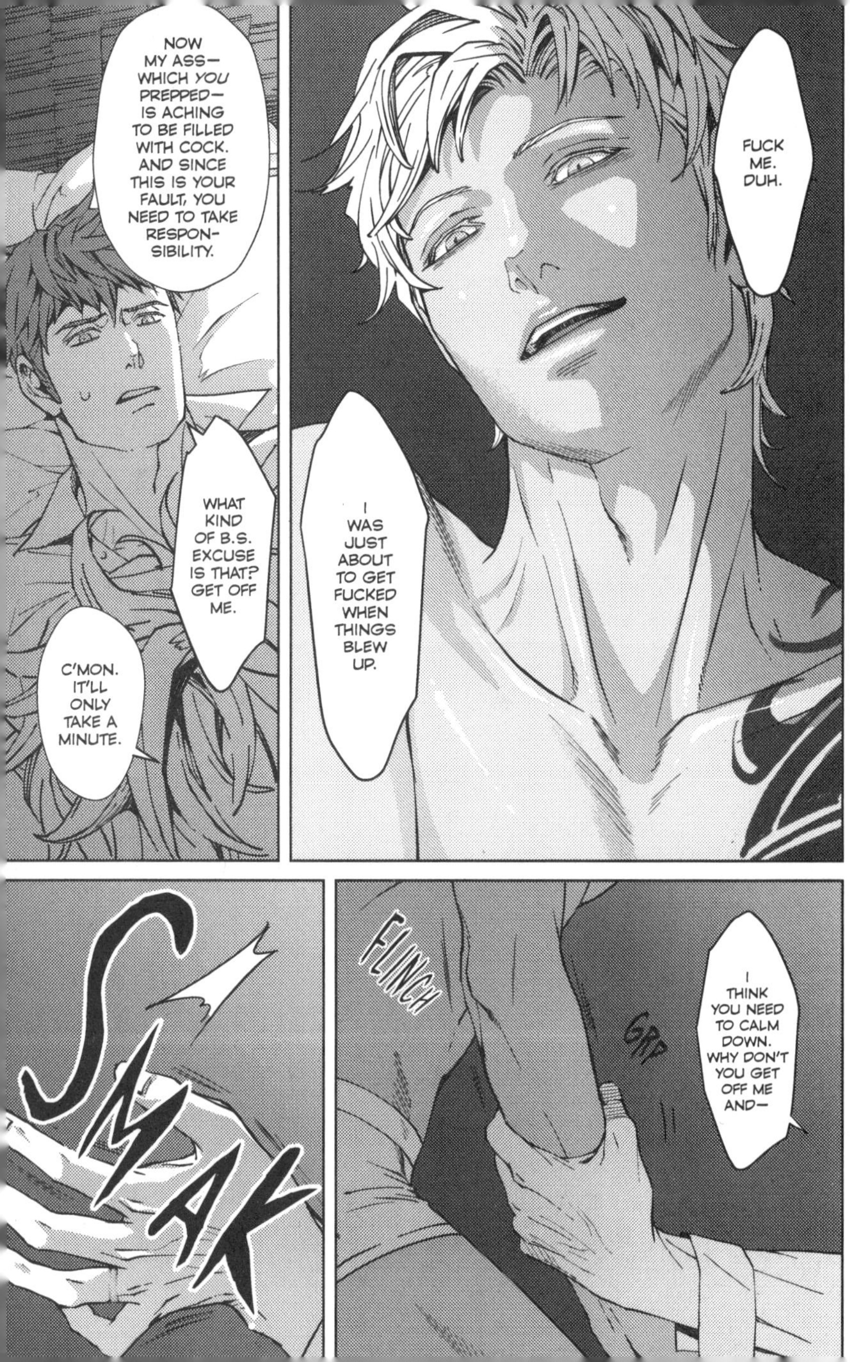
FUCK ME. DUH.
I WAS JUST ABOUT TO GET FUCKED WHEN THINGS BLEW UP.
NOW MY ASS—WHICH *YOU* PREPPED—IS ACHING TO BE FILLED WITH COCK. AND SINCE THIS IS YOUR FAULT, YOU NEED TO TAKE RESPON-SIBILITY.
WHAT KIND OF B.S. EXCUSE IS THAT? GET OFF ME.
C'MON. IT'LL ONLY TAKE A MINUTE.
FLINCH
GRP
I THINK YOU NEED TO CALM DOWN. WHY DON'T YOU GET OFF ME AND—
SMAK

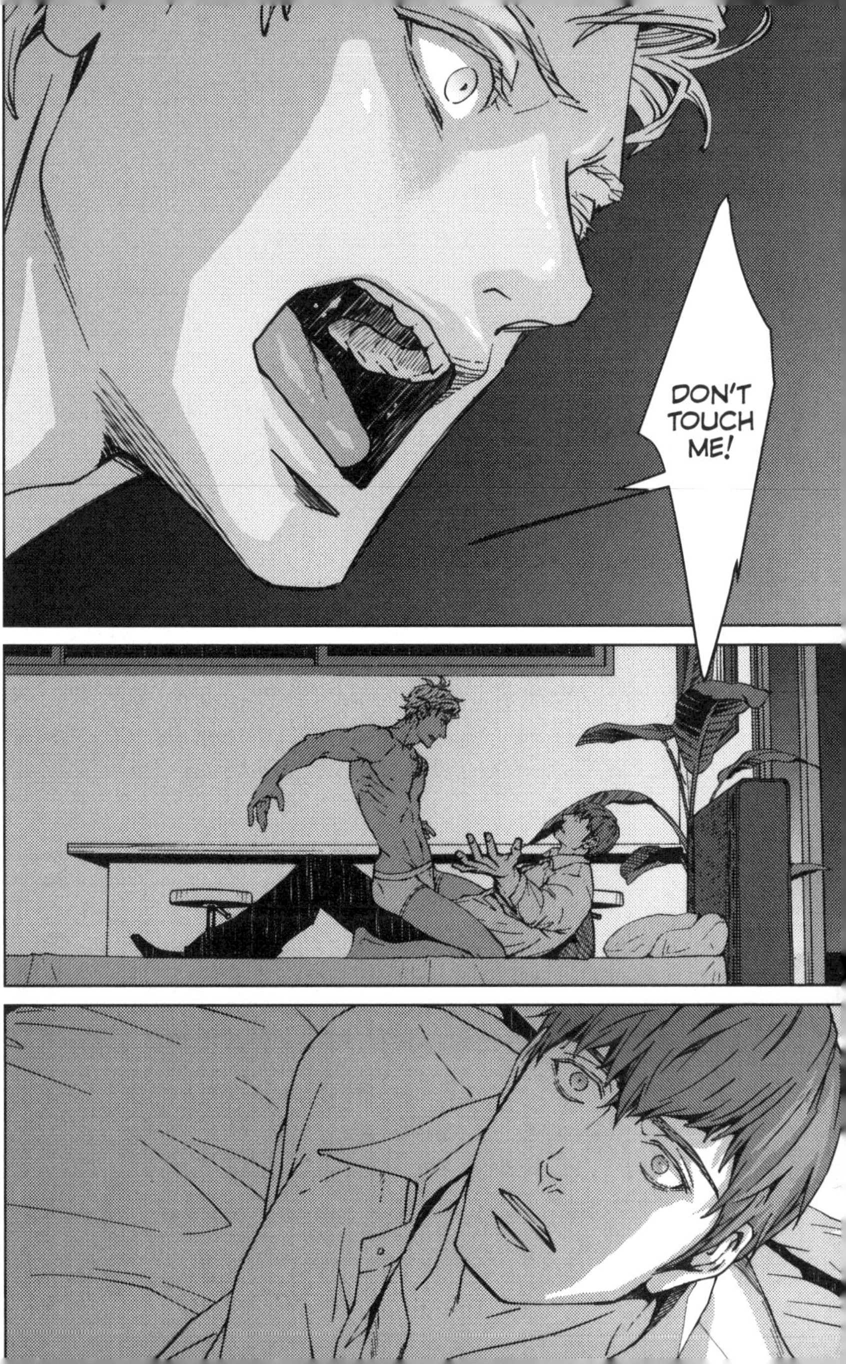
DON'T TOUCH ME!

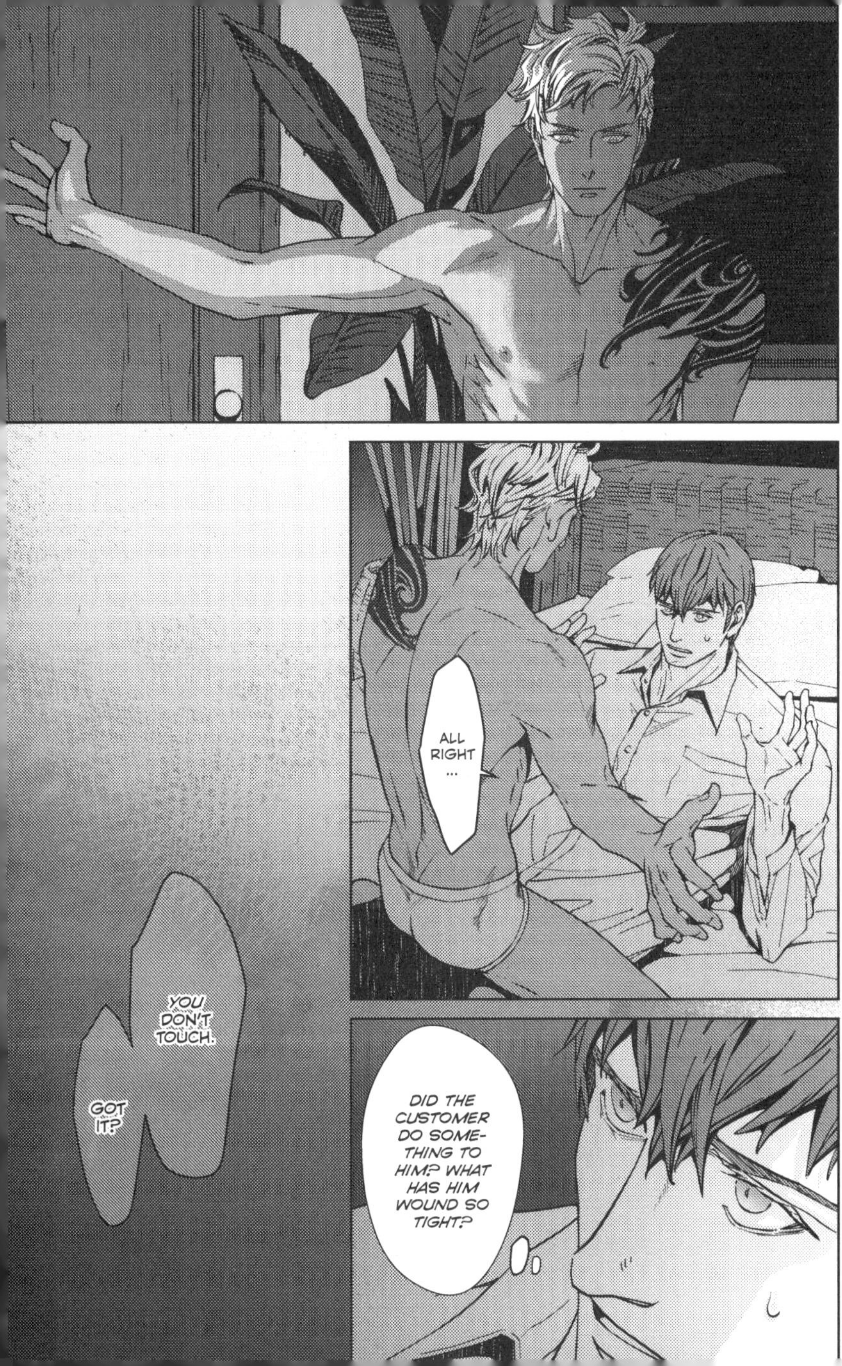
ALL RIGHT ...
DID THE CUSTOMER DO SOME-THING TO HIM? WHAT HAS HIM WOUND SO TIGHT?
YOU DON'T TOUCH.
GOT IT?

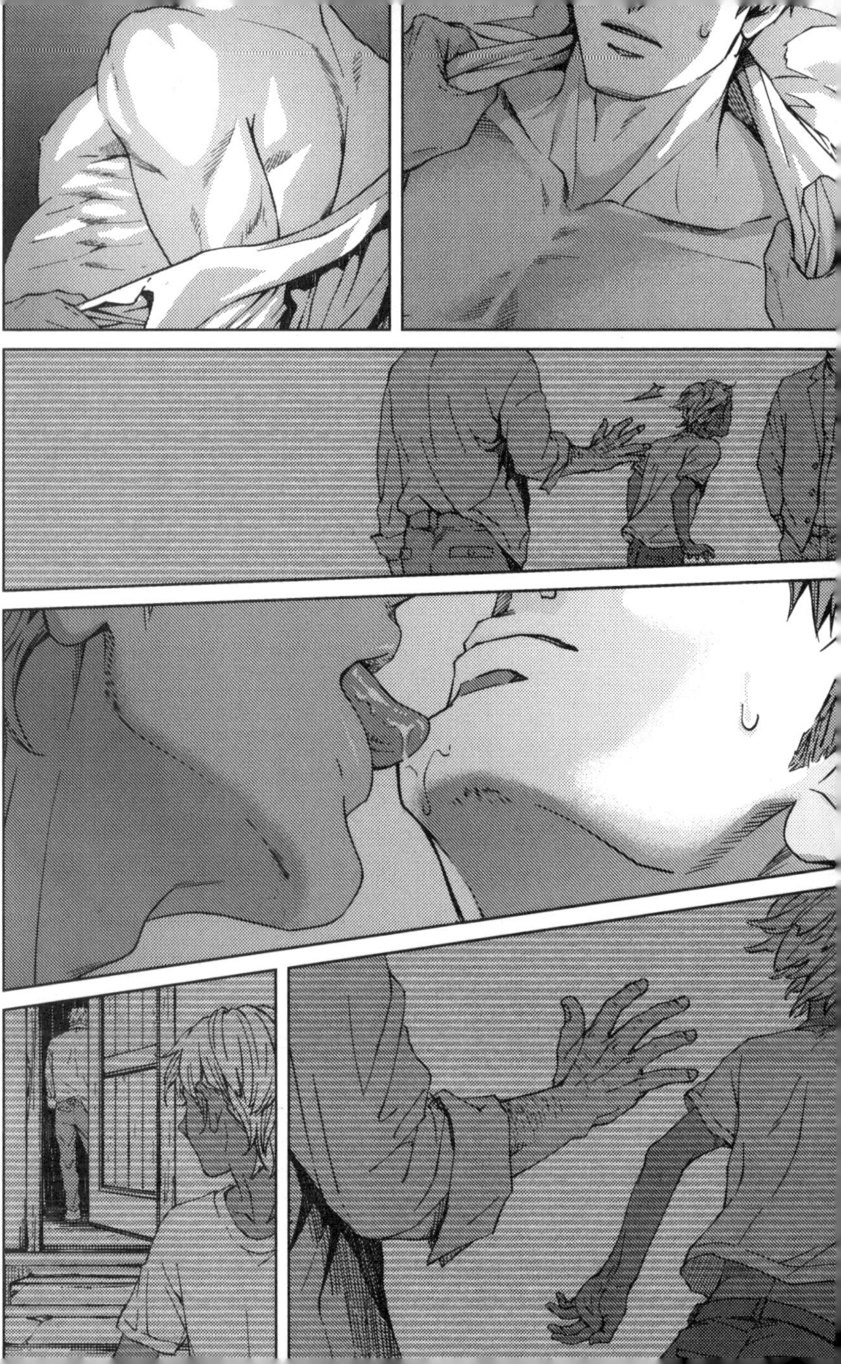

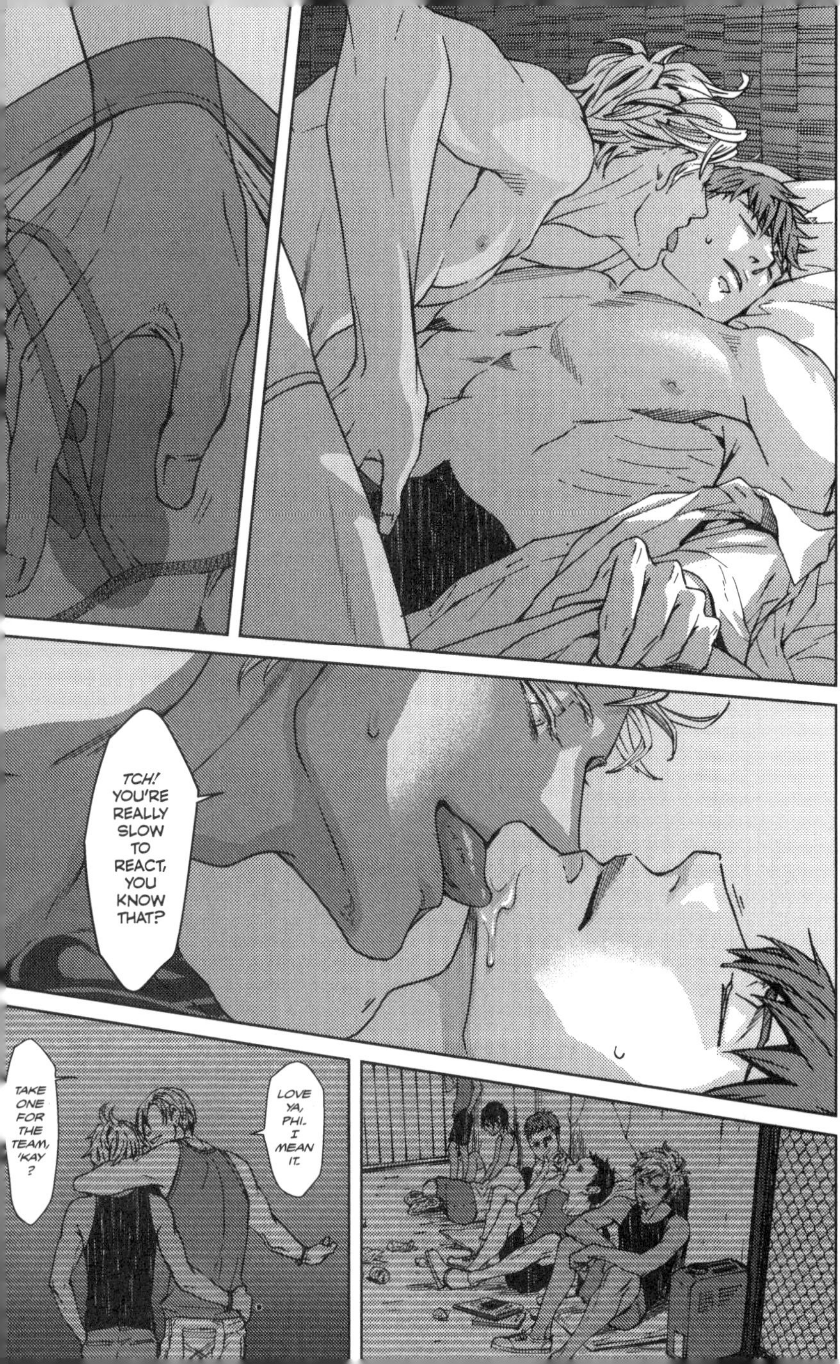
TCH! YOU'RE REALLY SLOW TO REACT, YOU KNOW THAT?
TAKE ONE FOR THE TEAM, 'KAY?
LOVE YA, PHI. I MEAN IT.

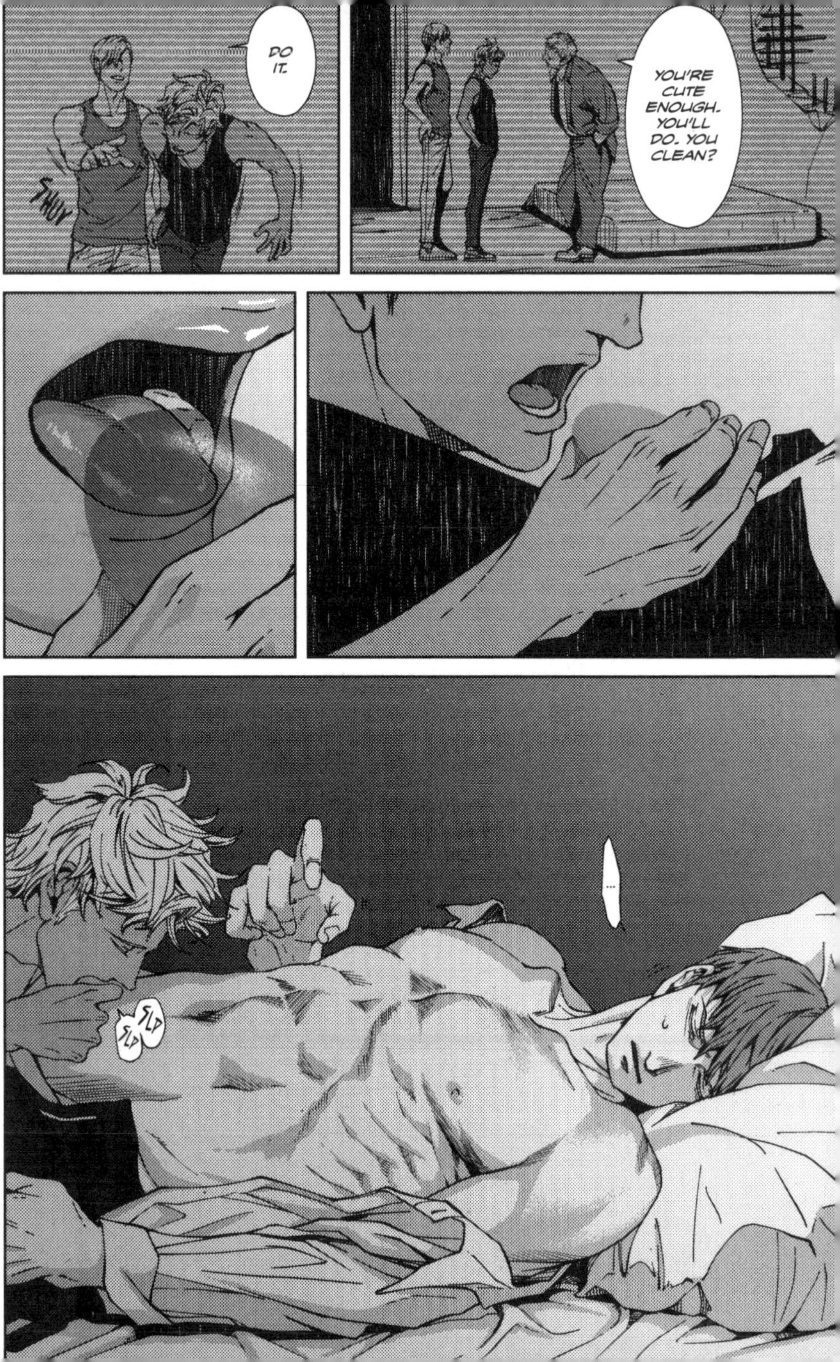
YOU'RE CUTE ENOUGH. YOU'LL DO. YOU CLEAN?
DO IT.
SHUV
...
SLP
SLP

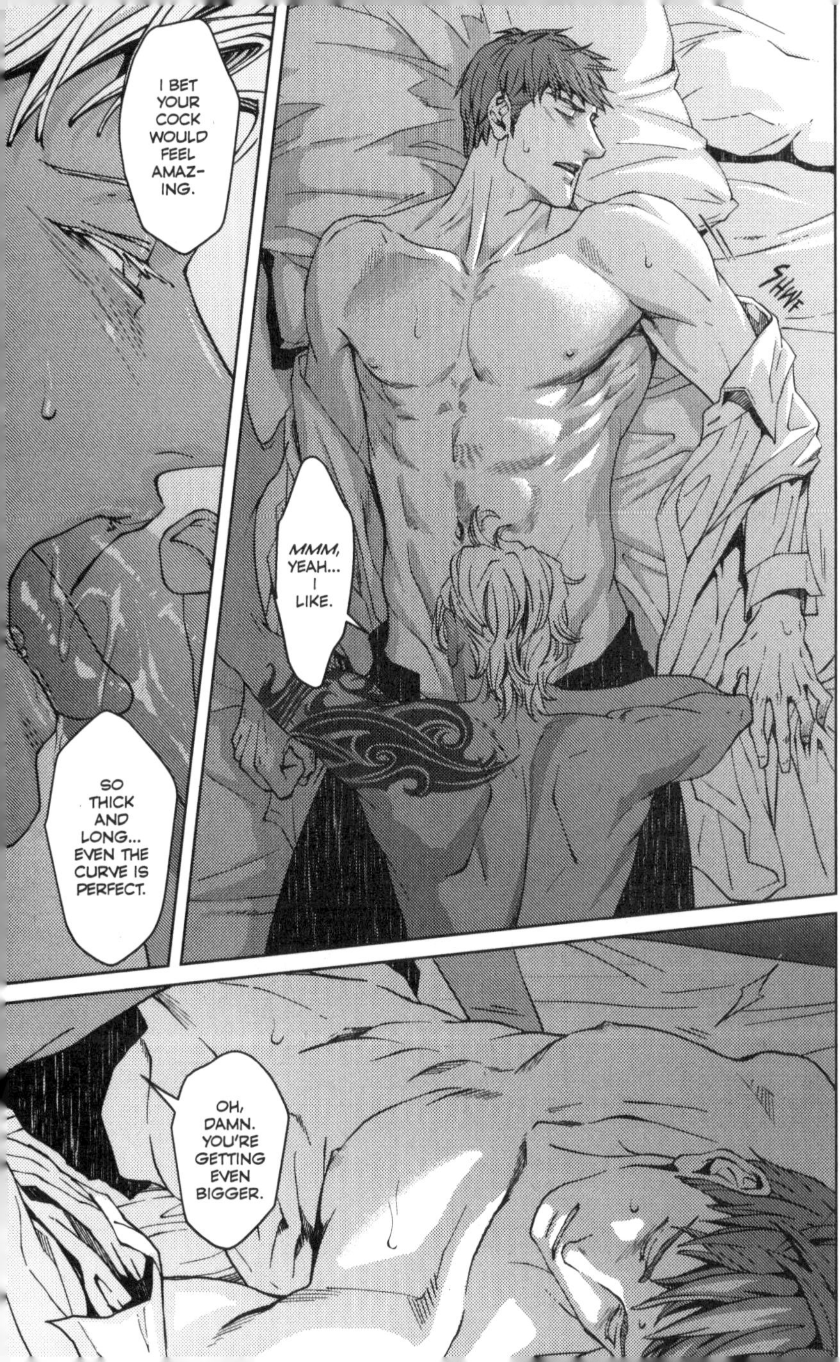
SHNF
MMM, YEAH... I LIKE.
I BET YOUR COCK WOULD FEEL AMAZ-ING.
SO THICK AND LONG... EVEN THE CURVE IS PERFECT.
OH, DAMN. YOU'RE GETTING EVEN BIGGER.

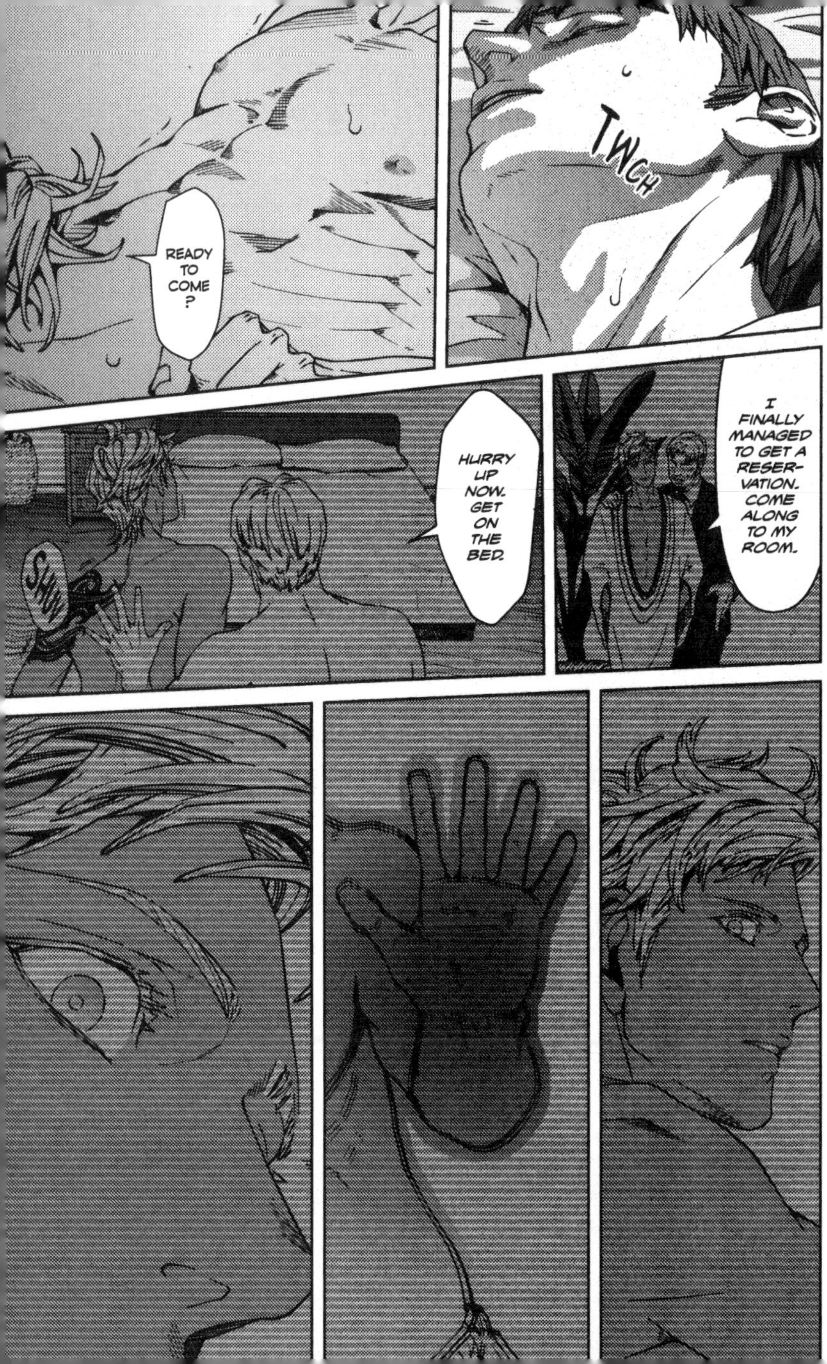
TWCH
READY TO COME ?
I FINALLY MANAGED TO GET A RESERVATION. COME ALONG TO MY ROOM.
HURRY UP NOW. GET ON THE BED.
SHH

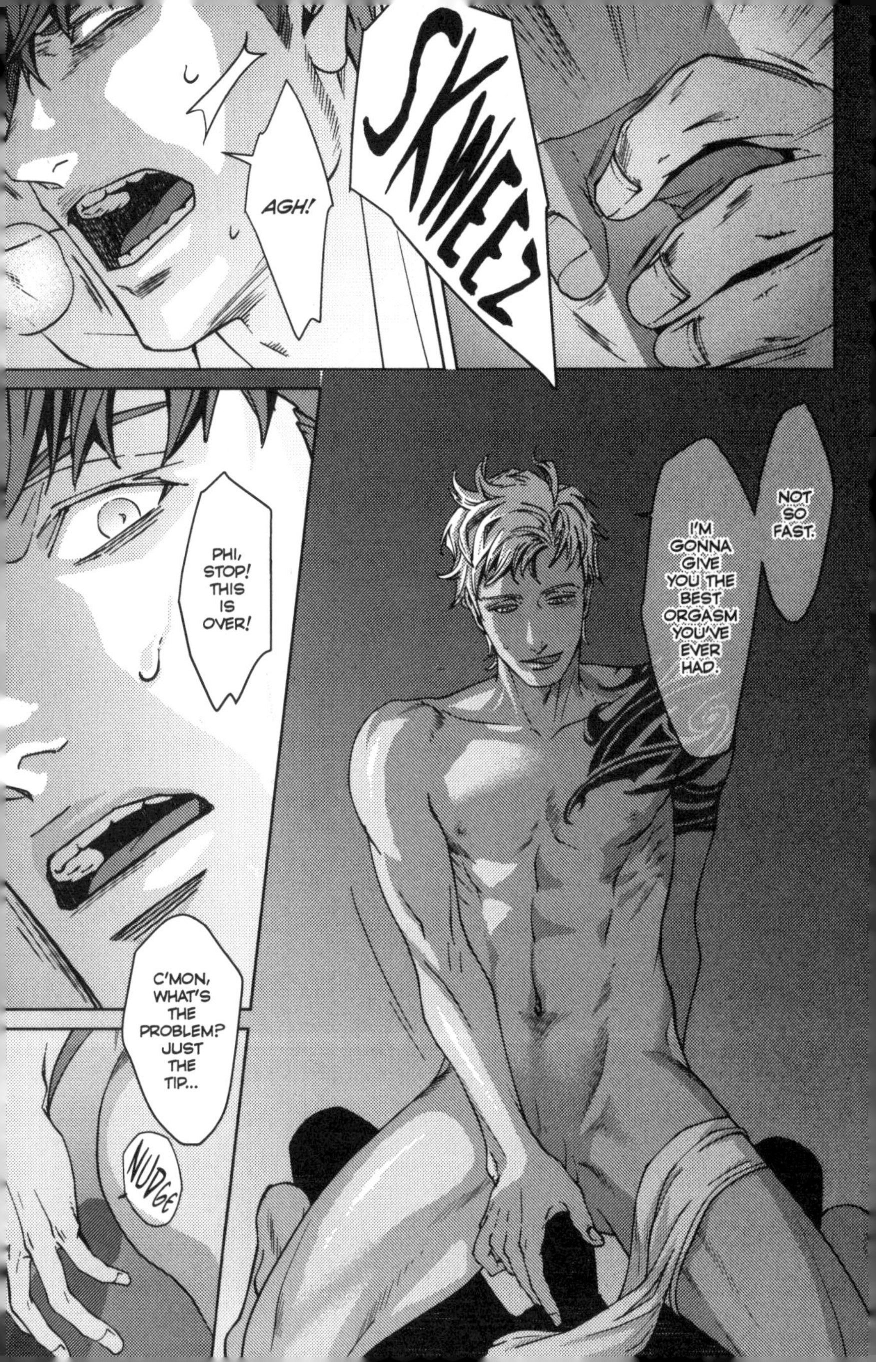
SKWEEZ
AGH!
NOT SO FAST.
I'M GONNA GIVE YOU THE BEST ORGASM YOU'VE EVER HAD.
PHI, STOP! THIS IS OVER!
C'MON, WHAT'S THE PROBLEM? JUST THE TIP...
NUDGE

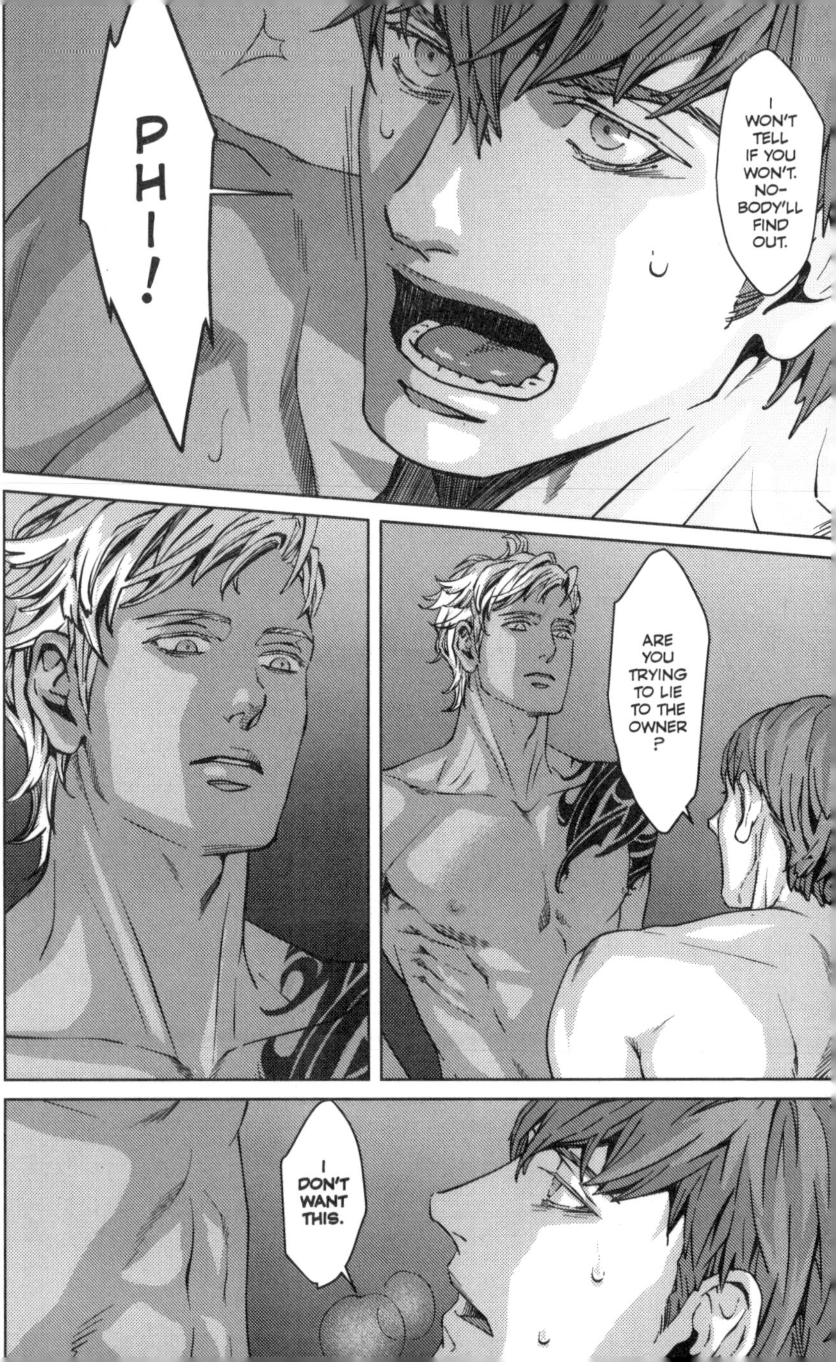
I WON'T TELL IF YOU WON'T. NO-BODY'LL FIND OUT.
PHI!
ARE YOU TRYING TO LIE TO THE OWNER?
I DON'T WANT THIS.

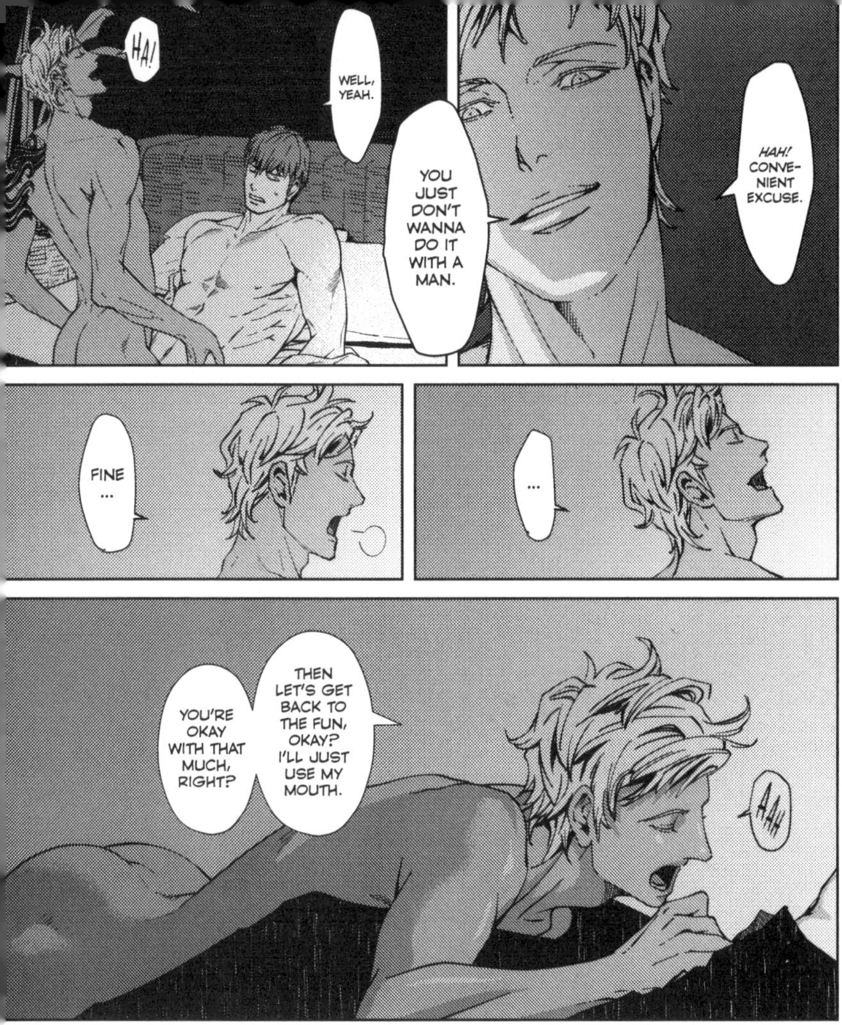
HAH! CONVENIENT EXCUSE.
YOU JUST DON'T WANNA DO IT WITH A MAN.
WELL, YEAH.
HA!
...
FINE ...
AAH
THEN LET'S GET BACK TO THE FUN, OKAY? I'LL JUST USE MY MOUTH.
YOU'RE OKAY WITH THAT MUCH, RIGHT?

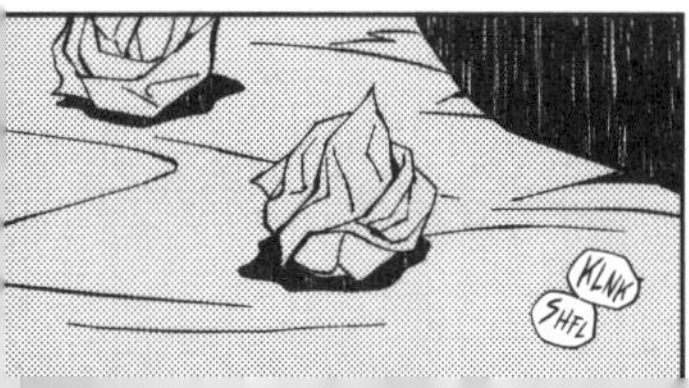
KLNK
SHFL

OF COURSE NOT.

THP THP

YOU LOOK PRETTY DIS-GUSTED. DIDN'T HAVE FUN, HUH?

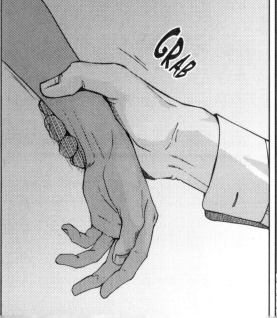

GRAB

ME, THOUGH... I NEED ME SOME! MY BODY'S STILL ACHING FOR COCK. MAYBE I'LL HEAD BACK OUT TO THE HALL AND GRAB ANOTHER ONE...

THP

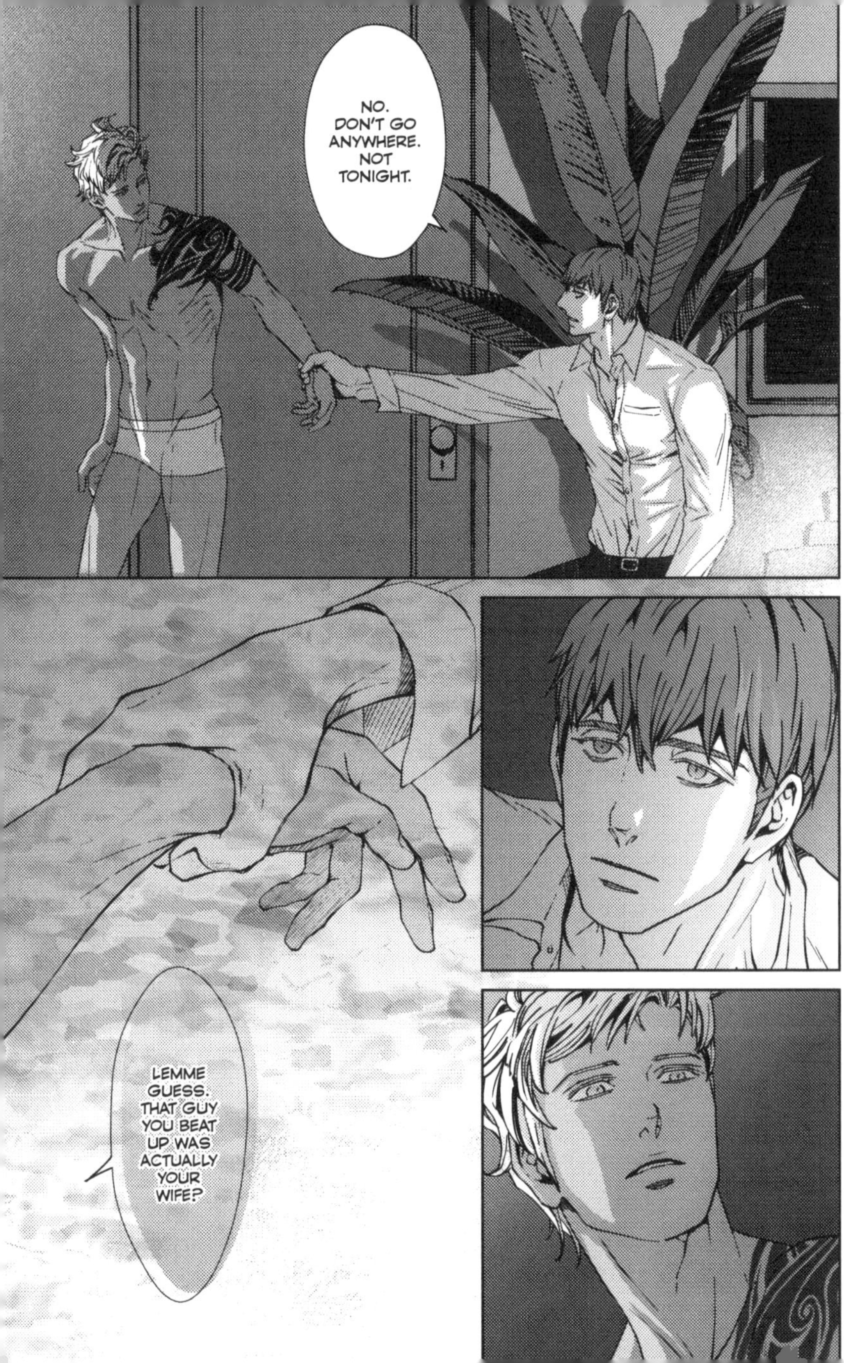
NO. DON'T GO ANYWHERE. NOT TONIGHT.
LEMME GUESS. THAT GUY YOU BEAT UP WAS ACTUALLY YOUR WIFE?

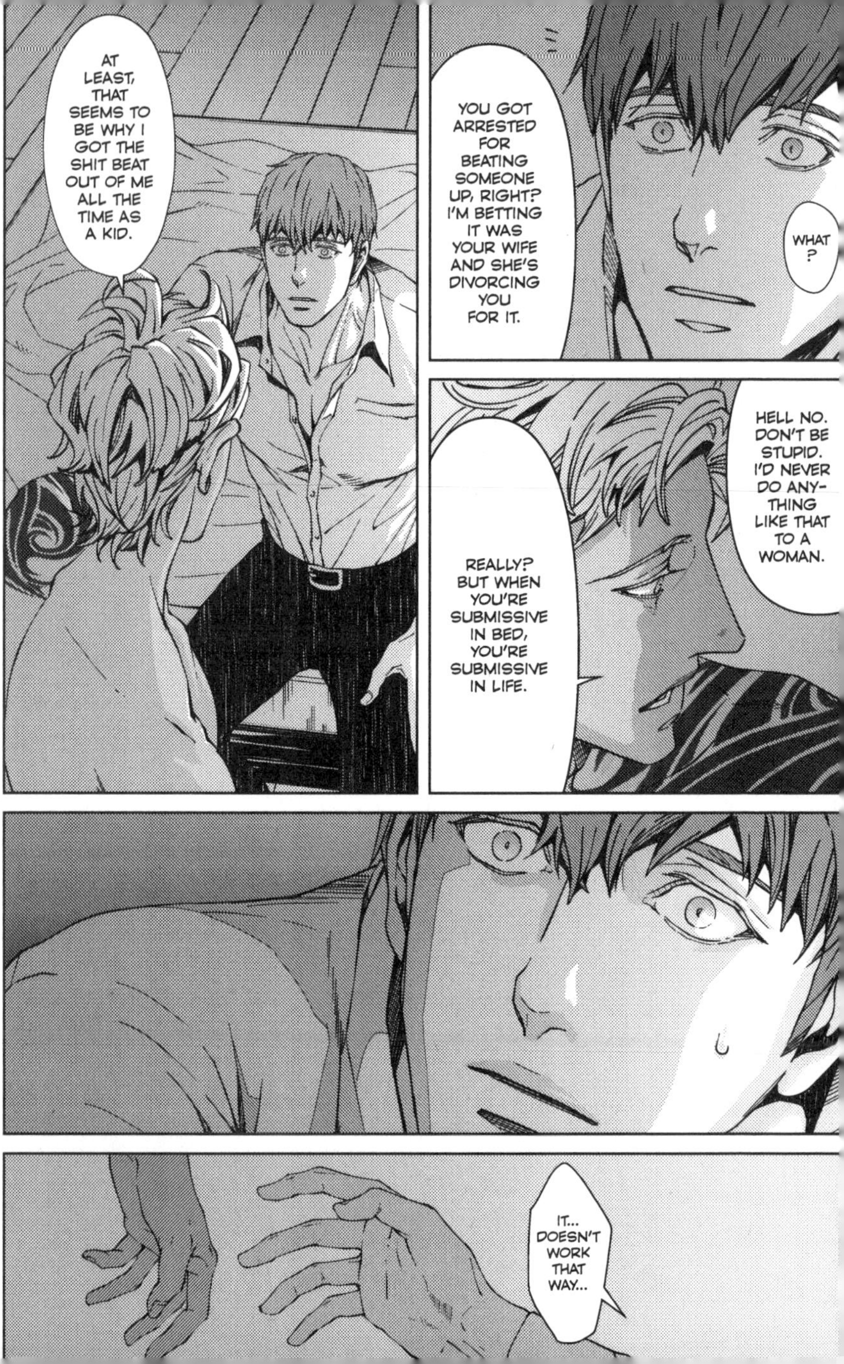
YOU GOT ARRESTED FOR BEATING SOMEONE UP, RIGHT? I'M BETTING IT WAS YOUR WIFE AND SHE'S DIVORCING YOU FOR IT.
WHAT?
HELL NO. DON'T BE STUPID. I'D NEVER DO ANY-THING LIKE THAT TO A WOMAN.
REALLY? BUT WHEN YOU'RE SUBMISSIVE IN BED, YOU'RE SUBMISSIVE IN LIFE.
AT LEAST, THAT SEEMS TO BE WHY I GOT THE SHIT BEAT OUT OF ME ALL THE TIME AS A KID.
IT... DOESN'T WORK THAT WAY...

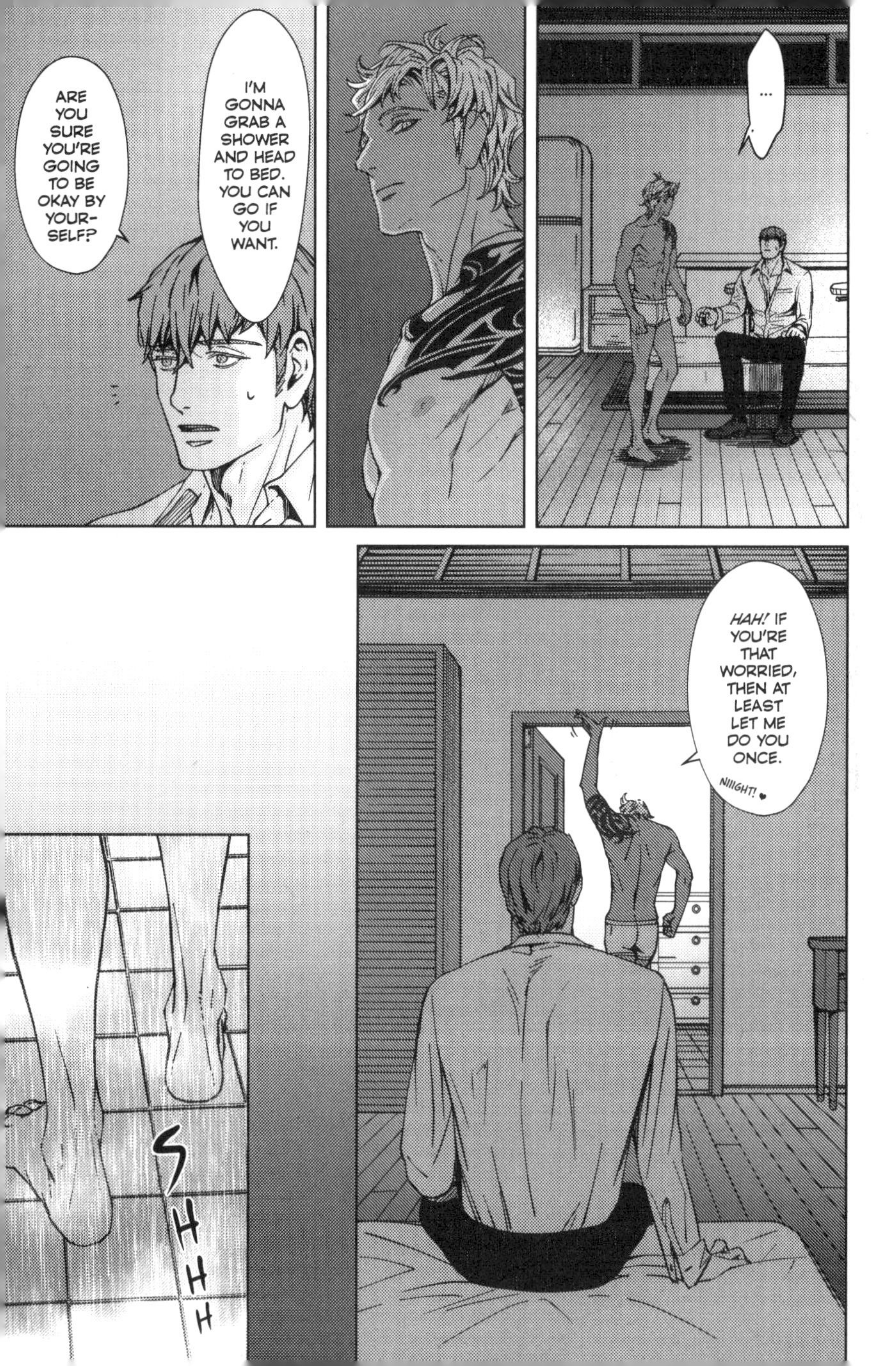
...
I'M GONNA GRAB A SHOWER AND HEAD TO BED. YOU CAN GO IF YOU WANT.
ARE YOU SURE YOU'RE GOING TO BE OKAY BY YOUR-SELF?
HAH! IF YOU'RE THAT WORRIED, THEN AT LEAST LET ME DO YOU ONCE.
NIIGHT! ♥
SHHH

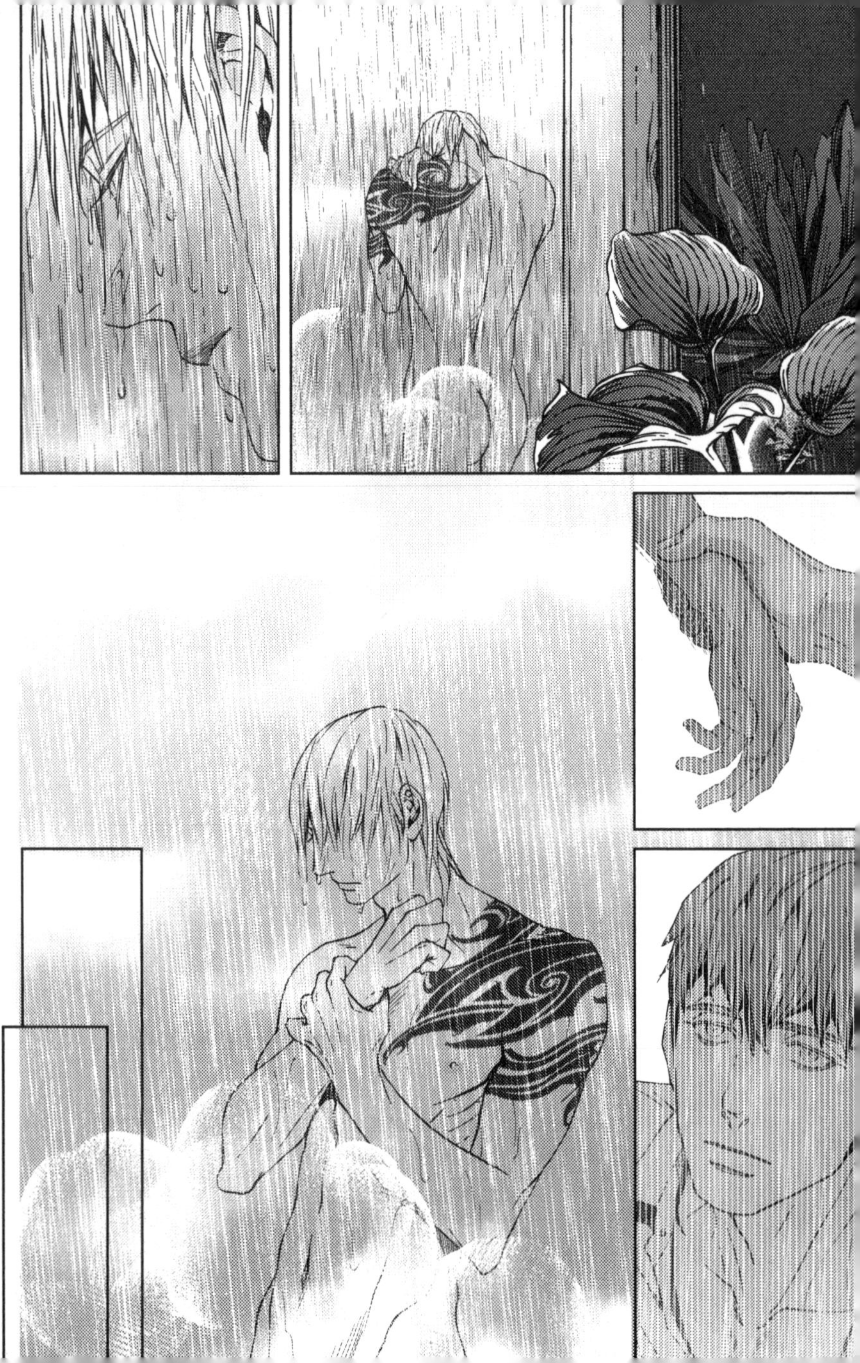

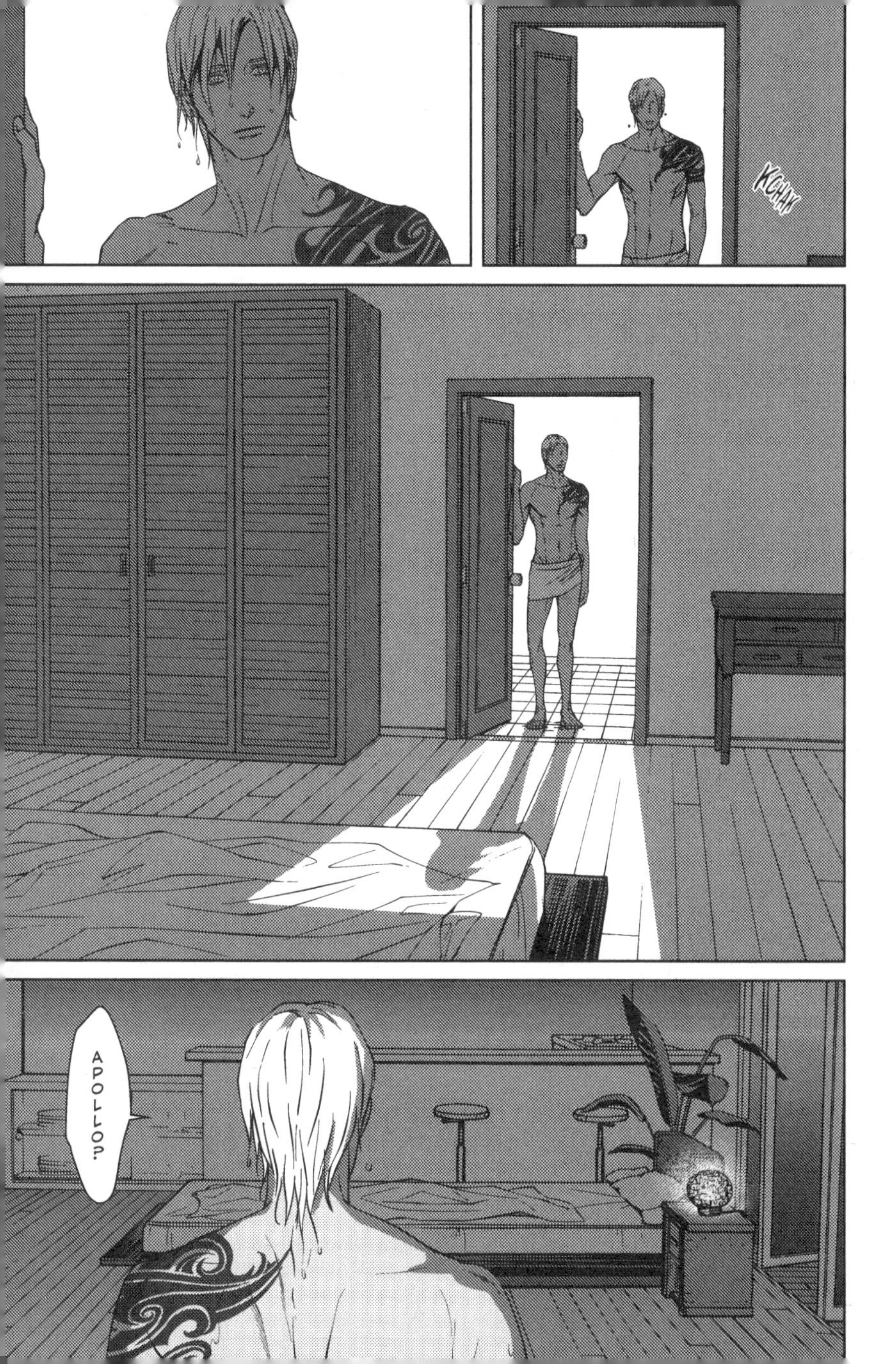
KCHAK
APOLLO?

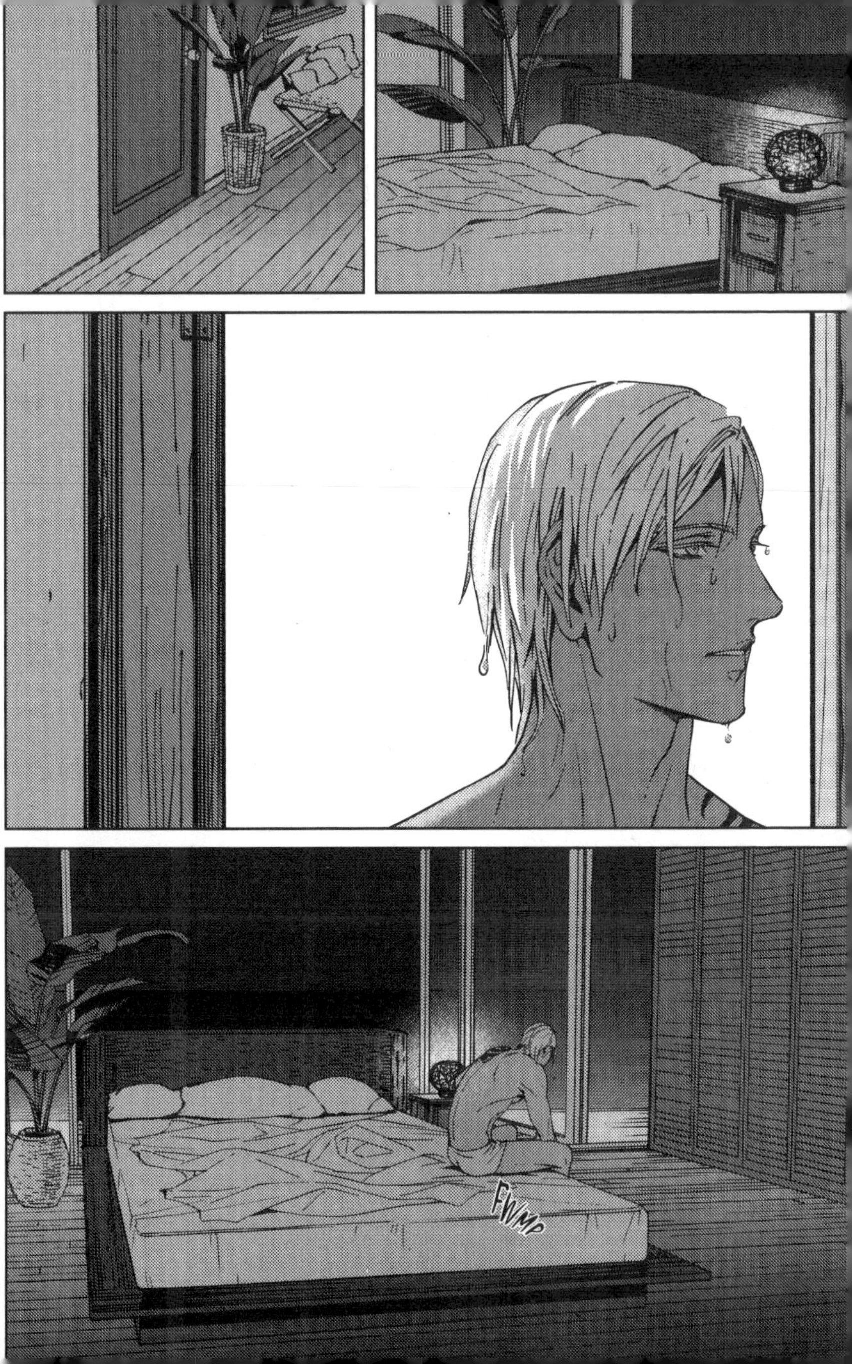
FWMP

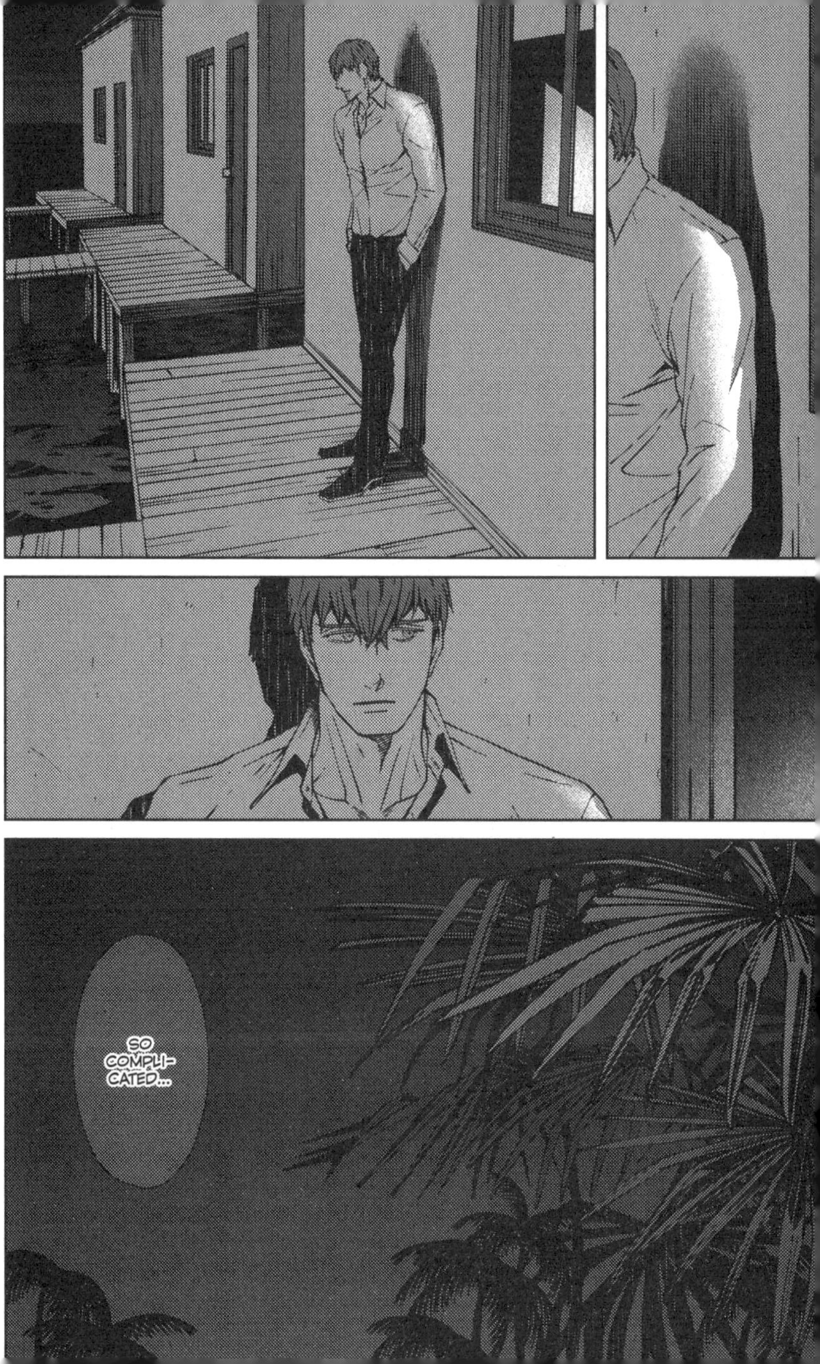
SO COMPLI-CATED...

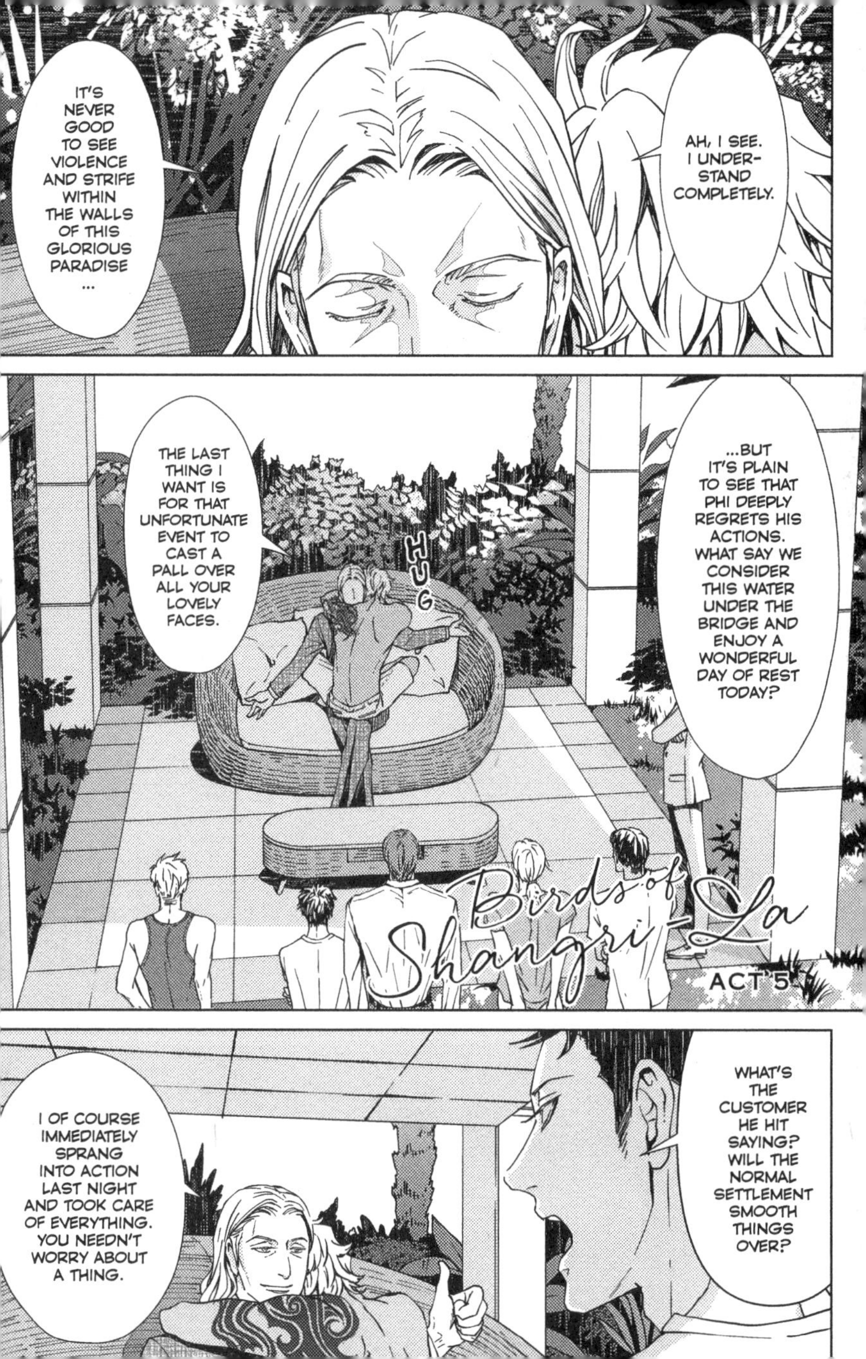
AH, I SEE. I UNDERSTAND COMPLETELY.
IT'S NEVER GOOD TO SEE VIOLENCE AND STRIFE WITHIN THE WALLS OF THIS GLORIOUS PARADISE ...
...BUT IT'S PLAIN TO SEE THAT PHI DEEPLY REGRETS HIS ACTIONS. WHAT SAY WE CONSIDER THIS WATER UNDER THE BRIDGE AND ENJOY A WONDERFUL DAY OF REST TODAY?
THE LAST THING I WANT IS FOR THAT UNFORTUNATE EVENT TO CAST A PALL OVER ALL YOUR LOVELY FACES.
HUG
Birds of Shangri-La
ACT 5
WHAT'S THE CUSTOMER HE HIT SAYING? WILL THE NORMAL SETTLEMENT SMOOTH THINGS OVER?
I OF COURSE IMMEDIATELY SPRANG INTO ACTION LAST NIGHT AND TOOK CARE OF EVERYTHING. YOU NEEDN'T WORRY ABOUT A THING.

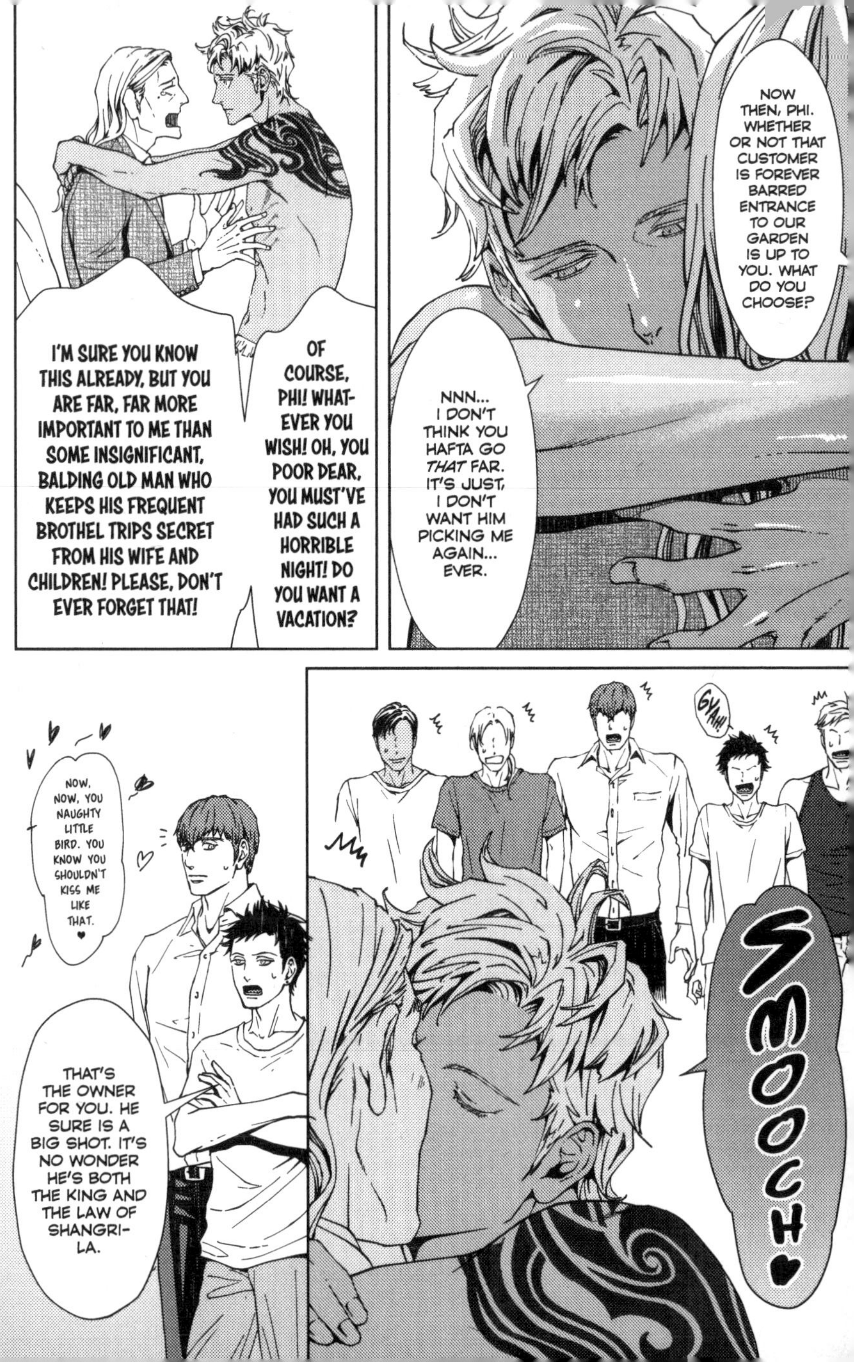
NOW THEN, PHI. WHETHER OR NOT THAT CUSTOMER IS FOREVER BARRED ENTRANCE TO OUR GARDEN IS UP TO YOU. WHAT DO YOU CHOOSE?
NNN... I DON'T THINK YOU HAFTA GO *THAT* FAR. IT'S JUST, I DON'T WANT HIM PICKING ME AGAIN... EVER.
OF COURSE, PHI! WHATEVER YOU WISH! OH, YOU POOR DEAR, YOU MUST'VE HAD SUCH A HORRIBLE NIGHT! DO YOU WANT A VACATION?
I'M SURE YOU KNOW THIS ALREADY, BUT YOU ARE FAR, FAR MORE IMPORTANT TO ME THAN SOME INSIGNIFICANT, BALDING OLD MAN WHO KEEPS HIS FREQUENT BROTHEL TRIPS SECRET FROM HIS WIFE AND CHILDREN! PLEASE, DON'T EVER FORGET THAT!
GYAH!
SMOOCH♥
NOW, NOW, YOU NAUGHTY LITTLE BIRD. YOU KNOW YOU SHOULDN'T KISS ME LIKE THAT. ♥
THAT'S THE OWNER FOR YOU. HE SURE IS A BIG SHOT. IT'S NO WONDER HE'S BOTH THE KING AND THE LAW OF SHANGRI-LA.

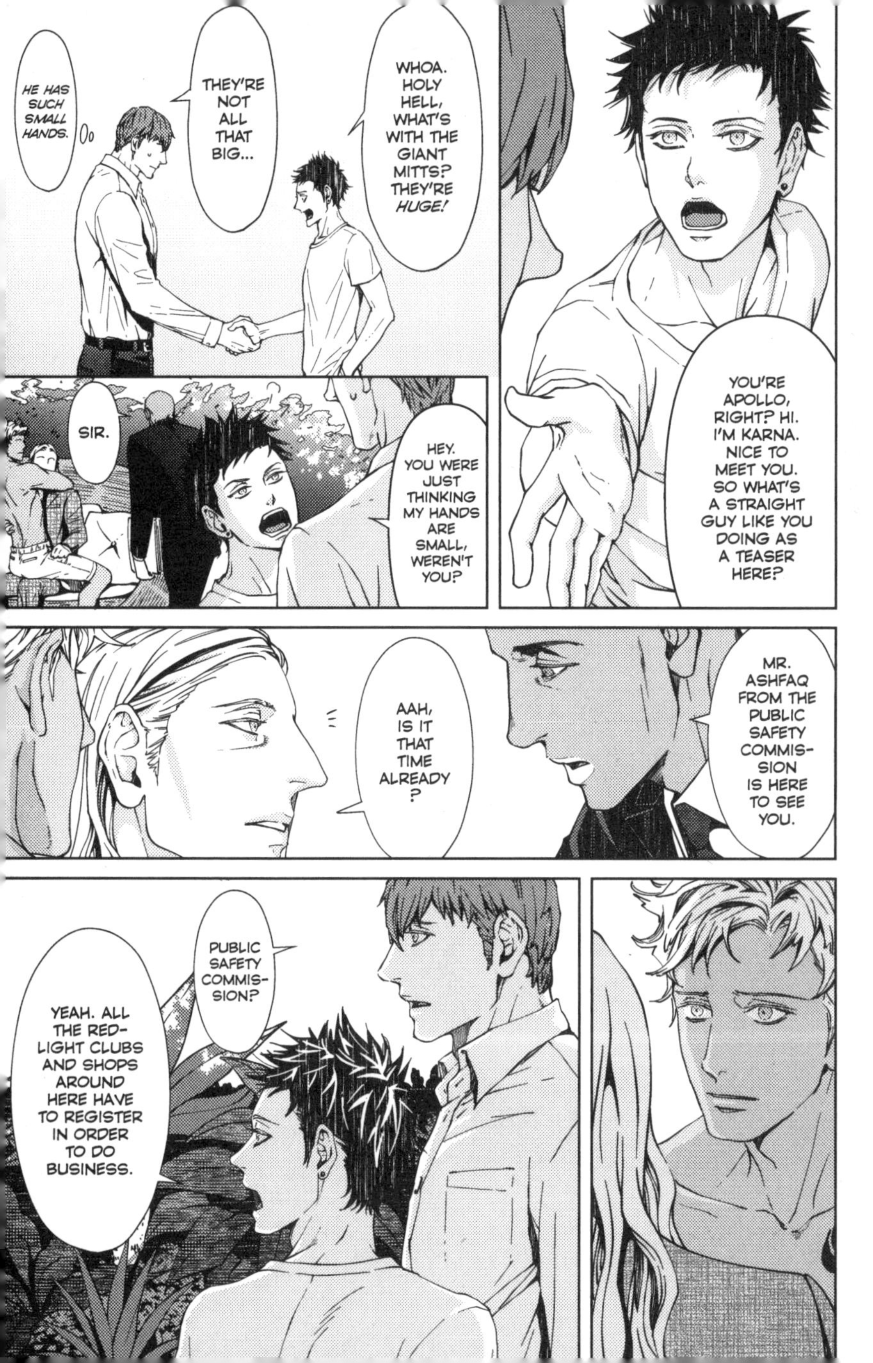
YOU'RE APOLLO, RIGHT? HI. I'M KARNA. NICE TO MEET YOU. SO WHAT'S A STRAIGHT GUY LIKE YOU DOING AS A TEASER HERE?
WHOA. HOLY HELL, WHAT'S WITH THE GIANT MITTS? THEY'RE *HUGE!*
THEY'RE NOT ALL THAT BIG...
HE HAS SUCH SMALL HANDS.
HEY. YOU WERE JUST THINKING MY HANDS ARE SMALL, WEREN'T YOU?
SIR.
MR. ASHFAQ FROM THE PUBLIC SAFETY COMMISSION IS HERE TO SEE YOU.
AAH, IS IT THAT TIME ALREADY?
PUBLIC SAFETY COMMISSION?
YEAH. ALL THE RED-LIGHT CLUBS AND SHOPS AROUND HERE HAVE TO REGISTER IN ORDER TO DO BUSINESS.

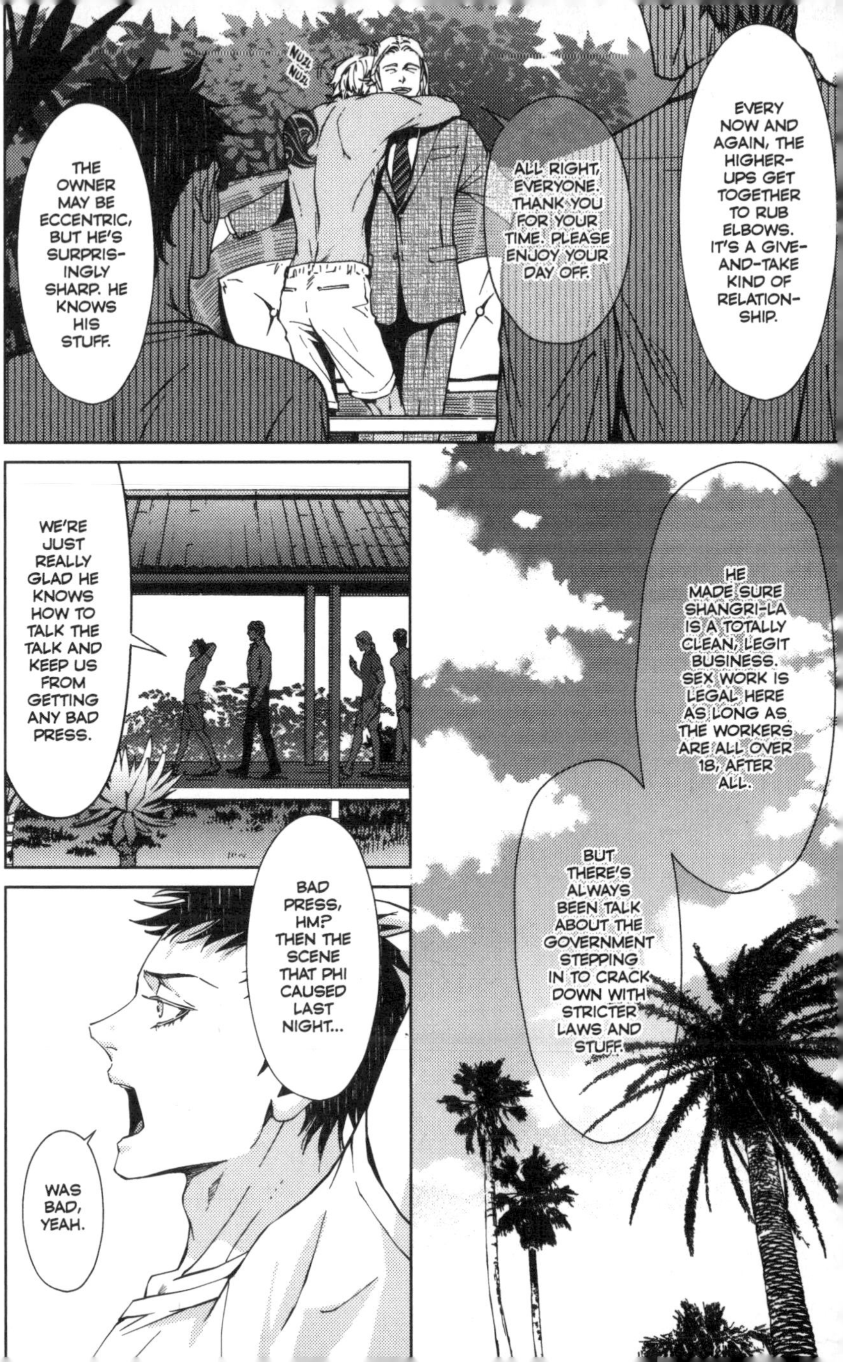
EVERY NOW AND AGAIN, THE HIGHER-UPS GET TOGETHER TO RUB ELBOWS. IT'S A GIVE-AND-TAKE KIND OF RELATIONSHIP.
ALL RIGHT, EVERYONE. THANK YOU FOR YOUR TIME. PLEASE ENJOY YOUR DAY OFF.
NUZL NUZL
THE OWNER MAY BE ECCENTRIC, BUT HE'S SURPRISINGLY SHARP. HE KNOWS HIS STUFF.
HE MADE SURE SHANGRI-LA IS A TOTALLY CLEAN, LEGIT BUSINESS. SEX WORK IS LEGAL HERE AS LONG AS THE WORKERS ARE ALL OVER 18, AFTER ALL.
BUT THERE'S ALWAYS BEEN TALK ABOUT THE GOVERNMENT STEPPING IN TO CRACK DOWN WITH STRICTER LAWS AND STUFF.
WE'RE JUST REALLY GLAD HE KNOWS HOW TO TALK THE TALK AND KEEP US FROM GETTING ANY BAD PRESS.
BAD PRESS, HM? THEN THE SCENE THAT PHI CAUSED LAST NIGHT...
WAS BAD, YEAH.

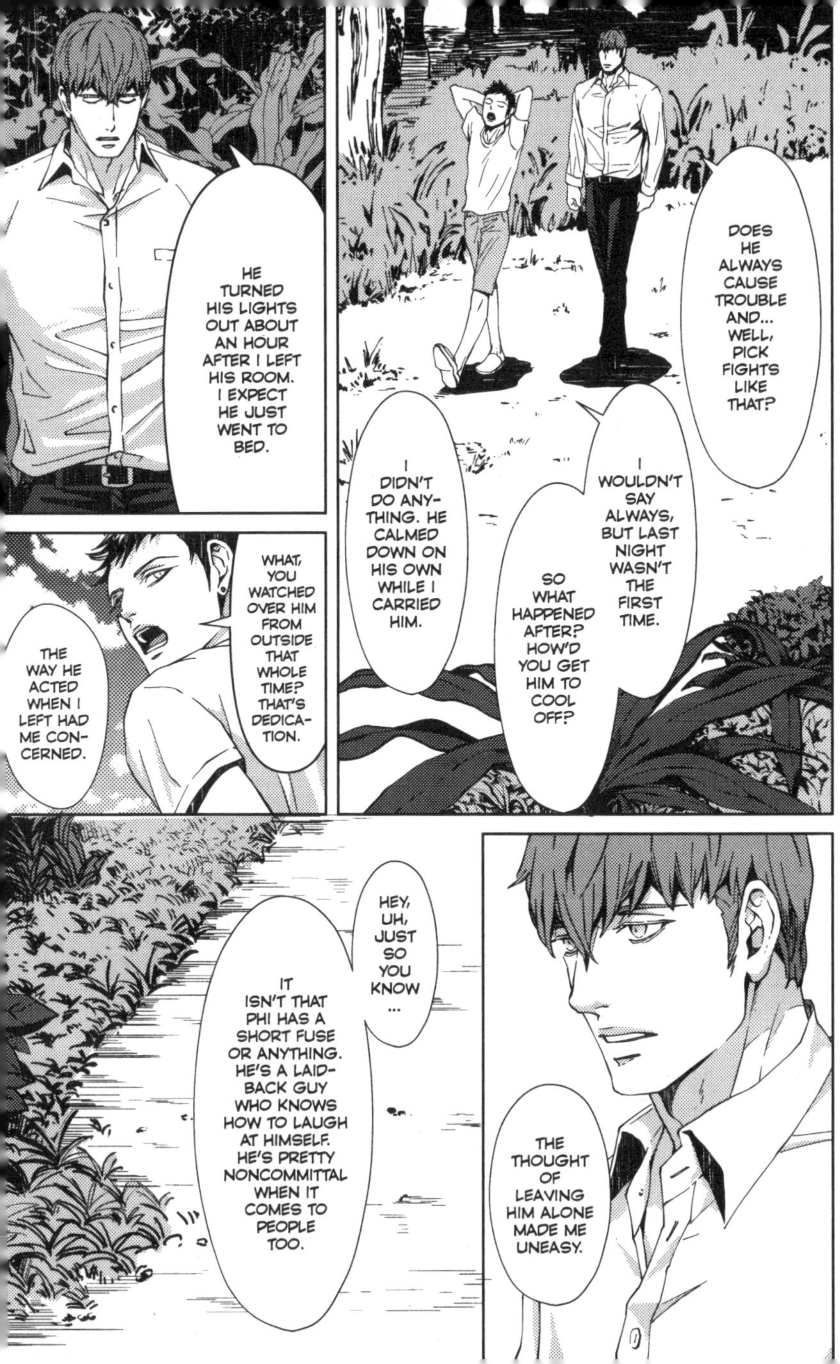
DOES HE ALWAYS CAUSE TROUBLE AND... WELL, PICK FIGHTS LIKE THAT?
I WOULDN'T SAY ALWAYS, BUT LAST NIGHT WASN'T THE FIRST TIME.
SO WHAT HAPPENED AFTER? HOW'D YOU GET HIM TO COOL OFF?
I DIDN'T DO ANYTHING. HE CALMED DOWN ON HIS OWN WHILE I CARRIED HIM.
HE TURNED HIS LIGHTS OUT ABOUT AN HOUR AFTER I LEFT HIS ROOM. I EXPECT HE JUST WENT TO BED.
WHAT, YOU WATCHED OVER HIM FROM OUTSIDE THAT WHOLE TIME? THAT'S DEDICATION.
THE WAY HE ACTED WHEN I LEFT HAD ME CONCERNED.
THE THOUGHT OF LEAVING HIM ALONE MADE ME UNEASY.
HEY, UH, JUST SO YOU KNOW...
IT ISN'T THAT PHI HAS A SHORT FUSE OR ANYTHING. HE'S A LAID-BACK GUY WHO KNOWS HOW TO LAUGH AT HIMSELF. HE'S PRETTY NONCOMMITTAL WHEN IT COMES TO PEOPLE TOO.

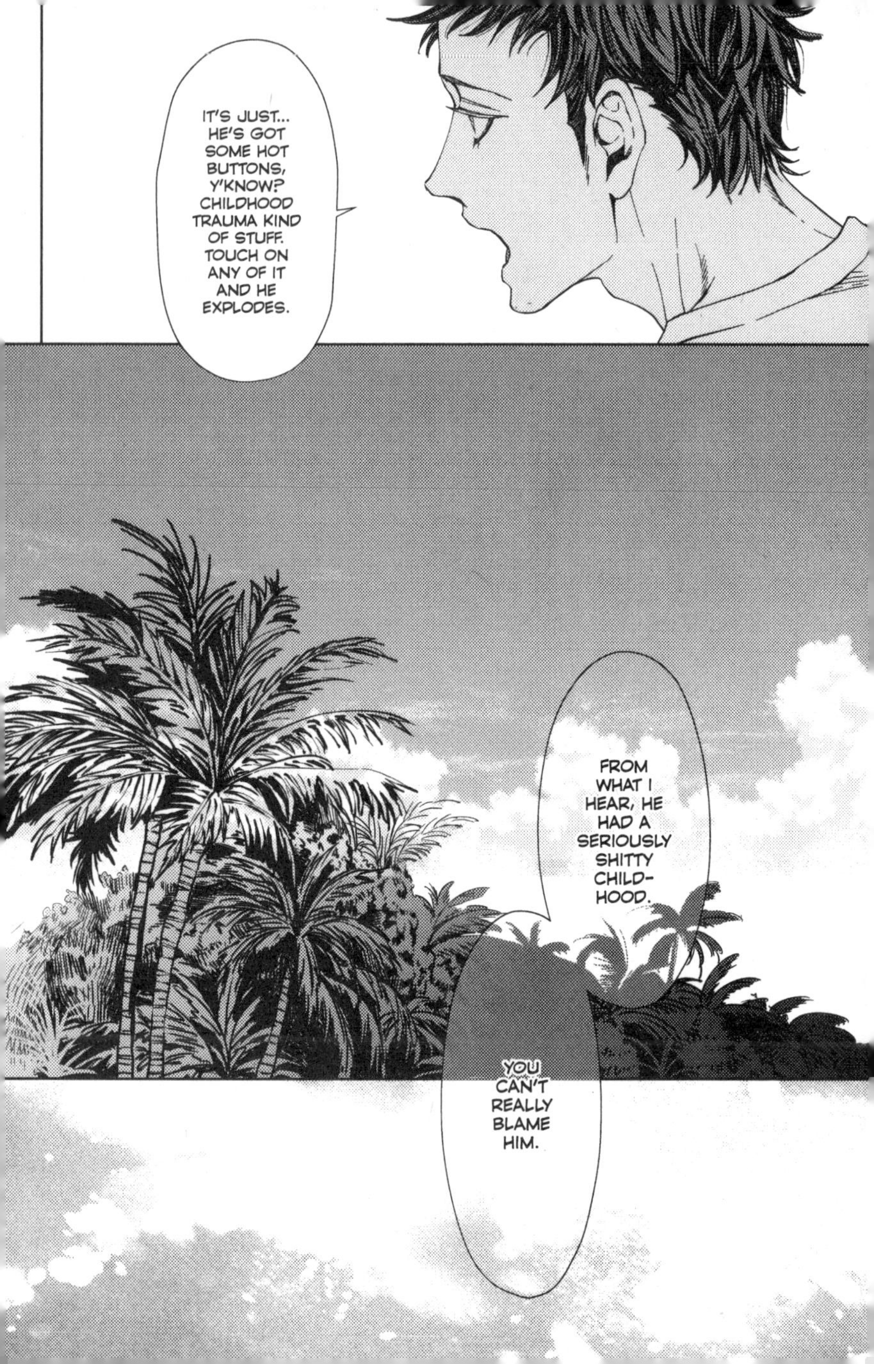
IT'S JUST... HE'S GOT SOME HOT BUTTONS, Y'KNOW? CHILDHOOD TRAUMA KIND OF STUFF. TOUCH ON ANY OF IT AND HE EXPLODES.
FROM WHAT I HEAR, HE HAD A SERIOUSLY SHITTY CHILD-HOOD.
YOU CAN'T REALLY BLAME HIM.

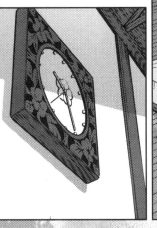

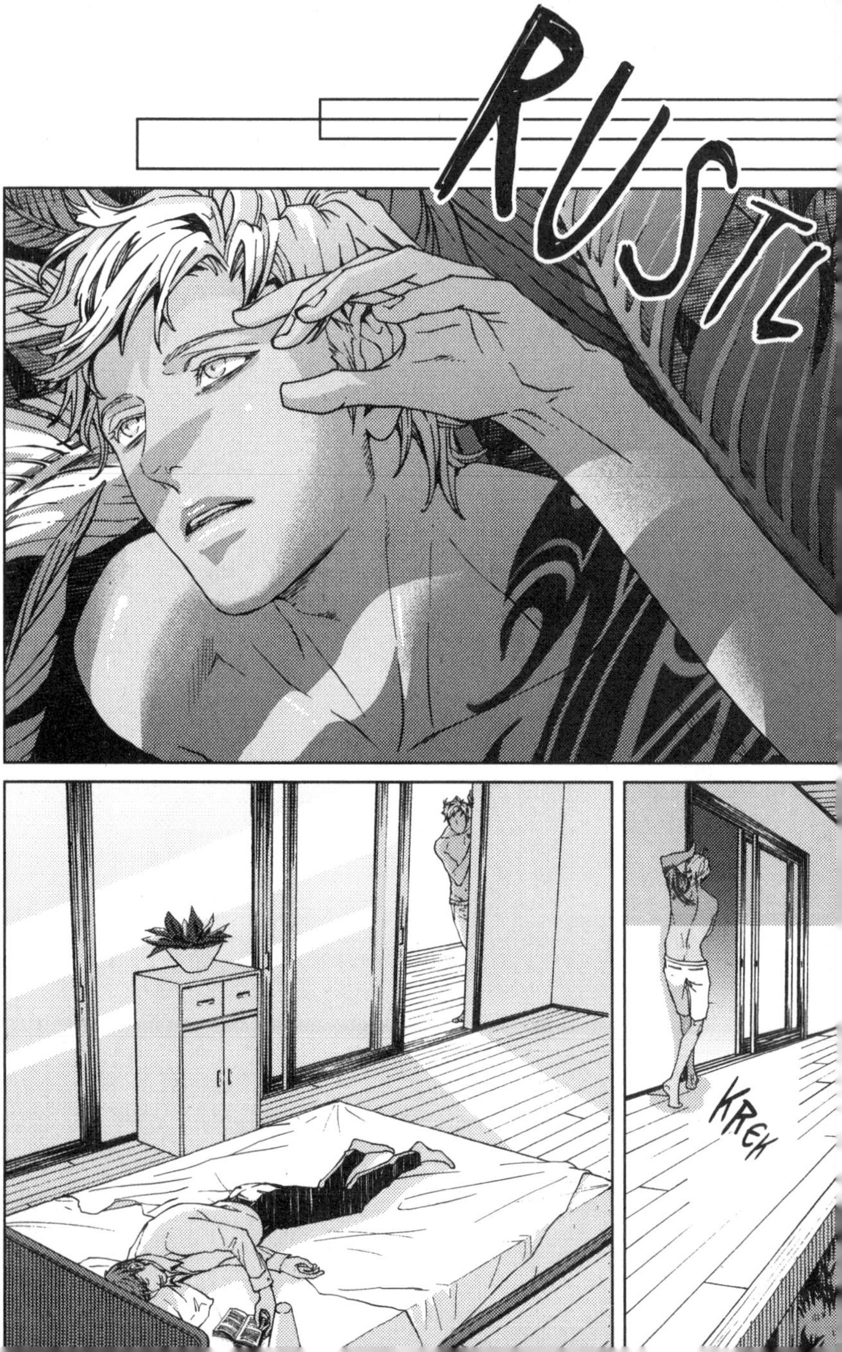
RUSTL
KREK

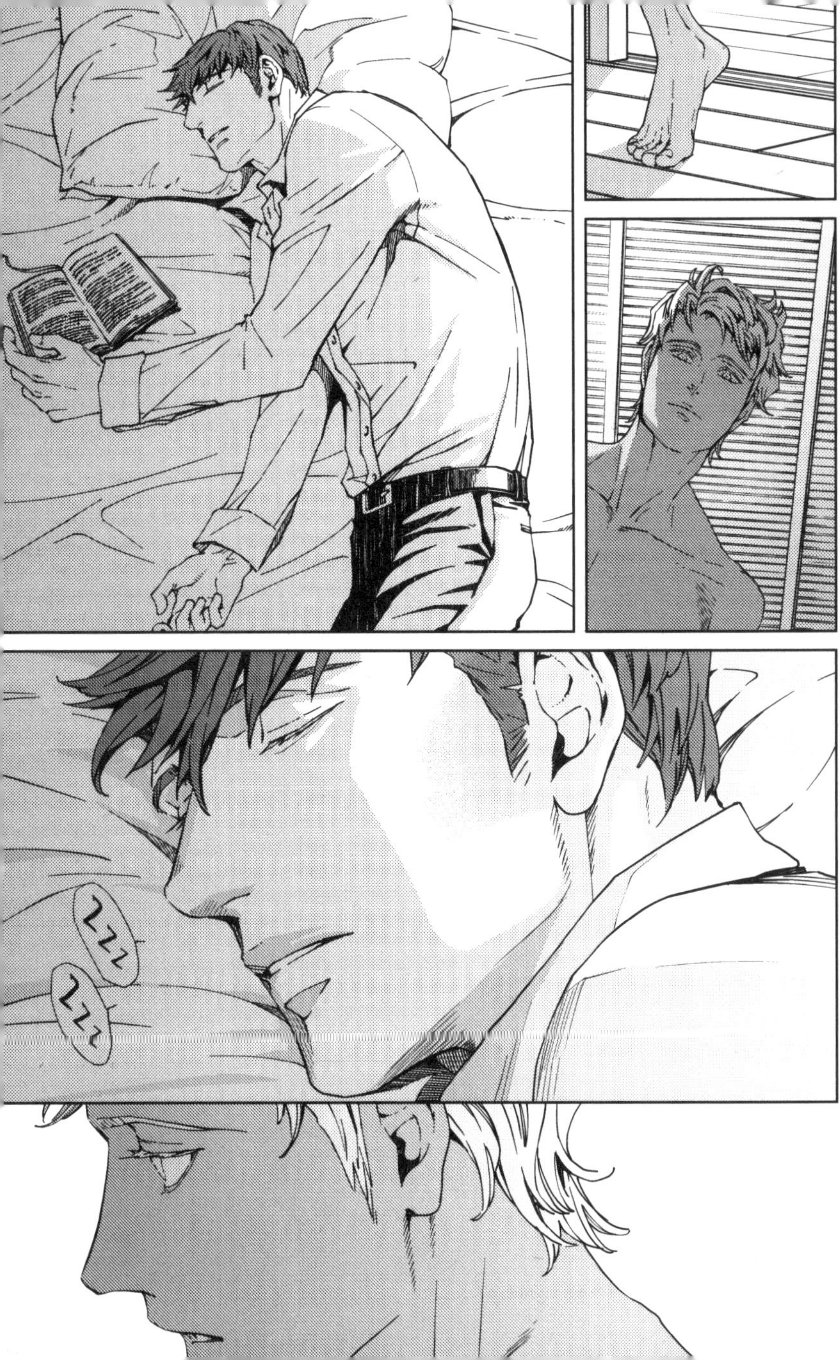
zzz
zzz

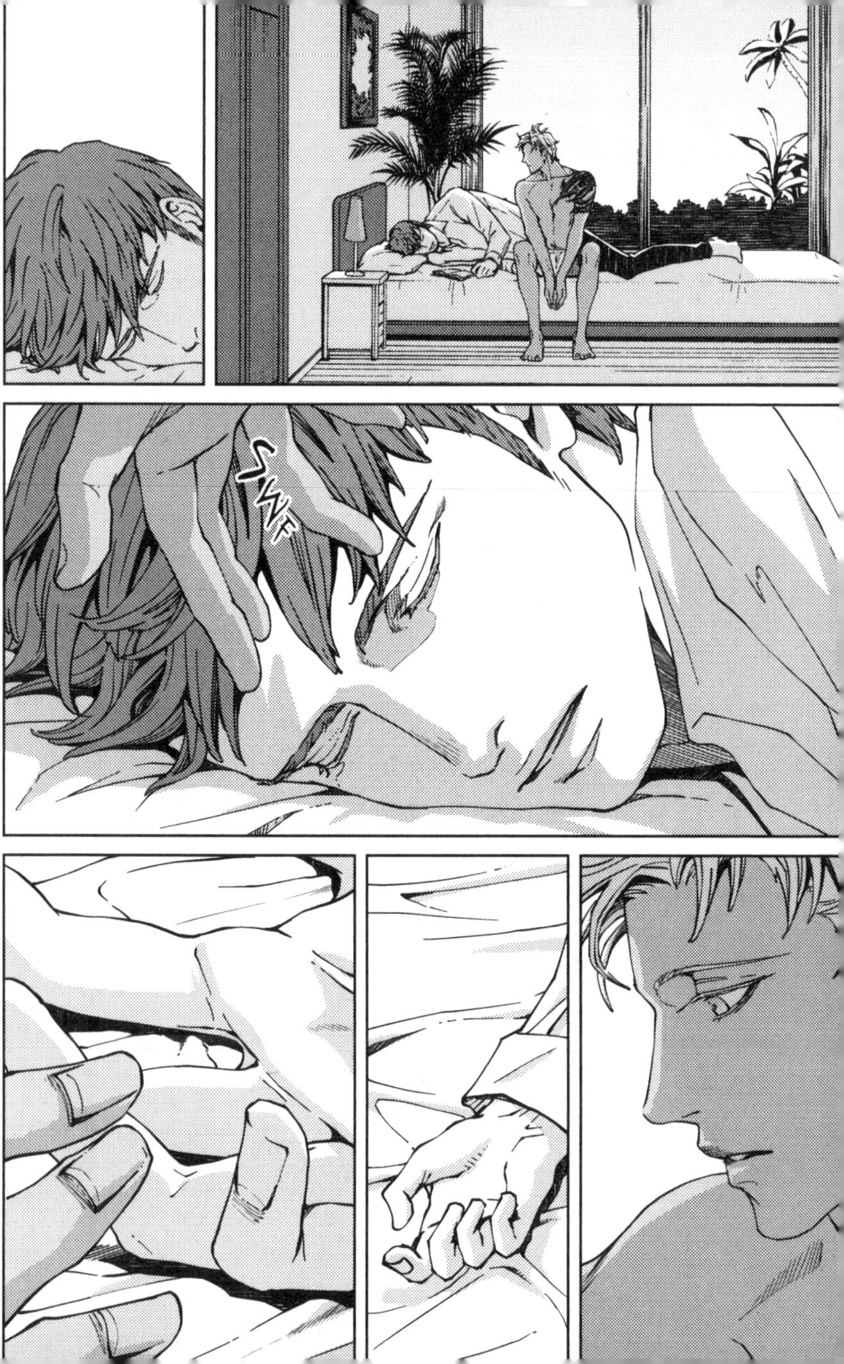
SWF

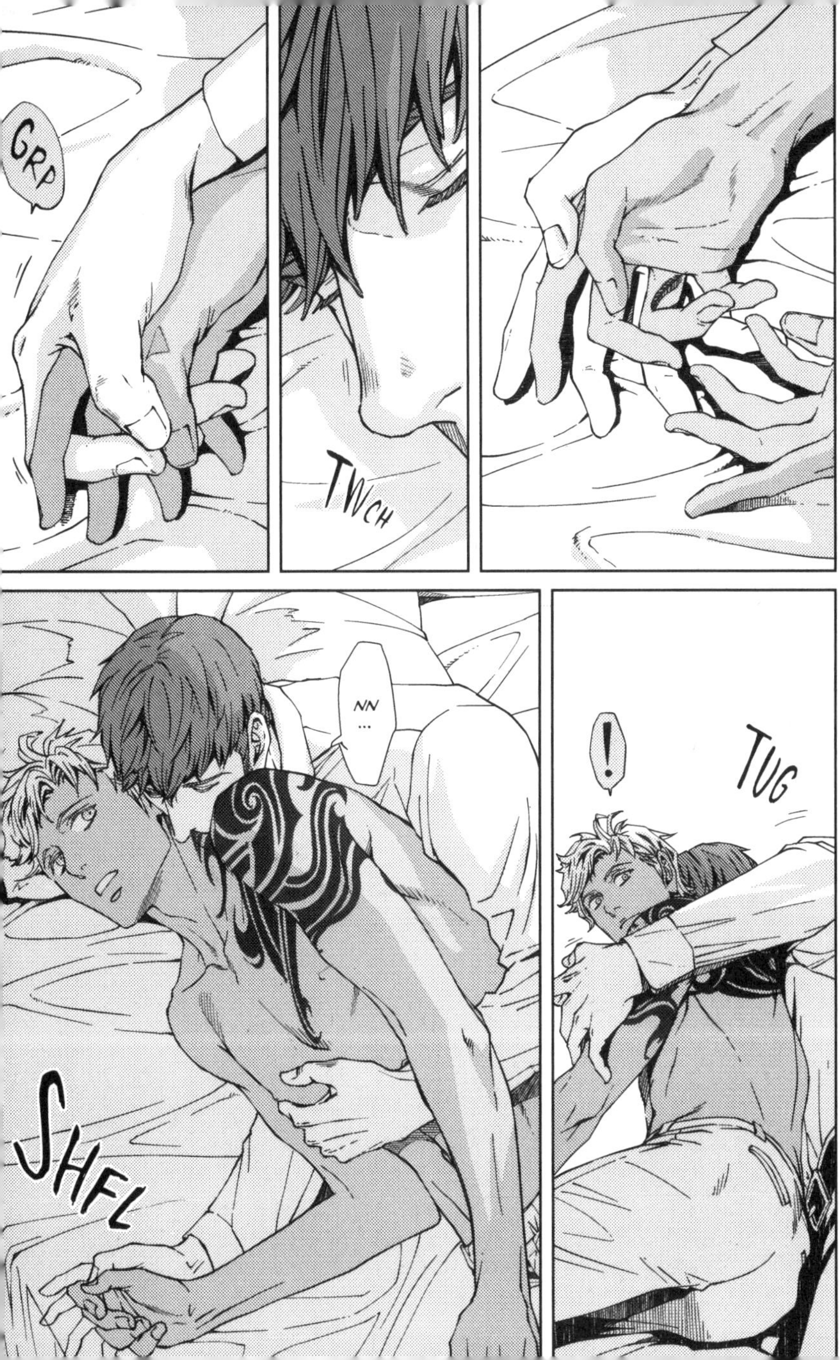
TWCH
GRP
!
TUG
NN ...
SHFL

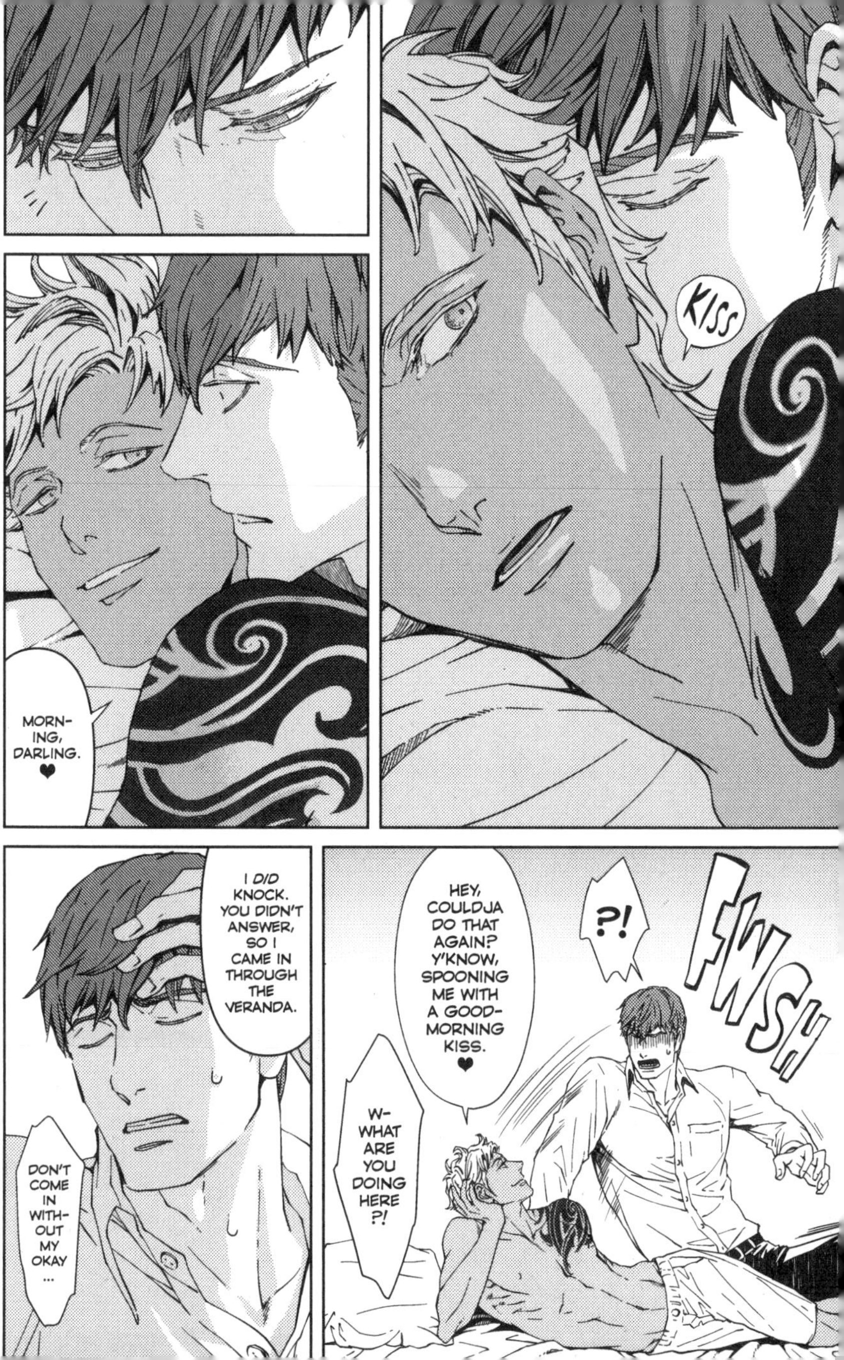
KISS
MORN-ING, DARLING. ♥
FWSH
?!
HEY, COULDJA DO THAT AGAIN? Y'KNOW, SPOONING ME WITH A GOOD-MORNING KISS. ♥
W-WHAT ARE YOU DOING HERE ?!
I *DID* KNOCK. YOU DIDN'T ANSWER, SO I CAME IN THROUGH THE VERANDA.
DON'T COME IN WITH-OUT MY OKAY ...

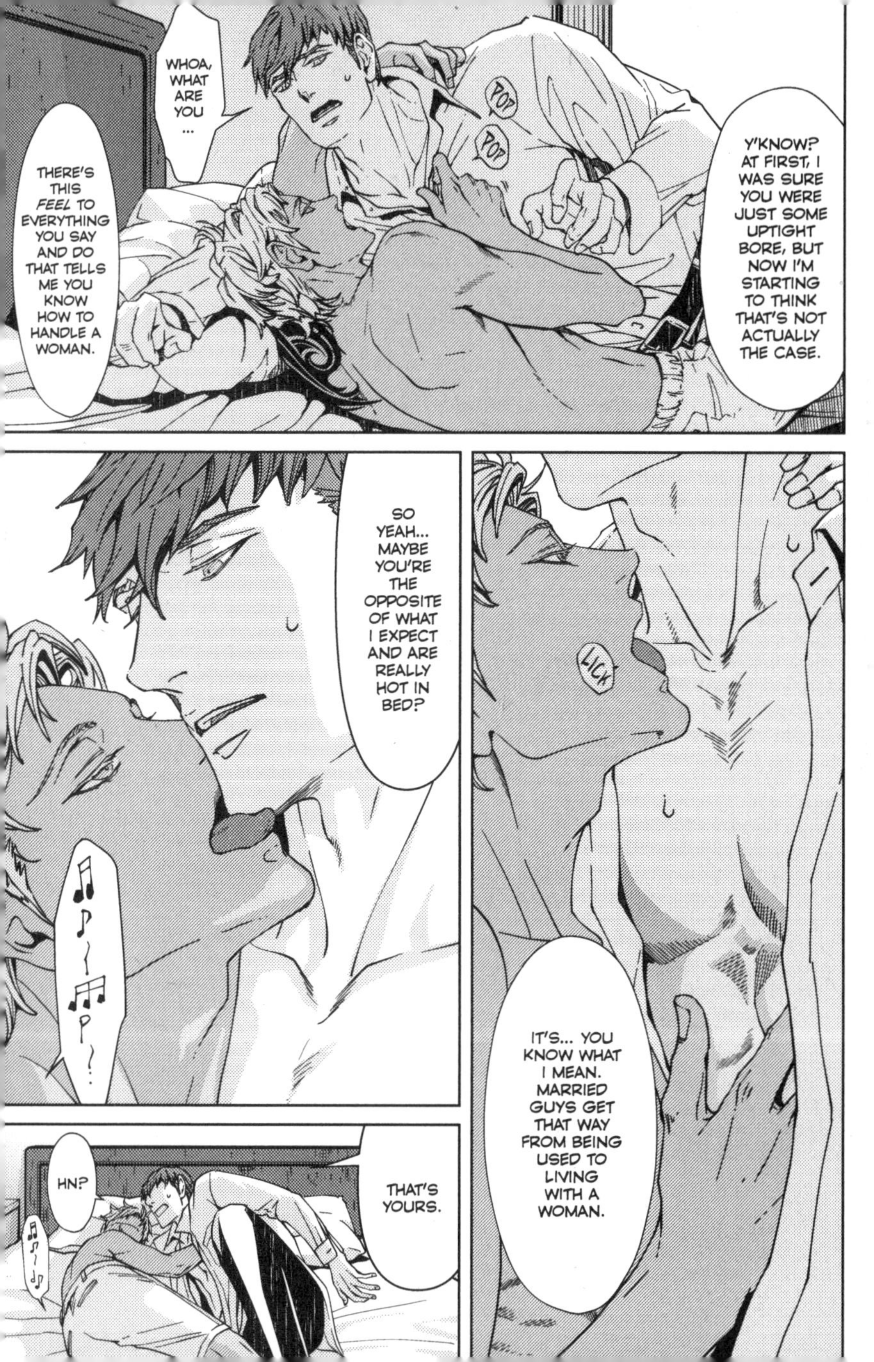
Y'KNOW? AT FIRST, I WAS SURE YOU WERE JUST SOME UPTIGHT BORE, BUT NOW I'M STARTING TO THINK THAT'S NOT ACTUALLY THE CASE.
POP
POP
WHOA, WHAT ARE YOU ...
THERE'S THIS *FEEL* TO EVERYTHING YOU SAY AND DO THAT TELLS ME YOU KNOW HOW TO HANDLE A WOMAN.
LICK
IT'S... YOU KNOW WHAT I MEAN. MARRIED GUYS GET THAT WAY FROM BEING USED TO LIVING WITH A WOMAN.
SO YEAH... MAYBE YOU'RE THE OPPOSITE OF WHAT I EXPECT AND ARE REALLY HOT IN BED?
THAT'S YOURS.
HN?

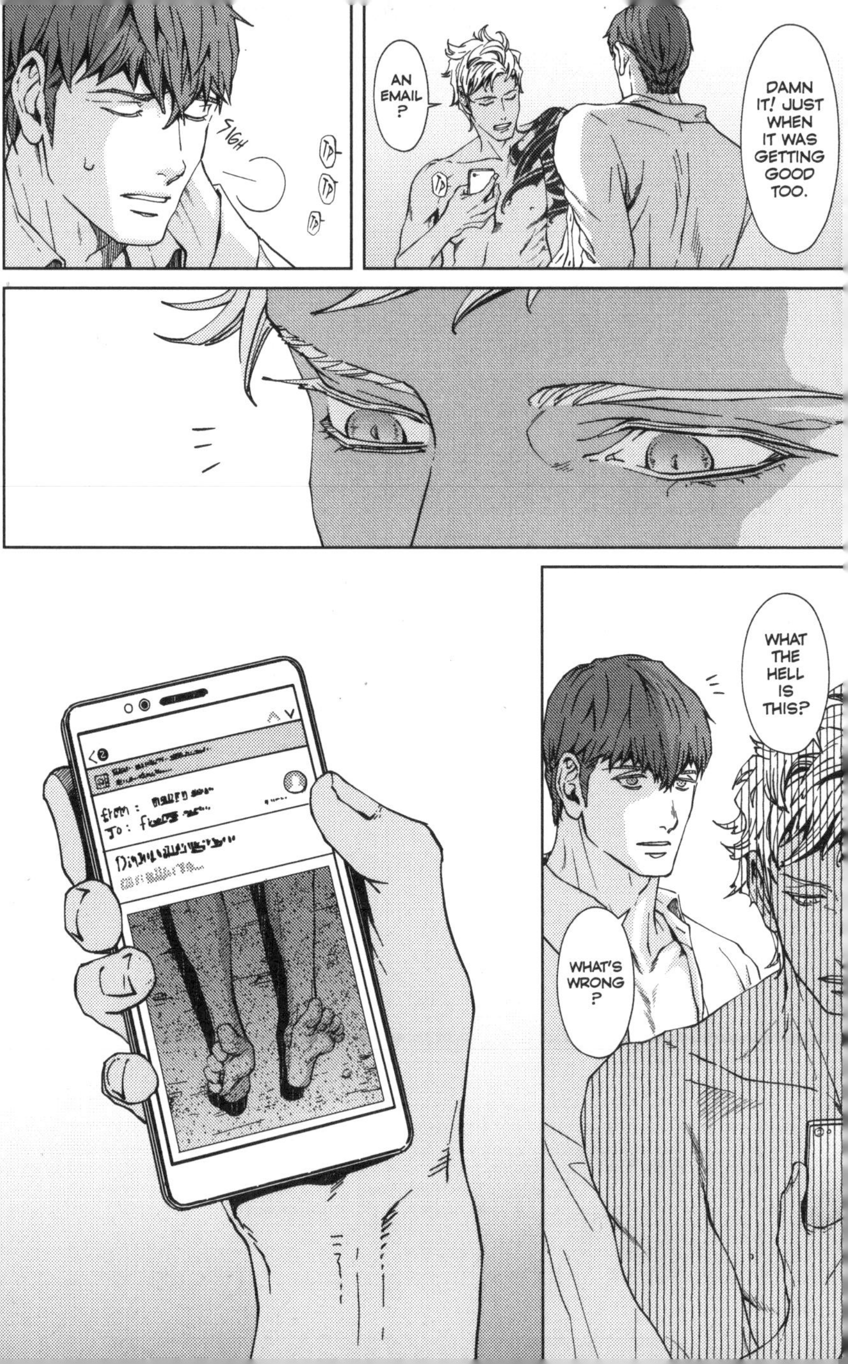
DAMN IT! JUST WHEN IT WAS GETTING GOOD TOO.
AN EMAIL?
TP
SIGH
TP
TP
TP
WHAT THE HELL IS THIS?
WHAT'S WRONG?
From :
To :

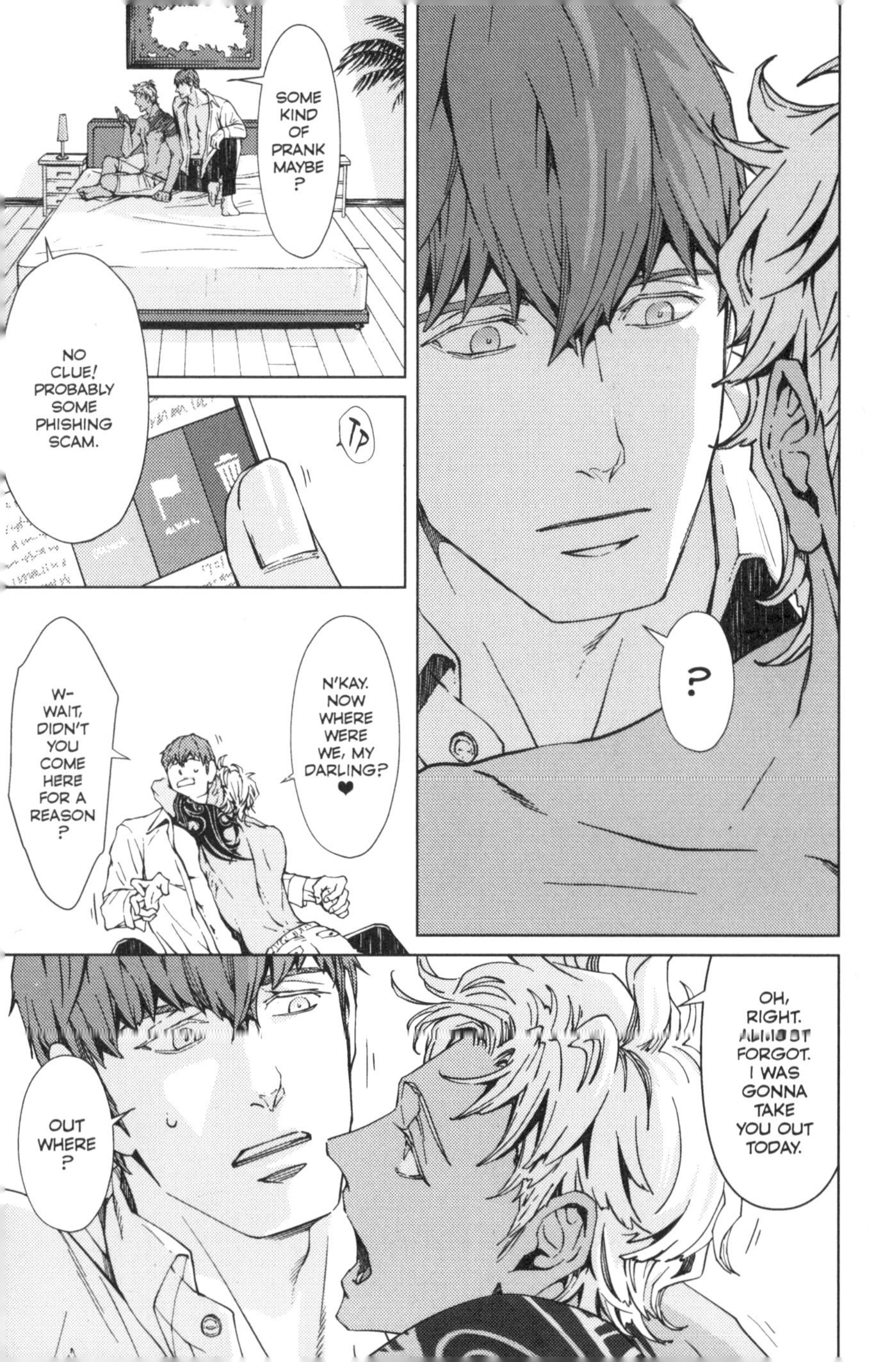
?
SOME KIND OF PRANK MAYBE?
NO CLUE! PROBABLY SOME PHISHING SCAM.
TP
N'KAY. NOW WHERE WERE WE, MY DARLING? ❤
W-WAIT, DIDN'T YOU COME HERE FOR A REASON?
OH, RIGHT. ALMOST FORGOT. I WAS GONNA TAKE YOU OUT TODAY.
OUT WHERE?

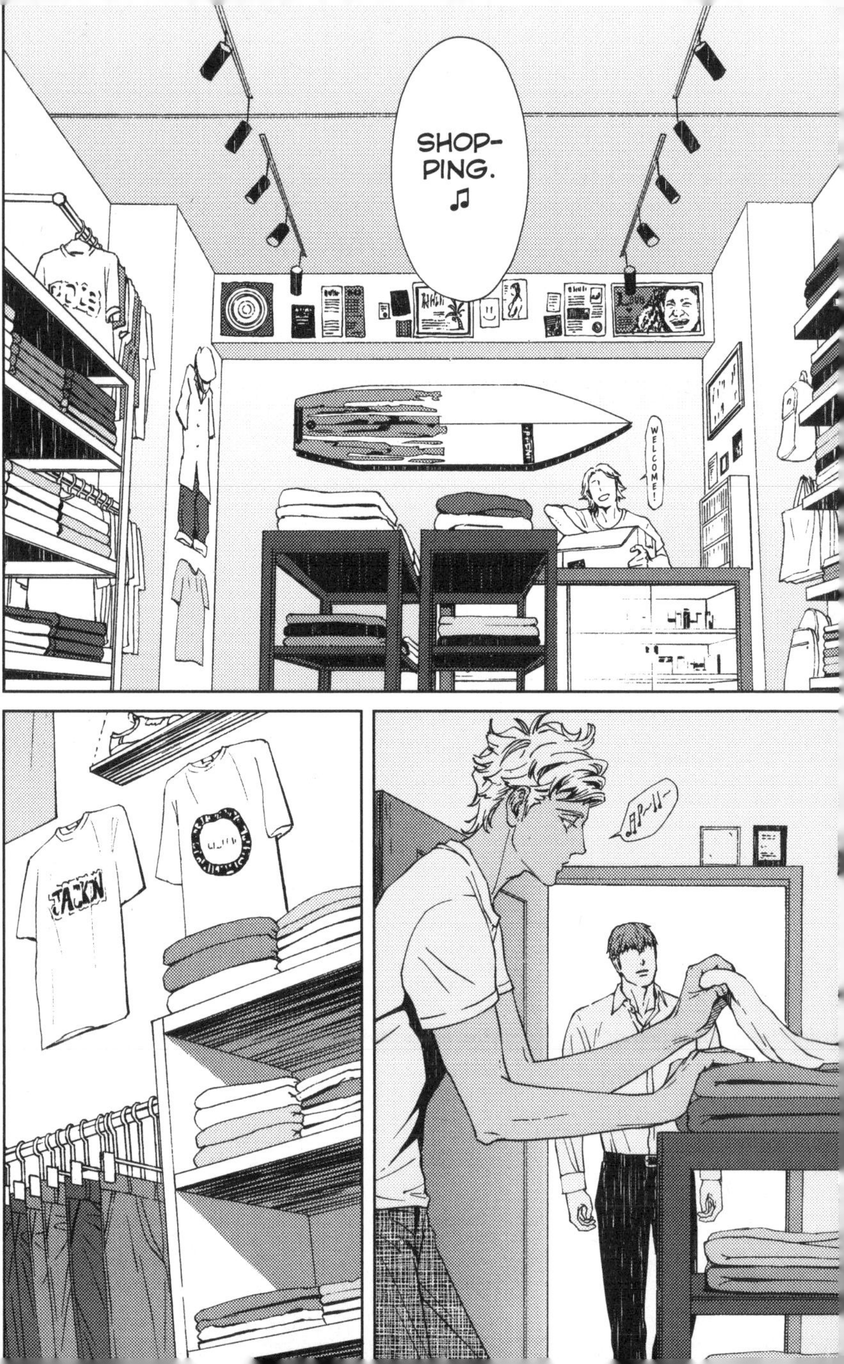
SHOP-
PING.
♫
WELCOME!

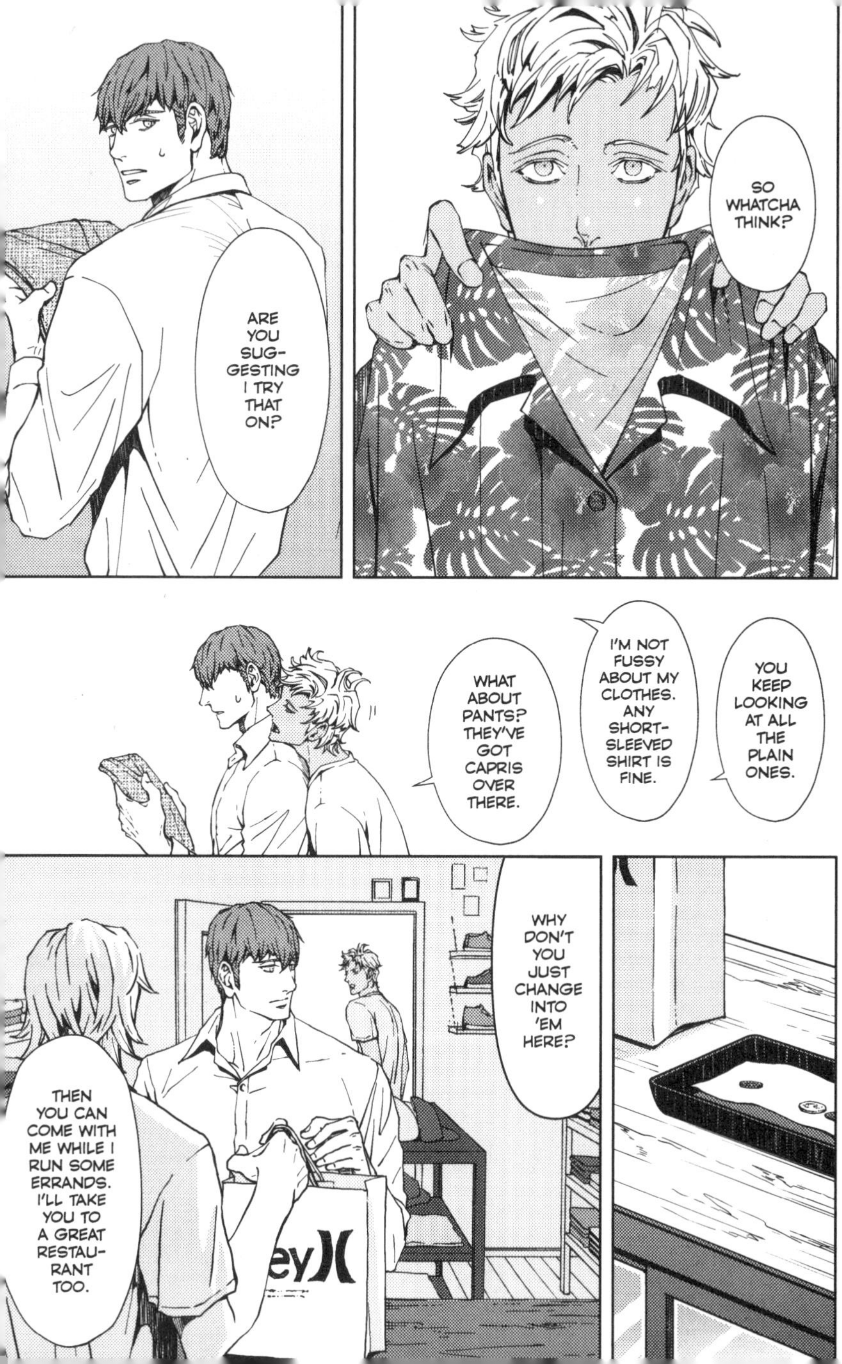
SO WHATCHA THINK?
ARE YOU SUG-GESTING I TRY THAT ON?
YOU KEEP LOOKING AT ALL THE PLAIN ONES.
I'M NOT FUSSY ABOUT MY CLOTHES. ANY SHORT-SLEEVED SHIRT IS FINE.
WHAT ABOUT PANTS? THEY'VE GOT CAPRIS OVER THERE.
WHY DON'T YOU JUST CHANGE INTO 'EM HERE?
THEN YOU CAN COME WITH ME WHILE I RUN SOME ERRANDS. I'LL TAKE YOU TO A GREAT RESTAU-RANT TOO.

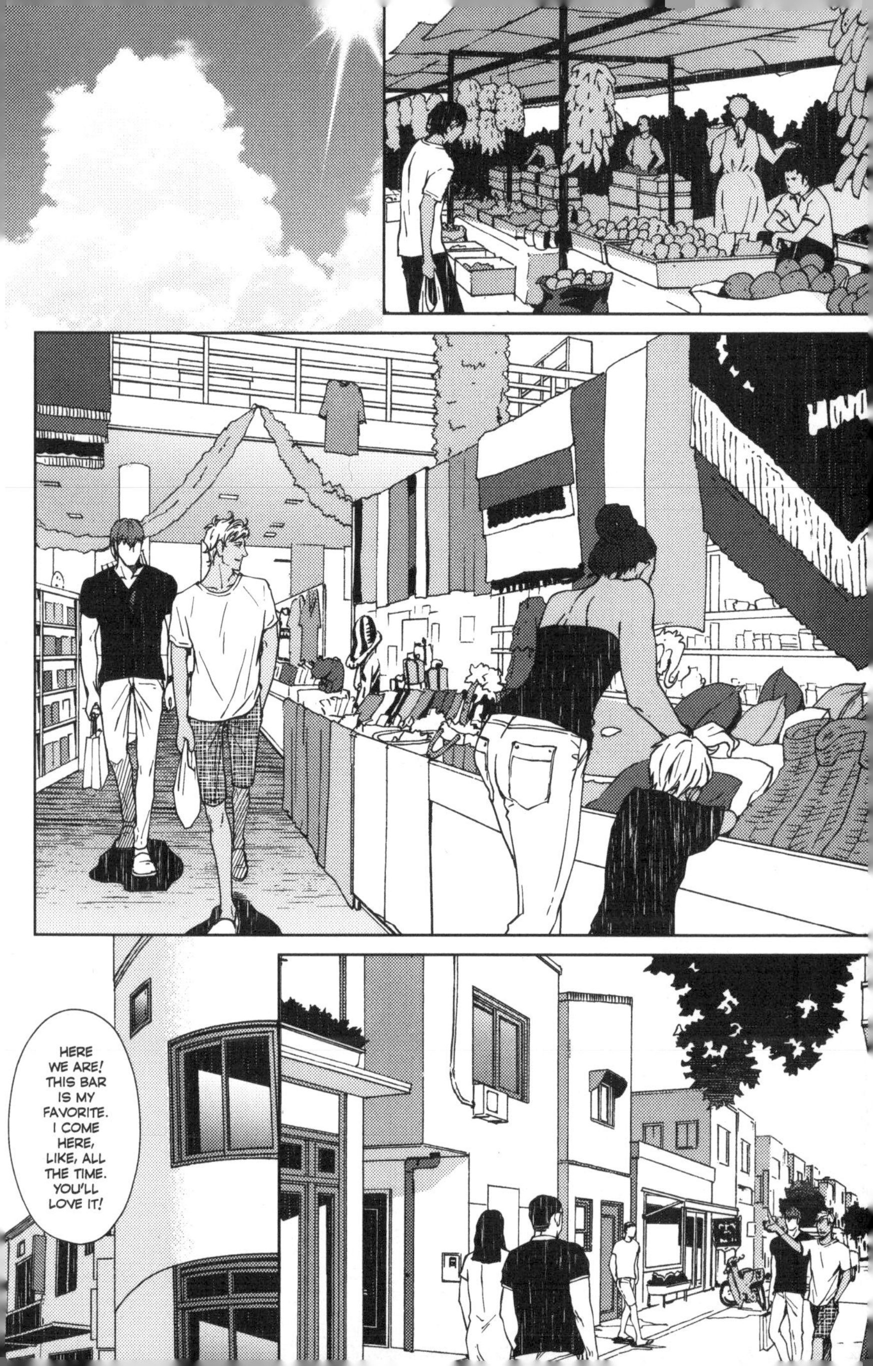
HERE WE ARE! THIS BAR IS MY FAVORITE. I COME HERE, LIKE, ALL THE TIME. YOU'LL LOVE IT!

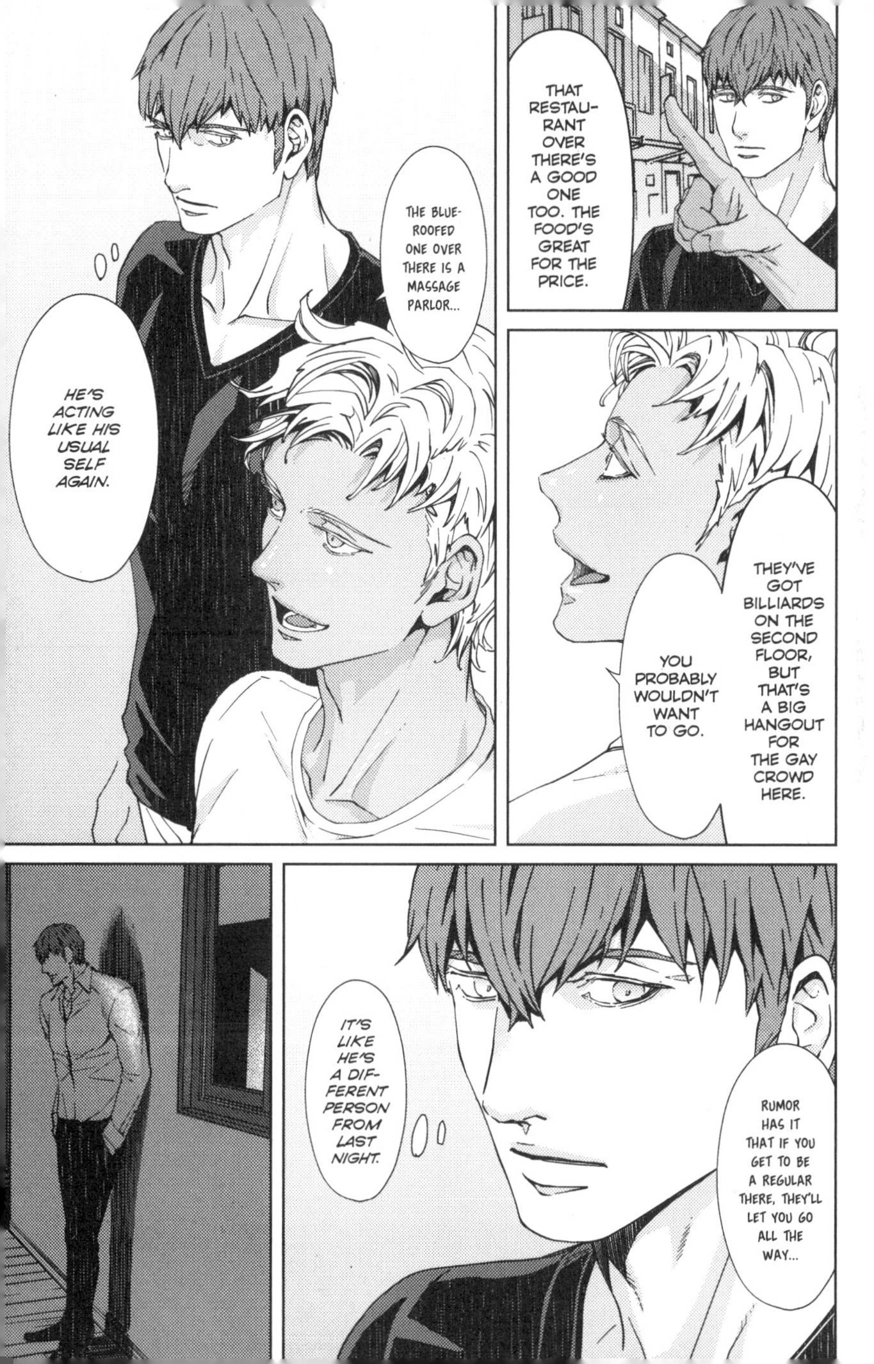
THAT RESTAU-RANT OVER THERE'S A GOOD ONE TOO. THE FOOD'S GREAT FOR THE PRICE.
THEY'VE GOT BILLIARDS ON THE SECOND FLOOR, BUT THAT'S A BIG HANGOUT FOR THE GAY CROWD HERE.
YOU PROBABLY WOULDN'T WANT TO GO.
THE BLUE-ROOFED ONE OVER THERE IS A MASSAGE PARLOR...
HE'S ACTING LIKE HIS USUAL SELF AGAIN.
RUMOR HAS IT THAT IF YOU GET TO BE A REGULAR THERE, THEY'LL LET YOU GO ALL THE WAY...
IT'S LIKE HE'S A DIF-FERENT PERSON FROM LAST NIGHT.

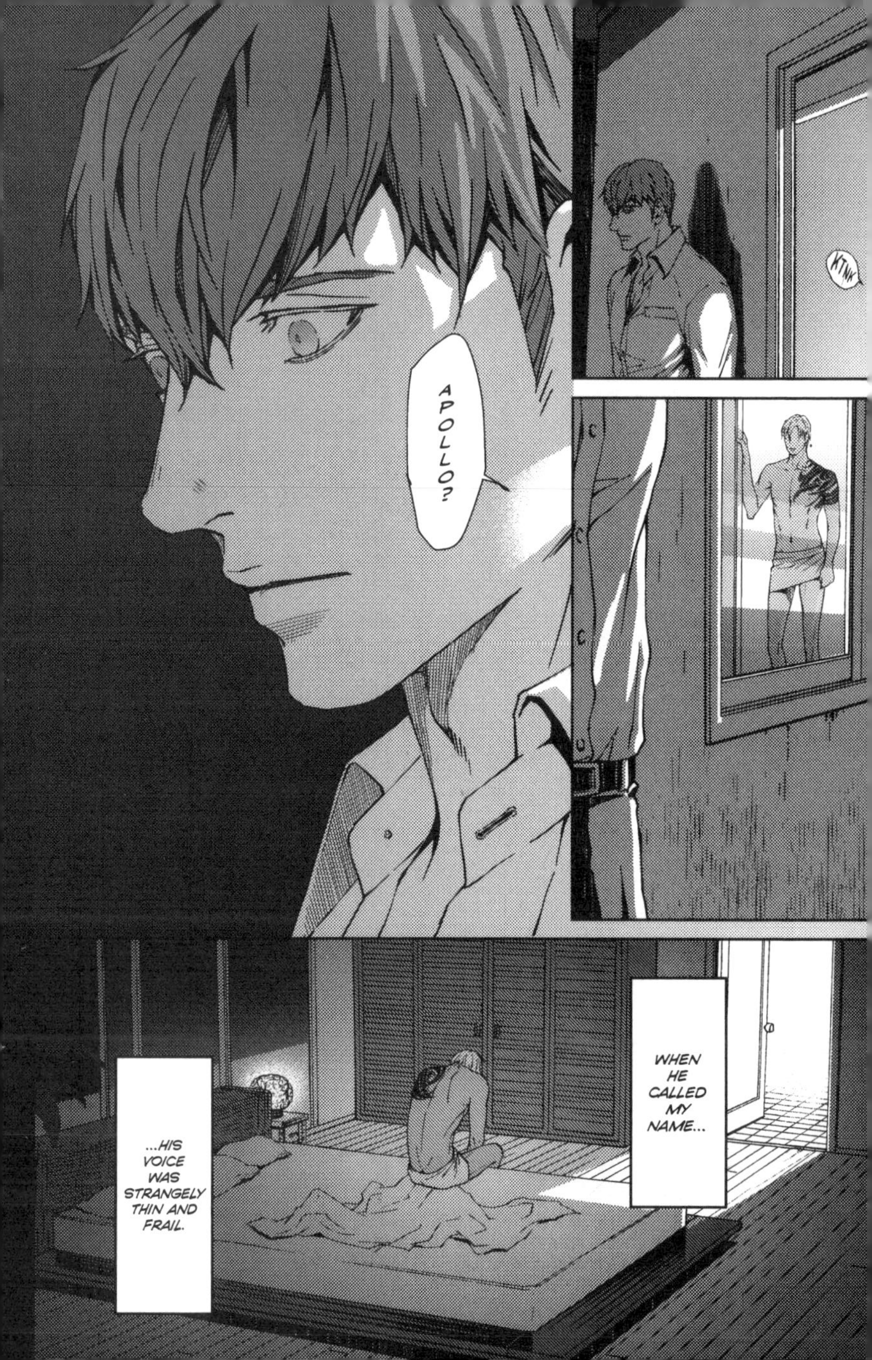
KTNK
APOLLO?
WHEN HE CALLED MY NAME...
...HIS VOICE WAS STRANGELY THIN AND FRAIL.

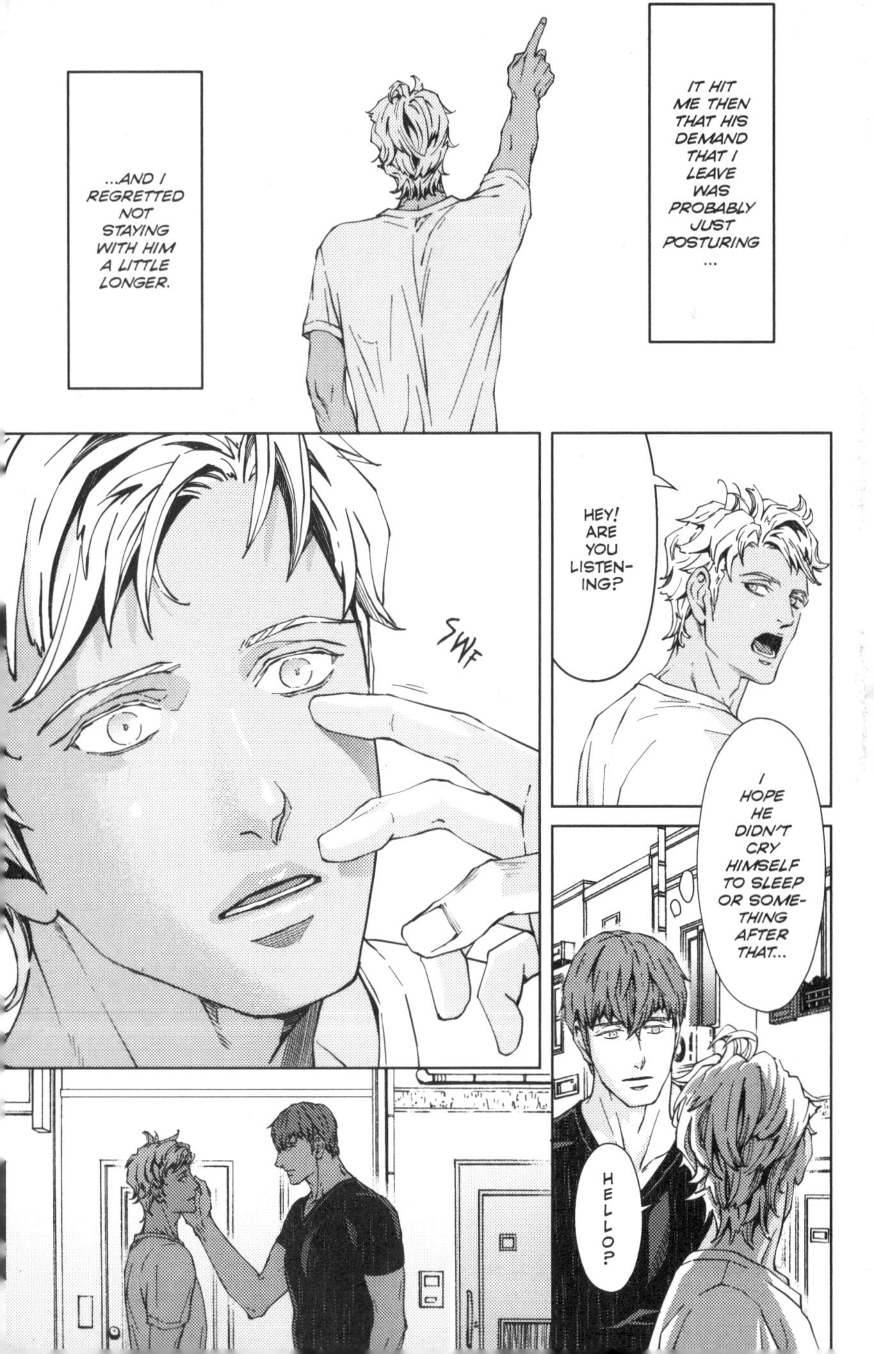
IT HIT ME THEN THAT HIS DEMAND THAT I LEAVE WAS PROBABLY JUST POSTURING...
...AND I REGRETTED NOT STAYING WITH HIM A LITTLE LONGER.
HEY! ARE YOU LISTEN-ING?
I HOPE HE DIDN'T CRY HIMSELF TO SLEEP OR SOME-THING AFTER THAT...
HELLO?
SWF

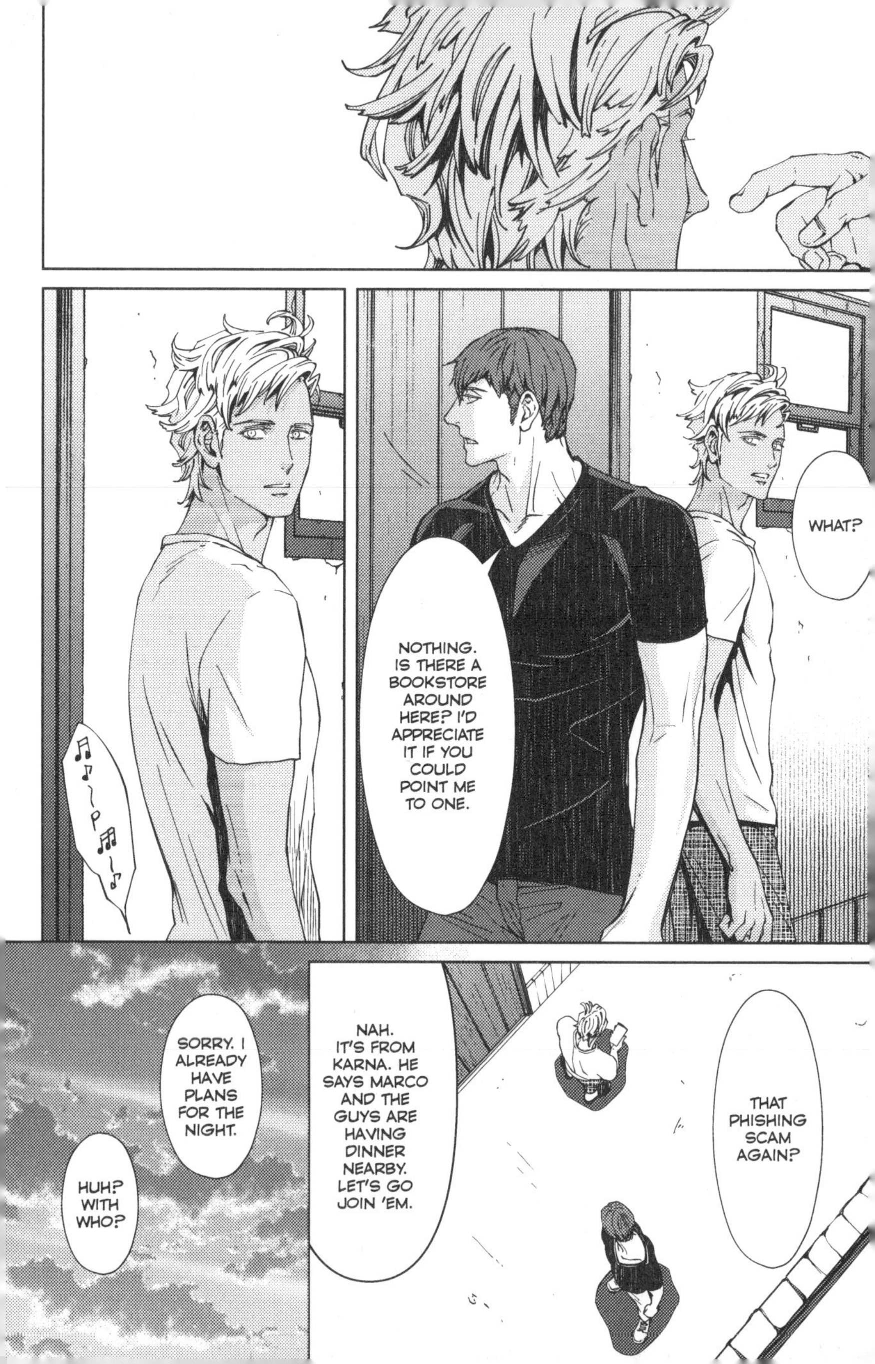
WHAT?
NOTHING. IS THERE A BOOKSTORE AROUND HERE? I'D APPRECIATE IT IF YOU COULD POINT ME TO ONE.
THAT PHISHING SCAM AGAIN?
NAH. IT'S FROM KARNA. HE SAYS MARCO AND THE GUYS ARE HAVING DINNER NEARBY. LET'S GO JOIN 'EM.
SORRY. I ALREADY HAVE PLANS FOR THE NIGHT.
HUH? WITH WHO?

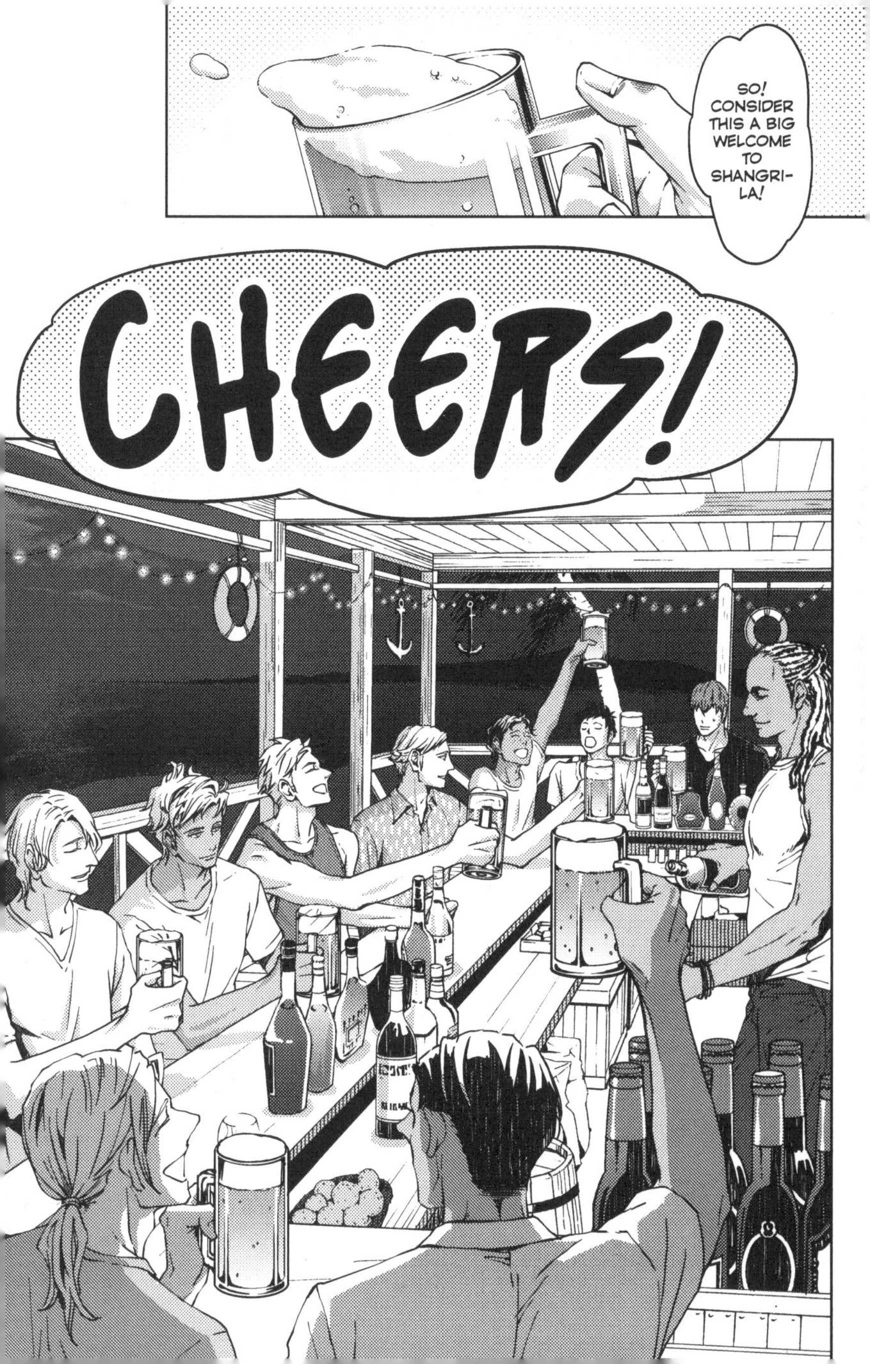
SO! CONSIDER THIS A BIG WELCOME TO SHANGRI-LA!
CHEERS!

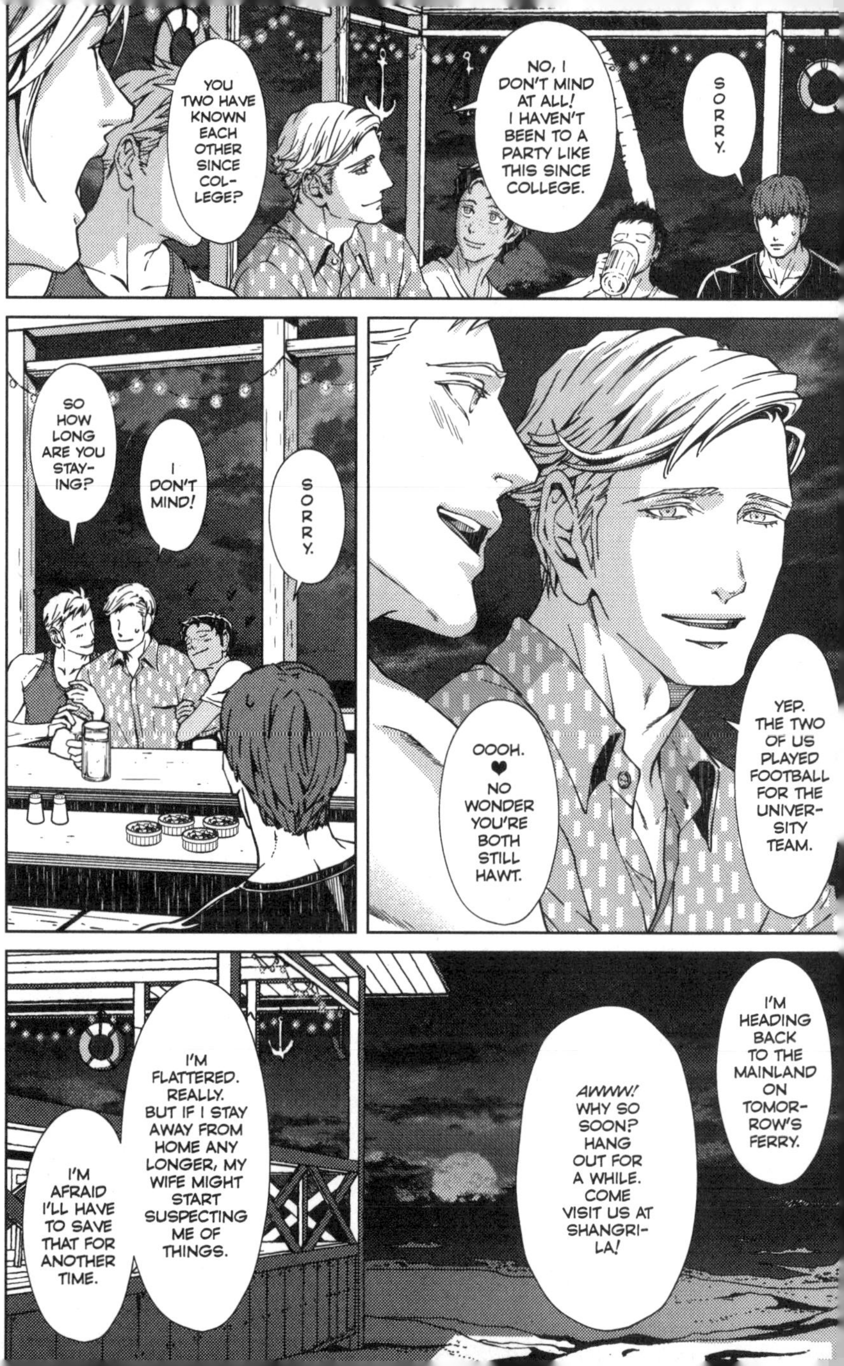
SORRY.
NO, I DON'T MIND AT ALL! I HAVEN'T BEEN TO A PARTY LIKE THIS SINCE COLLEGE.
YOU TWO HAVE KNOWN EACH OTHER SINCE COLLEGE?
YEP. THE TWO OF US PLAYED FOOTBALL FOR THE UNIVERSITY TEAM.
OOOH. ♥ NO WONDER YOU'RE BOTH STILL HAWT.
SORRY.
I DON'T MIND!
SO HOW LONG ARE YOU STAYING?
I'M HEADING BACK TO THE MAINLAND ON TOMORROW'S FERRY.
AWWW! WHY SO SOON? HANG OUT FOR A WHILE. COME VISIT US AT SHANGRI-LA!
I'M FLATTERED. REALLY. BUT IF I STAY AWAY FROM HOME ANY LONGER, MY WIFE MIGHT START SUSPECTING ME OF THINGS.
I'M AFRAID I'LL HAVE TO SAVE THAT FOR ANOTHER TIME.

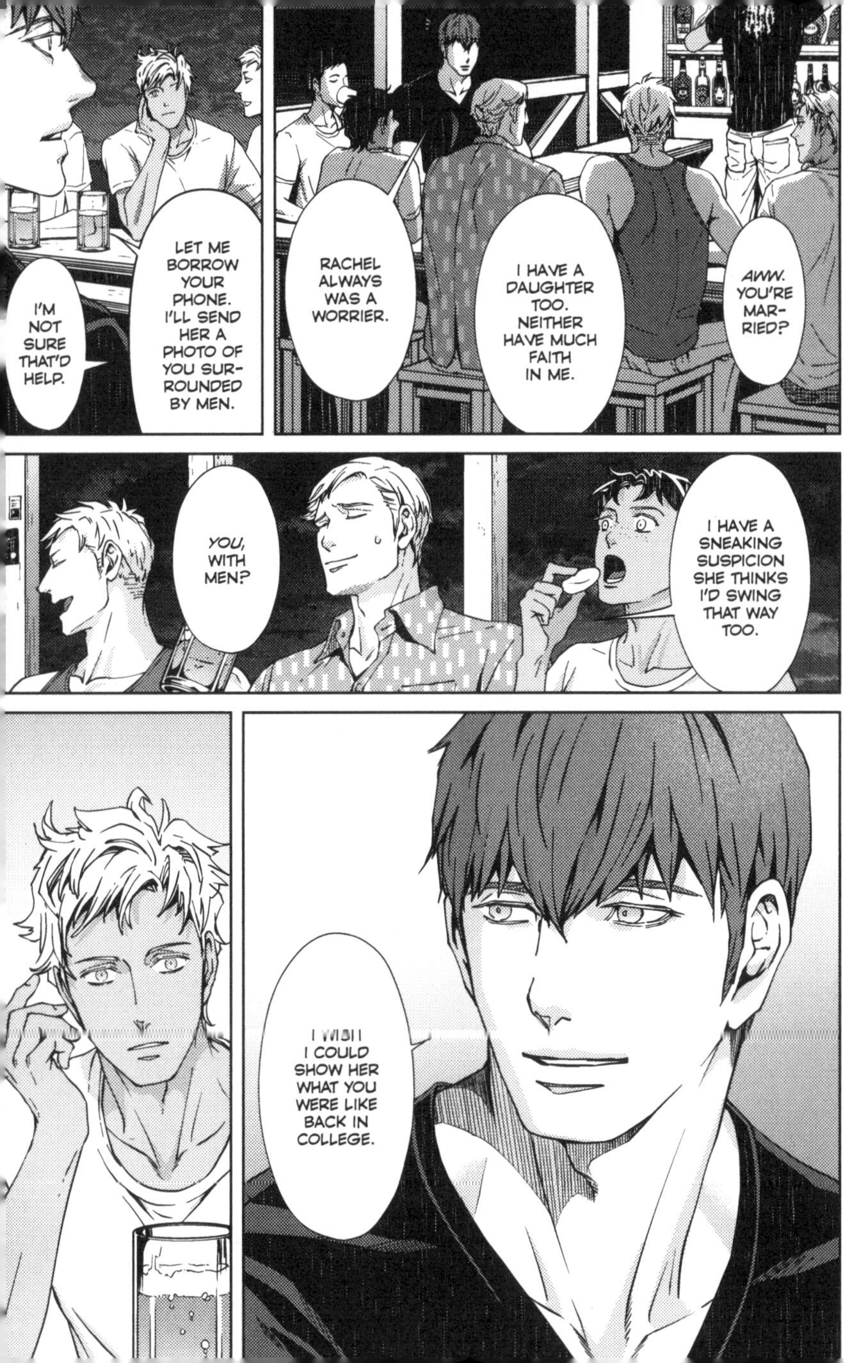
AWW. YOU'RE MARRIED?
I HAVE A DAUGHTER TOO. NEITHER HAVE MUCH FAITH IN ME.
RACHEL ALWAYS WAS A WORRIER.
LET ME BORROW YOUR PHONE. I'LL SEND HER A PHOTO OF YOU SURROUNDED BY MEN.
I'M NOT SURE THAT'D HELP.
I HAVE A SNEAKING SUSPICION SHE THINKS I'D SWING THAT WAY TOO.
YOU, WITH MEN?
I WISH I COULD SHOW HER WHAT YOU WERE LIKE BACK IN COLLEGE.

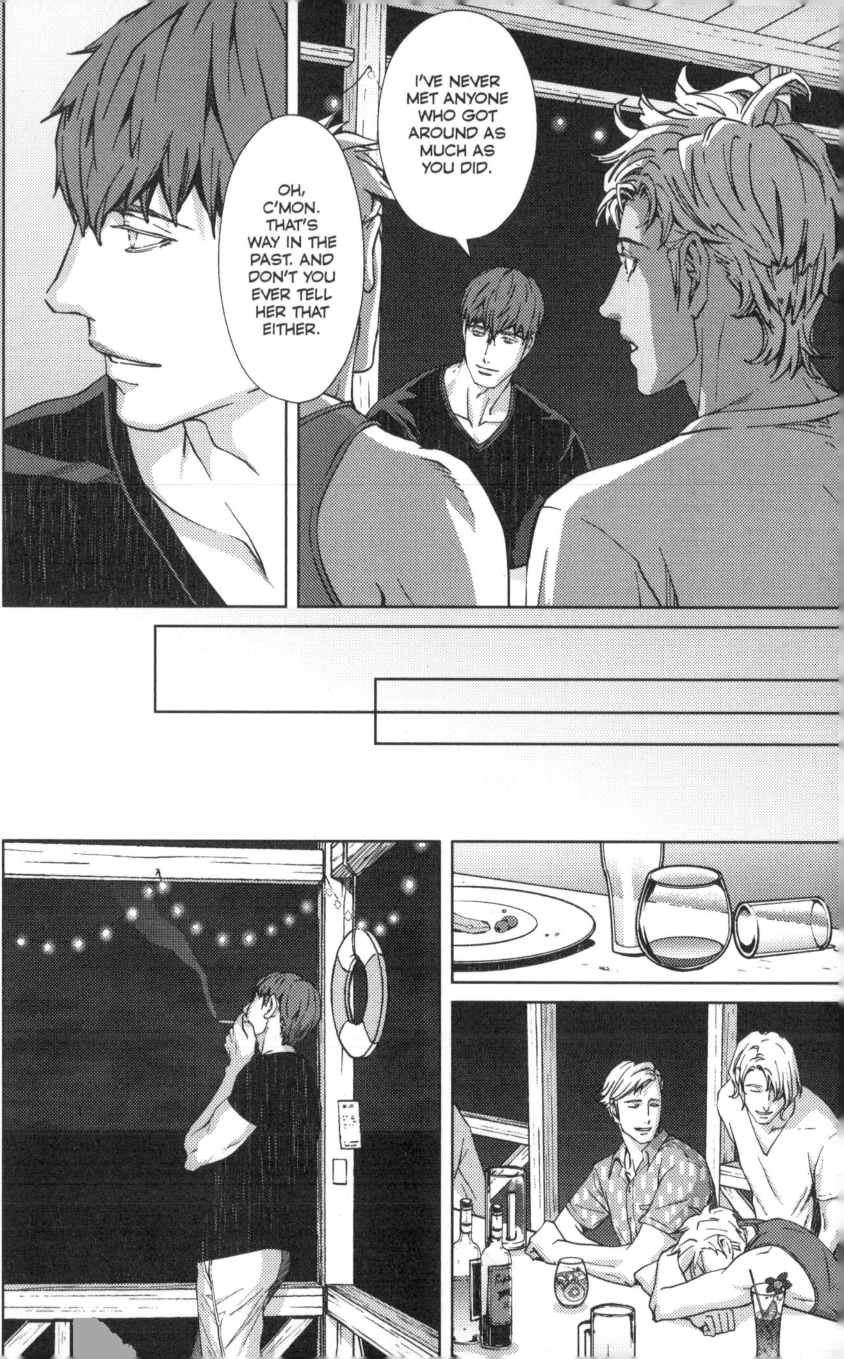
I'VE NEVER MET ANYONE WHO GOT AROUND AS MUCH AS YOU DID.
OH, C'MON. THAT'S WAY IN THE PAST. AND DON'T YOU EVER TELL HER THAT EITHER.

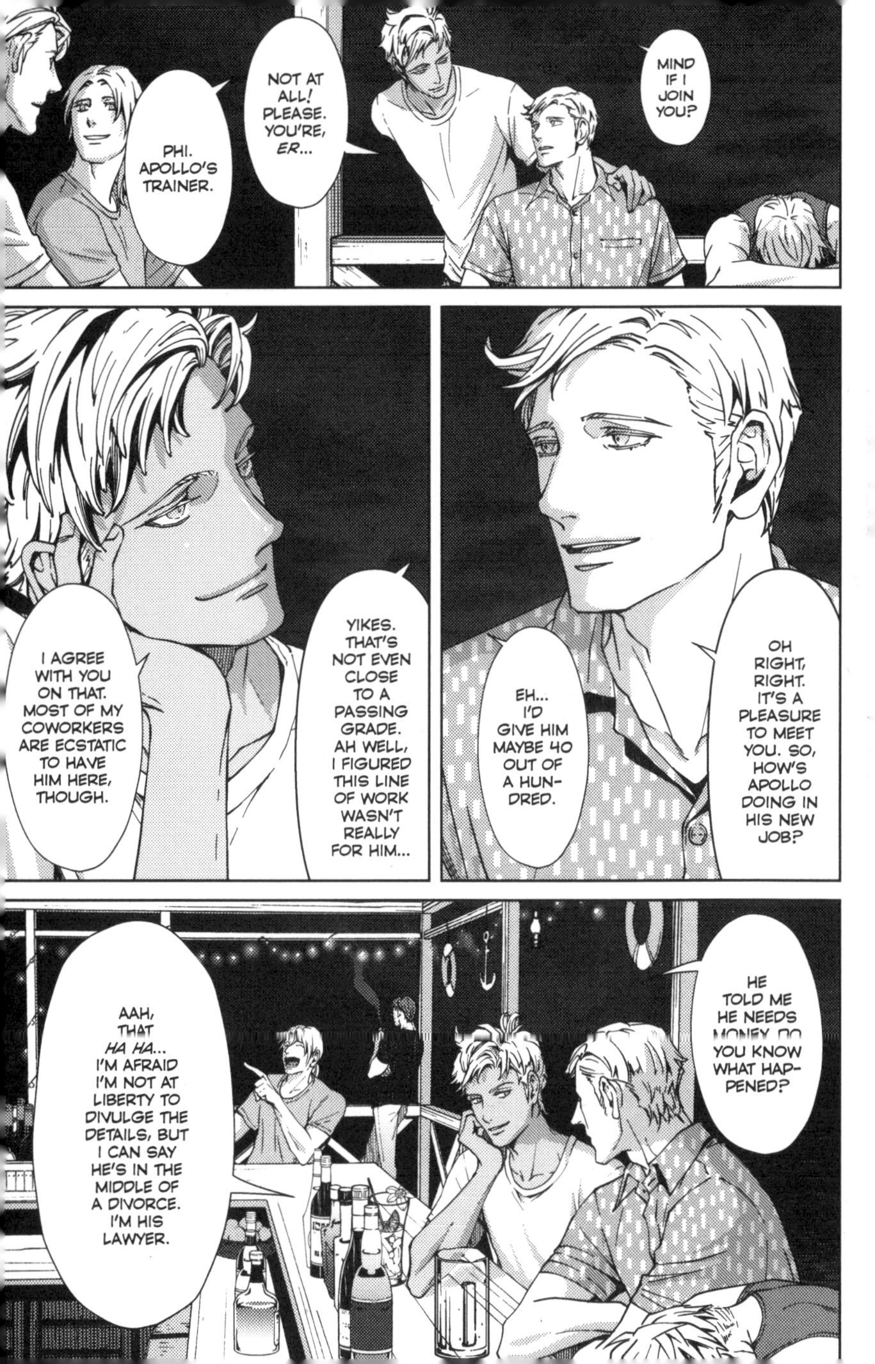
MIND IF I JOIN YOU?
NOT AT ALL! PLEASE. YOU'RE, *ER*...
PHI. APOLLO'S TRAINER.
OH RIGHT, RIGHT. IT'S A PLEASURE TO MEET YOU. SO, HOW'S APOLLO DOING IN HIS NEW JOB?
EH... I'D GIVE HIM MAYBE 40 OUT OF A HUNDRED.
YIKES. THAT'S NOT EVEN CLOSE TO A PASSING GRADE. AH WELL, I FIGURED THIS LINE OF WORK WASN'T REALLY FOR HIM...
I AGREE WITH YOU ON THAT. MOST OF MY COWORKERS ARE ECSTATIC TO HAVE HIM HERE, THOUGH.
HE TOLD ME HE NEEDS MONEY. DO YOU KNOW WHAT HAPPENED?
AAH, THAT *HA HA*... I'M AFRAID I'M NOT AT LIBERTY TO DIVULGE THE DETAILS, BUT I CAN SAY HE'S IN THE MIDDLE OF A DIVORCE. I'M HIS LAWYER.

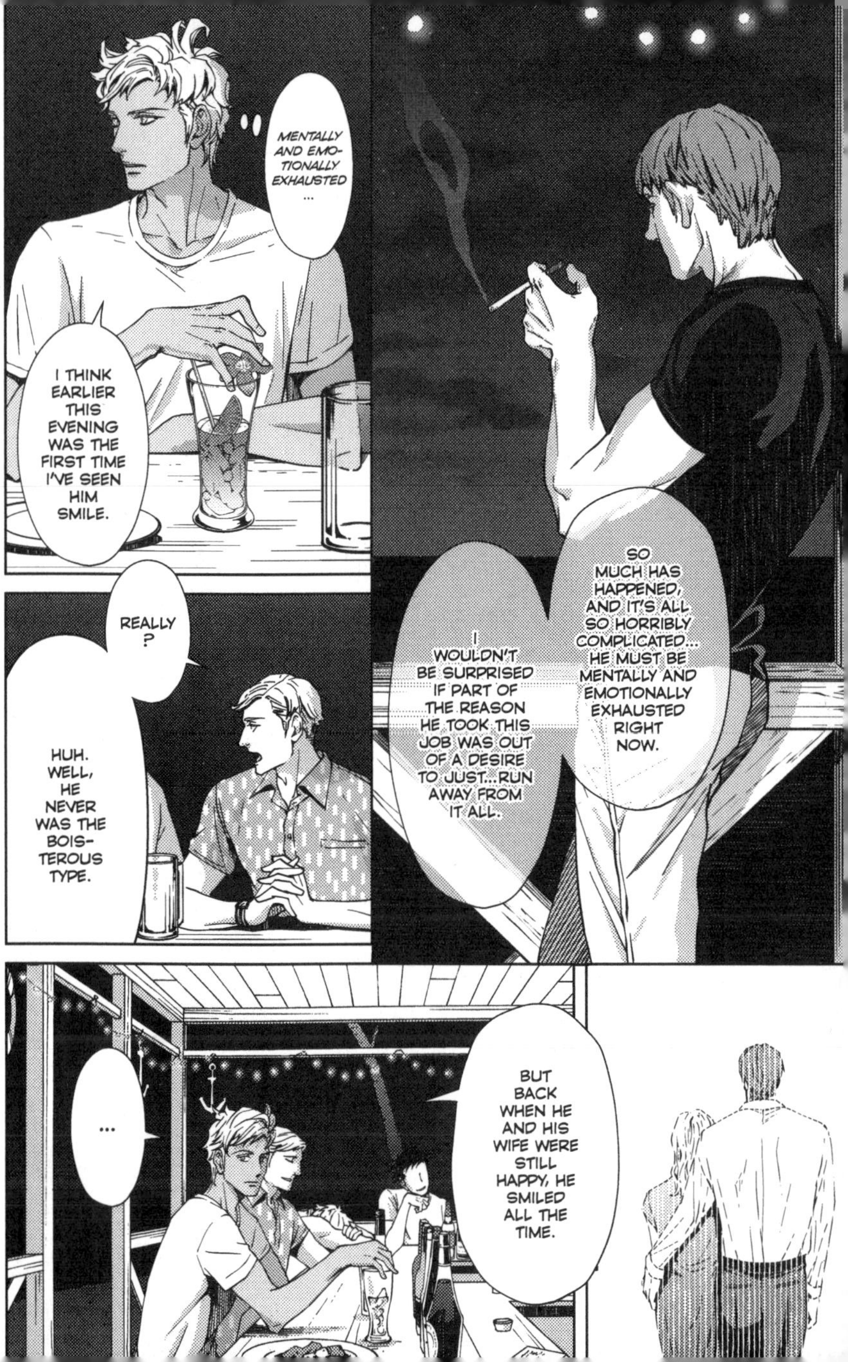
SO MUCH HAS HAPPENED, AND IT'S ALL SO HORRIBLY COMPLICATED... HE MUST BE MENTALLY AND EMOTIONALLY EXHAUSTED RIGHT NOW.
I WOULDN'T BE SURPRISED IF PART OF THE REASON HE TOOK THIS JOB WAS OUT OF A DESIRE TO JUST...RUN AWAY FROM IT ALL.
MENTALLY AND EMO-TIONALLY EXHAUSTED ...
I THINK EARLIER THIS EVENING WAS THE FIRST TIME I'VE SEEN HIM SMILE.
REALLY?
HUH. WELL, HE NEVER WAS THE BOIS-TEROUS TYPE.
BUT BACK WHEN HE AND HIS WIFE WERE STILL HAPPY, HE SMILED ALL THE TIME.
...

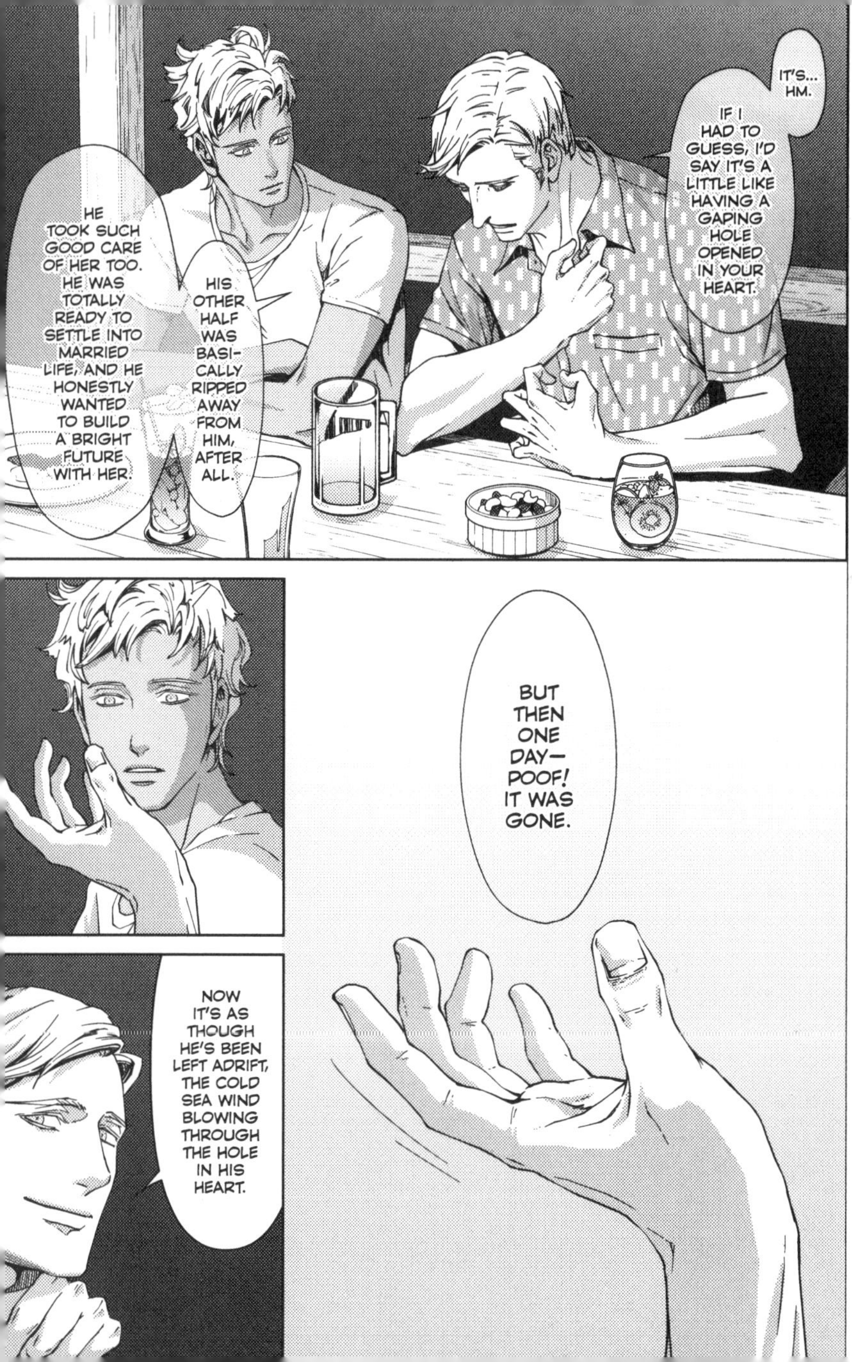
IT'S... HM.
IF I HAD TO GUESS, I'D SAY IT'S A LITTLE LIKE HAVING A GAPING HOLE OPENED IN YOUR HEART.
HIS OTHER HALF WAS BASICALLY RIPPED AWAY FROM HIM, AFTER ALL.
HE TOOK SUCH GOOD CARE OF HER TOO. HE WAS TOTALLY READY TO SETTLE INTO MARRIED LIFE, AND HE HONESTLY WANTED TO BUILD A BRIGHT FUTURE WITH HER.
BUT THEN ONE DAY—POOF! IT WAS GONE.
NOW IT'S AS THOUGH HE'S BEEN LEFT ADRIFT, THE COLD SEA WIND BLOWING THROUGH THE HOLE IN HIS HEART.

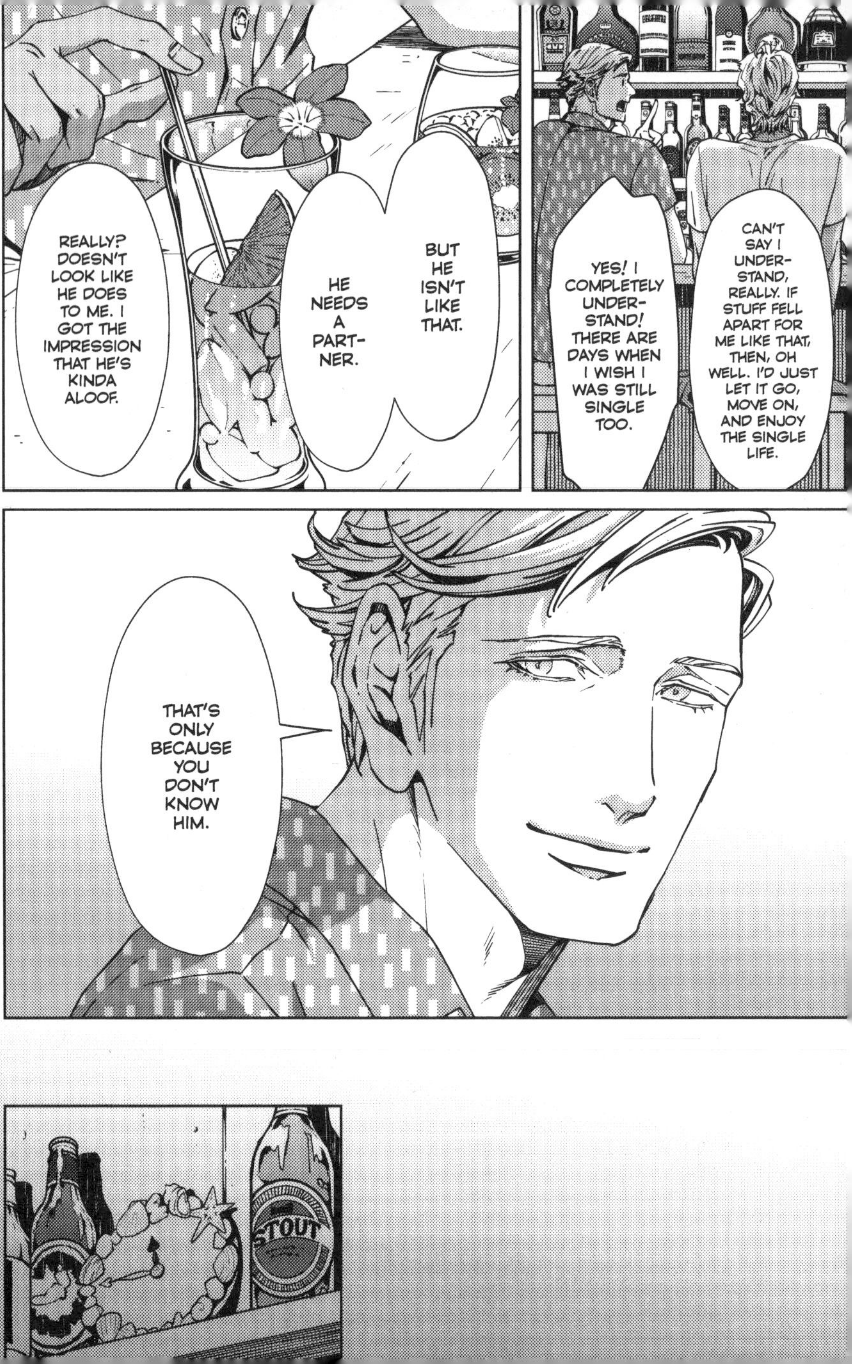
CAN'T SAY I UNDERSTAND, REALLY. IF STUFF FELL APART FOR ME LIKE THAT, THEN, OH WELL. I'D JUST LET IT GO, MOVE ON, AND ENJOY THE SINGLE LIFE.
YES! I COMPLETELY UNDERSTAND! THERE ARE DAYS WHEN I WISH I WAS STILL SINGLE TOO.
BUT HE ISN'T LIKE THAT.
HE NEEDS A PARTNER.
REALLY? DOESN'T LOOK LIKE HE DOES TO ME. I GOT THE IMPRESSION THAT HE'S KINDA ALOOF.
THAT'S ONLY BECAUSE YOU DON'T KNOW HIM.
STOUT

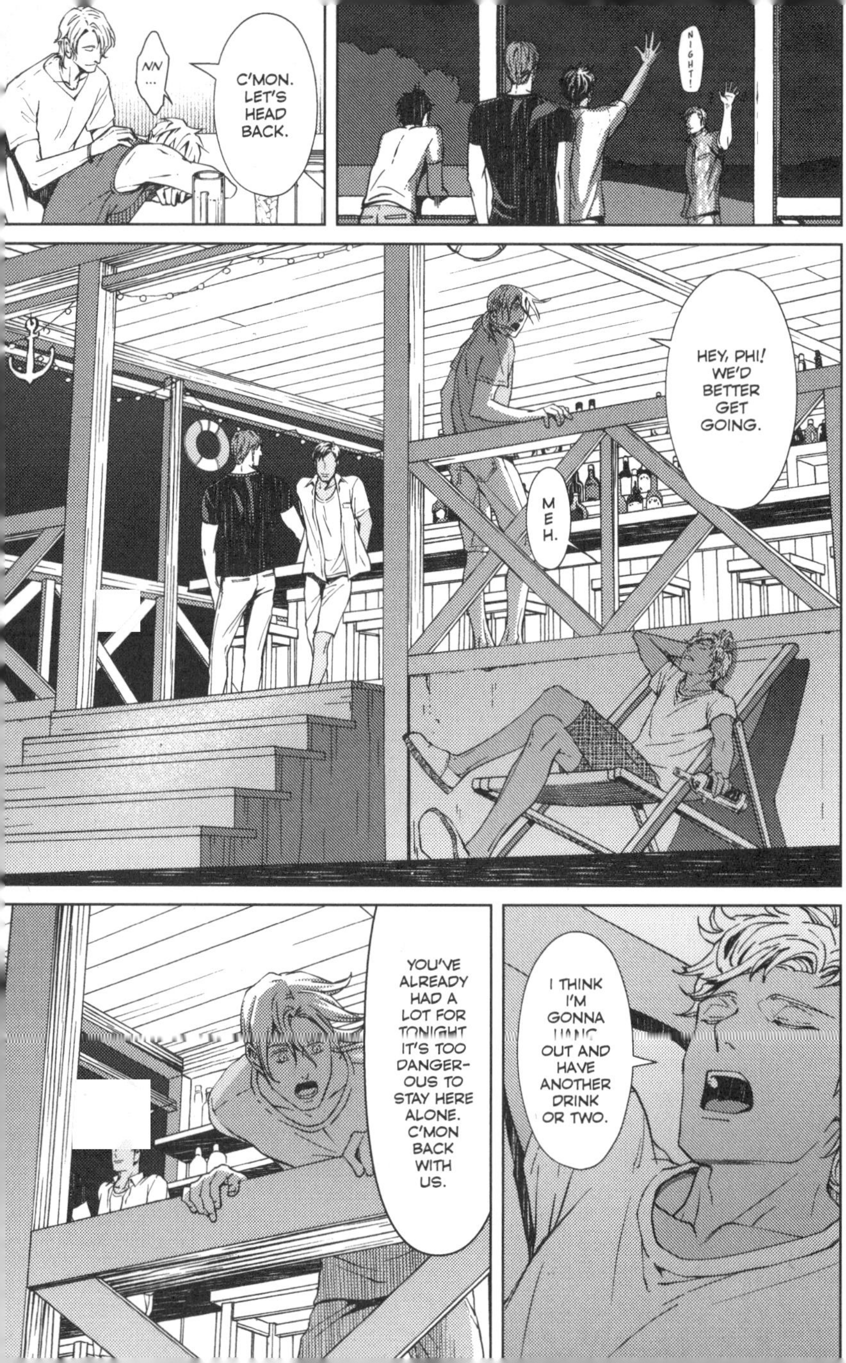
NIGHT!
NN...
C'MON. LET'S HEAD BACK.
HEY, PHI! WE'D BETTER GET GOING.
MEH.
I THINK I'M GONNA HANG OUT AND HAVE ANOTHER DRINK OR TWO.
YOU'VE ALREADY HAD A LOT FOR TONIGHT IT'S TOO DANGER-OUS TO STAY HERE ALONE. C'MON BACK WITH US.

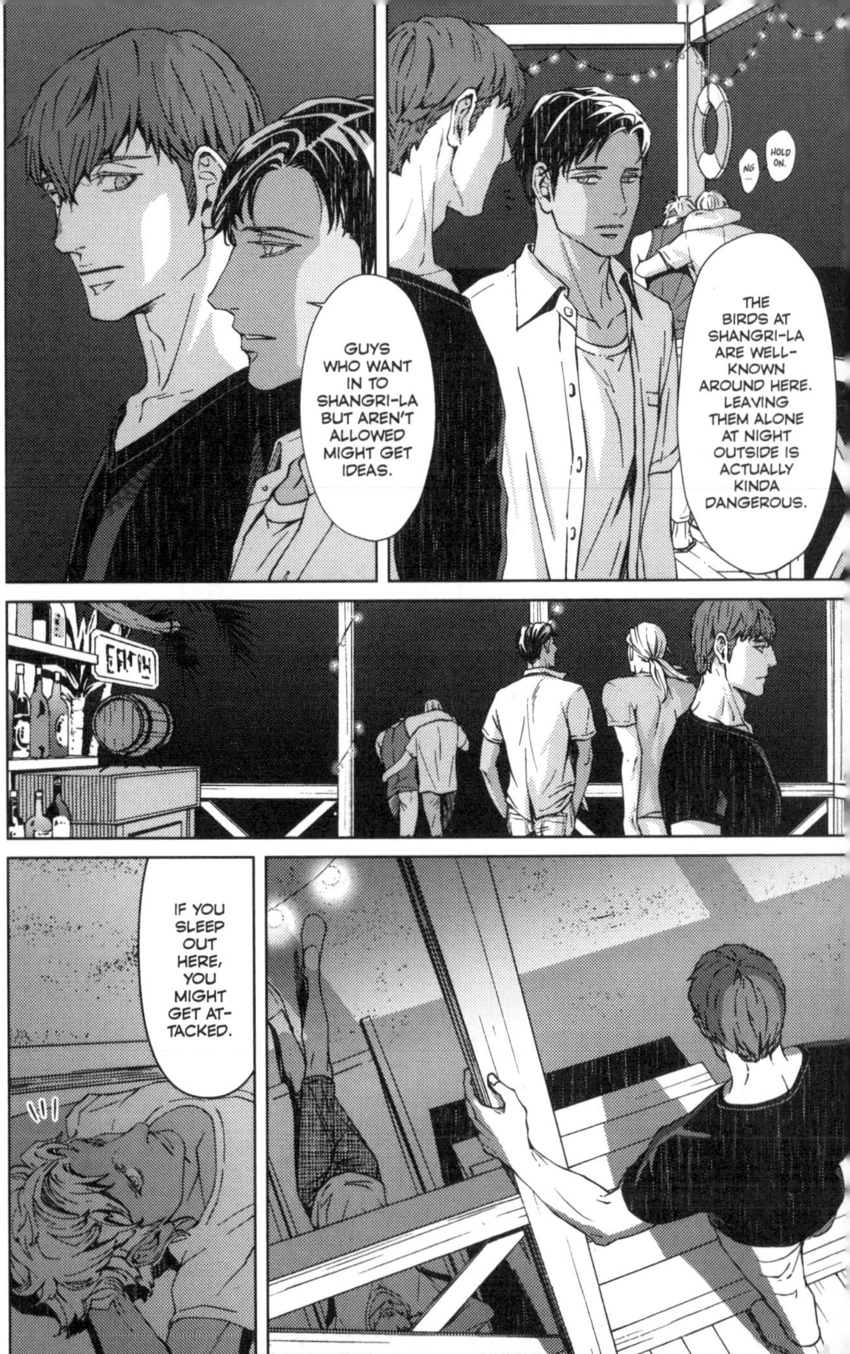
HOLD ON.
NG...
THE BIRDS AT SHANGRI-LA ARE WELL-KNOWN AROUND HERE. LEAVING THEM ALONE AT NIGHT OUTSIDE IS ACTUALLY KINDA DANGEROUS.
GUYS WHO WANT IN TO SHANGRI-LA BUT AREN'T ALLOWED MIGHT GET IDEAS.
IF YOU SLEEP OUT HERE, YOU MIGHT GET AT-TACKED.

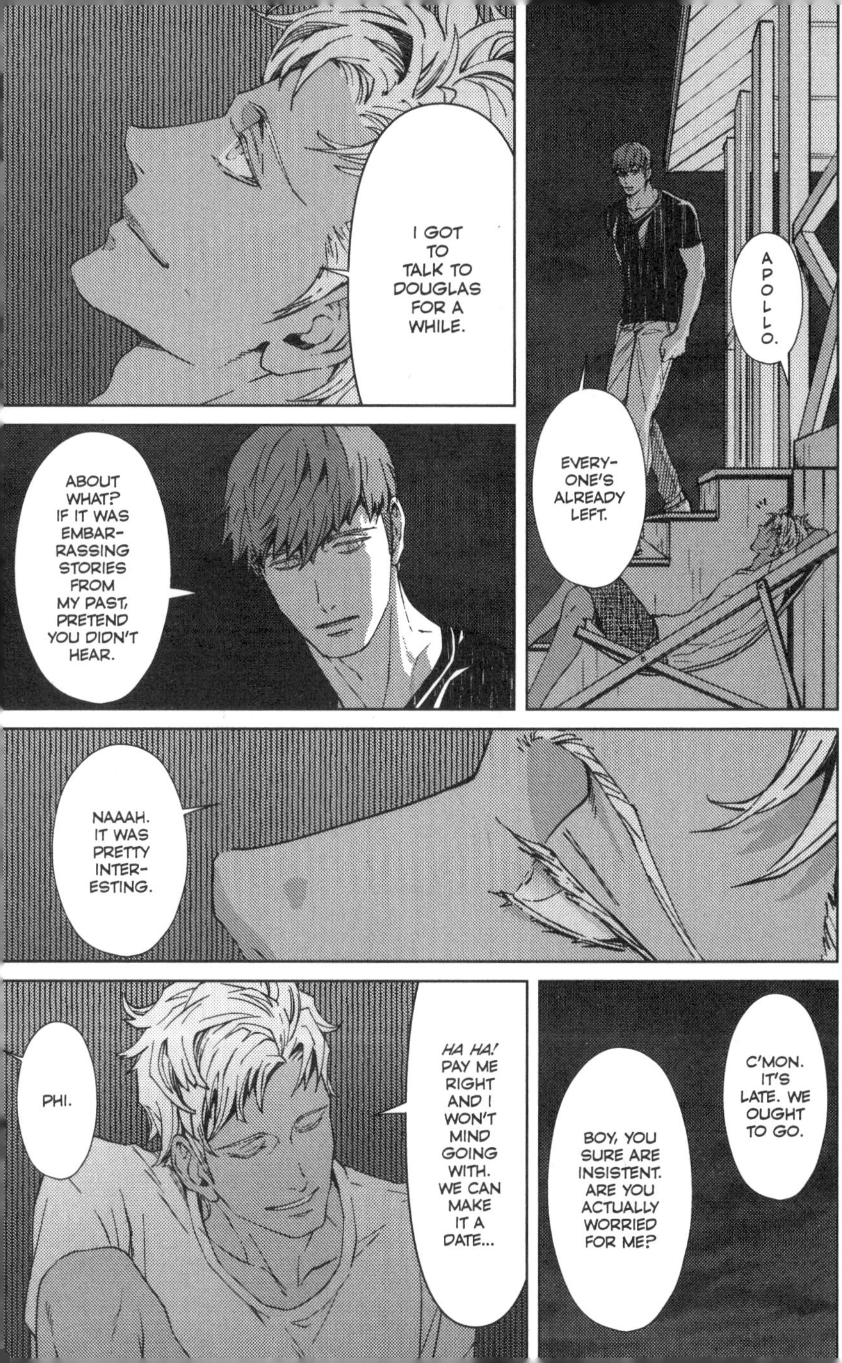
APOLLO.
EVERYONE'S ALREADY LEFT.
I GOT TO TALK TO DOUGLAS FOR A WHILE.
ABOUT WHAT? IF IT WAS EMBARRASSING STORIES FROM MY PAST, PRETEND YOU DIDN'T HEAR.
NAAAH. IT WAS PRETTY INTERESTING.
C'MON. IT'S LATE. WE OUGHT TO GO.
BOY, YOU SURE ARE INSISTENT. ARE YOU ACTUALLY WORRIED FOR ME?
HA HA! PAY ME RIGHT AND I WON'T MIND GOING WITH. WE CAN MAKE IT A DATE...
PHI.

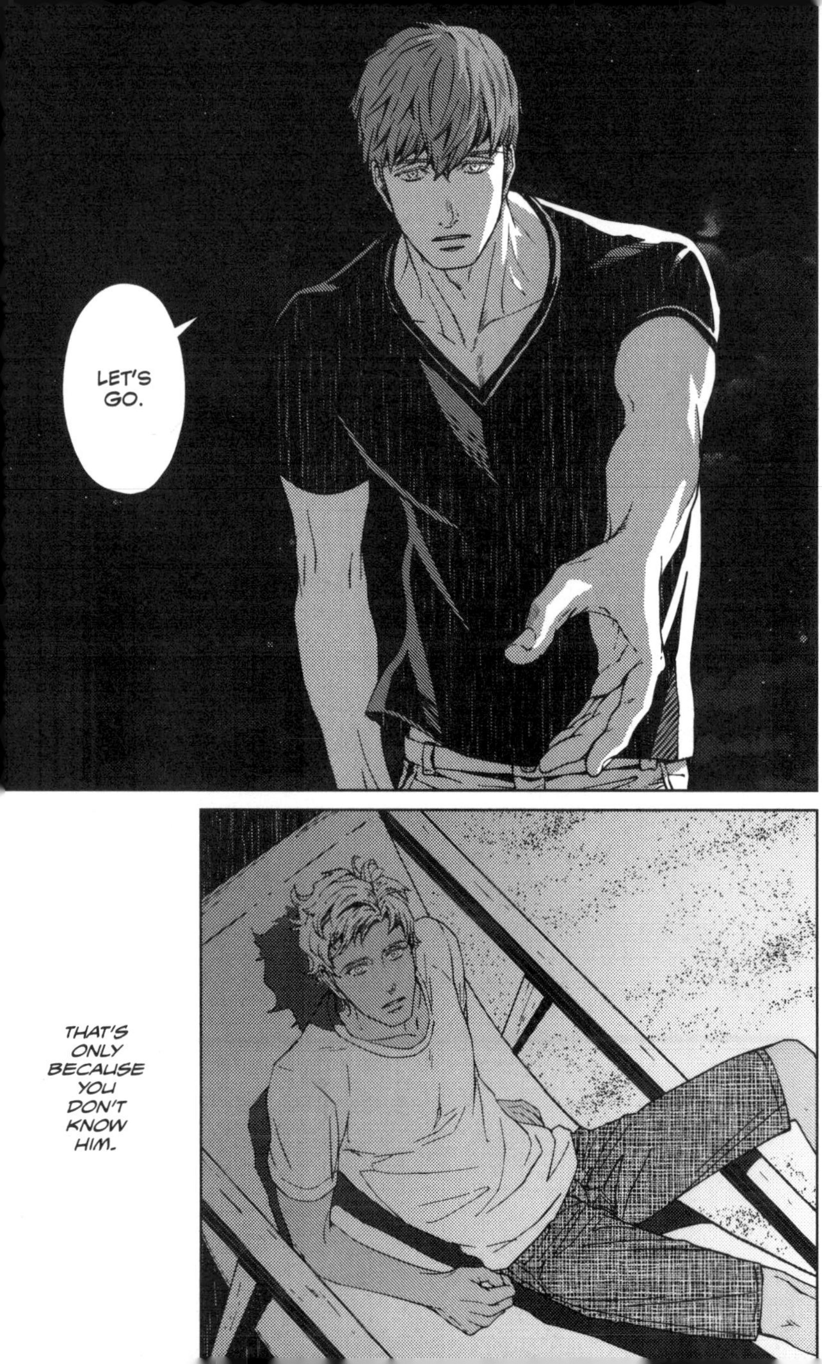
LET'S GO.
THAT'S ONLY BECAUSE YOU DON'T KNOW HIM.

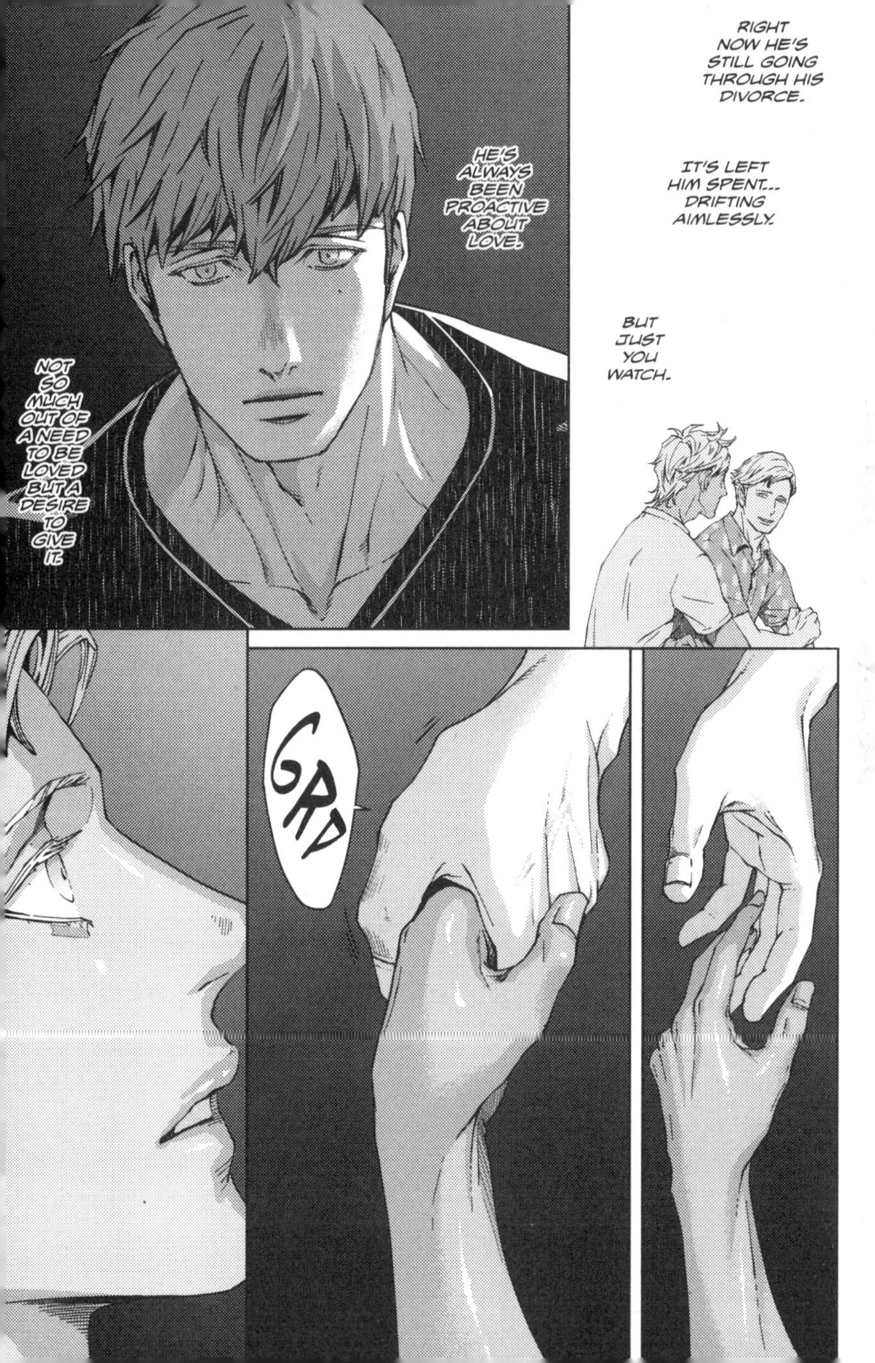
RIGHT NOW HE'S STILL GOING THROUGH HIS DIVORCE.
IT'S LEFT HIM SPENT... DRIFTING AIMLESSLY.
BUT JUST YOU WATCH.
HE'S ALWAYS BEEN PROACTIVE ABOUT LOVE.
NOT SO MUCH OUT OF A NEED TO BE LOVED BUT A DESIRE TO GIVE IT.
GRIP

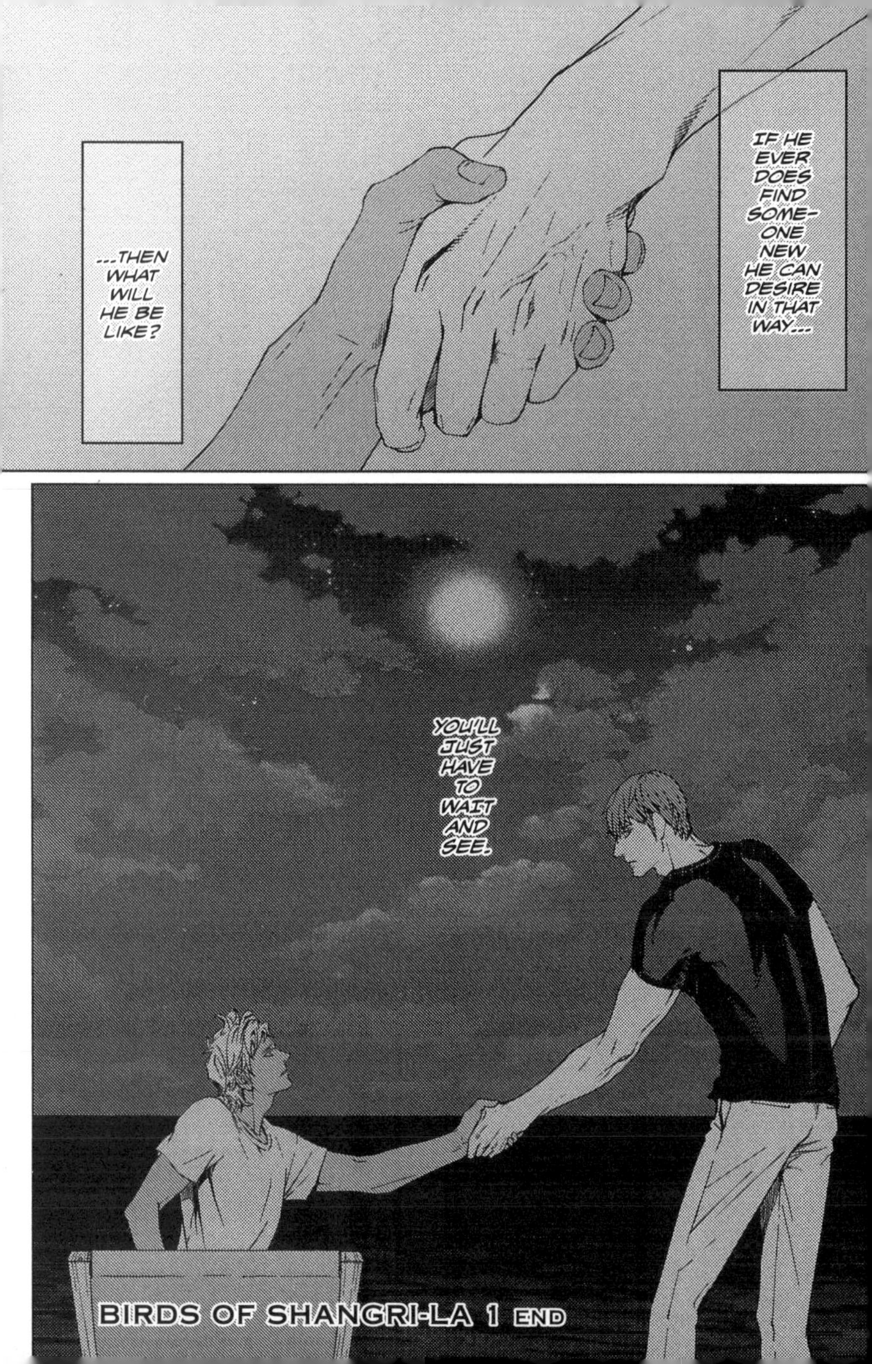
IF HE EVER DOES FIND SOME-ONE NEW HE CAN DESIRE IN THAT WAY...
...THEN WHAT WILL HE BE LIKE?
YOU'LL JUST HAVE TO WAIT AND SEE.
BIRDS OF SHANGRI-LA 1 END

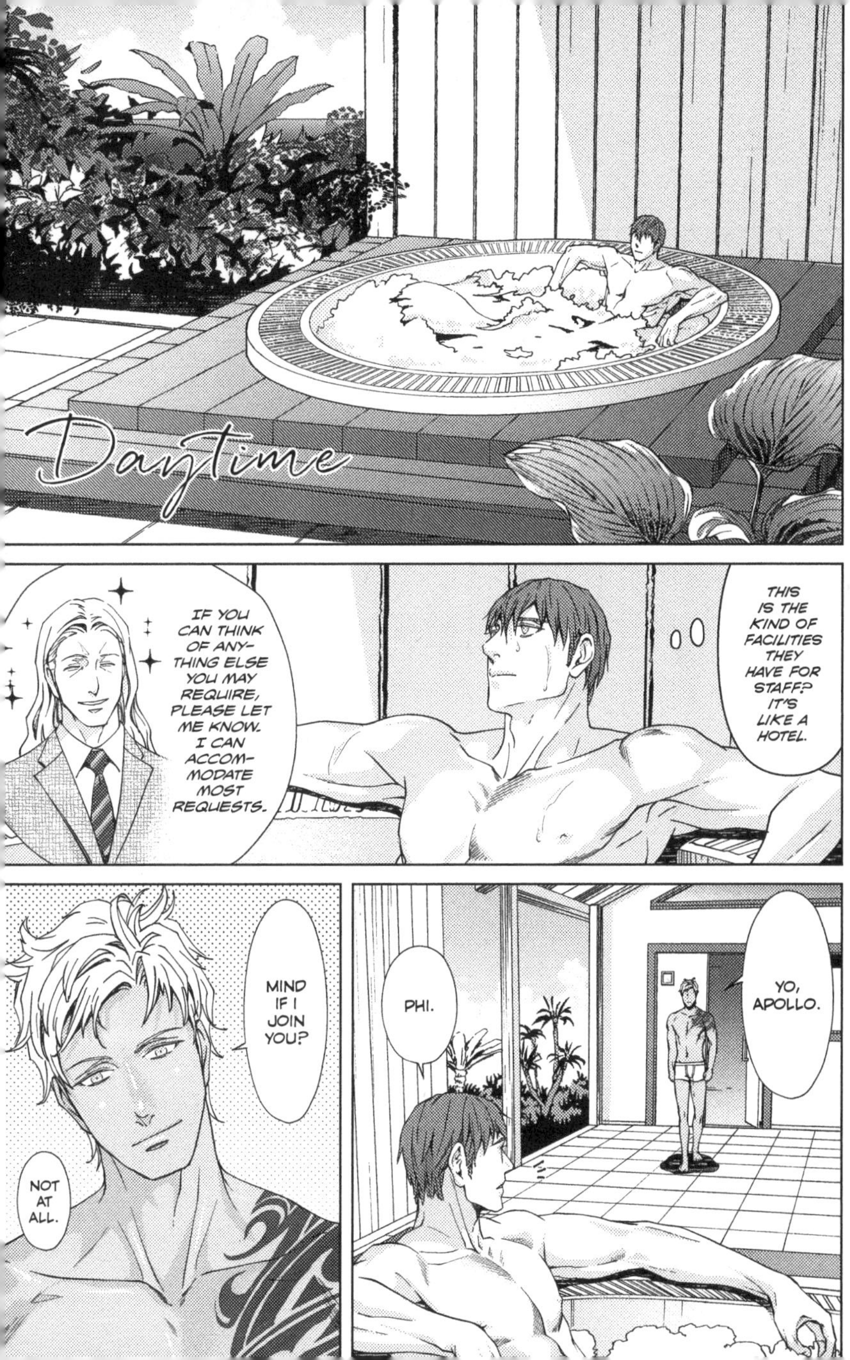
Daytime
THIS IS THE KIND OF FACILITIES THEY HAVE FOR STAFF? IT'S LIKE A HOTEL.
IF YOU CAN THINK OF ANY-THING ELSE YOU MAY REQUIRE, PLEASE LET ME KNOW. I CAN ACCOM-MODATE MOST REQUESTS.
YO, APOLLO.
PHI.
MIND IF I JOIN YOU?
NOT AT ALL.

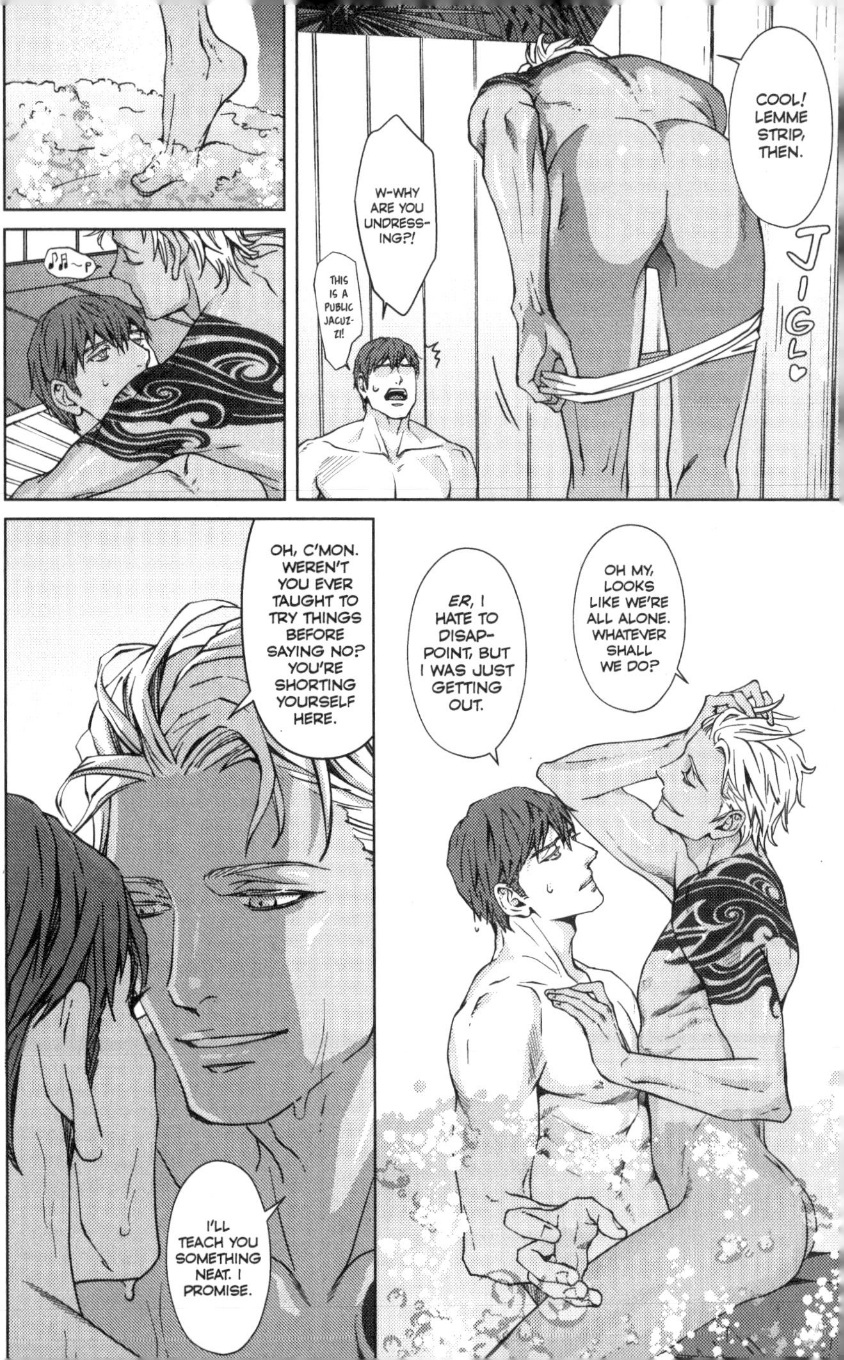
COOL! LEMME STRIP, THEN.
JIGL♥
W-WHY ARE YOU UNDRESS-ING?!
THIS IS A PUBLIC JACUZ-ZI!
♪♬~P
OH MY, LOOKS LIKE WE'RE ALL ALONE. WHATEVER SHALL WE DO?
ER, I HATE TO DISAP-POINT, BUT I WAS JUST GETTING OUT.
OH, C'MON. WEREN'T YOU EVER TAUGHT TO TRY THINGS BEFORE SAYING NO? YOU'RE SHORTING YOURSELF HERE.
I'LL TEACH YOU SOMETHING NEAT. I PROMISE.

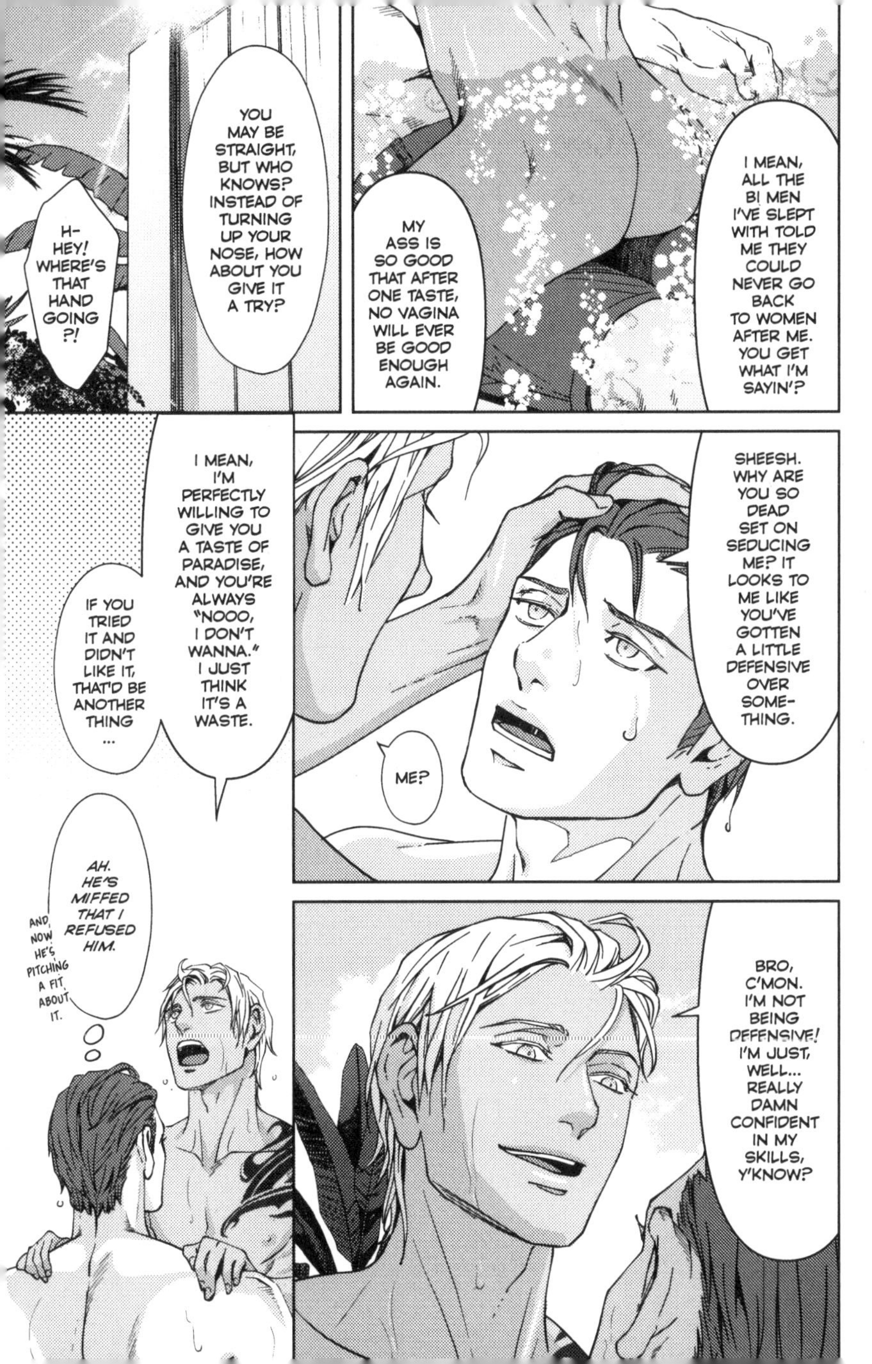
I MEAN, ALL THE BI MEN I'VE SLEPT WITH TOLD ME THEY COULD NEVER GO BACK TO WOMEN AFTER ME. YOU GET WHAT I'M SAYIN'?
MY ASS IS SO GOOD THAT AFTER ONE TASTE, NO VAGINA WILL EVER BE GOOD ENOUGH AGAIN.
YOU MAY BE STRAIGHT, BUT WHO KNOWS? INSTEAD OF TURNING UP YOUR NOSE, HOW ABOUT YOU GIVE IT A TRY?
H-HEY! WHERE'S THAT HAND GOING?!
SHEESH. WHY ARE YOU SO DEAD SET ON SEDUCING ME? IT LOOKS TO ME LIKE YOU'VE GOTTEN A LITTLE DEFENSIVE OVER SOME-THING.
ME?
I MEAN, I'M PERFECTLY WILLING TO GIVE YOU A TASTE OF PARADISE, AND YOU'RE ALWAYS "NOOO, I DON'T WANNA." I JUST THINK IT'S A WASTE.
IF YOU TRIED IT AND DIDN'T LIKE IT, THAT'D BE ANOTHER THING...
BRO, C'MON. I'M NOT BEING DEFENSIVE! I'M JUST, WELL... REALLY DAMN CONFIDENT IN MY SKILLS, Y'KNOW?
AH. HE'S MIFFED THAT I REFUSED HIM.
AND, NOW HE'S PITCHING A FIT ABOUT IT.

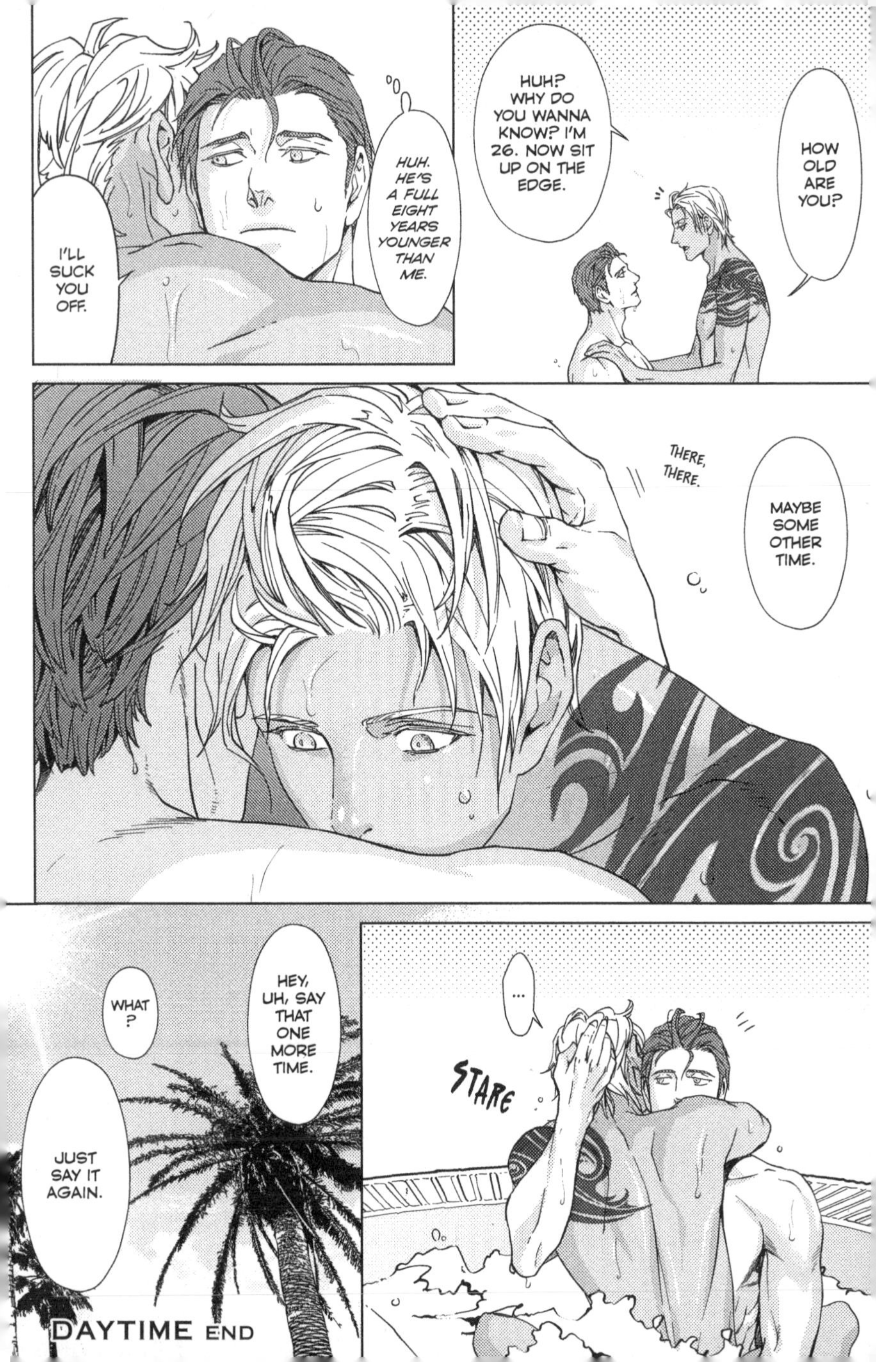
HOW OLD ARE YOU?
HUH? WHY DO YOU WANNA KNOW? I'M 26. NOW SIT UP ON THE EDGE.
HUH. HE'S A FULL EIGHT YEARS YOUNGER THAN ME.
I'LL SUCK YOU OFF.
MAYBE SOME OTHER TIME.
THERE, THERE.
...
STARE
HEY, UH, SAY THAT ONE MORE TIME.
WHAT?
JUST SAY IT AGAIN.
DAYTIME END

About the Author

Birds of Shangri-La is **RANMARU ZARIYA**'s
fourth English-language release following
Void, *Coyote*, and *Liquor & Cigarettes*.
She also publishes *doujin* (independent
comics) under the circle name "**ZARIA**."
You can find out more about her on
her Twitter page, **@zaria_ranmaru**.

Birds of Shangri-La
Volume 1
SuBLime Manga Edition

Story and Art by **RANMARU ZARIYA**

Translation—**Adrienne Beck**
Touch-up Art and Lettering—**Deborah Fisher**
Cover and Graphic Design—**Alice Lewis**
Editor—**Jennifer LeBlanc**

SHANGRI-LA NO TORI I © 2019 Ranmaru Zariya
All rights reserved.
Original Japanese edition published by FRANCE SHOIN

This English edition is published by arrangement with FRANCE
SHOIN Inc., Tokyo in care of Tuttle-Mori Agency, Inc., Tokyo.

Canna
Comics

Printed in the U.S.A.

Published by SuBLime Manga
P.O. Box 77010
San Francisco, CA 94107

10 9 8 7 6 5 4 3 2 1
First printing, November 2020

PARENTAL ADVISORY
BIRDS OF SHANGRI-LA is rated M for Mature and is
recommended for mature readers. This volume
MATURE contains graphic imagery and mature themes.

www.SuBLimeManga.com